Born in Scotland, Richard Jobson ⸺ ⸺ ⸺ ⸺ ⸺ as an apprentice to Aston Villa), m⸺ ⸺ ⸺ ⸺ el results he was appearing on *Top of the Pops* with his band The Skids), poet (two books and ten albums of poetry to his credit), an actor and a model. His career in broadcasting began when he was interviewed for Radio 4's *Loose Ends* and was immediately offered a job by the producer. Since then Richard has presented the ITV arts programme *01: For London*, as well as other popular-culture programmes for the BBC and Channel 4, and in 1992 he hosted the controversial discussion-led series *Men Talk*, a candid programme about men's sexuality. He has also written about London life for various newspapers and magazines.

THE *Virgin* INSIDER'S GUIDE TO LONDON

Richard Jobson

First published in Great Britain in 1993 by
Virgin Books
an imprint of Virgin Publishing Ltd
332 Ladbroke Grove
London W10 5AH

A catalogue record for this title is available from the British
Library.

ISBN 0 86369 676 7

Typeset by TW Typesetting, Plymouth, Devon
Printed and bound in Great Britain by
Biddles Ltd, Guildford and King's Lynn

TO FRANCESCA AND EDIE

ACKNOWLEDGEMENTS

Thanks to my editors at Virgin: Sally Holloway for her patience and faith in the project and Ríona MacNamara for reading my scrawl. Special thanks to Caroline McDonald for perseverance and support above and beyond the call of duty and to Cat Ledger for getting me on my bike.

CONTENTS

AUTHOR'S FOREWORD

I came to London for the first time when I was five years old and was sent to visit my grandmother, who lived in Earls Court and had a small shop on the Old Brompton Road. She was a mysterious woman who seldom visited my family in Scotland, and always said that she was too busy working and surviving the difficulties of city life to find the time to travel north. After only a few minutes in her shop I began to understand just what it was that kept her away from her grandchildren, and I stared in fascination at the steady stream of oddballs and 'professional' women who would come in to buy cigarettes or put up in the window small business cards advertising French lessons or the skills of a domineering headmistress. As a young man of five from the rural fields of Fife I found this new city very confusing but very exotic, and I still do.

Wandering the streets of Earls Court, which even then were the haunt of gay men, prostitutes and Australians, I discovered at an early stage a new courage and sense of independence. Every day my grandmother would throw me out of her shop because I spent too much time staring at her customers and eating her sweets, and reckless abandon, or a strong interest in what was going on around me, would draw me out to the mesmerising streets, parks and people of London.

In 1978 I came back to London with a bagful of clothes and a return ticket to Edinburgh. The return half of the ticket was never used: I love Scotland, but I am hooked on London. In my fifteen years here I have lived in almost every part of this big city, and always loved getting to know each area and its people as well as I could. I began to realise that London is really a series of villages and that if you stay long enough in, for example, Camden, you will find that there is enough there to ensure that you might never again need to visit another part of the city. Each area has its own attractions and is happily divorced from the rest of the capital, and a walk through the weekend markets of Camden, Notting Hill or Spitalfields will tell you that these are places seeking to create a new alternative to the uniformity of high-street culture which is taking over Britain.

On the surface of things London looks rather ugly, with its mix of dilapidated buildings and bad roads, and nothing ever seems to work very well here. Unlike other European capitals it has never attempted to make bold statements with gracious boulevards and architecture. But these cities lack London's ingenuity and its quality as a multicultural melting-pot of music, theatre and fashion. London is a city where young people create new and radical versions of their future. It is not easy to perform or create here, but for that reason there is a greater feeling of achievement and purpose for those who do win through. The city is constantly adapting to the changing times and while it can occasionally appear forbidding, it has more to offer than almost any other – you just have to dig a little deeper.

In this book I have tried to highlight the attractions of London's many villages and have concentrated on the bars, cafés, shops and public spots which are part of the real London. Although the book does cover 'Official London', I've also attempted to introduce you to the places and people overlooked or avoided by many other books. Some obvious tourist attractions are well worth seeking out and Londoners too often ignore them and are blasé about them; others are manufactured confections that you wouldn't bother about in your home town, so why bother about them here?

I have also tried to keep the layout of the book simple so that if you find yourself in an unfamiliar part of the city you can easily find somewhere to have a cup of coffee, a meal or a bit of peace and quiet. I've also tried not to make the book too bland – most of the places I have chosen are among the best of their type, but I have also criticised some for not delivering all they promise.

The book is as comprehensive as I can make it, but with a city as big and diverse as London there are bound to be omissions. *The Virgin Insider's Guide to London* is just my stab at the impossible: the rest is up to you. Go find London. It will not disappoint you.

HOW TO USE THIS BOOK

London is such a vast, sprawling city that it is impossible to generalise about its character. Therefore, this book treats it as the collection of villages it is, and attempts to give a taste of the many flavours of London life. Areas such as Soho, Notting Hill and Brixton all have their own atmosphere, and the best way to discover the special qualities of each village is to spend time tramping around, discovering the nooks and crannies of the place.

Each section of the book is divided into: **Sights and Sites**, **Eating and Drinking**, **Shopping**, and **Entertainment**. Every place mentioned is also listed in the **Gazetteer**. I have tried to give a contact number for each place, as well as telling you about which credit cards (if any) are accepted – though as this can change, it is best to check beforehand. For restaurants, cafés and so on I have also given the average price of a meal for two without wine or other drinks – but do remember that booze can add alarmingly to your bill. All details and prices in the text were correct, to the best of my knowledge, when the book went to press but are, of course, subject to change at any moment. Use them as a guide – no more.

If you're looking for a particular place – a gallery, shop, bar – go straight to the **Gazetteer**, which will direct you to the relevant section. You'll find a list of places, and can choose one from the nearest area.

Sights and Sites takes in well-known public monuments, as well as telling you about certain tourist traps which are a waste of time unless you like being crowded out by coach parties. I have also tried to rediscover smaller buildings or monuments, as well as streets, which are not covered by other guide books but which are interesting in themselves. This section can be used to find anything from a good example of period architecture to a quiet green space.

In **Eating and Drinking (Eating, Drinking and Sleeping** if hotels are covered), I thought that it was important to capture the wide variety of restaurants, both cheap and expensive, offered by London. If you're in an area such as Soho you'll be spoiled for choice, but most of London's villages also offer a wide variety of international cuisine.

In recent years bars have slowly begun to replace pubs, at least in the centre of the city, as places to hang out. And just as well, in my view – most pubs tend to offer bad service, bad food and a bad selection of drinks. They've managed to get away with it for so long because the British hate complaining – in their own country, at least. However, some pubs have enough character to survive the changing times and today it is possible (though not easy) to eat and drink well in a pub which is clean and where the people seem to know what they are doing. It's these that I have covered here.

One of the biggest problems I had while writing this book was in covering hotels. The type of cheap hotel found in most big cities is not easy to come across in London and if you don't find somewhere as soon as you arrive you could end up in some squalid place in Earls Court. The smaller, cheaper hotels and bed-and-breakfast establishments are mostly located in King's Cross and Bayswater. King's Cross is not a great place to visit as it is quite a dangerous locality where drug use and prostitution are rife, and the Bayswater hotels tend to be a bit grim and lifeless. The best area to find somewhere reasonable, decent and central to stay is probably Bloomsbury, where a mixture of University types and overnight stoppers use the family-run places along Goodge Street and around Bedford Square. I have, however, chosen certain hotels in other parts of London because of their character and charm. Some of them, such as Hazlitt's in Soho, have far more appeal and comfort, and are far more reasonable, than larger, lifeless but more recognisable establishments. You can walk out of the door of this hotel and straight into the culinary delights of an area offering perhaps some of the best and most varied cooking in the world. Most of the hotels I've chosen cost about £120 a night for a double room, which is a lot of money but sadly not that expensive by London's standards.

The **Shopping** section covers what can be a very exciting part of a visit to London. Different villages tend to offer different types of shops – for instance, Covent Garden has recently become to the nineties what Carnaby Street was to the sixties: a mecca for the stylish and the innovative. All of the major British and European designers have outlets here, and from the

Piazza to Neal Street, Covent Garden is a great place for window-shopping. The prices are quite reasonable for what you are getting, and bigger names such as Paul Smith and Armani have good stores here.

In Chelsea and Knightsbridge, from the top of Sloane Street all the way down the bottom of the King's Road, there is a hive of high-class fashion houses which attract the rich and the famous. Prices are high here but the big stores such as Harvey Nichols and Harrods offer a wide choice, and Peter Jones's department store a more down-to-earth one.

In general, in writing this section, I have given as many examples as possible of shops which are unusual or the best of their type. I've tried to keep away from high-street chain stores, although there are a few, such as Jigsaw and Kookai, which are too good to ignore.

The **Entertainment** section is a ragbag of theatres both commercial and fringe, cinemas, sports facilities, music venues and private art galleries. The theatre life in London is second to none. London also has excellent independent cinemas which offer you good service and amenities as well as a big screen, and each night you can hear music of every kind all over the city.

Though I have tried to cover the variety of nightlife available in London, to an extent this is an impossible task as clubs change all the time. I would recommend that you keep an eye open in clothes shops or cafés which often display small posters or flyers telling you where and when things are happening in Clubland. Check out weekly listings magazines such as *Time Out* as well.

The Entertainment section also covers commercial galleries such as those found in Cork Street and the Portobello Road which offer a rich variety of commercial art galleries where the quality is as high as the prices. (Details of public galleries can be found in **Sights and Sites**.)

In this section I have not given performance times or ticket prices for theatres and cinemas, as these are constantly changing according to time, season and production. It's always best to ring the number given.

TRANSPORT

SIGHTSEEING TOURS
If you have never been to London before and you want to get your bearings, there are a large number of companies of variable quality

operating coach tours around the city, stopping at well-known tourist spots and clogging up the roads, much to the annoyance of Londoners. There are a few more unusual or special-interest tours which might be more intriguing – what about the Angel and Joe Orton and Camden Passage Tour (071-226 8333), the In the Footsteps of Bertie Wooster Tour (071-272 6904) or the Marx and Engels in London Walk (081-349 3928)? Ask at your hotel desk for details, or check listings magazines such as *Time Out*.

TAXIS

As long as they have their orange light on, black taxis can be hailed anywhere on the street. The driver will wind down the passenger-side window and you should then tell him where you want to go Each driver has done 'the Knowledge', a rigorous training course, and will know central London intimately. Cab drivers are required by law to take the shortest route to your destination, though they don't always do so, often for legitimate reasons as the drivers know that certain roads are clogged up with traffic, roadworks et cetera. Each cab is metered, and there is a list of charges displayed in front of your seat, so you can see clearly what you will end up paying.

Minicabs are unlicensed cars generally cheaper than black cabs. They are not allowed to ply for trade on the street, and you have to ring them up. It's best to use only those companies recommended by a friend or by your hotel; though rare, there have been reports of assaults on lone female passengers, and not all minicabs are properly insured. It's also not unknown to spend a disproportionately long part of the journey time sitting at the side of the road while the driver consults a map.

TUBES

The tubes are easy to use but very crowded during the rush hours (8.30–9.30 a.m. and 5–6.30 p.m.), so avoid them then if you possibly can. At other times of the day the underground system is a fast and reliable way of getting around. Though you should of course take care of your possessions and be on guard against pickpockets and the like, London's tube is generally safer than, say, its New York equivalent. It's also a good idea to remember that the famous London Underground map, while an excellent guide to the system, is actually very unrepresentative of scale, and that in Central London it is often quicker to walk than to change trains – the couple of hundred yards between Embankment and Charing Cross, which look misleadingly far apart on the map, are a case in point. When going up and down escalators, do remember to stand on your right: this allows people to walk down the left-hand side of the stairs and is a universally observed rule.

BUSES

London's bus system looks intimidating to many and it can often appear very difficult to get the hang of the various routes. It's definitely worth persevering, though, as travelling by bus – especially on the top deck – gives a very good overview of the city. If you rely solely on the tubes it can be very difficult to get an idea of how London's various villages – Covent Garden and Bloomsbury, for instance – connect together. Bus route maps are available free of charge from most tube and train stations – just ask at the enquiries desk.

The night-bus system covers all of London and is a cheap way of getting home after a late night out, although buses to more outlying parts of the city tend to depart only once an hour or so. The stopping and starting place for all night buses is Trafalgar Square, and you can happily spend your waiting time here people-watching – the mixed crowd that gathers here can be fascinating. There's detailed guides posted at various stops that will tell you clearly which route to go for. Once your bus does arrive it'll probably be at least as fast as the tube, as the roads are nearly empty in the early hours. These buses are a great alternative to taxis if you're watching your budget.

RIVERBUSES

It's a great shame that the Thames is not used more as a means of transport, for it has the potential to put an end to much of the clogging-up of London's transport system. The Riverbus runs from Greenwich to Chelsea Harbour every hour or so, five days a week. It's not quite as fast as the tube, but it's more relaxing: you see London from a more unusual perspective and you always get a seat. The downside is that you can't go on deck and the view from some seats is rather restricted. At £4.80 for a one-way ticket from Greenwich to Charing Cross, the Riverbus isn't exactly competitively priced, either, but there's no doubt that it's a far more pleasant way to commute than crowded tubes or trains.

TRAVELCARDS

Travelcards are sold at all Tube stations and in some newsagents. They are an absolute must and can save you a great deal of money and trouble.

A one-day travelcard will allow you to use buses, trains and tubes (though not night buses) all day without paying any extra. If you're going to be in London for more than three or four days, a weekly or monthly travelcard is even better value, and these are valid on nightbuses as well. One of the less-publicised advantages of travelcards is that they allow you to indulge in the traditional Londoner's pastime of hopping on and off the famous open Routemaster buses, now sadly to be phased out.

AND IF ALL ELSE FAILS . . .
The maps in this book should be enough to serve most of your purposes, but no visitor should be without the Londoner's bible – the *London A–Z*. You'll need it if you've got on the wrong bus after all and ended up in Dagenham rather than Dulwich. You can buy it from just about any newsagent or bookshop, as well as in most stations.

USEFUL TELEPHONE NUMBERS

AIDS Telephone Helpline   0800-567 123
Alcoholics Anonymous   071-352 3010
Artsline (information on arts, entertainment
and facilities for the disabled)   071-388 2227
British Pregnancy Advisory Service   071-222 0985
Dental Emergency Care Service   071-400 0400
Great Chapel Street Medical Centre   071-437 9360
International Traveller's Aid   071-834 3925
Kidsline (Mon–Fri 4–6 p.m.)   071-222 8070
Lesbian and Gay Switchboard   071-837 7324
London Rape Crisis Centre   071-837 1600
London Tourist Board   071-730 3488
(Mon–Fri 9 a.m.–6 p.m.)
London Transport 24-hour information service   071-222 1234
Narcotics Anonymous   071-351 6794
Rapid Visa   071-373 3026
Riverbus Information   071-987 0311
The Samaritans (24 hours)   071-439 2224
Women's Aid   071-251 6537
General Information Service   0839-123 followed by
400 (what's on this week)
424 (kids)
403 (exhibitions)
480 (popular attractions)
428 (street markets)
407 (Sunday in London)
485 (pubs and restaurants)
411 (Changing the Guard)
Note: calls to this number cost
36 pence per minute cheap rate,
48 pence per minute all other times.

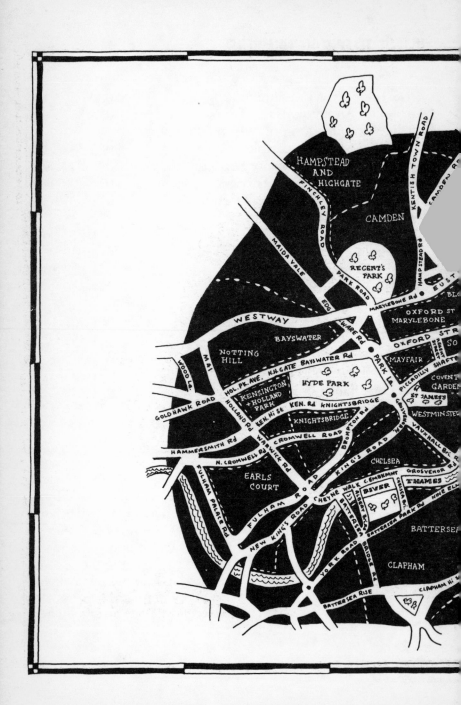

Central

Bloomsbury

BLOOMSBURY

*i*f I could choose where to live, the squares and avenues of Bloomsbury, Holborn and Fitzrovia would be my first choice. These relatively small districts manage to capture both the old London and the new without losing much of their character. Fitzrovia is made up of the backstreets and small houses north of Oxford Street, alongside the Tottenham Court Road and towards the Marylebone Road. Bloomsbury stretches deep into University land, east of Tottenham Court Road and from Kings Cross to Holborn Tube Station; and Holborn, the home of law firms, sits between Covent Garden and the City.

Bloomsbury, the most interesting area of the three, is more attractive than the rather grey Holborn because of its bohemian reputation, which dates from the early part of this century and the establishment of the Bloomsbury Group. This was an association of friends, mostly writers and artists, all of whom saw a deep understanding of art and beauty as essential for social progress – and most of whom were involved in promiscuous relations with their friends. Writers such as Virginia Woolf and E. M. Forster were major players in this nonsense, which led to a series of manifestos and organisations such as the Omega Workshop, founded in 1913 by Roger Fry, a key figure in London's new wave of artists and writers. Omega attempted to popularise new ideas in the decorative arts, such as putting Impressionist-style works on ceramic bowls or jugs. All the young designers at Omega were paid a wage, but more often than not their designs were copied by larger firms who had the technology to produce them for a mass market.

The next wave of writers to follow the Bloomsbury Group, such as Brendan Behan and Dylan Thomas, were regulars at the Fitzroy Arms (still there) in Fitzrovia, where they tried to drink themselves into oblivion.

As well as being University land, Bloomsbury is also hospital land, where researchers seek elusive cures for rare diseases. The famous Hospital for Sick Children in Great Ormond Street was founded in 1851. The first of its kind in Britain, it was sadly needed during Victorian times, when poor children were badly neglected. By the door of the outpatients' wing are two bronze sculptures by Gilbert Ledward. The Hospital for Tropical Diseases, part of University College Hospital, was founded at the turn of the century and is one of the world's centres for research into tropical diseases – a legacy of Britain's colonial days. The hospitals are all very much the product of the Victorian period, when medicine was relatively undeveloped and disease very much misunderstood. The buildings are odd and very dated, but their ominous appearance has a certain fascination.

Since the eighteenth century the area around Charlotte Street, known as Fitzrovia, has been an artists' quarter – Richard Winbon, the landscape painter, lived in Charlotte Street, as did John Nash, who moved to number 36 in 1824. John Constable lived at number 76 and finished his paintings 'The Lock', 'Salisbury Cathedral' and 'Hampstead Heath' here. London's major independent cinema, the Scala, was based in Charlotte Street before it moved to larger premises in Kings Cross (see Islington). Now the street is overpopulated with media people from Channel 4 and the advertising firm Saatchi & Saatchi, which ensures that there is a healthy selection of sandwich bars and restaurants.

Holborn, which stretches from High Holborn to Holborn Circus, north of the Strand and east of Covent Garden, takes its name from the Holbourne, a tributary of the river Fleet, which runs underground into the Thames. The area has always been home to a mixture of law firms and accountants, but it has also had some distinguished residents, including Samuel Johnson, Sir Francis Bacon and John Milton. Charles Dickens lived here for many years, and in *Great Expectations* the character Pip lived in the southern part of the area (see Dickens House).

In 1836 the University of London was founded and in 1911 was given a permanent home in Bloomsbury. The senate and administration buildings were completed in 1936.

Walking around Bloomsbury, Fitzrovia and Holborn, it is easy to imagine the grander times of the eighteenth century. The squares are magnificent, and the small streets have retained enough of their character to make it worthwhile just spending the day exploring them. The small shops and cafes buzz throughout the day because of the ever-increasing popularity of the area's centre, the British Museum – which can probably take most of the blame for turning this area into a cerebral bazaar during the day and a graveyard at night. There are places to go – small restaurants and bars which are good enough to command your attention – but despite the amount of students and art lovers who come here every day, this is really a place to visit only between 9 a.m. and 6 p.m.

HOW TO GET THERE

Tubes
- Chancery Lane
- Euston
- Euston Square
- Farringdon
- Goodge Street
- Holborn
- Kings Cross
- Russell Square
- Tottenham Court Road
- Warren Street

Buses
- Euston Road: 10, 14, 14A, 18, 30, 73, 74, 253
- Fleet Street: 4, 11, 15, X15, 17, 23, 26, 76
- Gray's Inn Road: 17, 45, 46, 171A, 243
- High Holborn: 8, 17, 22B, 25, 45, 46, 171A, 243, 501, 521
- Kingsway: 30,68, X68, 168, 188, 196, 501, 505, 521
- Oxford Street: 9, 19, 22B, 25, 38, 55, 98

FORBIDDEN PLANET

Central  BLOOMSBURY

SIGHTS AND SITES

The British Museum
Great Russell Street
WC1
071-636 1555

Open: Mon–Sat
10 a.m.–5 p.m., Sun
2.30–6 p.m.; first
Tuesday of each month
10–9 p.m.
Admission: free except
first Tuesday evening of
each month, £5

The British Museum is the most important museum in Britain, if not the world. The museum would not exist at all, of course, were it not for the all-conquering imperialism of the British Empire. This house of booty was stocked by gifts from men such as Sir Hans Sloane, the physician, who left his library, manuscripts and collection of artefacts to the nation in 1753, for the sum of £20,000. Excavations in the nineteenth century brought back so many priceless artefacts that when George IV gave the nation his father's library it was felt that a new and very large building was required. Sir Robert Smirke built this magnificent building between 1823 and 1847.

The collection of antiquities held here chronicles the evolution of Man from the Stone Age to the present day and is displayed here to maximum effect. The museum is so big that it would take weeks to get through it properly, so it's probably best to decide on a route and to stick to it. This can be difficult – I have found it is the easiest thing in the world to get side-tracked here. The two main highlights are the Egyptian galleries, which are lit up – to remarkable effect – on the pay-day each month, and the British Library reading rooms. Two of the four Magna Cartas, signed in the thirteenth century, sit alongside Shakespeare's first folio. The museum is obviously very popular, especially at the weekend, so it's best to come either early in the morning or in the late afternoon. Tours of the museum can be very entertaining as the guides are often actors who know how to tell a good story.

The British Library
Great Russell Street
WC1
071-636 1544

The circular reading room of the British Library, one of the great sights in London, is soon to disappear to the new modern library in St Pancras. It will remain in some shape or form, and in any case will carry on as it is until 1996, but the vast quantity of books – some eight million – will have to go. At present the clublike atmosphere here is a revelation and makes you want to sit and study.

The library is open only to those with a reading pass, but on weekdays at 2, 3 and 4 p.m., there are talks and introductions to the building and the collection. The talks are free – gather at the entrance.

Even when the books have gone it should be worth visiting here to see where and in what conditions the likes of Marx did their work, before comparing it to the new high-tech but soulless building at St Pancras.

BT Tower
Maple Street W1
071-356 5000

Designed by Eric Bedford and with a height of 620 feet, BT Tower was for a long time the tallest building in London. The circular restaurant at the top provided the best view in the city but has now been closed as a result of terrorist threats. It deals with radio, television and phone calls in and out of London. It's rumoured to go as deeply into the ground as it stands out of it.

Centre Point
New Oxford Street
WC1

Three hundred and sixty-five feet high and standing at what is supposedly the central point of London, this ugly monstrosity dominates the skyline of the West End and obscures the view of Holborn and Bloomsbury. Centre Point was built in 1967, and the streets around were destroyed to make way for it – I only hope that I shall see it go in my lifetime.

Some people say that MI6 was based on Centre Point's top two floors before being relocated across the river, and others that there is a large nuclear bunker underneath the building. Whatever goes on here, it's kept quiet – the main building seldom has its lights on and I have never seen anybody go in there. Underneath there is the Centre Point Gymnasium, which caters only for men, and the Centre Point Snooker Club. In the pedestrian tunnel joining the east and west sides of the Charing Cross Road, homeless people sleep in cardboard boxes.

Dickens House
48 Doughty Street WC1
071-405 2127

Open: Mon–Sat
10 a.m.–5 p.m.
Admission: Adults £3,
concessions £2

In March 1837 Charles Dickens moved to Doughty Street, and during his stay here wrote *The Pickwick Papers*, *Oliver Twist* and *Nicholas Nickleby*, and began *Barnaby Rudge*. One of the great tragedies of Dickens's life, the death of his seventeen-year-old sister-in-law Mary Hogarth, took place in this house and distressed him so much that he was unable to write for many months afterwards.

His house was acquired by the Dickens Fellowship in 1925 and has been filled from basement to rafters with memorabilia of the great writer. First editions and velvet-covered desks are here, and in the base-

ment a kitchen like the one in Manor Farm in *The Pickwick Papers* has been built. It's a small place but definitely worth a visit.

Gray's Inn Square
Gray's Inn Road WC1

One of the four Inns of the Court which have the exclusive right to call trained men and women to the bar. The Inns began in the thirteenth century as places where members of the court could sleep and eat. They are now institutions which are very difficult to understand and even more difficult to join. Each Inn has a Great Hall as well as a chapel and a library. The Hall at Gray's Inn was built between 1556 and 1560 and in 1594 saw the first performance of Shakespeare's *The Comedy of Errors*.

The extensive grounds were laid out by Sir Francis Bacon in 1606 and were a fashionable place to walk during the day and to duel in the twilight hours. You can walk around the public grounds and squares but the buildings are closed to the public. Try applying at the porter's lodge – he might show you round.

Lincoln's Inn
Lincoln's Inn WC2

If you've read *Bleak House* by Charles Dickens you will recognise much of Lincoln's Inn, which has been in existence since the thirteenth century. The chapel (open Mon–Fri, 12.30–2.30 p.m.) has been ascribed to Inigo Jones and has a magnificent undercroft which catches every sound and throws it back in echo. In the Hall there is a large mural painted in the 1850s by G. F. Watts and entitled 'Justice – A Hemicycle of Lawgivers'. A few other details are worth looking at, such as Hogarth's historical painting, also in the Great Hall, and the windows by Bernard van Linge in the chapel.

Lincoln's Inn Fields were originally students' playing fields in the fourteenth century, and by the seventeenth century they were a very sought-after residential area, even though robberies, duels and executions took place here on a regular basis. Famous residents included Nell Gwynne, mistress of Charles II, and Prime Minister Ramsey MacDonald.

The gardens have been open to the public since 1894 and there is a piece of sculpture by Barry Flanagan, which is well worth taking a peek at. Hours are 10 a.m.–5 p.m. If you'd like a guided tour of the building, apply by letter to: David Corsellis, Assistant Under Treasurer, The Honourable

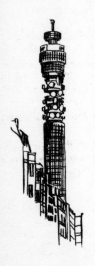

BT TOWER

Society of Lincoln's Inn, Treasury Office, London WC2A 3TL.

Percival David Foundation
53 Garden Square
WC1
071-387 3909

Open: Mon–Fri
10.30 a.m.–5 p.m.

In 1951, Sir Percival David's famous collection of Chinese books and ceramics from the Sung, Yuan, Ming and Chiing dynasties, stretching from the tenth to the seventeenth centuries, was collected here.

The library is intended for the use of scholars and students, but the display of ceramics is well worth a visit, for which you must apply beforehand in writing.

Pollock's Toy Museum
1 Scala Street WC1
071-636 3452

Open: Mon–Sat
10 a.m.–5 p.m.
Admission: adult £2,
under-18s 75p
Credit: A, Amex, V over
£10

This small museum, which takes up four floors of two small, eighteenth-century houses, was founded by Benjamin Pollock, who was responsible for promoting children's theatre and toy theatre in the nineteenth century. Originally based in Covent Garden, it moved here after it had outgrown its original premises. Its new home, above a shop selling traditional toys, has been laid out to resemble a series of children's rooms, with every imaginable plaything lying cluttered around. From jigsaws to puppets, the museum chronicles the evolution of the toy, but the most delightful displays are those of Benjamin Pollock's own toy theatres, which are beautifully crafted and quite mesmerising.

St Giles-in-the-Fields
St Giles High Street
WC2
071-240 2532

This church was founded at the beginning of the twelfth century in what was then open fields by Henry I's wife Matilda. Originally a leper hospital, it was rebuilt in the seventeenth century and again in 1734 when the architect Henry Flitcroft took the recently completed splendour of Saint Martins-in-the-Fields as his model. The Resurrection Gate has a beautiful wooden relief of the Day of Judgement, which dates from 1687.

Saint Giles is a great sanctum in this busy, hectic part of London, but unfortunately it is dwarfed by the dreadful Centre Point. There are regular services on Sundays and Wednesdays.

Saint Pancras New Church
Euston Row/Woburn
Place NW1
071-387 8250

This church, one of the finest examples of Ionic architecture in London, was built at the height of the Greek architecture craze of the 1920s and was William Inwood's winning entry in a competition to design a church to stand on the site. I have never understood the point of these competitions but they do seem to

be very popular, despite the fact that the public has no say in the design of the building they often end up paying for. Inwood's building is a success and does a great deal for what is a very drab area. It's rectangular, faced in stone and entered through a portico of six huge Ionic pillars. As a Christian church based on the pagan Tower of the Winds in Athens, the building caused an uproar in many circles when it was first built. I enjoy its enormity and foreboding atmosphere. Classical concerts are now a regular fixture here – ring to check.

Senate House
Malet Street WC1
071-636 8000

Closed to the public

This is the administrative heart of the enormous University of London, now so big that it extends into other cities. London was the last major city in Europe to found a university, and the Senate, designed in the brutalist style of Charles Holden, wasn't built until 1927. The building dominates the area and is thought by many to be a monstrosity. I think it holds the attention simply because of its unmistakable strength and modern character. It is said to be one of the four buildings in London which would remain standing after a direct hit by a nuclear bomb.

Sir John Soane's Museum
13 Lincoln's Inn Fields
WC2
071-405 2107

Open: Tues–Sat
10 a.m.–5 p.m.

In 1792 Sir John Soane purchased number 12 Lincoln's Inn Fields. He eventually acquired numbers 13 and 14 as well, and made them all into a single dwelling which was turned into a treasure trove for his enormous collection of artefacts, and is the most important testament to Soane's work. It now stands exactly as he left it and captures the spirit of the great man. His collection includes paintings, books, porcelain and drawings from nearly every period of antiquity, and on display are eight paintings from Hogarth's 'The Rake's Progress'. The most remarkable single item in the whole museum is an alabaster sarcophagus of Seti I, discovered in 1813 in Egypt's Valley of the Kings.

EATING, DRINKING AND SLEEPING

Bertorelli Room
19–23 Charlotte Street
W1
071-636 4174

This formal dining room is part of the more commercial wine bar Cafe Italien (see below), but the contrast between the two is very marked. The restaurant seems to be from another era, one where people ate

Open: Mon–Fri,
lunch midday–3 p.m.,
dinner 6–11 p.m.
Credit: A, Amex, DC, V
Average: £40

from solid plates with proper silver. The food here is exceptional and the service could be pre-war – you get the feeling that time has stood still.

The Bertorelli Room gets its name from the original owners, the four Bertorelli brothers, who were famous in London for taking Italian food upmarket, and also for appealing to the staid taste of the British. The food is very traditional Italian, but it seems to have been treated with a great deal of care and attention. I love the way they cook the veal in breadcrumbs – it's a dish available in most Italian cafes, but here it is very special. Also good is the ginepro – noisettes of lamb in a white wine sauce – and once you have tasted the tiramisu you'll understand why I like this place so much.

Cafe Italien

19–23 Charlotte Street
W1
071-636 4174

Open: Mon–Sat,
lunch midday–3 p.m.,
dinner 6.30–11 p.m.
Credit: A, Amex, DC, V
Average: £28

This brasserie-style restaurant serves up good, traditional Italian food in a setting that I always find relaxing and congenial, and is less formal and cheaper than its sister restaurant the Bertorelli Room (see separate entry). It specialises in pasta and fish dishes, and their Venetian-style liver, which can often be a disappointment in Italian restaurants, is also very good. Both the Cafe Italien and the Bertorelli Room are worth a visit if you're in the area and fancy some good food.

Chez Gerard

8 Charlotte Street W1
071-636 4975

Open: Sun–Fri, lunch
midday–2.45 p.m.,
dinner 6.30–11 p.m.,
Sat, dinner
6.30–11 p.m.
Credit: A, Amex, DC, V
Average: £40

This traditional French bistro has a solid reputation for serving up the best grilled steaks in the capital. A glass of Rhone wine and a platter of meat and chips seem to keep the local Channel 4 executives coming back for more. There's a set dinner menu which costs £15 per person. In the evening it can be a quiet, warm place, just right if you're in a romantic mood. French restaurants have been overtaken in popularity recently by Italian and, more recently, by what has been characterised as Modern British, but Chez Gerard still keeps going from strength to strength with few of the pretensions of its culinary brethren.

Cypriana

11 Rathbone Street W1
071-636 1057

Open: lunch, Mon–Fri
midday–2.45 p.m.;

The Charlotte Street area is renowned for its Greek restaurants, the majority of which are horrible and a rip-off, but Cypriana, which is basically a kebab cafe, has a menu which is a much better example of what Greek-Cypriot food is like. Prices are also far more reasonable; its competitors, although they seem to

dinner, Mon–Sat
5.30–11.15 p.m.
Credit: A, Amex, DC, V
Average: £20

First Out
52 St Giles High Street
WC2
071-240 8042

Open: Mon–Sat
11 a.m.–11 p.m., Sun
1–10.30 p.m.
No credit cards
Average: £15

The Greenhouse
Drill Hall Arts Centre,
16 Chenies Street WC1
071-637 8038

Open: Mon–Sat
midday–8 p.m.
No credit cards
Average: £15

Heal's Restaurant
Heal's, 196 Tottenham
Court Road W1
071-636 1666 ext.
5513

Open: Mon–Sat,
breakfast
10–11.30 a.m.,
lunch midday–3 p.m.,
tea 3–5.30 p.m.
Credit: A, Amex, DC, V
Average: breakfast £10,
lunch £40, tea £15

encourage people to be as noisy as they want and to smash as many plates as they can, also charge them the full whack. Cypriana offers the standard Greek dishes such as moussaka or humus, but they do taste like the real thing.

If you're looking to find out what is going on in the gay community, this cafe is the best place to come. It's quite difficult to find, tucked behind Centre Point on a street that is seldom used, but it is worth seeking out as the vegetarian food here is very good. The desserts are good too, particularly the banana cake, which is a treat.

They do have a takeaway service but the atmosphere in First Out is so good that it's usually better to eat in.

I'm never sure about the wisdom of descending into dark basements, but the Greenhouse, however dated it looks, manages to offer up enough choice for vegetarians to make the discomfort of this gloomy room bearable. The coffee is not too good but the dishes are, and the menu changes daily. The soups are always a safe bet and though the main dishes wander down the old vegetarian track of quiche and pizza, they are actually quite good here. Vegetable crumble and lasagne with lentils, vegetables and cheese are both delicious. There's also a big selection of herb teas at 45p a cup. The restaurant is unlicensed, but if you feel you really can't face nettle tea you can bring your own wine and they don't charge corkage.

If you're someone who goes shopping rather than browsing in Heal's furniture shop you won't find the prices in this restaurant too expensive, but I think it is dear for what it is. The menu in this well-designed restaurant varies between easily digested salads and ambitious main courses including lambs' sweetbreads served on a bed of noodles. Everything here is functional and simple, and aims to provide good food, good service and good wine, with a not-so-good bill at the end of it all. It's open for Continental breakfasts.

If you feel the need for something a little lighter you can try the Cafe at Heals, which is open all day for drinks and coffee, as well as breakfast and afternoon tea. They recommend that you book for lunch.

The Hotel Russell
Russell Square WC1
071-837 6470

Credit: A, Amex, DC, V
Average: £120 for a
double room
Bar and restaurant open
to non-residents

Designed by Charles Fitzroy Dell in 1898, this bizarre-looking 324-bedroom hotel was opened on Derby Day, 1900. A mixture of red-brick and terracotta gives you the impression that you are walking into a fantasy land. The entrance to the restaurant is framed by marble pillars and a very large and ornate chandelier. The hotel has none of the usual functional Englishness of the period and with its overwhelming interior design is really more French in style.

The King's Bar here is one of the best in London. Leather sofas, oak panelling and barmen who really know how to make a cocktail, something that's very rare in London, have made it popular with a new breed of Londoner. Regulars include journalist Julie Burchill, who lives nearby and comes here to hold court. Dress smartish and enjoy your £5 cocktail.

Indian YMCA
41 Fitzroy Street W1
071-387 0411

Open: breakfast
7.45–9.15 a.m., lunch
12.30–1.30 p.m.,
dinner 7–8 p.m.
No credit cards
Average: £8

Though it looks and feels a lot like having school dinners, it's worth coming here as the food is as good as any upmarket Indian restaurant in the area and incredibly cheap. It's a self-service canteen and you get your food piled high on a plate with rice and dhal which are especially good for mopping up the sauces. The place is especially popular with Indian students who say that the food is authentic and good. It's a can- teen rather than a restaurant, but if you don't expect restaurant service you'll get a very good deal here.

Museum Street Cafe
47 Museum Street WC1
071-405 3211

Open: Mon–Fri, lunch
12.30–2.15 p.m.,
dinner 7.15–11 p.m.
No credit cards
Average: £35

Reputations grow and then go these days, due to the ever increasing fashion-based attitude towards food, but although based in an area which dies in the evening, this small cafe-restaurant has gone from strength to strength – it is always difficult to get a seat here. All the food can be seen from where you are eating, so you know your meal will be fresh and cooked only after you have ordered it. The menu changes each day but generally has an Italian feel with good salad dishes and a strong fish dish such as grilled turbot or swordfish seasoned and served with a rocket salad – delicious. It all looks like art on a plate but without all the silly colour coordina-

tion normally associated with good food. There's no
à la carte; set lunches are £14 and dinners £19.50,
both for three courses. Starters include a salad with
chargrilled vegetables and parmesan shavings, and
for a main course there's a very tempting chargrilled
salmon with rosemary and anchovy mayonnaise.

Silva's
220 Shaftesbury Avenue
WC2
071-240 0028

Open: Mon–Sat
9 a.m.–7 p.m.
No credit cards
Average: £10

During a matinee interval at the Shaftesbury Theatre,
don't stay inside and drink their rubbish but go next
door to this small Italian cafe which serves up some
of the best cappuccino I have tasted in London. They
also have good snacks, such as a toasted cheese and
ham sandwich (£1.70) and coffee and apple cheesecake (£1.50) – a great if somewhat startling combination and definitely worth a go.

The Sun
63 Lambs Conduit
Street WC1
071-405 8278

Open: Mon–Sat
11 a.m.–11 p.m.,
Sun midday–3 p.m.,
7–10.30 p.m.
No credit cards
Average: £10

This free house, a favourite with University lecturers
and boffins from the British Museum, carries sixteen
different real ales – the largest selection in London –
with the added bonus of cheap food. It's also a
popular venue with the local besuited lawyers who
seem to be in here every lunchtime and evening –
maybe they use the place as an office. If you manage
to squeeze through the mass of pinstripe, then try a
pint of Breakspear and for safety's sake go for a
cheddar ploughman's which will absorb the beer and
get you ready for another. Typical pub meals are
available and there's toasted sandwiches, jacket potatoes and the usual chilli or curry, as well as two
daily vegetarian choices. The pub itself looks as if it
has seen better days but is a pleasant place.

Wagamama
4 Streatham Street WC1
071-323 9223

Open: Mon–Fri
midday–2.30 p.m.,
6.30–11 p.m.,
Sat 1–3.30 p.m.,
6–11 p.m.
No credit cards
Average: £12

Just off Bloomsbury Street, Wagamama is not obvious
to the passer-by as it is discreetly sheltered behind
glass doors. But the reputation of this basement
Japanese noodle bar is such that queues form at 11.30
a.m. – the place is always busy but the turnover is
fast enough to ensure that you will get a seat
eventually. In the evenings get here early, as otherwise you may have to queue for a fair old time. The
tables are laid out like a factory canteen and you
always have to share with others. The most important
thing, though, is not who you sit next to but the
delicious noodle dishes which are clean, filling and,
most importantly, reasonably priced. I am a bore and

always have the salmon ramen, which makes me feel hot and healthy.

There is a choice of Japanese beers, freshly squeezed orange or carrot juice and, of course, Japanese tea. There's a fantastic atmosphere in which to make those slurping sounds needed to get the noodles down.

SHOPPING

Atlantis
49a Museum Street
WC1
071-405 2120

Open: Mon–Fri
10 a.m.–5.30 p.m.
Credit: A, V

This strange-looking bookshop specialises in books about the occult and spirituality. Anything Aleister Crowley ever wrote is available here, which should indicate what kind of shop Atlantis is. Books on spiritual healing and mediums, and various magazines and obscure publications can be found here, and the shop also sells a wide range of second-hand books and limited editions from occult artists, all reasonably priced.

The Cinema Bookshop
13–14 Great Russell Street WC1
071-637 0206

Open: Mon–Sat
1.30–5.30 p.m.
Credit: A, V

The Cinema Bookshop sells a mixture of popular and cult film books, magazines and stills, as well as a very good selection of posters, and if you are looking for an unusual photograph of Monroe, Dean, Clift, Brando or Taylor they also have a good range of photographic prints. There is a vast library of film stills – mostly commercial portrait shots – and a selection of books on TV and soap stars, which are proving to be amazingly popular.

Cornflake Shop
37 Windmill Street W1
071-631 0472

Open: Tues–Thurs,
Sat 10 a.m.–7 p.m.,
Fri 10 a.m.–6 p.m.
Credit: A, V

The electronics shops on Tottenham Court Road and many of the small streets leading off it supposedly have the best hi-fi and electrical equipment at the cheapest prices in Britain. I have been walking up and down that street for fifteen years looking for a bargain and have never yet found a genuine one. What I have found, though, is this specialist shop which not only sells state-of-the-art technology for the home or personal studio, but which can also make things to your own requirements, however odd they might be. They do quality sound systems and a good CD system will cost upwards of £500. One special luxury is the multi-room system, where a single touchpad controls all hi-fi, music or television throughout the house. I have no idea what the name means, and neither did anyone in the shop.

Central

Dillons
82 Gower Street WC1
071-636 1577

Open: Mon–Fri
9.30 a.m.–7 p.m.,
Sat 9.30 a.m.–6 p.m.
Credit: A, Amex, V

This branch of Dillons has four floors of tightly packed bookshelves in which to discover everything from psychology books to science fiction. They've always had anything I've ever asked for, and new publications are always available here. Because it is so close to the University the store is very busy, and there's a very comprehensive selection of academic and non-academic books. It's a great place to browse. There's also a very large magazine section with a good selection of foreign titles.

Forbidden Planet
71 New Oxford Street
WC1
071-836 4179
Open: Mon–Wed, Sat
10 a.m.–6 p.m., Thurs,
Fri 10 a.m.–7 p.m.
Credit: A, Amex, V

Forbidden Planet has grown from a small basement operation to this glamorous new shop. Every comic still available can be bought here. There's a very large SF section which heavily features cult TV such as *Doctor Who*. Games, fanzines, rare comics, American imports, T-shirts and superhero suits make Forbidden Planet an unforgettable adventure. In the basement there's a huge selection of books, especially TV tie-in titles, and fanzines to appeal to everybody. TV chat-show host Jonathan Ross buys comics in bulk here and I've seen him talking with great passion to the other addicts, who can be an odd bunch.

French's Theatre Bookshop
52 Fitzroy Street W1
071-387 9373

Open: Mon–Fri
9.30 a.m.–5.30 p.m.
Credit: A, Amex, DC, V

Since the 1830s, French's has specialised in scripts and new plays, as well as books about the theatre. Anything from stage costumes and make-up to voice technique is dealt with here. The staff are incredibly knowledgeable and helpful, and will always be able to point you in the right direction. They have a comprehensive catalogue, and also have a mail-order service which can be very useful.

Heal's
196 Tottenham Court
Road W1
071-636 1666

Open: Mon
10 a.m.–6 p.m.,
Tues–Fri
9.30 a.m.–6 p.m.,
Thurs 9.30 a.m.–7 p.m.,
Sat 9 a.m.–6 p.m.
Credit: A, Amex, DC, V

Heal and Son Ltd first arrived in London in 1805, and since then six generations of the family have run this magnificent store. The store is a good barometer for looking at what is going on in the world of design and I think it's better, though more expensive, than Habitat next door, as it seems to take more chances with new and more radical designs. Everything you could ever want for the home is here on the various floors. Unfortunately, you have to pay a high price for what you get here, but I still feel that you are getting something special and not mass-produced. Stores like this are always best at sale times (January and July) when prices drop dramatically and you can allow yourself to at least think about buying that sofa. There is also a restaurant (see separate entry).

James Smith & Sons
53 New Oxford Street
WC1
071-836 4731

Open: Mon–Fri
9.30 a.m.–5.30 p.m.,
Sat 10 a.m.–5.30 p.m.
Credit: A, V

Nothing much has changed at Smith's since it first opened in 1830. Umbrellas of every description and colour adorn the windows, and you can buy a good, stout umbrella here for £20 or, if you prefer, you can go for something a bit more special, such as a silver-handled brolly at a cool £400. In general a good-quality man's umbrella costs from £25 upwards, and handmade umbrellas from £45. The staff are all very helpful in an old-fashioned kind of way and will give you as much time as you need to make your decision.

Nice Irma's
46 Goodge Street W1
071-580 6921

Open: Mon–Wed, Fri
10.30 a.m.–6.30 p.m.,
Thurs 10 a.m.–7 p.m.,
Sat 10.30 a.m.–5 p.m.
Credit: A, Amex, V

Nice Irma's offers a cheap and occasionally elegant way to furnish your home using Indian-style rugs and cushion covers, and various other knick-knacks from Asia. Compared to the nearby stores Heal's (see separate entry) and Habitat, prices are much more approachable, and the quality is as good. The accessories range from lamps to plates and glasses, all of which are hand-made and mostly from India, and a selection of curtain' and furnishing fabrics. They're decent enough, though I get the feeling you might tire of this stuff quite quickly.

The Print Room
37 Museum Street WC1
071-430 0159

Open: Mon–Fri
10 a.m.–6 p.m.,
Sat 10 a.m.–4 p.m.
Credit: A, V

The Print Room has a beautiful collection of antique maps and prints, all of which are for sale at prices ranging from £2 to £5,000. Political caricatures, topographical prints and portraits dating from the sixteenth to the nineteenth centuries are all available, and there is a good selection of work by famous print-making artists such as Hogarth, Rowlandson and Gillray. A grotesque but very funny caricature can make a perfect present.

Skoob Books
15 & 17 Sicilian
Avenue WC1
071-404 3063

Open: Mon–Sat
10.30 a.m.–6.30 p.m.
Credit: A, Amex, V

This second-hand shop is so popular with people in the know about books that the good bargains go immediately. But that's what makes Skoob so exciting, since they refill the shelves as soon as they are emptied. There is quite a broad choice of subjects, but they always have a brilliant selection of poetry in hardback editions at a good price. It's also the only second-hand bookshop in London to have a substantial mathematics, science and computer section – this is at number 17, along with books on the ancient world and spiritual life; number 15 holds mainly titles on literature and the European humanities.

Vanbrugh Rare Books
40a Museum Street
WC1
071-404 0733

Open: Mon–Fri
10.30 a.m.–6 p.m.,
Sat, Sun 11 a.m–6 p.m.
Credit: A, Amex, DC, V

Museum Street is probably the most interesting small street in Bloomsbury. A mixture of good specialist bookshops and decent cafes makes it a good stop-off point before or after a visit to the British Museum. One of the few remaining bookshops in London able to describe itself as truly antiquarian, Vanbrugh Rare Books specialises in seventeenth-century English books but stocks others dating from the fifteenth to the early nineteenth centuries. Prices range from £20 to £20,000. They also sell a large selection of prints ranging in price from £20 to £20,000, any of which would be a welcome present. Books, maps and prints are all beautifully arranged, and the shop looks like it's come straight from the seventeenth century. Six to eight times a year they print an excellent catalogue (free), and they also have a mail-order service.

ENTERTAINMENT

The Cartoon Gallery
44 Museum Street WC1
071-242 5335

Open: Mon–Sat
10.30 a.m.–5.30 p.m.
No credit cards

This specialist cartoon gallery sells comical and satirical cartoons at prices ranging from £50 to about £300. It's run by the cartoonists themselves and there is definitely an air of enthusiasm about the place. Artists such as Mel Calman, Posy, Larry and Heath make up an impressive list, and the quality of work here, in a genre that is often underrated and taken for granted, is very high. There is an in-house framing service, and books and cards are also for sale.

Central YMCA
112 Great Russell Street
WC1
071-637 8131

Open: Mon–Fri
7 a.m.–10.30 p.m.,
Sat, Sun 10 a.m.–9 p.m.
Credit: A, V

Inside one of London's best and biggest sports complexes is a mixture of every possible indoor activity, as well as various places where you can have beauty, health or physiological treatments. The swimming pool is Olympic sized and the main gym is clean, modern and safe. It's all incredibly popular with students from the nearby University of London as it's reasonably cheap. Members can bring in guests who for £6 can use all the facilities. Daily memberships are worth checking out – give them a call.

Karsten Schubert
85 Charlotte Street W1
071-631 0031

Hidden among Channel 4 high-flyers and the offices of Saatchi & Saatchi, Karsten Schubert has given Charlotte Street something to be proud of. His gallery is probably one of the most radical in London, for

Open: Mon–Fri
10 a.m.–6 p.m.,
Sat 10 a.m.–midday
No credit cards

Renoir Cinema
Brunswick Centre,
Brunswick Square WC1
071-837 8402

Credit: A, V
Admission: £5

Schubert has never troubled himself with what will sell and keep the critics happy.

The shows here are always controversial and challenging, and you shouldn't go in there expecting pretty pictures.

It's a great shame that many people think that the Renoir is too out of the way to visit, as it's an excellent cinema showing good English and foreign-language films. It's also untrue, for the Renoir is in walking distance of Russell Square and Holborn tubes, and it also serves the local community who live around and above this basement cinema house. Frequently they have theme weekends here, which could feature, for example, a Roman Polanski or Orson Welles triple bill. The management has realised that you can get to see most older commercial films on video nowadays and instead shows a great deal of classic cult films such as Rohmer's *A Winter's Tale*. There is a coffee bar here which is adequate but not particularly inspiring.

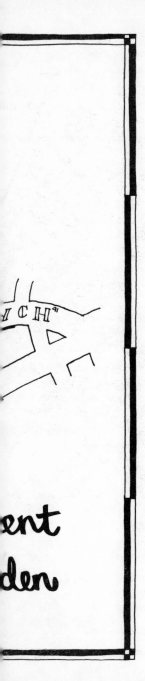

COVENT GARDEN

*t*he area between Long Acre, St Martin's Lane and the Strand was once pastureland enclosed by a fence. Until 1552 the land was owned by Westminster Abbey and known as a Convent Garden, though the area now known as Covent Garden stretches as far west as Charing Cross Road, as far north as High Holborn and as far east as Kingsway. This pastoral image was changed when the new owner, the Earl of Bedford, employed the palladio-inspired skills of Inigo Jones to design a square consisting of St Paul's Church and three rows of tall terraced houses looking inwards to the large open courtyard which is now the Piazza. It was a style of building entirely new to the city and became an instant success with the rich and famous who immediately bought or rented property on the square.

Around 1670 the fifth Earl of Bedford allowed market-stall holders to sell flowers and fruit in the area. Eventually shops were built in and around the Piazza, and by 1748 shops and coffee houses had sprung up all over the area and were patronised by the likes of Fielding, Boswell, Garrick and Hogarth. At the same time the area had become a bohemian quarter popular with actors and artists and served by an astonishing number of brothels, Turkish baths and gambling dens.

In an attempt to bring some order to the anarchic ways of the market, the sixth Duke of Bedford commissioned architect Charles Fowler in 1830 to design an appropriate building in

which tradesmen could carry out their work. At the time the market was thought of as a great building, but 25 years later it was nearly obsolete, unable to cope with the influx of traders from other markets which had been closed down. This resulted in even more lack of control and regulation, and eventually the Bedfords sold on responsibility for the market to a private company, leaving little more in the area than their motto – 'Que sera sera' (what will be, will be) – high on the Piazza wall. The Fowler Building was renovated rather than rebuilt and when the fruit and veg market moved to Battersea in 1974 the ruling council converted the area into the tourist attraction and shopping area it is now.

The restored Covent Garden is a mixture of the banal and the mysterious. Rather tacky market stands selling London memorabilia to anyone daft enough to buy it lie side by side with quality shops selling individually created, often somewhat expensive items. The latter may not be cheap, but they at least try to maintain a standard which has been slipping in London for some time. Over the past few years Covent Garden has overtaken the Kings Road or Knightsbridge as the most fashionable area to open up a clothes store. From the Piazza to Neal Street, new ideas in shopping open and close so quickly that it would be difficult to record them in this book. It would be a mistake to go looking for Covent Garden's seething underbelly, though, because it doesn't have one. With shops selling everything from ancient African and South American jewellery to homoeopathic remedies, Covent Garden has become a quaint consumer's zone with little of its promiscuous and licentious history apparent. All the tight regulation the Bedfords failed to achieve has now been realised by a new band of entrepreneurs who see their investment in the area as a long-term thing.

Covent Garden's main attraction is still the Opera House, with its gargantuan debts and questionable policies, but it's the numerous bars, cafes and shops which have revived the place. The streets around Neal Street and Neal's Yard (see separate entries) are the new centre of Covent Garden and it is here that you will find the most interesting shops. The recently developed Thomas Neal Mall on Shorts Garden is a mixture of furniture, art and fashion shops which has yet to capture the public's imagination, but the future of London shopping does seem to come in the shape of something not unlike an American mall. Such places have their good and bad points, but it's too early as yet to say if they will work in this country.

HOW TO GET THERE

Tubes
- Covent Garden
- Holborn
- Leicester Square
- Russell Square
- Tottenham Court Road

Buses
- Charing Cross Road: 24, 29, 176
- Kingsway: 30, 68, X68, 171, 188, 196, 501, 505, 521
- New Oxford Street: 8, 19, 22B, 25, 38, 55, 98
- Strand: 6, 9, 11, 13, 15, X15, 23, 77A, 176, 177X, 196

THE HAT SHOP

SIGHTS AND SITES

St Paul's Church
Bedford Street WC2
071-836 5221

Open: ring to check

This church was the pivotal point of Inigo Jones's layout of the Covent Garden square. The Earl of Bedford, a parsimonious man, commissioned Jones to do the work and told him that the church, which was for local parishioners, should be little more than a barn. Jones told the Earl that he would build the handsomest barn in England. The building was gutted by fire in 1795 but was rebuilt to Jones's design. It has recently had its outer walls repaired and cleaned and although it proudly overlooks the Piazza the entrance is through the churchyard to the rear where a delightful garden, well maintained and stocked with flowers, has benches where you can sit and read or have a sandwich and enjoy a brief moment of tranquillity in the city. St Paul's is known as the Actors' Church, and simple wooden tablets at the west end tell which thespians worshipped here or had their burial services here. They range from Ellen Terry to Ivor Novello, Marie Lloyd and Vivien Leigh. The public is welcome but as the church is not always open it is best to check before you go.

EATING AND DRINKING

Ajimura
51–53 Shelton Street
WC2
071-240 9424/
071-240 0178

Open: lunch, Mon–Fri
12–3 p.m.;
dinner, Mon–Sat
6–11 p.m.
Credit: A, Amex, DC, V
Average: restaurant
£60, sushi bar £30

This restaurant has been here for around eighteen years and although it is expensive it always seems to be very busy – especially with Japanese businessmen. Thankfully there is no karaoke machine so you don't have to watch drunken men singing badly, but there is a very good sushi bar. Separate from the restaurant, it is more comfortable and less formal, and what you see is what you get.

I've been told by Japanese people that the food in the main restaurant is reliable but unimaginative, but after a few cups of sake your own imagination will run wild anyway. Their set lunches are reasonable at around £10 for two courses, and their pre-theatre menus are small but good enough if you want something decent in a hurry. Set dinners cost between £19 and £38 per person, and sushi between £7.50 and £16.

Arts Theatre Cafe
6–7 Great Newport
Street WC2

This cafe, one of London's great undiscovered secrets, features a genuine Italian rustic menu mixing meats and pasta at a reasonable price. It's essentially

071-497 8014

Open:
midday–10.50 p.m.
No credit cards
Average: £23

an afternoon cafe, but food is available in the evening. It's a bit dark inside and you will have to mix with the punters and schoolkids coming to see the musical comedies which are the speciality of the small but reasonably comfortable theatre, but it's worth it.

For a time the Arts Theatre was known as an experimental venue where plays such as Beckett's *Waiting for Godot* had their London premieres. I always blush when I come in here, as it was the scene of my West End debut in the days when I considered myself an actor. The play I was in was absolutely terrible, and I was worse. The whole thing must have been a nightmare for the audience, but it did appeal to some strange-looking men in raincoats. If you did happen to catch the performance, do not allow the horrific memory to put you off trying either the theatre or the cafe.

Cafe Pelican
45 St Martin's Lane
WC2
071-379 0309

Open: Mon–Sat
11 a.m.–1.30 a.m.;
Sun,
11 a.m.–11.30 p.m.
Credit: A, Amex, V
Average: £45

Opening early enough for a late breakfast, French-style, this large brasserie looks rather grand towards the rear and has a front which gives you the feeling you might be sitting in rue Saint-Germaine. The coffee here is exceptional, something rare in London, and it is possible to have just a cappuccino and a snack in the front if you don't fancy a full meal. The back section is much posher and there's often a pianist there, giving the place a genuine French feel. The food itself is standard brasserie fare – anything from an omelette to a steak sandwich. Though it stays open late, be warned that the kitchen closes at midnight.

Cafe Pelican was the first restaurant in London to offer free valet parking, LA-style, to its customers.

Cafe Sante
17 Garrick Street WC2
071-240 7811

Open: Mon–Sat
8 a.m.–11.30 p.m.,
Sun 10 a.m.–7 p.m.
No credit cards
Average: £15

This sandwich bar is that rare thing – one with space. The seating arrangements are admirable, as the tables are spread out with enough room between them for privacy. The sandwiches are generous and far from basic, though primarily vegetarian. The best are the mozzarella and tomato on ciabatta and the curried chicken on granary, and they come in at an average of £2.50. The coffees are decent and the home-made dish of the day, which normally has an Italian feel, is great value at around £4. After a trip to the Photographers' Gallery in Great Newport

Street, this is a nice place to sit and mull over what you've seen.

The Chandos
29 St Martin's Lane
WC2
071-836 1401

Open: 9 a.m.–11 p.m.
Credit: A, V
Average: £10

One of the better drinking holes in Central London, this Victorian pub-restaurant has been lovingly restored to its former glory. It's perfectly situated in the heart of St Martin's Lane, next to the ENO (see separate entry) and within blinking distance of Trafalgar Square. It is an establishment where it is possible to eat breakfast from 9 a.m. and have afternoon tea and sandwiches after a walk around the National Gallery (see Westminster and St James's). The ground-floor bar is panelled and the wall and chairs look as if they have always been there, though they are in perfect condition. The pub grub is a mixture of bar meals and more substantial food such as lasagne, smoked mackerel salads and ploughman's, and upstairs they serve a full lunch every day. The menu is all very reasonably priced at around £5 for a full lunch, which goes down well with some of the pub's 'museum ale'.

Chez Solange
35 Cranbourn Street
WC2
071-836 0542

Open:
midday–12.15 a.m.
Credit: A, Amex, V
Average: £30

I'm never sure why I like this place as I always leave it thinking that it was too expensive and the food wasn't that good. It has the atmosphere of an old restaurant, which is what it is, but seems to be attempting to attract an older age group, making it all a bit formal and dull. The good thing about the menu is that it is not new French cooking but the older, more dignified stuff like calf's liver and steaks and, of course, onion soup.

Some nights they have a piano player who gets better as the evening progresses – perhaps he's putting away the drink – and who is definitely worth listening to. Chez Solange is definitely recommended for a romantic and unshowy evening.

Cordon Brown
32 Bedford Street WC2
071-836 7486

Open: Mon–Sat
7.30 a.m.–11.30 p.m.
No credit cards
Average: £25

Probably the best breakfast in Central London is available here. There's six different variations on the theme of bacon and egg, starting at £2.40 and ending up at just under a fiver. It's all quick, clean and very good, the type of breakfast normally available only in New York. The coffee at £1 is worth its price, which is rare in this city, and if you feel like coming back in the afternoon for lunch the salt-beef sandwiches, club sandwiches and avocado and prawn baps are generous and good. The cafe is licensed, so you can relax with a drink here rather than just hitting the spot and running. In the evening Cordon Brown functions as a pasta bar, serving dishes such as stuffed calamari and mussels.

Freud's
198 Shaftesbury Avenue
WC2
071-240 9933

Open: Mon–Sat
11 a.m.–11 p.m.,
Sun 5.30–10.30 p.m.
No credit cards

Hidden beneath the furniture store of the same name, this bar is far from obvious as you walk along the Covent Garden end of Shaftesbury Avenue. As you go down the wrought-iron stairs you could be forgiven for thinking you're about to enter some subterranean world from which you might never escape. If, in fact, you were to be detained here for a considerable time, it might not be so bad once you had recovered from the usually unexciting exhibition of paintings on the wall and thought about trying a honey muffin and a cappuccino, or one of the many imported European beers (all around the £2.50 mark). They serve pancakes and bagels and home-made lemonade and milkshakes are also available. At the weekend the place is overcrowded and because it is a basement this makes it too smoky and stuffy for me. The best time to go is in the afternoon before people finish work.

Haagen Daz
The Piazza WC2
071-240 0436

Open: 10 a.m.–11 p.m.
No credit cards

The Haagen Daz chain of ice-cream parlours has been staggeringly successful all over Britain, and everybody in the country seems recently to have become addicted to the rich, delicious ice cream it sells. This branch is big enough to have a food section, serving typical Italian-American diner food – pasta, fresh fruit salads and doughnuts, as well as tea, coffee and orange juice. But what you really come for is the ice cream – try a sinfully delicious tub of chocolate chip, pistachio or, better still, chocolate and pear. Truly wicked is the Cookie Crunch – two scoops of chocolate-chip ice cream on a cookie, topped with chocolate fudge sauce, whipped cream and chocolate vermicelli.

The Ivy
1 West Street WC2
071-836 4751

Open:
lunch 12–3 p.m.;

The Ivy was once the most fashionable restaurant in London, a favourite with everyone from Ivor Novello to Noël Coward, but as theatrical habits changed in the fifties and sixties the quality failed to impress a new generation until Chris Corbin and Jeremy King of the Caprice in St James's (see Westminster and St

Central

COVENT GARDEN

dinner 5.30–12 a.m.
Credit: A, Amex, DC, V
Average: £60

James's) mounted a rescue operation. The original decor remains but for the inclusion of the odd contemporary painting by the likes of Patrick Caulfield.

It's practically impossible to get a seat unless you book a month in advance and are prepared to be put into the forgotten section by the door – this table is in fact the best as everyone who comes here has to shuffle past. From George Michael to Harold Pinter, the Ivy chairs have held the brainy bums as well as the silly, and its function rooms have seen some very starry parties. It continues to hang on to its reputation as the people running it keep their ears to the ground and know who's in and who's out.

The menu is simple and unpretentious and favours fish, especially fish cakes and rocket salads. A brilliant Chateaubriand is available at £30 for two, and it's served up with the best chips in· town. It's also important to taste the Ivy sweets, especially the white chocolate mousse or the tiramisu, which are great.

Joe Allen
13 Exeter Street WC2
071-836 0651

Open: Mon–Sat
midday–12.45 a.m.;
Sun midday–11.45 p.m.
No credit cards
Average: £25

American-style restaurants in London can be incredibly naff with little more attempt at authenticity than a burger and a cocktail list and a few pictures of old Hollywood stars. Joe Allen's is the most successful of all the attempts to capture a slice of the States, triumphing where thousands have failed because of their menu, which changes daily, and their classic meat dishes such as steaks and burgers. A conscious effort has been made to add a fresh fish dish each day, and the pecan pie is as good as any you'll find Stateside. It's best to come here at night after a show so you can watch a steady stream of theatricals from the nearby Strand Theatre and from Shaftesbury Avenue arrive. What's really amusing is to seat yourself next to some of these luvvies and get a taste of the backstabbing, fear and loathing that goes on in their profession.

The Lamb and Flag
33 Rose Street WC2
071-497 9504

Open: Mon–Fri
11 a.m.–11 p.m.,

This ancient and tiny pub offers basic English fare upstairs, reasonably priced and average enough to be eaten without complaint. The dishes vary each day but almost always consist of stews and pies served with the traditional two veg and chips, all priced between £2.50 and £4. Bar snacks are available downstairs until 5.30 p.m. The pub serves Directors

Sat 11 a.m.–10.45 p.m.,
Sun 12–3 p.m.,
7–10 p.m.
No credit cards
Average: £10

and Courage Best from clean kegs, which makes a considerable difference, and attracts a mixture of low and high life which is probably its main attraction. It's fashionable with the nearby publishing houses and also with the stallholders from the markets off the Piazza. It can get a bit cramped in the evening, and if it's a hot day the street outside becomes crowded with noisy Englishmen doing their utmost to be noticed. I wouldn't recommend it to lone women, though.

Neal Street Restaurant
26 Neal Street WC2
071-836 8368

Open: Mon–Sat, lunch
12.30–2.30 p.m.,
dinner 12.30–11 p.m.
Credit: A, Amex, DC, V
Average: £80

As soon as you walk in the door you can sense that this restaurant is going to cost you money. Terence Conran's design is expensive-looking, and the David Hockney-designed menus sit comfortably with a clientele made up mainly of actors and their agents, and local advertising and design people. The restaurant has been fashionable for years and manages to maintain a reputation with dishes based on proprietor Antonio Carluccio's speciality, mushrooms. The food is mostly Italian, though it incorporates other cuisines, and the wine list, which has a distinct Italian bias, is exceptional. Especially good is the selection of New World wines.

Orso
27 Wellington Street
WC2
071-240 5269

Open: midday-midnight
No credit cards
Average: £45

This big restaurant, much loved by theatrical and television types who enjoy an evening's table-hopping, is subtly placed back from the street and down in a basement.

When I came here last I tried the sword fish which had been grilled but was too dry, and the vegetables looked a bit tired to me, but the people around me were throwing bucketloads of pasta down their throats and seemed much happier. The wines are not too expensively priced and if you pick the right night to go you could find yourself sitting next to Marie Helvin. She seems to be there every time I am, picking at a salad and looking better than she should at her age.

Rock and Sole Plaice
47 Endell Street WC2
071-836 3785

Fish and chip shops-cum-restaurants don't always offer much more than a greasy plate or a packet of something which can't do your cholesterol level much good, but this traditional chippie has made an effort to turn itself into something a bit more special. Its fast, friendly service is matched by the enormous portions

Open:
11.30 a.m.–11 p.m.
No credit cards
Average: £10

– a plate of cod and chips can cost as little as £4, and a decent piece of Dover sole £8–£9, which is pretty good going considering that some local restaurants will charge three times that. It's not licensed, though you're welcome to take your own, and seats around thirty people; when the sun is shining a few tables and chairs are placed outside. It's a great place to take kids when you're in a hurry and can't face a McDonald's, and it also does takeaway.

SHOPPING

Anello and Davide
35 Drury Lane WC2
071-836 1983

Open: Tues–Fri
9 a.m.–5.30 p.m.,
Sat 9 a.m.–5 p.m.
Credit: A, V

This otherworldly shoe shop has been serving the theatrical and dance worlds for a considerable time and has now taken its more extravagant designs and made them available to the public. As well as the two-toned spats and buttoned boots (£90), there is a selection of basic daywear for both men and women at prices which are quite reasonable, especially considering the location of the shop. A pair of basic character shoes cost £35, and bridal shoes, dyed to the colour of your choice, are £36 and up. Prices rise into the hundreds for those who fancy a career as toe-tappin' dancers.

Cenci
31 Monmouth Street
WC2
071-836 1400

Open: Mon–Fri
10.30 a.m.–7 p.m.,
Sat
10.30 a.m.–6.30 p.m.
Credit: A, Amex, DC, V

This excellent second-hand shop sells good-quality men's and women's clothes from the fifties and sixties. The window displays always look good here, and always succeed in enticing me into the shop. There are great bargains to be had here, and there is always a fantastic selection of Mod clothing. If you're in the mood to smarten up but don't like much of what is on offer in the shops today, you can pick up a good wool suit here for between £50 and £90.

Charles H. Fox Ltd
22 Tavistock Street
WC2
071-240 3111

Open: Mon–Fri
9.30 a.m.–1 p.m.,
2–5 p.m.
Credit: A, V

Established in 1878, this specialist shop is where the pros come for their stage, film and TV make-up. They have a big range of foundations and professional translucent powders, such as Kryolan. Just about everything you'll need, from liquid body make-up for those sexy scenes to UV day-glo creams and a mind-boggling range of real-hair moustaches can be had here. Until their recent return to high fashion, this was the only place in London to get decent false eyelashes. Don't be put off by the specialist nature of the shop, for the staff are very helpful and there is a range of books in stock which will show you just what can be achieved with these pots and creams.

Destroy

57–59 Neal Street
WC2
071-379 1896

Open: Mon–Sat
10.30 a.m.–7 p.m.,
Sun 1–6 p.m.
Credit: A, Amex, DC, V

John Richmond has fast become the only new designer of the past four or five years to succeed in capturing the public's imagination with a line of clothes that mix urbane streetwear with a streamlined elegance. His shop in Soho has been a great success and Destroy, in the hub of Covent Garden's hippest shopping area, has two floors featuring his new, cheaper diffusion line, Destroy. The clothes, for both men and women, have a rather lounge-lizardy feel to them, and are well designed and rather special. Richmond has always had a clientele of pop stars and fashion people but this new and more accessibly priced range, with a shirt or a pair of trousers costing around the £60 mark, should ensure that his clothes are worn even by us mere mortals.

Dover Bookshop

18 Earlham Street WC2
071-836 2111

Open: Mon–Sat
10 a.m.–6 p.m.
Credit: A, Amex, DC, V

This specialist bookshop sells a wide range of illustrations and designs which are copyright-free and so can be used freely by designers and craftspeople. Their list is very impressive and includes everything from Amish quilt patterns to Japanese floral stencils and Celtic designs. The Dover Bookshop has been here for seven years, since film director Ken Russell visited the original shop in Australia and advised them to open another in London. Russell is still a regular client, as is fellow director Peter Greenaway and sculptor Eduardo Paolozzi and a whole host of artists, designers and advertising people.

Flip

125 Long Acre WC2
071-836 7044

Open: Mon–Sat
10 a.m.–7 p.m.;
Sun midday–6 p.m.
Credit: A, Amex, V

More observant folks have told me that this second-hand shop's window display changes all the time, but it always looks like the same old American workwear to these tired old eyes. Prices for antique jeans start at about £15 and go as high as £25 or £45. The traditional American workwear is still as popular as ever in London and this two-level store's mixture of ginghams, jackets and jeans keep it a favourite with clubbers. If you feel able to sift through the mass of clothing in an attempt to find a pair of old Levis that actually fit and are not falling apart, then it's worth a visit – Flip is cheap but very hard work.

Freud's
198 Shaftesbury Avenue
WC2
071-831 1071

Open: Mon–Fri
10 a.m.–6 p.m.,
Sat 11.30–6 p.m.
Credit: A, V

This store sells the best reproduction Charles Rennie MacKintosh chairs money can buy, with the original long elegance and quality cherished by the much-loved designer. The store also stocks good-quality Italian electric fans and a decent selection of candlesticks, but it's really the chairs that are the thing, especially the Hill House, named after the building near Glasgow which MacKintosh designed for the Blackie publishing dynasty. It's made of solid maple and retails at around the £250 mark. Their bestseller is Ingram Street, a high-backed oak tearoom chair which retails at £250.

The Hat Shop
58 Neal Street WC2
071-836 6718

Open: Mon–Sat
10 a.m.–6 p.m.
Credit: A, Amex, V

It seems you have to be a certain type of person to want to wear a hat, and if you are, then this is the shop for you. It's tiny and overflowing with every type of hat imaginable. From a fez to a deerstalker, everything you might want to cover your bonce with is here and advice is readily available from the experts behind the counter. They might not tell you if you look stupid in a hat, but they will guide you to one which makes you look less foolish than you might do. Prices range from £15, and the place gets so packed that they have to let people in in batches.

Jones
13 Floral Street WC2
071-240 8312

Open: Mon–Sat
9.45 a.m.–6.30 p.m.,
Sun midday–5 p.m.
Credit: A, Amex, V

Jones is a favourite with pop stars who feel they need the security of designerwear on their bums and backs to make them stand out from the rest of us mere mortals. Both men's and women's clothes are available here, and Gaultier and Miyake are sold alongside the Jones label, which is a lot cheaper and more wearable than the big-name imports.

   You need courage and a big bank balance to enter this shop but it's worth the effort, if only for a possible glimpse of Jason Donovan or Mick Jagger spending their fortunes.

Kookai
The Piazza WC2
071-379 1318

Open: Mon–Sat
10 a.m.–8 p.m.,
Sun midday–6 p.m.
Credit: A, Amex, DC,
Switch, V

Covent Garden's Piazza has in recent years become very commercial: apart from the market stalls the shops here are mainly commercial chains such as Hobbs, Body Shop, Cable & Co. and Monsoon. Kookai is part of a very successful French womenswear chain which is beginning to make its mark on the British market with a very successful combination of French style and reasonable prices. Jeans, woollens, knitwear, leggings, leather skirts, printed dresses and blazers are all well designed and priced from £30 to £300. The clothes are sexy and very wearable, and are definitely influenced by what is going on in the world of high fashion. They appeal to every age group and can be mixed with enough individual flair to make you feel you're not one of the crowd – scene rather than herd, so to speak.

N. Mann
7 Monmouth Street
WC2
071-836 9049

Open: Mon–Thurs
9.30 a.m.–6 p.m.,
Fri 9.30 a.m.–5 p.m.
No credit cards

Since 1860 five generations of the Mann family have worked as framers here, and of all the many places in London offering a framing service, Mann's is definitely the best. There is a good range of traditional and modern frames available, from rich nineteenth-century oak to modern aluminium. The prices depend on the amount of work to be done but start from £10 and can go up as high as £300. Prints, oil paintings and good drawings of the Covent Garden area are also available in this good shop.

Monsoon
23 The Market WC2
071-836 9140

Open: Mon–Sat
10 a.m.–8 p.m.,
Sun midday–6 p.m.
Credit: A, Amex, DC,
Switch, V

The award-winning designer Rifat Ozbek learned his trade working at Monsoon, which, before the recent hippy revival, catered almost exclusively for those who still loved long, flowing skirts and dresses. Now this look is finally back in style and Monsoon's print frocks, in everything from cotton to Viyella, and hand-embroidered Indian silk shirts are selling like hotcakes. This new shop, on the ground floor of the Royal Opera House, is spacious and well-organised, making it easy for you to match one item with another. Considering the work that goes into the clothes, these gorgeous, deeply coloured clothes are not expensive: skirts range from £35 to £40 and dresses from £60 to £200.

Morning
20 Wellington Street
WC2
071-379 8249

Open: Mon–Sat
10.30 a.m.–6.30 p.m.
Credit: A, Amex, V

For ten years Italian designer Susie Callas has kept Covent Garden women happy with her stylish clothes. Classic suits that would look good on any occasion, from the office to an evening at a restaurant, as well as very feminine and sexy evening wear, are all made from fabrics which hang beautifully on the body and which tend to need little in the way of fussy styling. Prices range from £100 to £300, and the quality is always high.

Moss Bros
21–26 Bedford Street
WC2

Moss Bros is the most famous place in the world to hire men's and women's formal dress. The highland, livery and military wear is absolutely brilliant and no

Central

071-240 4567

Open: Mon–Wed, Fri,
Sat, 9 a.m.–6 p.m.;
Thurs 9 a.m.–7 p.m.
Credit: A, Amex, DC, V

matter how detailed your requirements they never seem to let you down. For big occasions book your clothing early, but you don't usually need to worry as whatever you want they will probably have it in any size. Quality items for sale can be found on the shelves, but you need to look hard – while some are quite good other items are on the naff side. Stick to the hired stuff or go there for a haircut and enjoy the five-star treatment at a reasonable price. The price of hiring can vary but you must always leave a deposit or pay in advance. Highland wear can cost as much as £50–£75 for an evening, black tie between £38 and £40 and women's wear from £50 for a cocktail frock to £120 for very heavily beaded gowns.

Mysteries
11 Monmouth Street
WC2
071-240 3688

Open: Mon–Sat
10 a.m.–6 p.m.
Credit: A, Switch, V

This large New Age and psychic centre sells every-thing to do with the supernatural, the paranormal and astrology. The very long list of services available includes tarot and palm readings (£15) as well as past life readings, which involve a form of mild hypnotism under which you remember and work through trau-matic past-life experiences (£40). The staff are helpful and more than willing to explain everything to you, but I have to say that faced with a choice of natural healing, biorhythms, herbal remedies and pendu-lums, I chose the exit.

The Natural Shoe Store
21 Neal Street WC2
071-836 5254

Open: Mon, Tues
10 a.m.–6 p.m.,
Wed–Fri
10 a.m.–7 p.m.,
Sat 10 a.m.–6.30 p.m.,
Sun midday–5 p.m.
Credit: A, Amex, DC, V

This hippie heaven sells earth-loving footwear such as Indian moccasins and bumby-soled sandals which are supposed to improve the circulation, and is a good place to get your summer Bass Weejun loafers (£79.95) which look good with anything. Caterpillar boots cost around £65. Strangely enough, once you have admired the eco-conscious interior, recycled timber and low-voltage lighting, you will see lots of leather and suede – they are not quite so right-on here as they might think. But on the shelves there's bound to be something perfect for the mood you're in, man.

Neal's Yard
Neal's Yard WC2
Open: Mon–Fri
10.30 a.m.–5.30 p.m.,
Sat
10.30 a.m..–4.30 p.m.

This strange little backstreet yard is a mecca for those who prefer food in its pure and most natural form. There's a wonderful bakery which sells an abundance of freshly baked bread, as well as wholefood ware-houses and small eating houses which cook the food on the premises. Vegetarian and vegan food available includes gado gado at £2.60, pizzas, croissants and soups, as well as the usual vegetable curries and soups. The prices are slightly high – around £4 for a small dish of food – as the vegetables and grains have all been grown organically and you have to pay for that peace of mind. The cheese shop used to be the highlight of the Yard, with a huge selection including Stiltons and Cheddars in great blocks, but has now moved around the corner to Shorts Garden (see separate entry). In the afternoons the healthy and the food fundamentalists gather here to look at each other's pale skin and talk about how well they all look. They seem to enjoy the pitta-bread sandwiches, salads and fruit drinks served up rather ironically in polystyrene tubs and cups. They also run the severe danger of being overrun by twelve-year-olds on skateboards coming to buy up Slam City Skates (see separate entry).

The main attraction now is the Neal's Yard Apothecary (071-379 7222), which sells a vast selection of massage oils and creams, vegetable soaps and ointments which might make you feel twenty years younger. The now famous blue bottles keep the prices up but these magic solutions seem to have a cure for every pain. The apothecary also has Therapy Rooms, offering a wide range of alternative remedies, where they'll deal more intensively with your problem (071-379 7662).

Neal's Yard Dairy
17 Shorts Gardens
WC2
071-379 7646

Open: Mon–Sat
9 a.m.–7 p.m.,
Sun 11 a.m.–5 p.m.
Credit: A, V

When this cheese shop moved to this new address in 1992, the people who run it used their thirteen years' experience to design the perfect place to store and sell cheeses. Inside this wonderful store is shelf upon shelf of cheeses stacked on top of each other and long counters of soft cheeses. Downstairs is the maturing cellar where the soft cheeses such as Milleen, Gubbeen and Caerphilly mature. There are also little chunks of cheese laid out for you to try.

The staff in the Neal's Yard Dairy are enthusiastic and helpful and are more than willing to advise you on the best way to store or serve your purchases. I never feel under any pressure to buy in here. Choosing your cheese is made more fun by the practice of labelling every piece with its place of

origin – for example, Mary Holbrook's delicious Emlett (£1.65 a half pound) is made in the Mendip Hills from unpasteurised ewe's milk, and Stilton from Colston Bassett in Nottinghamshire is £4.45 a pound.

The shop also stocks yogurts and delicious breads from & Clarke's famous bakery (see Notting Hill). They also do mail order and will give you a catalogue to take away and browse over.

Paul Smith
41–44 Floral Street
WC2
071-379 7133

Open:
Mon–Wed, Fri, Sat
10.30 a.m.–6.30 p.m.;
Thurs
10.30 a.m.–7 p.m.;
Sat
10.30 a.m.–6.30 p.m.
Credit: A, Amex, DC, V

From his Nottingham base, the eponymous Paul Smith has created a multi-million-pound empire out of providing contemporary menswear with a twist. It's all a bit overrated, I think, but there's still no competition to touch him in the off-the-peg shirt-and-suit market, and he's big all over the world, from Japan to the USA. You can get an entire outfit here, from socks and underwear (more affordable than you might think) to suits and ties, and his clothes are also for sale in other shops. An easy-to-wear outfit for any occasion can be found in the basement, and his shirts and leisurewear are often fun enough to warrant paying his rather exorbitant prices. Suits range from £500, shirts cost £65, boxer shorts £25 and raincoats upwards of £300. He has just launched a sedate range of womenswear which should see him conquer that market as well.

The Russian Shop
99 The Strand WC2
071-497 9104

Open: Mon–Sat
9.30 a.m.–5.30 p.m.
Credit: A, Amex, DC, V

Tucked between the Savoy Hotel and Simpsons restaurant, this craft shop specialises in all types of goods from Eastern Europe, including the famous dolls which fit inside each other. Called matrioshkas, they vary in price according to size, but can be as little as £5.50 or as much as £400. Kilims, glass ornaments, laquered boxes and drawings of the Steppes are all on display here. Everything is made from natural materials and according to traditional manufacturing methods.

Shelly's
14–18 Neal Street
WC2
071-240 3726

Open:
Mon–Wed, Fri, Sat
9.30 a.m.–6.30 p.m.,

Shelly's provide the best selection of Dr Marten air-sole shoes in London. From cherry-red classics and twenty-hole boots to new, more adventurous designs, this shop is always so far ahead in both style and price that you wonder what the competition is doing. The boots and shoes are not made from the best leather and suede, but offer up-to-the-minute designs for a fraction of the big-house prices, from

Thurs
9.30 a.m.–7.30 p.m.
Credit: A, Amex, DC, V

names as big as Katherine Hamnett, Jean-Paul Gaultier, John Richmond and Vivienne Westwood. Despite the success of his company, Shelly, the man behind the operation, still works from a grotty storeroom above his Oxford Street shop.

Slam City Skates
16 Neal's Yard WC2
071-240 0928

Open: Mon–Sat
10 a.m.–6.30 p.m.
Credit: A, V

Slam City Skates is the only specialist skateboard shop left in London after the skateboarding craze of 1986–88. The shop sells only 'proper' skateboards, not plasticky toy ones, and prices for a full set-up range from £90 to £200. As well as the boards themselves, Slam City Skates also stocks spares and protective gear such as helmets, gloves and kneepads, and a range of snowboards and snowboarding gear, from £200 upwards. The staff here are all very knowledgeable about what's happening on the skateboard scene and are very willing to advise. But the real reason Slam City Skates is always packed out with clubbers is because of the street fashion clothes. There's a good variety of Stussy gear (shirts cost about £50 and T-shirts about £30), Vans shoes (about £50), Anarchic Adjustment, Jive, Ben Davis and their own label, Insane, which covers the whole range of street fashion from T-shirts at £25 to jackets at £250.

Stanford's
12–14 Long Acre WC2
071-836 1321

Open: Mon, Sat
10 a.m.–6 p.m.,
Tues–Fri 9 a.m.–7 p.m.
Credit: A, V

This long-established shop is the best map and travel bookshop in London, and if you are about to set off on your travels or simply enjoy reading about remote parts of the globe, you simply must come here. The ground floor is laid out by continent, with everything from relevant fiction to travel journalism on the shelves. There is also a great variety of Bartholomew world maps and globes to choose from which can be very amusing as, due to recent political upheavals, they always seem to be out of date. In the British section in the basement there is, among other things, a comprehensive selection of British Ordnance Survey maps, essential if you're about to take up rambling. The staff are very helpful, too.

Theatre Zoo
21 Earlham Street WC2
071-836 3150

Open: Mon–Fri
9 a.m.–5.30 p.m.

Make-up artists from the film, theatre and TV world all come here to pick up the latest tools and tricks, but Theatre Zoo is also open to the general public. As well as selling cosmetics, wigs, costume jewellery and a great selection of beards and moustaches, the shop also hires out a huge range of fancy-dress and

Credit: A, V

costumes at £30 a time. There is also a terrific range of masks here, which are always topical and wickedly caricature well-known political and media people.

The Tintin Shop
34 Floral Street WC2
071-836 1131

Open: Mon–Sat
10 a.m.–6 p.m., Sun
midday–5 p.m.
Credit: A, V

This bright, modern shop with pale wood and glass counters is stuffed full of all kinds of merchandising relating to the cartoon hero Tintin. The shop has been here since 1990 and stocks keyrings, diaries, packs of envelopes, T-shirts and the famous cuddly sweater, which costs about £100. Of course, the full range of Tintin books is also available, as well as other books by the great master Herve. It's an odd little specialist store which rides on the wave of adult nostalgia for the boy detective.

Venus
19 Shorts Gardens
WC2
071-379 1426

Open: Mon–Sat
midday–6 p.m
Credit: A, V

This treasure of a shop, tucked away in the basement of a store selling ethnic pieces and gifts, it stocks beautiful clothes from Britain's best designers, and all at incredibly low prices for what they are. Suzie, the owner, has been here since 1990 and has built up a regular clientele who come here to flick through the rails of Vivienne Westwood, John Galliano, Bella Freud, Arabella Pollen, Ben de Lisi. You can get jackets and dresses here for £60 to £100 – they're not second hand but they are a season or so out of date, though with clothes as good as these that doesn't really make much difference. If you always wanted a designer piece but couldn't afford it, grab what you want as soon as you can, for turnover, not surprisingly, is very fast.

William Hunt
68 Neal Street WC2
071-836 0809

Open: Mon–Sat
10 a.m.–7 p.m.,
Sun midday–5 p.m.
Credit: A, Amex, DC, V

This simple small shop offers a decent contemporary selection of menswear. Italian striped cotton trousers and very British John Smedley sea island cotton shirts (£55) lie beside trousers in anything from tartan to suede (around £65). Waistcoats here cost about £95. Everything seems to have been carefully mixed and matched so that the less adventurous can leave the shop with a couple of wearable outfits and still have some change in their pockets.

**YHS Adventure
Shop**
14 Southampton Street
WC2
071-836 8541

Run by the Youth Hostelling Association, this shop sells all the equipment, clothing, literature and accessories you could ever want for a holiday walking, climbing or camping. The clothes are made from tough, practical fabrics such as Goretex and are sturdy and practical with few concessions to fashion. There's

Open: Mon–Wed
10 a.m.–6 p.m.,
Thurs, Fri
10 a.m.–7 p.m.,
Sat 9 a.m.–6.30 p.m.
Credit: A, Amex, DC,
Switch, V

a vast range of sleeping bags, tents and rucksacks available, and there is information available on all outdoor activities. There is also a large selection of books covering the practical rather than the literary side of travel. The Adventure Shop is very popular with students, who know that the goods and equipment on offer are the cheapest of their sort in London.

ENTERTAINMENT

**The English
National Opera**
The Coliseum,
St Martin's Lane WC2
071-836 3161

The London Coliseum was commissioned in 1904 by Oswald Stoll, the most powerful actor-manager of his day, as a home for variety. Stoll and his architect Frank Matcham toured Europe to research modern ideas for his dream theatre, which from the beginning attracted the attention of the public with its enormous tower featuring figures representing Art, Music, Science and Architecture, and topped by a revolving dome. The London Coliseum was the first theatre in England to have lifts and a revolving stage. With a capacity of 2,558 it is also the largest theatre in the capital.

The history of the theatre is littered with names such as Edith Evans, Ellen Terry, Lillie Langtry and Sarah Bernhardt, who all performed here, but perhaps the Coliseum's greatest moment was in 1918, when the great Diaghilev brought his Ballet Russe here to thunderous applause. Between 1931 and 1968 the theatre was frequently used as a cinema as well as a venue for operettas by the Sadlers Wells Company. In 1968 it became the home of the Sadlers Wells Opera, known since 1974 as the English National Opera, which is permanently based here and puts on several productions a year, all in English.

The ENO is known for its often controversial productions such as its scratch 'n' sniff version of Prokofiev's *The Love of Three Oranges*, and classic operas such as *Madam Butterfly, Cosi fan Tutte* or even Wagner's *Ring* cycle are given a thorough examination and often radical production, attracting a varied audience ranging from young families to aficionados. Recent directors such as Ken Russell (in his restaging of Gilbert and Sullivan's *Princess Ida*) have employed filmic ideas, which seem to suit the huge auditorium, to good effect here. The Coliseum also plays host to a number of visiting companies –

one of the most exciting recently being the Alvin Ailey American Dance Theater.

The ENO is cheaper than the Royal Opera House and far less pompous. Coffee and sandwiches rather than champagne and smoked salmon are available at the interval. If you are new to opera then there can be no better introduction than a trip to the ENO.

Jubilee Hall
The Piazza WC2
071-836 4835

Open: Mon–Fri
6.30 a.m.–10 p.m.,
Sat, Sun 10 a.m.–5 p.m.
Credit: A, Amex, V

Considering its central location, this is an enormous gym. It's divided up so that badminton, indoor football or basketball enthusiasts can exercise at the same time as the aerobic and meathead body-builders next door. The best time to go is between 9 a.m. and lunchtime – any later than that and it's impossible to move as the place fills up with serious body-beautiful types and hordes of over-the-top business people who spend an awfully long time staring at themselves. If you need to get in shape various instructors will take you on a tough circuit at an extra cost, and there are various classes which you can join – take your pick of anything from dance to martial arts.

It's relatively cheap for a West End sports club – membership costs between £45 and £500 a year, with day membership at £5 and monthly membership £40. The small cafe is clean and good. The only problem is the other people – too many of them.

**The Photographers'
Gallery**
5 & 8 Great Newport
Street W1
071-831 1772

Open: Tues–Sat
11 a.m.–7 p.m.
No admission charge

The shows here change constantly, and in my experience have never compromised or gone for easy commercial photographs. Recent work shown has varied from collections of London pictures to avant-garde work by unknown or very well-known photographers, and there seems to be a policy of showing the work of those trying to do something new with the medium. Photographs are for sale in the print room and include everything from straight Victorian work to contemporary prints, and start at about £50. They also frame and mount work here, which costs, depending on the size, from £30. Other spaces in the gallery focus on British photographers working in anything from fashion to landscape.

The Poetry Society
22 Betterton Street WC2
071-240 4810

The Poetry Society was founded with the intention 'to promote poetry'; it publishes the quarterly magazine *Poetry Review* and runs the biggest national poetry competition which is usually launched in April

Open: Mon–Fri
9.30 a.m.–5.30 p.m.
Credit: A, V

and which has a November closing date. They hold regular readings here – ring for details – and also have regular talks which are not always about poetry but are sometimes concerned with literature in general.

**The Royal Opera
House**
Covent Garden WC2
071-240 1066

The first theatre to stand on this site was built in the eighteenth century for the pantomimic and harlequin John Rich, who moved here from his Lincoln's Inn Fields venue to create the most luxurious theatre London had ever seen. The history of the theatre throughout this time is fascinating: Handel is said to have written *Samson, Solomon* and many other oratorios specifically for Covent Garden. All the great English actors, from Garrick to Macklin and Reg Woofington, appeared in the theatre, and Goldsmith's *She Stoops to Conquer* and Sheridan's *The Rivals* were both premiered here.

The second theatre was built here in 1809 after Rich's creation was destroyed by fire. The architect Robert Smirke modelled his building on the Temple of Minerva in Athens. The price of theatre tickets was raised to pay for the new building, prompting eleven days of continuous rioting. During this period Mozart's *Don Giovanni* and *The Marriage of Figaro* received their first British performances. However, Smirke's theatre also burned down and in 1858 was replaced E. M. Barry's new design, which survived virtually unchanged until the 1980s, when a huge extension was planned for the Royal Opera and the Royal Ballet.

The Royal Opera House's 2,141 seats have in their time seen remarkable performances such as Benjamin Britten's *Troilus and Cressida* or the extraordinary choreography of the late Sir Kenneth Macmillan. However, it is a controversial venue because of its pricing policy: it is virtually impossible for normal working people to afford tickets here unless they are prepared to sit in the gods or queue for hours on the off chance of snapping up some returns. Many of the seats and boxes are given over to corporate entertainment, which is a great shame.

**Theatre Royal
Drury Lane**
Catherine Street WC2

Once upon a time this theatre was the main attraction in Covent Garden. Built in 1663, it was one of two Royal Patent theatres – the other being Lincoln's Inn

Central

071-836 3687

Credit: A, Amex, DC, V

Fields Theatre, now gone – and has a formidable reputation, and not only for its productions. In 1665 Nell Gwynne appeared here in Dryden's *Indian Queen*; in 1716 a man tried to assassinate George III there; and in 1737 there was a riot after footmen were refused free admission. Henry Holland built what was thought to be the loveliest theatre in Europe here in 1794, but this masterpiece was burned down in 1809, supposedly as Sheridan watched from a nearby coffee house. The building which stands today is the work of Benjamin Wyatt, who in 1811 created a theatre of ovular domes which begin at the Doric vestibule with a domed entrance hall leading up the staircase to domed foyers.

Drury Lane became famous for its musical productions, the longest-running being *My Fair Lady*, with 2,281 performances. It is said to have a ghost which appears only in the Circle during matinees and which is thought to be the spirit of a man whose skeleton was found behind one of the walls, a knife between the ribs.

*M*ayfair is the area which stretches from Marble Arch to Hyde Park Corner and from Oxford Street to Regent Street and on to Piccadilly. It gets its name from the fair which was held in Shepherd Market in the eighteenth century until the complaints of new and wealthy residents, refugees from the declining Covent Garden and Soho, forced it to move. The new and fashionable developments of gracious Georgian squares became home to those anxious to live on the other, richer side of Regent Street.

Apart from Shepherd Market, which has kept something of its village-like atmosphere – despite the open practice of prostitution in its streets – Mayfair has since become sedate and a bit of a bore. Old stables and mews buildings have all been converted into bijou apartments, and the grand houses are now the offices of modern-day property speculators and estate agents.

The famous Berkeley Square is the most overrated of all London's squares. There's no doubt that the Georgian character of the building on the west side (which dates from the 1730s) has a lot of virtues, but mostly the square's 30 plane trees are overshadowed by anonymous office blocks. There are two or three bars and clubs here, playgrounds for the rich and famous – the best known are Annabel's and the Clermont at number 44, and Morton's, the favourite haunt of the music-industry bigwigs. The area also has a few haute-cuisine restaurants and specialist shops, which are all very expensive, but the heart

of the district is Bond Street and Cork Street, where there are enough interesting things to keep you hooked on window-shopping. Nothing is cheap here but the shops are not as intimidating as they might look.

The history of Mayfair's buildings and people is a quiet one but a walk about will take you through some of the wealthiest and grandest shopping and residential streets in London.

HOW TO GET THERE

Tubes
- Bond Street
- Green Park
- Hyde Park Corner
- Marble Arch
- Oxford Circus
- Piccadilly Circus

Buses
- Davies Street (northbound only): 8
- New Bond Street (southbound only): 8
- Oxford Street: 2A, 2B, 6, 7, 8, 10, 12, 13, 15, 16A, 23, 73, 88, 94, 98, 113, 135, 137, 137A, 139, 159
- Park Lane: 2A, 2B, 10, 16, 36, 73, 74, 82, 137, 137A
- Piccadilly: 9, 14, 19, 22, 38
- Regent Street: 3, 6, 12, 13, 15, 23, 53, 53X, 88, 94, 139, 159

BROWN'S HOTEL

SIGHTS AND SITES

Bond Street, W1

Bond Street is Mecca for art dealers and fashion folks, and is supposedly the home of the best of London's taste. This may have been true at one time but the street is beginning to look a little tired now that the halcyon days of spend, spend, spend are over. Bond Street is definitely one of the best streets in London for window-shopping, though the side streets and off-shoots such as South Molton Street, Dering Street and Avery Row are where the most interesting things are to be found.

Towards the southern end of Bond Street stands the beautiful jewellery store Asprey's, unaffected by fashion and worth a look if only for the displays in its windows. Around the corner on Bruton Street is the Time/Life building, designed by Michael Rosenauer and featuring a frieze by Henry Moore which you can see from the street. Further up on the right are Sotheby's auction rooms, which can be as thrilling as great theatre when something rare is up for sale.

If the shops and their prices become too much for you to bear, I recommend you head for Hanover Square, one of the capital's most wonderful Georgian squares and now the home of the likes of the Conde-Nast empire. The green patch in the middle is a welcome oasis where you can regenerate your shopping batteries.

Mount Street Gardens, W1

Between Grosvenor Square and Berkeley Square, and tucked behind the Gothic revival building which is the Church of the Immaculate Conception, the Mount Street Gardens are a tranquil spot in the big city. The sound of the Latin Mass can occasionally be heard here when the Jesuit fathers are in full voice. It's a remarkably well-kept garden which has never been damaged, although there is a school next door – which means that it might be a good idea to avoid coming here at lunchtime or during early-morning break. It's not too far from Bond Street so you can walk up here to rest your feet after a day's shopping.

The Museum of Mankind
6 Burlington Gardens
W1

The Ethnography Department of the British Museum (see Bloomsbury) has been based here since 1970, when it was moved from the main museum building as a result of lack of space. The building was designed

071-437 2224

Open: Mon–Sat
10 a.m.–5 p.m.,
Sun 2.30–6 p.m.
No admission charge

**The Royal
Academy of Arts**
Burlington House,
Piccadilly W1
071-439 7438

Open: 10 a.m.–6 p.m.;
cafe 10 a.m.–5 p.m.
Admission: £4
Credit cards: A, Amex, V

by Sir James Pennithorne in 1869 and was originally owned by the University of London. The exotic, tribal exhibits from the British Museum's collection are quite astonishing, and the small size of the place makes it easy to take it all in without being too easily distracted. There is a very good book and gift shop as well. The Cafe de Colombia (see separate entry) is also one of the best venues in London for lunch or an afternoon snack.

The Royal Academy was founded in 1768. George III was its first patron, supporter and protector, Sir Joshua Reynolds its first president. Since then it has consistently held its ground as the place for the finest traditional art shows each year. It is not only an exhibition hall but a school, where the likes of Constable and Turner learned their craft.

The main RA collection, the result of gifts and donations, is impressive, but it is its annual Summer Exhibition which captures the public's attention. For over 200 years artists – many of them amateurs – have been submitting contemporary paintings, drawings, engravings, sculptures and architectural plans to the committee of the RA, who then make their selection. Members of the Academy can submit work without it being judged, and as many of them are getting on a bit the quality of the work can be very variable. It can be quite surprising to find the work of an unknown artist hanging beside a painting from some-one quite established, and to find that the second is not really any better. All the work is for sale, at prices that range from £200 to £20,000.

Other shows throughout the year consist either of members' work or major international exhibitions, often sponsored. Recent highly successful shows have included exhibitions of new German art, Pop art and the sacred art of Tibet. The Monet show had people queueing around the block to get in. There is also a new wing which has given rise to much controversy because it has the smell of modernism about it, but I think it adds a new dimension to the space and is a good-sized gallery for the smaller exhibitions.

The Academy shop, which is not great by current art-world standards, normally sells items tied in with the major show of the time. The cafe is overpriced and forgettable, but not bad if you're desperate.

Burlington House, which is home to the Academy, is the last of Piccadilly's great noblemen's houses. The original was built in 1665 but has continually been altered and added to. In 1854 it was bought by the government for £140,000, and is now a scholarly home for academics who work for the various societies based here, such as the Geological Society, the Royal Astronomical Society and the Society of Antiquarians. It has a nice courtyard, and an outdoor cafe has recently been opened here. It's modelled on the one indoors and is just as expensive.

Shepherd Market, W1

It was here that the original May Fair was held until it was suppressed in the eighteenth century. Its renowned drunkenness and debauchery upset Mayfair's new gentry so much that they used all their powers to end it, shutting off the area to the lower classes for ever more. Today the eighteenth-century feel of the area is remarkable and is one of the few surprises left in Mayfair. The small cafes and grocery shops sit comfortably in the tight streets alongside apartments advertising anything from a massage to a spanking. The authorities seem to tolerate the open prostitution that goes on here, probably due to the fact that some of the highest in the land are said to be regular visitors. Definitely worth a wander round to soak up the atmosphere.

EATING, DRINKING AND SLEEPING

Al Hamra
31–33 Shepherd Market W1
071-493 1954

Open: midday–midnight
Credit: A, Amex, DC, V
Average: £30

Middle Eastern cuisine has never caught the British imagination in the way that Asian and European cooking have, but in recent years more and more people have been tempted into Lebanese, Egyptian and Moroccan restaurants. Al Hamra has been in Shepherd's Market for years and was once the place where rich Arabs would eat before hitting Mayfair's casinos. Those days are over but the restaurant is still worth a visit. Meze – a selection of starters – is brilliant value at £20 a head.

Brown's Hotel
19–20 Dover Street W1

Brown's Hotel is a taste of the Britain you no longer thought existed. Opened in 1837 and taking up

071-493 6020

Open: restaurant – lunch
12.15-2.30 p.m.,
dinner 6–10 p.m.,
Sun 6.30–9.30 p.m.
Credit: A, Amex, DC,
MC, V
Average: double room
£175 plus VAT;
dinner £60;
tea £12.95
Restaurant and bar open
to non-residents

fourteen elegant townhouses, it's the last word in class. Its 120 rooms and suites all have their own character and the style of the hotel itself is a vague cross between town and country, English style. I have never eaten in the restaurant but am told that it's very good – a traditional French-style restaurant with expensive trimmings.

The very best thing worth coming to Brown's for, though, is the tea. Quiet dark rooms with wood panelling come alive with the sound of tail-coated waiters bustling to and fro with silver trays loaded with cucumber sandwiches and warm scones and preserves. Tea begins at 3 p.m. and high tea at 4 p.m. It's worth arriving on time as it's becoming increasingly difficult to get a table here – Brown's has become very popular with old and young in the middle of affairs, or with very tired-looking art dealers trying in vain to sell to a customer over a cup of Earl Grey. The teas range from Lapsang Souchong to English Breakfast, and there is always an abundant selection of cream cakes which spoil any attempt at playing it cool as they fall out of your mouth and into your lap. Definitely recommended for the naughty, the secretive or the bohemian.

Cafe de Colombia
Museum of Mankind,
6 Burlington Gardens
W1
071-287 8148

Open: Mon–Sat
10 a.m.–4 p.m.,
Sun 2.30–5 p.m.
No credit cards
Average: £30

This museum cafe is a major surprise. Its mixture of space and discreet modernism, on the comfortable side of high-tech, provides an airy room with a sense of ease which most such places can only dream of. The staff are all young and helpful and the food suits the space perfectly: the prosciutto, ciabatta, olives and salad makes a perfect plateful at £15, and the lemon tart at £5 is the best in London. The food is generally cold and snacklike, so don't come here to have a full meal. It's licensed, but drink is not the best start to a cultural afternoon though it might help you at some of the nearby Cork Street galleries. There's also a choice of espresso or cappuccino, made with real Colombian coffee – it's on the strong side but will keep you going for the rest of the day.

Casper's
6 Tenderton Street W1
071-493 7923

Open: Mon–Sat,

This is not a place to go unless you're in the mood for something a bit silly – in fact, something really, really stupid. Casper's is a grill room set in a dimly lit basement, and on every table sits a telephone. The idea is that if you like the look of someone you can

lunch midday–3 p.m.,
dinner, Mon–Thurs
6.30–11.30 p.m.,
Fri, Sat
6.30 p.m.–2 a.m.
Credit: A, Amex, DC, V
Average: £35

have a chat with them simply by dialling their table number. The owners say that people are franker and not so uptight on the telephone, and when I visited the place was full of slobbering, salivating Sloanes (upper-middle-class Londoners) throwing their tongues down the line at each other in some kind of ritualistic intercourse.

The food leans towards the New American, incorporating everything from Mexican to Cajun influences. Nothing's bad but nothing's particularly memorable either – apart from the sight of the people at table 12 using the telephone to talk to the people on table 13. The atmosphere of the place made me want to drink, which is not a bad idea as Casper's stocks a large selection of European and American beers and also has a decent wine list incorporating the best of the New World wines.

The Connaught
Carlos Place W1
071-499 7070

Open: grill room –
Mon–Fri, lunch
12.30–2.30 p.m.,
dinner 6–10.30 p.m.;
restaurant – Mon–Sun,
lunch 12.30–2 p.m.,
dinner 6.30–10.15 p.m.
Credit: A, MC, V
Average: double room
£214–£235 plus VAT;
dinner £75
Restaurant open to
non-residents

The restaurant at the Connaught is one of the most beautiful dining rooms in London. It's absolutely enormous and its extensive panelling gives it an air of magnificence. The hotel itself was built in 1896 to the designs of Isaacs and Florence, and immediately became a hit with the landed gentry, who often kept suites here. During World War II the Connaught was the home of General de Gaulle and its reputation for serving the high and mighty is as strong as ever today.

The Connaught restaurant and grill rooms are probably the most respected of all hotel dining rooms in Britain. The chef, Michel Bourdin, presides over a kitchen famous for its ability to mix the simple with the extraordinary. Anything from a Welsh rarebit to exquisite lamb is available, and more adventurous dishes, such as sole quenelles with a lobster and champagne sauce, or the pâté de turbot froid au homard sauce pudeur, are all specialities which come highly recommended.

Le Gavroche
43 Upper Brook Street
W1
071-408 0881

Open: Mon–Fri,
lunch midday–2 p.m.,
dinner 7–11 p.m.

Le Gavroche is first choice for food aficionados as it is the home of the famed French chef Albert Roux. I first ate here as a 21st birthday treat and was put at a table next to a gathering which included Lord Carrington and the Queen Mother, who seemed to be enjoying her grub and a tipple. I was amazed when a legion of French waiters descended on us, whisking away plates, cleaning tablecloths, filling

Credit: A, Amex, DC, V
Average: £140–£200

glasses and disappearing as quickly as they had arrived. As I was the birthday boy I had no idea what it cost, but I did sneak a look at the wine list which was frighteningly expensive. They do have a set menu for lunch (£36) and dinner (£59) which might not shock you so much, but if you do go here you must remember that you are getting, and paying for, the best.

The man who controls the seating arrangements here, Silvano Giraldin, is a master of courtesy and will always help you to choose the best wine to accompany your meal. For all its splendour, Le Gavroche is not pompous. Everyone is treated very specially here and it is an experience you will not forget.

Ye Grapes

16 Shepherd Market
W1
071-499 1563

Open: Mon–Sat
midday–11 p.m.,
Sun midday–3 p.m.,
7–10.30 p.m.
Credit: A, V
Average: £20

Since the days of the original May Fair there has always been a pub on this site and this free house, built in 1882, has become the local for residents of Shepherd's Market. The interior is traditionally Victorian, with leather, brass and lots of glass everywhere. There's a very good atmosphere in Ye Grapes but it is the restaurant upstairs, the Vinery, which has captured everyone's imagination, serving a selection of good pasta dishes and Chianti. The main dishes are priced at a very reasonable £6, which must make this place one of the best-value eateries in Mayfair.

The Green House

27a Hays Mews W1
071-499 3331

Open: lunch – Mon–Fri
midday–2.30 p.m.,
Sun 12.30–3 p.m.;
dinner 7–11 p.m.,
Sat, Sun 7.30–11 p.m.
Credit: A, Amex, DC, V
Average: £60

The Green House made an important decision in 1991 to change the menu and create a slightly less stuffy atmosphere less directed at the mothers-and-daughters brigade it used to attract. The new chef, Gary Rhodes, brought with him a whole new way of thinking about British food which has worked extremely well. The food leans towards meat in a manner that would make Mrs Beeton bubble with pleasure and pride that her influence is still felt, especially in the offal dishes which should convert anyone to the delights of liver and lights. The best traditional puddings in the capital are made here – bread-and-butter pudding is the highlight. The Green House is not just a nostalgia trip, but a great place to go to taste the quality end of British food.

The Guinea

30 Bruton Place W1
071-499 1210

These mews would once have served many of the big houses as stables and servants' quarters, but are now some of central London's most desirable places

Open: Mon–Sat
11 a.m.–11 p.m.;
lunch, Mon–Fri
midday–2.30 p.m.,
dinner, Sat
6.30–11 p.m.
Credit: A, Amex, DC, V
Average: £50

to live. There has been a tavern of sorts here, just off Berkeley Square, since the fifteenth century, and the Guinea has now become a major attraction for local workers, who can enjoy a good bottle of wine here as well as a selection of Young's beers. Food is also available, and the menu includes fresh lobster, prawns, smoked salmon and an enormous piece of sirloin that would fill you for a month. Everything is fresh and cooked to order and you get an old-fashioned British service without a microwave, ka-raoke machine or stripper in sight.

The Hard Rock Cafe
150 Old Park Lane W1
071-629 0382

Open: Sun-Thurs
11.30 a.m.–12.30 a.m.,
Fri, Sat
11.30 a.m.–1 a.m.
Credit: A, Amex, V
Average: £25

This American burger bar has been open since 1971 and is probably the most famous eatery in London. Every day people queue outside to get a table and the food itself is not at all bad. Main courses such as pork ribs, steaks, burgers, fries and chicken, as well as vegetarian dishes, are available all day and cost between £5 and £15. A cheeseburger, fries and salad will set you back £6.50, and fillet steak, also served with fries and salad, is £12.95. The bar is long and stocked with everything you could possibly want to drink and there is a good range of cocktails, begin-ning at around £4. The walls are covered with rock memorabilia such as Pete Townshend's guitar, B. B. King's semi-acoustic and Ringo Starr's jacket. I can't see the attraction of the Hard Rock Cafe myself, but people love it and it's wildly successful.

Kaspia
18 Bruton Place W1
071-493 2612

Open: Mon–Sat,
lunch midday–3 p.m.,
dinner 7–11.30 p.m.
Credit: A, Amex, V
Average: £100

Kaspia is one of the strangest and most wonderful restaurants I have ever been to in London. A friend's birthday dinner here involved drinking variously flavoured vodkas and eating caviar – something I thought I'd never touch. It was brilliant – and after about fifteen minutes, a glass of champagne and a blini I was in heaven. Kaspia is incredibly expensive, though. Set menus are available and vary between £27 and £55 per person. They also sell vodka at about £16 a carafe.

The King's Arms
2 Shepherd Market W1
071-629 0416

Open: Mon–Fri
11 a.m.–11 p.m.,

This busy old free house has been in existence in one form or another for centuries. It's very popular with people from the local offices, especially at lunchtimes when traditional bar food such as sausages and chips and ploughman's are available. Downstairs they serve a selection of salads and upstairs you get a choice of eight meals. But it's the beer which most people come here for, as The King's Arms stocks a fantastic selection of bitters and lagers including Everard's Tiger, Wadsworth 6X and Webster's Yorkshire. There's a small, dimly lit gallery where you can sit and watch customers in peace, and for such a busy little place the atmosphere is always quiet and serious.

The Queen's Cafe
Cork Street W1
Open: Mon–Fri
8 a.m.–6.30 p.m.
No credit cards
Average: £8

Set in the heart of Cork Street, the Queen's has for years been feeding not only bespoke-suited art dealers but also students and artists visiting their galleries. There is nothing particularly special about the place but it does offer wholesome breakfast dishes or well-filled sandwiches throughout the day at prices around the £2-£5 mark. The cappuccinos and espressos are fine but the tea, as in most Italian cafes, is just terrible. A prawn and avocado sandwich at £2 will put you in the mood to deal with another gallery or provide cover so that you can eavesdrop on art-world gossip. Lunchtimes here are frantic but early mornings and late afternoons are a bit more peaceful and you might get a seat at one of the booths.

The Red Lion
1 Waverton Street W1
071-499 1307

Open: Mon–Fri
11.30 a.m.–11 p.m.,
Sat, Sun
11.30 a.m.–3 p.m.,
7–11 p.m.
Credit: A, Amex, DC, V
Average: £40

This pub is a magnificent example of a seventeenth-century inn and in fact it looks better than many so-called modern bars and pubs. The management runs a good house serving a delicious mixture of real ales and European lagers. There is also a very good restaurant here, popular at lunchtimes with actors and their agents. The food is traditional English – steaks, chips and meat pies – but the service is fast and French. It's a bit on the expensive side (main courses £13-£19, starters at £3-£7) but there are also bar snacks available.

The Rose and Crown
2 Old Park Lane W1
071-499 1980

Open: Mon–Fri
11 a.m.–11 p.m.,
Sat midday–11 p.m.,
Sun midday–3 p.m.
Credit: A, Amex, V
Average: £12

For the past 300 years any pub standing on this site has been said to be haunted by the ghost of those hanged at the Tyburn gallows: prisoners were often put into the cellars overnight to await their delivery to their final dispatching place at what is now Marble Arch. If he has time the barman can tell you stories of mediums and exorcists who arrive here to tackle the spirits but instead wind up enjoying the choice of real ales and club sandwiches. Hot meals are served every lunchtime except Sunday, and in the evenings sandwiches and salads are available instead.

Sat 11 a.m.–3 p.m.,
5–11 p.m.,
Sun 11 a.m.–3 p.m.
Credit: A, Amex, DC, V
Average: £12

Scott's Restaurant
20 Mount Street W1
071-629 5248

Open: Mon–Sat, lunch
12.30–2.45 p.m.,
dinner 6–10.45 p.m.;
Sun, dinner 7–10 p.m.
Credit: A, Amex, DC, V
Average: restaurant
£80, oyster bar £60

Scott's oyster bar and its brasserie/restaurant are very popular with politicians, publishers and the art world. The oyster bar is small and grand enough to make the prices asked here seem understandable, if not cheap. Everything served here is bought in from France, and the waiters have that very special French arrogance which can be quite charming. The walls are hung with paintings which change monthly and which are all for sale at gallery prices.

On my only visit to the restaurant I was in the company of Dame Barbara Cartland, who insisted that every dish was pink, so we had fish soup, salmon and pink sorbet.

SHOPPING

Belvoir Watson
15 Cork Street W1
071-491 0635

Open: Mon–Fri
11 a.m.–5.30 p.m.,
Sat by appointment
Credit: Amex

The lush interior of this jeweller in the heart of Cork Street subtly serves to highlight the contemporary silver and jewellery made here. It's beautifully and intricately made and leaves you in no doubt about the skill and artistry of the craftsmen. The shop gallery has been open since about 1989 and the pieces on show – everything from pillboxes to necklaces – range in price from £50 to £50,000; the last time I was there they were displaying a beautiful coffee set at £25,000.

Browns
23 South Molton Street
W1
071-491 7833

Open: Mon–Wed, Fri,
Sat 10 a.m.–6 p.m.,
Thurs 10 a.m.–7 p.m.
Credit: A, Amex, DC,
Switch, V

The men's and women's branches of Browns are now the only thing worth talking about on South Molton Street, which was once the home of modern fashion in London until bad times and the arrival of cheap high-street chains chased it away. Browns, however, has carried on the tired flag of designer fashion and Donna Karan, Sonia Rykiel, Comme des Garçons, Romeo Gigli and Azzedine Alaia can all be found here. The shops are simple and expensive and the quality is clear for all to see. Sales take place in the New Year and in summer. They are worth waiting for as prices are reduced dramatically, and if you're willing to risk losing that precious garment, prices get knocked even further down for those prepared to wait.

Burlington Arcade
Piccadilly W1

Designed in 1869 by Samuel Ware, this beautiful Regency arcade is famous for its small shops selling everything from knitwear to jewellery. It was commissioned by Lord George Cavendish of Burlington

House to prevent passers-by from throwing their rubbish into his garden, and since then it has been the custom to ensure that nobody runs, sings or carries open umbrellas or heavy packages in the arcade. The security men, known as beadles, stand at either entrance. They're always ex-servicemen, so don't break the rules as they will know a thing or two about the best way of dealing with you.

Church's Shoes
136 New Bond Street
W1
071-499 9449

Open: Mon–Wed, Fri,
Sat 9.30 a.m.–6 p.m.,
Thurs 9.30 a.m.–7 p.m.
Credit: A, Amex, DC,
JCB, V

A legend in the shoe trade, Church's sell men's leather, suede and crocodile-skin brogues, all of which are cut as well as any shoe can be without being specifically fitted. Prices range from £150 for dark chocolate tasselled loafers to £140 for a heavy leather semi-brogue.

The staff here are all old-style salesmen who know your requirements better than you do, and the customers are a mixture of the old-boy brigade and slick Bond Street art dealers spending the profits of a good day or trying a little retail therapy to forget a bad one. It's the place to get reliable, quality shoes you can put on and forget about.

Comme Des Garçons
59 Brook Street W1
071-493 1258

Open: Mon–Wed, Fri,
Sat 10 a.m.–6 p.m.,
Thurs 10 a.m.–7 p.m.
Credit: A, Amex, DC, V

In the early eighties I found myself on a French beach playing a saxophone as the photographer Peter Linberg attempted to catch a moment for a new Comme des Garçons advertising campaign. Being young, foolish and somewhat pretentious I went along with this and had no problem running up and down in one of their £700 overcoats and £800 suits. Comme des Garçons have fused Japanese minimalism with a fifties European cafe-jazz look, usually in black and white and incorporating some incredibly irregular patterns. In my opinion the women's clothes, while they sometimes have a sexiness about them, are very rigid, but some people swear by them.

S. Fisher
22 & 32 Burlington
Arcade W1
071-493 4180

Open: Mon–Wed, Fri,
Sat 9.30 a.m.–6 p.m.,
Thurs 9.30 a.m.–7 p.m.
Credit: A, Amex, DC, V

Fisher's specialises in cashmere jumpers and cardigans in every colour you could ever imagine. The garments are a dream to see and handle and the roll-necks and crew-necks come in at a cool £160. They also have an extensive selection of sea island cotton tops, again in every colour imaginable, starting at £40 – a long-sleeved polo version will cost you £59.95. Both men's and women's garments are available and would always make wonderful presents.

Freedman and Tarling Ltd

27 Cork Street W1
071-734 9212

Open: Mon–Fri
9 a.m.–6.30 p.m.,
Sat 10 a.m.–5 p.m.
Credit: A, Amex, DC, V

Freedman and Tarling manage to combine old-school men's tailoring with a new retail sensibility, making and selling men's clothes to everyone from bankers to pop stars. This relatively new shop has opened up in an old tailor's cutting and fitting room, and has managed to hang on to the spirit of the old place as well as adding its own particular charm. Off-the-peg shirts, blazers, trousers, woollens and ties are all available, and any man who wanted to dress smartish would find it very difficult to leave here without one of their woven or knit ties (from £30). The shirts are generously made and have a good-size collar rather than the small one that seems to have been fashionable for the last few years. Waistcoats and jumpers are all made from pure wool or cashmere and the colours include violets, lemons, whites, green checks, salmon pinks and intense blues that you will not find elsewhere. Prices for these start at £60 and go right up to £650, and trad blazers with gold buttons are upwards of £400.

George F. Trumper

9 Curzon Street W1
071-499 1850/
071-499 2932

Open: Mon–Fri
9 a.m.–5.30 p.m.,
Sat 9 a.m.–1 p.m.
Credit: A, Amex, DC,
MC, V

This Victorian/Edwardian men's perfumery deserves a special mention. Hand-made glass and leather bottles contain ointments and cream which, while they may not have the secret of eternal youth, might just make you or your man look that wee bit better. Aftershaves cost £11 and up, but it is the badger brushes, which cost between £15 and £150, which might ruin you. A close shave . . . If you make an appointment they can cut your hair into a shape that might make you think you have grown up at last – Trumper's is a very grown-up kind of place and very, very British.

W & M Gidden Ltd

15d Clifford Street W1
071-734 2788

Open: Mon–Fri
9 a.m.–6 p.m.,
Sat 10 a.m.–3 p.m.
Credit: A, Amex, DC, V

Gidden's is one of London's very best equestrian shops, stocking everything you could ever want or need for yourself and your horse. They do their own line in saddlery – prices range from £590 to £4,000, with riding boots at £225 – though their outfits, while they definitely cut a dash, are a bit expensive considering that you'll be running around the countryside in them. There's a bit of the fashion victim in everyone, though, even horsy people. The shop also sells quality leather goods such as wallets and belts. Despite the fact that they supply the Royal family,

Gidden's is by no means snooty and the staff are very helpful.

Gray's Antique Market
58 Davies Street W1
071-629 7034

Open: Mon–Fri
10 a.m.–6 p.m.
Credit: ask

The 180 stalls here sell anything from small antique cars such as E-Types or XJSs to beautiful hand-made Italian glass bowls and Victorian lace. It's an Aladdin's cave in which you're bound to find something you love. The traders are very experienced and always know when someone hasn't a clue what they're talking about, so if you're determined to haggle, be careful. Don't let yourself be bullied into buying something you don't want or are not sure about – remember that these guys sell for a living. Monday is supposed to be the best day to try for a bargain, though, so you never know what might slip through their fingers.

Hermes
155 New Bond Street
W1
071-499 8856

Open: Mon–Sat
9 a.m.–5.30 p.m.
Credit: A, Amex, V

If you feel like treating yourself and don't care about the bill, Hermes is the place to do it. Over the years this fashion house has taken classic clothes designs and given them an ever-so-slightly softer look, and its range moves between the formal and the casual with the assurance that comes from really knowing its customers. A silk handkerchief or one of their famous scarves will add elegance to your most tired outfits, and a new outfit from here will cost you anything between £400 and £2,000. Hermes also has a magnificent range of accessories, from handbags to silk ties, all of which are fabulously seductive, but remember that the prices will be very high.

Heywood Hill Booksellers
10 Curzon Street W1
071-629 0647

Open: Mon–Fri
9.30 a.m.–5.30 p.m.,
Sat
9.30 a.m.–12.30 p.m.
No credit cards

Though it opened only in 1936, this bookshop is rich in history. The Mitfords constantly referred to it in their diaries, and Nancy Mitford actually worked here from 1942 to the end of World War II. It really is one of the very last real booklover's shops, and is beautifully laid out, with new and rare books on offer covering everything from the latest children's writing to the classics. The staff are very accommodating and will order any books they don't actually have in stock, and they also have the contacts to find any first editions you want at a good price. The shop offers a book-binding service which is a great way of saving a much-loved volume that is falling to pieces.

The Irish Linen Company
35 Burlington Arcade
W1
071-493 8949

Open: Mon–Fri
9 a.m.–5.30 p.m.,
Sat 9 a.m.–4.30 p.m.
Credit: A, Amex, DC, V

The most beautiful table linen and bedsheets in the world are available here, but at a very high price. Double-damask napkins sell at £85 for six and linen sheets cost about £250 a pair, and there are also some magnificent hand-sewn Irish linen tablecloths which would make any dinner table look sumptuous.

All the items are of the very highest quality and should last you a generation – as well they might, considering the price. They are all potential heirlooms.

Penhaligon's
17 Burlington Arcade
W1
071-629 1416

Open: Mon–Sat
9.30 a.m.–6 p.m.
Credit: A, Amex, DC, V

This perfumery looks perfect in the setting of the arcade. Both men's and women's toiletries and accessories are sold here and would all sit wonderfully on any dressing table. The items are all crafted with an old-fashioned care but unfortunately do not carry old-fashioned prices – most of the small bottles cost over £100. English Rose eau de toilette is £32 for 100 ml, and there is a full range of creams and lotions in each fragrance.

Polo – Ralph Lauren
143 New Bond Street
W1
071-491 4967

Open: Mon–Wed, Fri,
Sat 10 a.m.–6 p.m.,
Thurs 10 a.m.–7 p.m.
Credit: A, Amex, DC,
MC, V

In the middle of London's most fashionable and traditional street an American designer is very successfully managing to sell Englishness to the English. Ralph Lauren can provide a complete wardrobe for those who aspire to a cross between the Ivy League preppy look and a touch of 1920s Oxbridge. His women's clothes are less stuffy than their English equivalents, and have a subtle enough twist about them to sell to the younger and hipper crowds. His men's button-down shirts (£75) seem to be worn by everybody these days and though they aren't really that great, the little motif carries enormous cachet for some people. His winter wear is as good as any other designer's, if not better, and more importantly, carries the logo.

Savile Row, W1

Savile Row, named after Lady Dorothy Savile, wife of the third Earl of Burlington, is world-famous for being the centre of men's tailoring. Before the tailors arrived, though, it was a fashionable residential street: the dramatist Sheridan lived at number 14 in 1813, and George Baseri, the architect, lived here between 1826 and 1845. The aristocracy and the new gentry who moved into the area in the early nineteenth century all needed clothing, but the sweatshops of the East End were too rough for them, and the tailors saw an ideal market waiting to be satisfied. At number 30 is Anderson & Shepherd, regarded as the best of all the tailors, but with terrifying prices. It's here that the Royal family and many leading politicians come to be booted and suited.

Smythson
44 New Bond Street
W1
071-629 8558

Open: Mon–Fri
9.15 a.m.–5.30 p.m.,
Sat 10 a.m.–1 p.m.
Credit: A, Amex, V

Established in 1887 and with a royal warrant, Smythson's have the facilities to print headed paper or business cards but are most famous for their wonderful diaries and notebooks. I have managed to keep a Smythson diary for the last ten years – it's not too big and has a classy look about it that I like. They stock various sizes, as well as notebooks and specialist reference diaries such as fishing, shooting, dinner dates diaries, and even a New York or London black book, to keep your most special numbers in. The memorable S symbol is blazoned over their loose sets of playing cards and poker sets.

ENTERTAINMENT

Annabel's Club
44 Berkeley Square W1
071-629 2350

Open: from 8 p.m.
Credit: A, Amex, V

Named after owner Mark Birley's wife, Annabel's is supposed to be the best nightclub in the world – by those few pampered men and women who have never been in a real nightclub. It caters for the very, very rich and offers them the chance to drink gallons of champagne and cavort on the dancefloor without anyone taking too much notice – it can be pretty grim to see newpaper editors, finance moguls or members of the government behave in this way after too much of the good stuff. The club is also popular with Iraqis and Iranians who don't seem to mind being in the same room as each other. I cannot actually see the attraction of Annabel's, but then again I'm not wealthy and I like good music. Annabel's is worth mentioning for the beautiful building which houses it, described by Nicholas Pevsner, the great chronicler of English architecture, as one of the finest terraced houses in London.

Anthony D'Offay
20–23 Dering Street
W1
071-499 4100

This outstanding gallery represents some of the most important artists working today. Every D'Offay exhibition is a major event and the shows always manage to stir up some controversy, mainly because they tend to involve radical artists, and also because

Open: Mon–Fri
10 a.m.–5.30 p.m., Sat
10 a.m.–1 p.m.
No credit cards

Circa
59 Berkeley Square W1
071-499 7850

Open: Mon–Sat
11 a.m.–11 p.m.;
coffee from 10 a.m.;
lunch
midday–3.30 p.m.;
light snacks
3.30–9.30 p.m
Credit: A, Amex, V

The Embassy Club
6 New Bond Street W1

Open: 10 p.m.–3 a.m.
Credit: A, Amex, V
Admission: £12

The Fine Art Society
148 Bond Street W1
071-629 5116

Open: Mon–Fri

they never pander to ideas of what is fashionable in the art world. Artists who have shown here recently include Gilbert and George, Richard Long and the world's greatest artist, Anselm Kiefer. The D'Offay gallery, despite its standing, welcomes any visitors, though it tends to get quite crowded.

Circa, nestling in the Saatchi & Saatchi building, is definitely worth a mention. It's a good place for an afternoon coffee or a drink. The bar looks a bit dated, but even so continually attracts new customers by allowing nightclub entrepreneurs to organise regular nights here.

In the early evening and at lunchtime Circa is a favourite with the advertising boys next door, but it's better at night – there's an admission charge after 10.30 p.m.

Club nights change, so you might want to ring first to check what's going on.

This club has managed to survive for decades by changing with each successive fashion. In the inter-war years it was a favourite haunt of the then Prince of Wales, the Mountbattens, Lady Diana Cooper and Cecil Beaton. When I first went there, in 1979, naked men and women danced on the bar and the dance-floor was full of young and old men kissing and gyrating to some kind of high-energy dance music. I was quite shocked by it all. Since then it has been a New Romantics club, a Gothic palace and a home for the pre-Ecstasy club craze which saw a return to good music and bad behaviour.

The various bars here all have their own atmos-phere. Occasionally there is live music here but this happens less and less as nobody seems to be able to play live any more. There is a strong door policy to keep trouble away, but no membership, only a good sense of fun, is required.

As I write the Embassy is closed for refurbishment but will reopen soon in some new guise.

Mayfair's most beautiful gallery deals in the work of nineteenth-century Orientalists and portrait painters in general but specialises in the work of British painters between 1860 and 1960. Nothing ever looks out of place in the Fine Art Society and all the work

9.30 a.m.–5.30 p.m.,
Sat 10 a.m.–1 p.m.
No credit cards

has the stamp of quality. A lithograph by Wilkie will start at about £400, and a painting by Lavery can cost anything from £600 to £85,000. There is a particularly Scottish influence in the Fine Art Society – they have other galleries in Edinburgh and Glasgow – and many of the Scottish colourists are represented here. However, the gallery's idea of modern stops at World War II. The Fine Art Society was a favourite with the painter Sickert and with Wilde, and Tennyson gave one of his famous readings here. The only person to have a reading here since was me, in 1986 – my proudest moment.

Hamilton's Gallery
13 Carlos Place W1
071-499 9493

Open: Mon–Fri
10 a.m.–6 p.m., Sat
11 a.m.–5 p.m.
Credit: A, Amex, V

This building was once the swimming pool and sauna used by the Connaught Hotel but for over a decade Hamilton's has used this beautiful space to mount photographic exhibitions. I was lucky enough to meet Horst P. Horst here, as well as Helmut Newton and David Bailey, all of whom have exhibited and sold their work very successfully from Hamilton's. Each new show attracts London's glitterati who come in force to look and to buy, meaning that photography has become increasingly collectable. A Mapplethorpe platinum print will set you back £10,000, while a good Horst print will be more than £2,000.

**Marlborough Fine
Art Ltd**
Albemarle Street W1
071-629 5161

Open: Mon–Fri
10 a.m.–6 p.m.,
Sat 10 a.m.–midday
Credit: A, Amex, V
accepted for prints only

One of the most influential – and expensive – galleries in the world, the Marlborough has been home to the work of Francis Bacon, Lucien Freud and Frank Auerbach. It's an odd feeling to walk off the street and into a small room where you can look really closely at the work of modern masters. The gallery has kept clear of anything too modern, though in 1989 they took on the young Scottish artist Stephen Conroy and sold every piece before his show even opened.

If you're interested at all in painting, this wonderful gallery should be high on your list. The people here never ask questions and have none of that Cork Street pomposity which can be so intimidating.

**Mayfair Hotel
Gymnasium**
Mayfair Hotel, Stratton
Street W1
071-629 7777

The Mayfair was the toast of the town during the thirties and has managed to sustain its reputation by constantly updating the services available to its clients. Open to non-residents as well as residents, this gymnasium is part of its health club, which also

Open: Mon–Fri
6 a.m.–9 p.m., Sat, Sun
9 a.m.–6 p.m.
Credit: A, Amex, V
Admission: £20

has a sauna and a pool. The weights room is small but rarely crowded, as in my experience it is almost never used by the guests. The staff will provide you with anything you need. Membership, which gives you access to the gym, pool and sauna, costs £550 per year; monthly membership is £60 and two months cost £100.

Raab Gallery
9 Cork Street W1
071-734 6444

Open: Mon–Fri
10 a.m.–6 p.m.,
Sat 10 a.m.–4 p.m.

A new arrival on the art world's street of shame, this gallery has a policy of showing the work of artists with a touch of glamour and something distinct to say. Opening at a time when most other galleries were struggling to survive, Raab's mixture of the very serious and the very odd has brought it a high media profile as well as a steady flow of sales. A recent showing here of the work of French photographers Pierre et Giles had people falling in from the street, and the Scottish realist Ken Currie has attracted much acclaim, helped by Raab's conviction that he is one of Britain's most important living artists.

William Jackson Gallery
4 New Burlington Street
W1
071-287 2121

Open: Mon–Fri
10 a.m.–6 p.m.,
Sat 10 a.m.–1 p.m.
No credit cards

One of the most enterprising galleries in Mayfair, this was once the Scottish Gallery, dealing particularly in twentieth-century work from north of the border. Jackson, who was part of the Scottish Gallery, broke away and has done very well here so far. He now shows exactly what he wants, in the way he wants, consulting only the artist instead of a committee. The artists he shows are still Scottish and he has put together some fantastic shows by people such as Adrian Wiszniewski. The prices here are reasonable by Cork Street standards and the attitude is less stuffy.

BROWN'S

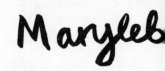

Maryleb

Oxford Street

*U*ntil the late nineteenth century Oxford Street was most famous for its places of entertainment, such as the Pantheon (now Marks and Spencer), and the notorious Figg's School of Arms, a boarding house opposite Poland Street, specialising in female fighting and bear and tiger baiting, and run by the famous prize fighter James Figg. The most popular place, however, was Tyburn, now Marble Arch, where the gallows attracted thousands to the public hangings which took place here between 1388 and 1738. The condemned would be brought here by cart and given their last drink of ale at the church of St Giles-in-the-Field. Hanging days were public holidays, as the authorities felt that the sight was a good deterrent to crime, and thousands of people, dressed in their holiday clothes, would jostle for good viewing positions while hawkers and stallholders sold all sorts of refreshments. Nowadays, however, Marble Arch is little more than a huge junction between roads from the south, west and north of London.

Apart from its size, very little distinguishes Oxford Street from any other London street, but for a time it was the most wondrous and exciting of them all. However, apart from the big department stores – Selfridges, Marks and Spencer (see separate entries) John Lewis, Debenhams, British Home Stores, D. H. Evans – I have always found Oxford Street to be vile, lined with the worst kind of shops selling second-rate goods to unsuspecting shoppers. It is the roads off the main street which are more enjoyable and fruitful – the backstreets to Soho (see Soho) and down into Bond Street (see Mayfair) are well worth a visit.

To the north things aren't much better – the streets are mainly residential and have become very dull. From the fourteenth century until recently, Marylebone, named after the church of St Mary's which stood by Tyburn stream, was infamous for its violence and danger. Most of the squares and long, wide streets housing firms of solicitors and doctors' practices – including the highly regarded Harley Street – were developed during the eighteenth century. Now it is very difficult to imagine this sad array of office conversions as a place where people lived in gracious villas – the character of the place has been all but destroyed.

HOW TO GET THERE

Tubes
- Baker Street
- Bond Street
- Edgware Road
- Goodge Street
- Great Portland Street
- Marble Arch
- Oxford Circus
- Marylebone
- Regents Park
- Tottenham Court Road
- Warren Street

Buses
- Baker Street (southbound)/Gloucester Road (northbound): 2A, 2B, 13, 74, 82, 113, 139, 159, 247
- Edgware Road: 6, 7, 15, 16, 16A, 23, 36, 98
- Marylebone Road: 18, 27, 74
- Oxford Street: 6, 7, 8, 10, 12, 13, 15, 16A, 23, 25, 55, 73, 88, 94, 113, 135, 137, 137A, 139, 159, 176
- Portland Place: 135, C2
- Tottenham Court Road: 10, 14, 14A, 24, 29, 73, 134

Cavendish Square, W1

Cavendish Square forms an elegant centre point to the area known as St Marylebone. Before entering take a look at the Barbara Hepworth sculpture standing eerily on the side of the John Lewis department store. St Peter's Church, which stands on the north side of the square, is a miniature version of St Martin-in-the-Fields, built in 1724. The east window, by the pre-Raphaelite artist Burne-Jones, is worth going to have a look at.

Harley Street, W1

Harley Street was named after the second Earl of Oxford, Edward Harley, and until the early nineteenth century was mainly residential. Britain's greatest painter, J. M. W. Turner, lived at number 64, portrait painter Allan Ramsay at number 67, and prime minister William Gladstone had a house at number 73. Now, however, sick people from all over the world come here to consult with eminent specialists and medical experts, and the area has probably brought as many people to London as Buckingham Palace. The practices are for the most part very private and very expensive.

Portland Place, W1

In the eighteenth century this street, laid out by the architect brothers Robert and James Adam, was the grandest in London, and inspired Nash to use its style for his remarkable procession of buildings leading from Regents Park to Carlton Terrace. The most impressive building amongst all the embassies and institutions based here is the Royal Institute of British Architects at number 66. Exhibitions are often held here – recent shows have included architect Will Alsop and Scottish artist Bruce McLean's entry for the competition to rebuild part of Berlin.

Further down the road stands Broadcasting House, the impressive twentieth-century home of BBC Radio. The architect G. Val Myers had a difficult brief – the new building had to be in keeping with the street, but also needed to create a soundproofed environment for 22 recording studios. When it was opened in 1932 the building was likened to the prow of a ship; the façade has remained unchanged but the inside of the building has been in need of constant updating, The external sculpture is by Eric Gill, who

BROADCASTING
HOUSE

took Shakespeare's character Ariel, from *The Tempest*, as his symbol of broadcasting.

Next door is All Souls Church, Langham Place, which was designed by John Nash in 1822–5. It was ridiculed when it was first built but is now regarded as a masterpiece. Live classical music is often performed here in the afternoon – it's usually free and well worth going to, especially on a wet day.

Ever since the atrocities in Tiananmen Square, there has been a constant vigil outside the Chinese embassy, one of the many on Portland Place.

Regent Street, W1

Regent Street is the main artery of John Nash's development, started in 1811, which sweeps from Regents Park down to St James's Park. The Georgian splendour of the buildings created a link between the two parks and transformed London into an elegant capital. While this new London was being built Nash had to contend with tremendous financial problems, and used his own money to build the Quadrant, just above Piccadilly Circus, which was designed to keep the heads of London's wealthy shoppers dry but which ended up as a favourite haunt of prostitutes.

Regent Street is now occupied mostly by woollen and cloth shops, but you can still imagine the bohemian gatherings which would take place at the Cafe Royal (see Soho) and to acknowledge the genius of Liberty's design (see Soho), which remains as good as ever. There is a smattering of good shops such as Gap Kids and Hamleys, and during November and December Londoners flock here to watch the Christmas lights being turned on.

The Wallace Collection

Manchester Square W1
071-935 0687

Open: Mon–Sat
11 a.m.–5 p.m.,
Sun 2–5 p.m.
No admission charge
(donations welcome)

Bequeathed to the nation in 1897 by Lady Wallace after the death of her husband and opened to the public in 1901, the Wallace collection was the creation of five generations of collectors. It holds paintings by Fragonard, Reynolds, Watteau, Delacroix, Gericault, Rembrandt and Velasquez, and Frans Hal's famous 'The Laughing Cavalier' is here. Sir Richard Wallace was cautious about what he bought and tended to look for the unusual, such as the Irish Bell of Mura which was reputed to have fallen from heaven. It's not a place to come to see modern art as the work here covers the seventeenth, eighteenth and nineteenth centuries. There are few such eclectic collections in the world and it is a pity that so few people come to this grand house to view it.

The house itself is in magnificent condition and has recently been redecorated. It is one of London's truly wonderful places, and the fact that it is something of a secret adds to its mystique. Vivienne Westwood came here for the Boucher and Fragonard-inspired fabrics in her recent collections. There's also a shop selling cards and slide reproductions of about half the paintings in the collection.

EATING AND DRINKING

The Crown and Sceptre
86 Great Titchfield Street W1
071-636 7940

Open: Mon–Sat
11 a.m.–11 p.m.,
Sun midday–3 p.m.,
7–10.30 p.m.
No credit cards
Average: £12

Standing on the corner of Great Titchfield Street and Foley Street, this pub was a big favourite with journalists from ITN before they moved to Gray's Inn Road from their headquarters in nearby Wells Street. When the hostage John McCarthy, who used to be a regular here, was released, the outside of the building was covered with yellow ribbons. Since ITN moved the pub hasn't been quite the same, but it's still an excellent place to come for a decent pint of real ale and a pub sandwich. There's also pub meals available such as roast beef served with potatoes, veg and Yorkshire pudding at £5.

The Dome
290 Regent Street W1
071-636 7006

Open: Mon–Sat
8 a.m.–11 p.m.,
Sun 10 a.m.–6 p.m.
Credit: A, Amex, DC, V
Average: £20

Of all the Dome brasserie-bars, this is the most convincing, and looks like an authentic Boulevard St Germaine bar where French intellectuals might once have shared a cigarette and a brandy. The Dome is open for breakfast in the mornings – le vrai déjeuner anglais costs £4.25, and a croissant and confiture is £1.25. The food is basic – saucisse de Toulouse or steak – and the main dishes are well priced at under £10. They are perfectly complemented by a glass of fitou or pinot noir. It's also a great place to come for a drink, which cannot be said about the other Domes in London. In the evenings it gets very busy, especially with BBC people.

Efes Kebab House
80 Great Titchfield Street W1
071-636 1953

Open: Mon–Sat

There are not many Turkish restaurants in central London as they tend to be situated in areas such as north or east London where there are large Turkish communities. This is one of the best known in the city centre and has become a popular hangout for those who care little for the burgeoning vegetarian

Central

midday—11.30 p.m.
Credit: A, Amex, V
Average: £28

movement. Though it calls itself a kebab house it is very much an upmarket place rather than a takeaway shop. The lamb dishes and the meze are delicious and well worth visiting the restaurant for – set menus are £14 or £15 a head. Efes is very popular with BBC people from around the corner in Broadcasting House, and the walls are plastered with photographs of DJs who eat here regularly.

There is a posher branch of this restaurant round the corner in Great Portland Street which is popular with the local doctors and their clients. It's just as good but is more expensive.

Kerzenstuberl
9 St Christopher's Place
W1
071-486 3196

Open: Mon–Fri, lunch
midday—2.15 p.m.,
Mon–Sat,
dinner 6–11 p.m.
Credit: A, Amex, DC, V
Average: £30

It can come as quite a shock to find this remarkably untrendy Austrian restaurant, where the staff are decked out in breeches and blouses, tucked in beside one of the most fashionable small streets in the capital. The husband-and-wife team who run the place have taken great pride in re-creating a little piece of old Vienna here and in serving very good food. The trad Austrian tucker consists of heringsalat (£3.80) and wiener kesselgulasch (£8.80), a goulash served up with gherkins. Vegetables cost £2.50. The apple strudels (£3.20) are not to be missed.

Maison Sagne
105 Marylebone High
Street W1
071-935 6240

Open: Mon–Fri
9 a.m.–5 p.m.,
Sat 9 a.m.–1 p.m.
No credit cards
Average: £10

Nothing much has changed in this small patisserie since it first opened in the 1920s. It's very popular with local doctors from Harley Street and broadcasters from the BBC local radio station across the road. Uniformed staff direct you to your table, where you can sit and enjoy hot, strong coffee and a choice of cakes and pastries which would make you want to stay all day. A cappuccino and croissant (£1.10) is just right to set you up for the day. The word has got out that the best omelette in London is available here, and so it's very busy at lunchtime. It's worth coming for afternoon tea, too.

Massarella's Ice Cream Parlour and Creperie
Selfridges, Oxford Street
W1
071-629 1234

Open: Mon–Wed, Fri,

This Italian-style ice-cream bar really delivers the goods and is deliciously cool on a hot summer's day – the only problem is that you have to share the experience with some of Selfridge's thousands of daily shoppers.

After a hard day's shopping or browsing, try the chocolate fudge sundae or La Rocce which taste out of this world.

Sat 9.30 a.m.–7 p.m.,
Thurs
9.30 a.m.–7.45 p.m.
Credit: A, Amex, DC, V
Average: £8

Nico Central
35 Great Portland Street
W1
071-436 8846

Open: lunch, Mon–Fri
midday–2 p.m.,
dinner,
Mon–Sat 7–11 p.m.
Credit: A, Amex, V
Average: £60

**Ranoush Snack
and Juice Bar**
43 Edgware Road W2
071-723 5929

Open:
8.30 a.m.–2 a.m.
No credit cards
Average: £8

Raw Deal
65 York Street W1
071-262 4841

Open: Mon–Fri
11 a.m.–9.30 p.m.,
Sat midday–10.30 p.m.
No credit cards
Average: £10

Woodlands
77 Marylebone Lane
W1
071-486 3862

Coffees and cappuccinos cost about £1 and, if you feel the need for something a little more substantial and less sinful than ice cream, sweet and savoury crepes come in at between £3.25 and £4.25.

Nico Landenis has the most formidable reputation of any chef in London, and for two reasons: his food is thought to be the best in the capital and his abrupt style of dealing with philistines, vegetarians and children is supposedly terrifying.

Everything, including the luxurious wine list, is expensive here, but the food is really wonderful. Confit of duck in a mustard sauce is about £10, boudin of pheasant with chestnuts on a bed of mashed potatoes with chopped shallots is £12 and the spectacular puddings are £5.

Edgware Road has long been the place where people from the Middle East have settled. Most of the shops and bars are run by Arabs and of the several restaurants, this is the best. It's more like a cafe than a formal restaurant and the clientele are quite young and laid back. One counter sells only freshly squeezed juices such as carrot or orange, and the other is for snacks which you can eat in or take away. There is a fairly wide selection of felafel, sandwiches and sweet pastries to choose from, and sweets are available at £14 a kilo. The chandeliered and marbled room, throbbing with Arab pop music, is worth spending some time in.

This long-established vegetarian restaurant is a big favourite with people from local offices such as Marks and Spencer's headquarters. The choice of salads is formidable, and there is a choice of two hot dishes each day – mushroom pancakes or mixed vegetables in red wine – which come in at under a fiver. The delicious non-sugary puddings are never more than a couple of quid and there's also a fresh juice bar where you can get takeaway cups of orange juice.

This is the big sister of the Woodlands opposite the Comedy Theatre in Panton Street (see Westminster and St James's). The Theatreland branch is basic and fantastic for vegetarians, but this one is a bit more upmarket. It has been criticised for keeping its prices too high and its portions too small, but it's

Open: lunch
midday–3 p.m., dinner
6–10.45 p.m.
Credit: A, Amex, DC, V
Average: £12

nevertheless a favourite with those who love South-ern Indian cooking. If you don't know about this type of food, ask – you'll get an array of snacklike starters to try out. In fact the best way to eat here is to try the rice dishes and spiced pancakes and then gently push yourself through the menu. Though the place is licensed, nobody ever seems to drink much here.

The Yorkshire Grey
46 Langham Street W1
071-636 4788

Open: Mon–Sat
11 a.m.–11 p.m., Sun
midday–3.30 p.m.,
7–10.30 p.m.
No credit cards
Average: £12

This old Victorian pub is a favourite with technicians from the BBC. It's on the corner of a small, quaint street called Middleton Buildings and in many ways has kept its early Victorian character. The beers here are a mixture of the not-so-good British lagers and some very good real ales. The bottled beers are reasonably priced at around £1.25 and they make an effort to sell some decent house wines. Pub food is also available at lunchtimes and in the evening – it's standard fare such as sausages and mash and steak and kidney pie, and is not at all bad.

SHOPPING

Alfie's Antique Market
13-25 Church Street
NW8
071-723-6066

Open: Tues–Sat
10 a.m.–6 p.m.
Credit: ask

This is the largest indoor market in Britain and the variety of goods on show here is breathtaking. It's a little bit out of the way – at the top end of the Edgware Road – but it's worth the journey to have a look at the selection, which varies from top-class antiques to bric-a-brac. As always in this type of place, you have to look closely at what's available to dig out any bargains, but there are good deals to be had.

The only bad point about this place is the lack of anywhere decent to have a cup of coffee or some-thing to eat – the cafe in the market, serving snacks and hot meals, is very basic. It compensates for this, though, by having a drinks licence and a rooftop terrace.

BBC Shop
4–5 Langham Place,
Upper Regent Street W1
071-927 4970

Open: Mon–Fri
9 a.m.–5.30 p.m.,
Sat

This is the London showcase of BBC Enterprises – books, videos and cassettes relating to successful TV programmes are all on sale here. It's the place to come if you have been looking for a Monty Python or Goons script. A video of *Fawlty Towers* will cheer up anyone feeling a little blue. They also stock a remark-able set of recordings, done in the sixties and seven-ties, of Shakespeare's plays performed by some of

9.30 a.m.–5.30 p.m.
Credit: A, V

Biggles
66 Marylebone Lane
W1
071-224 5937

Open: Mon
10.30 a.m.–4 p.m.,
Tues–Fri
9.30 a.m.–6 p.m.,
Sat
9.30 a.m.–4.30 p.m.
Credit: A, Amex, V

The Button Queen
19 Marylebone Lane
W1
071-935 1505

Open: Mon–Fri
10 a.m.–6 p.m.,
Sat
10 a.m.–1.30 p.m.
Credit: A, V (over £10
only)

Cycle Logical
136–138 New
Cavendish Street W1
071-631 5060

Open: Mon–Sat
9.30 a.m.–6 p.m.,
Sun 11 a.m.–5 p.m.
Credit: A, V

the great actors. It's a good place to pick up an interesting and useful present.

This bright little shop boasts the finest selection of sausages in London, and not a rusk or an E-number in sight. There's a sausage here for everyone – from traditional Cumberland and Toulouse sausages to duck and orange, Armenian lamb and chicken, banana and sweetcorn sausages, with prices averaging about £2.50–£2.80 a pound. Occasionally they even have free-range Welsh boar sausages, but they sell out almost immediately. In 1993 they hope to open up the back of the shop so that customers can sample the wares on site – that'll be well worth checking out. They also stock a good range of condiments such as beer and peppercorn mustard and garlic jelly.

The Button Queen is one of London's hidden treasure troves and on the list of every designer and fashion student in the country. In April and May each year final-year students from the London College of Fashion and colleges as far away as Newcastle flock here to find the perfect buttons to set off their exam outfit. Wooden toggles are 50p each, modern gilt and diamante jewel-like buttons are £37 each, and antique cut steel buttons in steel mounts will set you back £240 for six. Much of the stock, though, is very affordable. You may be surprised to learn that buttons are in the top five collectable items in the States, and every so often a formidable blue-rinsed matron arrives, hunting for a rare treasure. But the Button Queen is not just for collectors – it has supplied buttons to costume designers on films such as *The Field* and the TV series *The House of Elliott*, as well as to ordinary punters.

If you're a cycle purist who likes to talk, think and philosophise about the wonders of the two-wheeled machine, Cycle Logical is the place for you. From Colagno ten-speed racers to the latest developments in the state-of-the-art mountain bikes in which they specialise, everything is available here and will cost you anything between £199 and £1,900. The workshop in the basement is a good place to have your bike serviced or customised with a few of the latest gadgets.

Central

Frumkin & Co. Ltd

66 Great Titchfield
Street W1
071-580 9701

Open: Mon–Fri
9 a.m.–5.30 p.m.
No credit cards

This is one of the strangest off-licences you are ever likely to see. Inside it is not exactly the grandest-looking place in the world, especially considering the fact that there is so much champagne for sale here – but the bohemian shambles of it all has a certain charm.

Prices obviously vary but it is possible to find bargains here such as a bottle of Lanson Black Label for under £15. They always have a discount deal available on certain labels, and these deals change regularly – it's worth checking what the current bargains are.

Hennes

481 Oxford Street W1
071-493 8557

Open: Mon–Wed, Fri
10 a.m.–6.30 p.m.;
Thurs 10 a.m.–8 p.m.,
Sat 9.30 a.m.–6 p.m.
Credit: A, Amex, V

This quality Swedish fashion company is one of the great European success stories of recent years. They have over 200 branches scattered around Europe, and this store is a brilliant showcase for their cheap family clothes. They are never far behind the big designers and in fact these days they see what is going on a bit before the acknowledged taste-makers. A skirt here can cost as little as £15, and a well-designed jumper will rarely be more than £35. Hennes is also the only shop other than Gap to have realised that there is a big market for well-designed kids' clothes, and has recently moved into baby clothing.

Marks and Spencer

173 Oxford Street W1
071-437 7722

Open: Mon–Wed, Sat
9.30 a.m.–6.30 p.m.,
Thurs 9.30 a.m.–8 p.m.,
Fri 9.30 a.m.–7 p.m.;
food hall, Mon–Fri from
8.30 a.m.
Credit: M&S charge
card only

This is my favourite of all M&S's London branches. It's big enough to get lost in but everything is laid out so that you can find what you're looking for very quickly.

M&S are an incredible success because they keep abreast of the times, which cannot be said for many other big Oxford Street stores, and they manage to sell high-quality, well-designed clothes at reasonable prices. Their woollens, underwear and socks are of the highest quality, and are incredibly good value for money.

The food hall in the basement has everything from a takeaway sandwich to fresh fruit and a wine counter. The food is expensive, but the prepackaged dishes will serve you well when you don't have the time to cook.

Mulberry

11–12 Gees Court W1
071-493 2546

This shop is a great nostalgia trip back to the days of Victorian England and traditional values, when people cared about quality rather than the transient world of fashion. Mulberry, however, has managed

Open: Mon–Wed, Fri,
Sat 9.30 a.m.–6 p.m.,
Thurs 9.30 a.m.–7 p.m.
Credit: A, Amex, DC, V

to marry the two ideas together with great success – their goods can look very trad but if you look closely many of the clothes incorporate new ideas in a very subtle way. The clothes always stay very much within the country look but each season brings a subtle change. Their autumn and winter clothes are the best, especially the big wool duffel coats (£375) which would keep an army warm. The very Englishness of the clothes has always been popular with the Japanese, who like a trip back to days when England was not just Britain PLC.

Though the clothes are highly regarded, it was their range of leather bags and accessories that really made Mulberry's name. They also do their own range of personal planners which are larger and more practical than Filofaxes but are expensive – a big leather one with fillers costs £179.

St Christopher's Place, W1

This small street has managed to attract a very varied selection of stylish shops, and though there has been a high turnover of businesses recently, they have managed to keep the chainstores out. A mixture of cocktail bars and restaurants has failed to make the street come alive at night, though, and it remains a discreet street for afternoon shoppers – though the shops remain open until 7.30 on Thursday evenings. Best bets are Whistles (see separate entry), The Hat Shop (at number 18), Paddy Campbell (8 Gees Court) and Mulberry (see separate entry).

St Christopher's Place has always been South Molton Street's poorer cousin (see Mayfair), but stores like Mulberry have brought a traditional English look back to the place. It's an image that's very popular with us Brits, who love wallowing in our own past.

Selfridges

400 Oxford Street W1
071-629 1234

Open: Mon–Fri
9.30 a.m.–5.30 p.m.,
Sat 9 a.m.–6 p.m.
Credit: A, Amex, DC,
Selfridges Gold Card, V

This beautiful big store was the brainchild of Gordon Selfridge, who was so impressed with Whiteley's (see Notting Hill and Bayswater) in Bayswater that he copied the idea and opened Selfridge's, one of the grandest department stores in the world, in 1909. The fashion department seems to have control of the window displays, which are always quite startling – especially at Christmas – and one of the few things on Oxford Street worth looking at. It also has a clock with an eleven-foot-high figure called the Queen of Time, by Gilbert Bayes and A. D. Millar, over the main entrance.

If you do come here try to make sure you have a few hours to waste as a good wander round takes time. I find the whole experience overwhelming and tend to spend most of my time here in the basement ice-cream bar, Massarella's (see separate entry). Between cafes, wine bars and restaurants, there are eleven places to eat here.

The Shaker Shop
25 Harcourt Street W1
071-724 7672

Open: Mon–Sat
10 a.m.–6 p.m.
Credit: A, Amex, V

The Shaker Shop is instantly seductive: its simplicity and clean, basic air reflects the Shaker ideal of function as beauty. The shop sells a good range of furniture made to Shaker designs, which means utility is always the first consideration. Any pieces under £200 are available in kit form, so you can take them home and assemble them yourself. Apart from the furniture, there's a good stock of Shaker lanterns (£43-£50) and traditional wrought-iron sconces with a heart motif (from £13). Best of all, though, are the famous Shaker boxes, hand-made from cherry wood and with very delicate tapering swallowtails secured with copper tacks. The Shakers believe that when you take off the lid, the box should sigh – a sign of good workmanship. Also good are the baskets, made by craftspeople who have restored originals for Shaker museums in America, and lots of traditional homespun bedlinen.

Virgin Megastore
14–30 Oxford Street
W1
071-631 1234

Open: Mon–Sat
9.30 a.m.–8.00 p.m.,
Sun midday–7 p.m.
Credit: A, Amex, DC, V

Although this store started out simply as a record store it has taken stock of the changing market and opened departments dealing with computer games and videos, as well as a very good book and comic department. There's now a vast and comprehensive selection of these, as well as every record or CD you could possibly want. There's good classical, jazz and world music sections here, and the staff are knowledgeable and helpful. I worked here for a day during a charity stint and was amazed by the shop. It's quite an enchanting place and is very well stocked and managed by young people who are in touch with the customers. The new classical section is soundproofed off, as this store has its own radio station playing rock and dance music non-stop all day. You can listen to certain records before you buy, and you can actually buy empty cassette and CD boxes here – great if your music collection has fallen to bits over the years. You can even buy airline tickets at Virgin.

Upstairs there is a small cafe, which closes an hour before the main store, where you can examine your purchases over a decent cup of coffee and one of their well-laden sandwiches.

Whistles

12–14 St Christopher's
Place W1
071-487 4484

Open: Mon–Wed, Fri,
Sat 10 a.m.–6 p.m.,
Thurs 10 a.m.–7 p.m.
Credit: A, Amex, DC, V

Whistles started off cleverly mixing their own-label designs with those of designers such as Patrick Cox (shoes) and John Galliano (dresses), but since the store has become very popular they have concentrated more and more on their own designs. They stock beautiful and stylish knitwear which will not leave you with much change out of £150, but it is always a reliable place to pick up a dress for work or for evening without having to remortgage the house. Whistles girls always look très elegante without appearing to have made too much of an effort.

ENTERTAINMENT

The Wigmore Hall

Wigmore Street W1
071-935 2141

Credit: A, Amex, DC, V

This concert hall was built in 1901 by Friedrich Bechstein and was originally known as Bechstein Hall – it took the name of the street on which it stands in 1917 when it was sold to the department store Debenham's. It has recently been refurbished and is looking better than it ever has. The surrounding streets were once famous for their piano shops, a number of which remain, upholding the musical tradition of the area. The Wigmore Hall is thought to have some of the best acoustics in London and the regular concerts held here are well attended by those who recognise the authentic purity of the building. It's open all year, though there are no concerts in August. During the rest of the year there are about eight concerts a week – ring for details.

Soho W1

SOHO

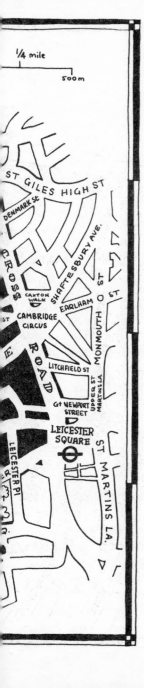

Soho is a half square mile of contradictions – a place where Italians, French, Cypriots, Poles, Sicilians, Maltese, Chinese, Bengalis and occasionally the English do business but seldom mix. It offers every kind of shop or restaurant and is the home of the British media, but visiting the area can be a very difficult and exhausting exercise, and very expensive if you get it wrong.

Soho is the most exciting area in London and can be the most dangerous. It is still the porn and prostitution capital of Britain, and working women live in and trade from apartments alongside those of local residents, who seem much more interested in getting on with their own lives than in causing any outcry. Although about 80,000 people come into Soho each day, only about 4,000 live there. It's a strange place to choose as a home but it holds a charm and history which shows that this small area has never been sedate and could never be boring.

Soho is also the birthplace of British pop music and a melting pot for Jewish and French immigrants: in the nineteenth century it was alleged to be the worst slum in the capital. Over the centuries it has been home to London's aristocratic, intellectual and artistic life – it was, and still is, a resting place for eccentrics and lunatics.

The name Soho supposedly comes from a French hunting call used in the seventeenth century. In many ways this is apt, because Soho is separate from the rest of London in that it is so un-English. The Scottish painter Sir David

Wilkie, who spent a considerable time drinkingand eating in what was the King's Arms in Poland Street, said it was a rare thing to see an Englishman, while there was an abundance of Corsicans, Italians, French, Germans, Welsh and Scots. It seems that ever since Charles II's son, the Duke of Monmouth, built his grand house on Soho Square, the area has had an association with immigrants seeking refuge. The King welcomed the fleeing Huguenots who settled in Soho, bringing with them a cosmopolitan air which had never been seen before. Their craftmanship and exotic tastes changed the face of the village of Soho, and up until the middle of the twentieth century the area was regarded as a French quarter. The Huguenots were followed in the eighteenth century by French Catholics fleeing the Revolution, and during the military rule of Napoleon III French liberals made Soho their new home.

The visionary William Blake was born in 1757 on Broad Street, now Broadwick Street. He summed up the quarter beautifully when he said that Soho was the ideal place to work: 'For life in Soho is meant to be lived to the full, not recorded for the benefit of posterity.'

Times were changing rapidly in Soho. James Boswell discovered in 1775 that it was not a good idea to try to sleep off a hangover in his lodgings in Gerrard Street, for it was 'impossible to have a lie-in in Soho, for, like it or not, one was woken by the sound of street sellers shouting their wares, the clatter of carriages on cobblestones or the steady beat of a hammer from Huguenot craftsmen'.

The list of people who made their homes in Soho at various times is illustrious. In the eighteenth century the young Mozart lived at number 20 Poland Street, and later the Romantic composer Liszt lodged in Great Marlborough Street and Wagner in Old Compton Street. During the 1820s Shelley lived in Poland Street while William Hazlitt lived and drank his tea, miserably, at 6 Frith Street.

In the middle of the nineteenth century Soho went through a radical change when the few remaining aristos headed for Fitzrovia: north of Soho, across Oxford Street and around Charlotte Street. The buildings they left behind were eventually knocked down and replaced by smaller, tighter apartment buildings and tenements into which were squeezed Soho's soaring population of poor. By 1850 families were crammed in eight to a house, and were even living in dank kitchen cellars accessible only by ladders let down from the street. The Liberal leader Gladstone used to walk around talking to the 80,000 or so prostitutes in the area and offering them a bath, a meal and a bed for the night – all to be prepared by his long-suffering wife. It was meant to be in the spirit of charity, but Gladstone supposedly only ever asked the pretty ones.

Towards the end of the nineteenth century attempts were made to clean up Soho. High rents were forcing craftspeople out of their homes and workshops, to be replaced by bordellos and gambling dens; at this time Greek Street was thought to be the most criminal street in London.

After World War I Soho once again became a bohemian gathering place, centred on the Cafe Royal, one of the few good venues in Nash's beautiful Regent Street, which had not seen such decadence since Oscar Wilde had gone to jail. The new bohemians were the painter Nina Hamnett, Mark Gertler, Roger Fry, Augustus John and Duncan Grant, who were replaced in the even madder and frenzied fifties by the young turks Bacon, Freud and Auerbach. Clubs such as the Colony Rooms, run by the legendary Muriel Belcher who was rude to everyone, entertained Sohoites such as George Melly and Colin MacInnes, who so brilliantly caught the period in his book *Absolute Beginners*.

The arrival at around this time of Italian immigrants, who settled mainly into Old Compton Street and Frith Street, brought another style of life to the now squalid area. The Italians' celebratory approach to life rubbed off on many of the locals, who enjoyed the 'arrival of delis such as the Parmigiana and the Camisa. Overlooking these changes was John Logie Baird, who in 1924 rented a two-room attic at 22 Frith Street, where he set up a laboratory in which he eventually demonstrated his new invention, television, on 27 January 1927. Later Wardour Street was to become the home of the British film production and distribution network.

World War II brought with it hostility to the local Italians, who faced attacks in the press and the internment of most of their young men. Some people can still remember the day the ship carrying the internees to Canada was sunk by a German torpedo, leaving 730 men dead.

As youth culture began to make its way into the Soho nights the first pop music clubs such as the 2i's gave young British acts the opportunity to impersonate their American heroes, drink their espressos and park their Vespas outside. New clubs sprang up overnight: the 100 Club on Oxford Street, which is still going strong; the Marquee, which was a jazz haunt before it moved and became the haunt of rock music; Cy Laurie's all-night rave-ups at Mac's in Windmill Street; the Metro in Old Compton Street; and of course the now legendary Ronnie Scott's. Swinging London was about to explode.

As Carnaby Street swung to the sound of a retailing revolution something

just as dramatic was happening much more discreetly on the other side of Shaftesbury Avenue. The Chinese who had arrived in Britain during the Opium Wars in the 1840s – a mere 545 of them – had settled in London's docklands. They had never been made to feel welcome in Britain, but the return from Asia of soldiers who had developed a taste for Chinese cuisine gave them the idea that a move uptown might be a good idea. They settled in the slumlands of Gerrard Street, and the thriving businesses there today are a testament to a very tight-knit community which is extremely proud of its achievements.

Throughout the sixties and seventies racketeering and prostitution were still rife in Soho, until public opinion put pressure on the authorities to clean up the streets and make them safer. This they managed to do without destroying the atmosphere of the area.

In recent years new restaurants have opened and closed overnight but the good ones have survived the high rents, the rates and the recessions which have all threatened the existence of Soho as a place where people want to spend time. The biggest fear of Sohoites is that the area will be changed into an office monoculture with no room for the small specialist shops, the market stalls and the delis which make the place what it is. The mixture of clubland and theatreland prevails against all the odds, making the fascinating small quarter vibrant and essential to London life. Soho's pubs, though, still need to wake up to the fact that people's drinking habits have changed, that they now want to visit a toilet that doesn't smell as if a pig was in there before them, and that drinking alcohol does not mean that you want to sit beside ashtrays piled high with rubbish while being abused by some drunken idiot who has been allowed to sit beside you. However, despite this one gripe, don't let anyone tell you that Soho isn't what it used to be – it's better than ever.

Soho's mixture of misfit and bohemian shows no sign of disappearing. From the masquerades and balls held in Soho Square's Carlisle House in the eighteenth century to the transvestisism of Madame JoJo's (8 Brewer Street) or the hip-hop attitude-slinging of the Wag Club (33 Wardour Street), Soho has always been the centre of London's nightlife. Thomas de Quincy gathered the material for *Confessions of an Opium Eater* here and left Soho with the permanent reputation of being subversive and anti-social, though it is in fact the most social district of London.

During the fifties the proliferation of jazz clubs made the area the most musically important and influential in Britain, and many of the new immigrants coming to the country from the Caribbean found a home for their music here. Colin McInnes' *Absolute Beginners* captured the explosive atmosphere of the period, when new coffee bars such as the Moka Bar in Frith Street and the 2i's in Old Compton Street rocked the streets for the first time, and the marriage of music and fashion introduced style as well as recreational drugs to London's youth culture.

In recent years rents and rates have risen dramatically and though some clubs have survived, more and more seem to open on Monday and close on Tuesday. The good ones, though, such as the Wag, Cafe de Paris and Gossips (69 Dean Street), still deliver to a more than willing public. It helps to know what's going on and the best way to find out is to go to Soho's record shops.

The authorities have tried their best to close down the illicit goings-on in some of the seedier topless bars which set out to rip you off, but the sex industry has simply responded by becoming more streamlined and very efficient, though still seedy. Keep clear of such places as they offer nothing but trouble.

Leicester Square has a mixed bag of clubs. On the southern tip the Comedy Store has nightly performances by 'stand-up comedians varying from the terrible to the very good. Their regular improvisation night can be awesome, but could turn out to be a nightmare – call 0426 914433 for details. The former Empire Ballroom, now relaunched as Equinox (071-437 1446), is aimed at tourists and is more a disco than a club. Maximus, 14 Leicester Square, can vary from being a brilliant gay club, the Love Ranch, to a boring rap club. The Limelight (136 Shaftesbury Avenue, 071-434 0572), held in an old Victorian church, should be brilliant, but has never quite got it right. A dance club needs focus, and this is too complicated a venue, where every room seems to lead on to another. Not really worth visiting is the Hippodrome (071-437 4311), which is aimed purely at tourists, and the Marquee, which continues to attract rock 'n' rollers in search of a drunk, sweaty evening.

The other type of club which flourishes in Soho is the private members' club, places where people who do not enjoy pubs or public places can eat and drink in comfort without the hassle of worrying about England's restricted drinking laws. The most famous drinking club is the Colony, where the likes of Francis Bacon and Dylan Thomas came to get drunk and insulted by the late owner Muriel Belcher. It's nothing special – a small room with a bar, a piano and a strange-looking man called Ian Board, who has taken over from Belcher as insulter. People still come here to get drunk, and the latest recruit is soul singer Lisa Stansfield who seems to enjoy the bawdy mixture of slumming it and slamming it.

Fred's at 4 Carlisle Street, next door to the offices of satirical magazine *Private Eye*, is an upmarket bar frequented by media folk in search of a new job, a new idea or a new launching pad for their egos.

The Groucho Club (44 Dean Street) is Soho's most elite and expensive establishment, and is home to people from the worlds of television and publishing. Its good food and very good bar makes it a very popular venue where deals are done and ideas kicked around by the masters of the media universe.

HOW TO GET THERE

Tubes
- Leicester Square
- Oxford Street
- Piccadilly Circus
- Tottenham Court Road

Buses
- Charing Cross Road: 14, 19, 22B, 24, 29, 38, 176
- Oxford Circus: 7, 8, 10, 25, 73, 176
- Regent Street: 3, 6, 12, 13, 15, 15B, 53, 53X, 88, 94, 139, 159
- Shaftesbury Avenue: 14, 19, 22B, 38

ED'S EASY DINER

Carnaby Street, W1

This street was the home of French Huguenot craftsmen until the late nineteenth century when shopkeepers and tradesmen took over the properties and changed the street from a largely residential area to a commercial one. Along with the Kings Road, Carnaby Street epitomised Swinging London in the sixties, but after the early seventies it went into a terminal decline, summed up perfectly in the Jam's song 'Carnaby Street, Not What It Used to Be'. And it isn't – it still attracts thousands of visitors every day, but what is on offer is mainly a collection of tatty shops attempting to capitalise on the nostalgia of the street.

The streets leading off Carnaby Street have attempted to bring a serious dose of eighties and nineties fashion to the area, now mysteriously known as West Soho. But the fun and frivolity of shops such as Pam Hogg (5 Newburgh Street) and Junior Gaultier (28 Fouberts Place) is not enough to conceal the death throes of what was once London's premier fashion street. Carnaby Street has now been replaced by Covent Garden's Neal Street as the hippest and most current place around.

Chinatown
Gerrard Street W1

The area south of Shaftesbury Avenue and centred around Gerrard Street is known universally as Chinatown. At one time Gerrard Street was an artistic ghetto housing the likes of John Dryden at number 24, and in the 1920s and 1930s the street was famous for its nightclubs; later, in the fifties, it became home to a line of seedy strip shows. Chinatown developed after the second wave of Chinese arrived in Britain in the fifties and sixties, fleeing poverty in Hong Kong and China. The original Chinatown, which was in Limehouse, could not cope with the numbers which arrived off the boats and Tong Yan Kai (Chinese Street), as Chinatown is known, came about after the overpopulation of Limehouse caused the new immigrants to look for somewhere cheap to settle. At the time of their arrival Gerrard Street and its surroundings were terrible slums and it is an indication of the effort that the Chinese people have put into this area that it now attracts more visitors than almost anywhere else in the West End.

Gerrard Street has recently been done up to look 'authentically' Chinese, which is a bit of a joke to the locals who see it as a very English view of China. Nevertheless, for all its stereotyping this is one of the best areas in London to eat in. The choice of restaurants is huge and all of them are good. They range from Wong Kei, beside the Wag Club on Wardour Street, which is famous for its rude waiters and canteen-like atmosphere, to more formal restaurants and places where you can simply have some tea and Chinese buns. Chinatown is a great place to go at lunchtime for dim sum – tiny steamed dumplings with various fillings which you pick from a trolley wheeled round the dining room. Most of the larger restaurants do dim sum and it's a cheap and novel way to fill up for an afternoon's shopping.

Every February the London Chinese celebrate their new year in a way which should put the rest of us (except the Scots) to shame. A cavalcade of colour takes to the streets as the lion dance is used to chase away evil spirits, and for a moment it seems as if London is the most exciting city in the world.

Chinatown has shops dealing in martial-arts accessories, Chinese videos, books covering anything from philosophy to medication, and even travel agencies – anything related to the Chinese lifestyle can be had in this area. But the most important reason for coming here is food, which in this area is mainly Cantonese – the other regions of China are not well served here or anywhere else in London.

Leicester Square, WC2

In the seventeenth century, Robert Sidney, Earl of Leicester, acquired this piece of land and built Leicester House on the north part of it. On the southern side, fields were laid out to complement the house which, although plain, was one of the largest and most expensively furnished in London. Lord Leicester would allow no shops to be built there during his lifetime but eventually his son permitted booths to be erected on the square. Famous writers, actors and professional people, as well as traders, were attracted to the houses which were built in the grand style of Pall Mall. William Hogarth produced 'The Rake's Progress' while living at number 30; Sir Joshua Reynolds bought number 47 in 1760 and lived there until his death in 1792. His house was regarded as one of the most stylish residences on the square, and he spent much of his fortune on redesigning the interior to suit his tastes; he regularly entertained visitors such as Boswell, Edmund Burke, Goldsmith and Garrick here, and it was here that Reynolds and Johnson formed The Club, which met every Thursday at the Turk's Head in Gerrard Street to discuss and debate every conceivable subject.

The increasing volume of traffic and its growing population saw the square grow quite seedy during the nineteenth century. Cholera outbreaks chased the wealthy away during the Victorian era, but the lure of Theatreland, which had sprung up along Shaftesbury Avenue, now the most fashionable area of London, proved too great for them to resist for long. Late-night restaurants and cafes opened, capturing the spirit of the times as they kept their doors open into the small hours to entertain the beau monde.

Leicester Square's most exotic days are now long gone, but it still has a strong attraction for many people. During summer nights it's alive to the sound of buskers, who are tolerated by the police, and because it's a pedestrian precinct it has a relaxed, almost Continental feel to it on balmy evenings. The cinemas here are about the best in London – they are so big that it is almost always possible to get a seat here. Another thing worth looking out for is the cut-price ticket booth, which sells very cheap same-night seats for almost all plays and shows in the capital. The clubs in and around the square change with every musical fashion, but there will always be something to interest you. There is not much here in the way of proper food, but then you're only a stone's throw away from Chinatown which has a huge variety of restaurants and cafes which are cheap and can be very, very good.

Notre Dame de France
5 Leicester Place WC2
071-437 9363

.Services: English –
Mon–Fri 12.15 p.m.,

The original church was built in the nineteenth century to serve London's large French Catholic population, and occupied the site where the famous Panorama building once stood. The building was damaged during the war, but was rebuilt in 1953 using original Chartres stone. The hall below once played host to alternative rock bands but this has now been stopped,

French – Sat 6 p.m.,
Sun 10 a.m.,
11.30 p.m.

presumably by its ecclesiastical owners who thought all that racket unsuitable for a holy place.

The most interesting thing about the church is the tapestry behind the high altar. It was made at Aubusson to the design of the French genius Jean Cocteau, who also designed the walls of the Lady Chapel, which feature long, linear figures ascending to a greater place. The church is one of the very few places in Britain where Cocteau's work can be seen.

Shaftesbury Avenue, W1 and WC2

Shaftesbury Avenue is the centre of Theatreland, where plays are put on at great expense in the hope that they will run and run. They seldom do. The street, the dividing line between Soho and Chinatown, was built in 1886 to ease the serious congestion in the West End. Some of London's worst slums were demolished to make way for it. The years between 1888 and 1907 saw theatre become extremely popular in London and as a result an increasing number of theatres were built here. The Apollo, the Globe and the Queen's, as well as the now-destroyed Shaftesbury Theatre, rose almost overnight to satisfy the public's thirst for entertainment, and until the new theatre of the fifties took attention away from commercial plays, to have a play in a Shaftesbury Avenue theatre was the zenith of achievement for actors and writers alike.

Soho Square, W1

It was in 1691, when the quality bricklayer Richard Frith bought the lease on the land known as Soho Fields that this square started to take shape. By the middle of the eighteenth century it was surrounded by good-sized houses, including Carlisle House and Monmouth House, though the original buildings did not last long – throughout the century new owners, including the Lord Mayor William Beckford, demolished and rebuilt their own style of homes. By the end of the century the aristocrats had moved to the grandeur of Mayfair, leaving the houses in the hands of foreign diplomats, country gentlemen and, eventually, a mixture of professional men.

In the nineteenth century Carlisle House was pulled down and replaced by the quieter St Patrick's Roman Catholic church. The house had been the place where the infamous Mrs Cornelys, an ex-lover of Casanova's, entertained London society in an outrageous manner to which it soon became accustomed.

Soho Square is now the home of CBS Records, 20th Century Fox, Paul McCartney's management and Bloomsbury publishers, as well as a host of advertising and media-related companies. The patch of grass in the middle is very popular with the women from the hostel on the corner of Greek Street, who seem to regard it as their front garden. It's an extraordinary place in which to watch London pass by.

EATING, DRINKING AND SLEEPING

Alastair Little
49 Frith Street W1
071-734 5183

Open: lunch, Mon–Fri
midday–3 p.m.;
dinner, Mon–Sat
6–11.30 p.m.
Credit: A, Amex, MC, V
Average: £70

Soho's premier chef has survived the recession, new trends and new attitudes to food by doing what he has always done – spending a lot of time in the kitchen. The menu in this place changes each day, but Little manages to sneak in a few of his classic dishes, such as wild mushroom risotto, or a warm salad of duck and chicken livers served with, believe it or not, poached egg and bacon. The unusual will always be on the menu, and the dishes will shock or at least surprise those culinary veterans who thought they had tasted it all. Downstairs is a secret little establishment which serves bar food at a quarter of the upstairs prices to half a dozen tables. I actually like it better down here, as the atmosphere makes you feel that some kind of conspiracy is afoot.

If you are into food and have the money to spend, this is the place to go. I find the crowd it attracts a wee bit full of themselves, but if you ignore them and just fill yourself you will leave happy.

Andrew Edmunds
46 Lexington Street W1
071-437 5708

Open: lunch
12.30–3 p.m.,
dinner 6–10.30 p.m.
Credit: A, V
Average: £30

This restaurant/wine bar is one of the strangest and most exciting discoveries in Soho. It attracts a mixture of advertising folk and artists, who all seem to ignore each other but are constantly disparaging one another's profession. The owner has a specialist print gallery next door which is well worth a visit – presumably before you sit down to eat and drink. I say this because although the food is very good here it seems as though most people are more concerned with getting drunk. The food is as varied as duck breast and mango, homemade ravioli and wild mushroom, or feta and eggplant terrine with salad. They always have a fresh tiramisu or a chocolate

mousse cake which you are encouraged to wash down with a muscat or vino santo. The wine list is second to none in Soho and this is probably the reason the place has remained so popular. There's also elderflower lemonade at £1.50, and house wine costs £8 a bottle.

The Bar Italia
22 Frith Street W1
071-437 4520

Open 24 hours
No credit cards

Opened in 1949 and owned by three generations of the charming Polledri family, this 24-hour cafe is the coolest hangout in Soho, a rendezvous for Italians after work, for sports fans who come to watch a big occasion on the extra-large screen, and for clubbers after a hard night's dancing. The huge television towards the back is never off and if it is not showing Italian football games it is blaring boxing matches or videos of old James Bond movies. Up above the coffee machine is a large poster of the undefeated heavyweight champion Rocky Marciano, sent by his wife. This was Marciano's favourite coffee bar when he visited London. It was also the centre of attraction for local mobsters and coffee drinkers during the infamous sixties and it was here that the duel between Albert Dimes and Jack Spot took place, eventually finishing with a stabbing in a local fruit and veg shop which used to stand on the corner.

The Bar Italia still serves the best coffee in Soho and a selection of sandwiches and pastries. The best coffee is Late Mochiato or an espresso.

Break For The Border
8 Argyll Street W1
071-734 5776

Open: bar, Mon–Sat
midday–11 p.m.,
Sun 7–11.30 p.m.;
restaurant 5.30–11 p.m.
Credit: A, Amex, V
Average: £25

This Tex-Mex restaurant is one of the noisiest establishments in London, so do not come here if you want to have a quiet chat. The emphasis is on drinking pitchers of beer or margueritas and shouting as much as possible. It's also very popular with rock 'n' roll types who bring a sleazy presence to the place as they hang out at the bar or booths and impersonate Keith Richards or Bono. The food suits the atmosphere, as it is not too fussy, and comes as very large portions of anything from a basic burger at £6 to fajitas and enchiladas at aroung £8. The music is always loud – too loud – but it's the place to be if you feel like getting off your head very quickly on an assortment of cocktails, tequila slammers and good cold beer.

Cafe Royal
68 Regent Street W1

It is difficult to imagine that this place, with its air of a fading upmarket French restaurant, was once the

071-437 9090

Open: brasserie –
Mon–Sat, lunch
midday–3 p.m.,
dinner 6–11 p.m.;
grill room – Mon–Fri,
lunch midday–3 p.m.,
dinner 6–11 p.m.,
Sat, dinner 6–11 p.m.;
drinks, Mon–Sat
midday–11 p.m., Sun
6–11 p.m.
Credit: A, Amex, DC, V
Average: brasserie
£16.50, grill room £80

Cafe Soho

13 Ingestre Place W1
071-287 8572

Open: Mon–Fri
7.30 a.m.–4 p.m.
No credit cards
Average: £8

The Coach and Horses

29 Greek Street W1
071-437 5920

Open: Mon–Sat
11 a.m.–11 p.m.,
Sun midday–3 p.m.,
7–10.30 p.m.
No credit cards

most fashionable spot in Victorian and Edwardian London. It was the brainchild of a French wine merchant who opened a cafe here in 1865 with a wine cellar and a billiard room in the basement. He later expanded into the adjoining buildings, creating a grill room which was much loved by Oscar Wilde, Augustus John and Whistler, who would swap ideas and gossip while sitting at the marble-topped tables. During the 1930s the next generation of intellectuals and society folks patronised the brasserie section which had replaced the former artists' meeting place. It is no longer a meeting place for intellectuals, though older and more glamorous types such as Shirley Conran and Joan Collins tend to patronise it, but it's worth a visit just to get a taste of the past. The drinks are expensive – a glass of champagne can cost as much as £7 – but they have a terrific list of around 40 cocktails at about the same price.

The husband-and-wife team of Lou and Pat have come up with the best sandwich bar in Soho. Situated down a small backstreet away from the hub of Soho life, it seems an unlikely venue for such a popular food bar but every day queues reach out into the street. The best sandwiches are tomato and mozzarella on ciabatta bread or prawn and avocado on granary, and are complemented by a well-made cappuccino or espresso. In the early morning, when you just might be able to get a seat, they do bagels or muesli.

This pub attracts a disparate bunch of Sohoites as well as voyeuristic tourists – the room upstairs is booked regularly by the satirical magazine *Private Eye* for its own even more disparate gatherings of writers and politicians.

The pub's attraction is difficult to see immediately, but the reputation of the owner, Norman Balon, must have something to do with it. His book, *You're Barred You Bastards*, is the tale of his life and the reasons why he is so rude to everyone, from the late Francis Bacon, who was a regular, to the naive tourist who asks the wrong question. I find Balon a bit of a bore but there are people who go back to his pub just to witness another ritual humiliation of some poor unsuspecting person. His status was blown up even

further recently with Keith Waterhouse's highly successful play *Jeffrey Bernard Is Unwell*, which told the tale of the drunken writer being locked up in the Coach and Horses for the night.

The pub has become as culturally important as the Tower of London to Soho aficionados, who see it as a metaphor for all that is exciting about life. The older generation of regulars have their own spots, so be careful where you sit or stand, as your seat might belong to some old soak whose talent for survival has made him a legend.

dell'Ugo
56 Frith Street W1
071-734 8300

Open: cafe – Mon–Sat
11 a.m.–11.30 p.m.;
restaurant – lunch,
midday–3 p.m.,
dinner 5.30 –11 p.m.;
bistro midday–3 p.m.,
7–11 p.m.
Credit: A, Amex, V
Average: cafe, £30;
restaurant, £60

The man behind the very successful 190 Queensgate restaurant in Kensington is responsible for taking on and revamping this site which was once the imaginative Braganza. Anthony Worrall Thompson has refocused the attention of his customers away from the decor and concentrated on his menu. The ground floor of this three-tiered establishment works as a cafe/bar serving up simple crostini or bruscettas piled high with salad.

The first floor is a bit more upmarket but again the emphasis is on the food menu, which mixes hot and cold dishes such as marinated mushrooms, grilled leeks or brimming plates of pasta – all very simple and delicious. There is always a special dish of the day, which is guaranteed to be a little bit more special and expensive but is probably worth a try. Leave a space for the puddings, which are Worrall Thompson's speciality.

The top floor is closest in style to Worrall Thompson's highly successful 190 Queensgate. The food is elaborate with a strong Italian flavour, again without being overly decorative, which shows a great understanding of the simplicity of British taste. The wine list is simple and easy to read, with prices ranging from £10 to £25. The whole place is light and welcoming – what more could you want?

The Dog and Duck
18 Bateman Street W1

Open: 11 a.m.–11 p.m.
No credit cards

There have been very few changes to this pub since it was built in 1773. Though there is not room to swing a cat you should manage to get in to get your drinks and slip out to the busy pavement without bumping into people or emptying glasses on them. The beer is a mixture of commercial lagers and real ale, and they have a decent selection of bottled beer served cold, which by English standards is not bad going. It's always crowded because of its size but you can go upstairs and find a seat and order a bar snack if you are desperate. It's worth coming here to see how a bar looked when Soho was becoming the exotic place we now know it to be.

The Dog House
187 Wardour Street
W1
071-434 2116

Open: restaurant –
Mon–Fri, lunch
12.30–3 p.m.,
dinner 6–11 p.m.;
Sat, dinner
5.30–11 p.m.;
bar midday–midnight
Credit: A, Amex, V
Average: £40

This Modern British restaurant is run by the people behind the successful First Floor in Notting Hill. The underground rooms and their alcoves are tightly packed but never dark or dank. At the moment the tables are garishly painted, which adds to the sense of wonder as you walk in. Very direct spotlighting creates a subterranean effect which changes the colour when seen from just about every angle. The food here is similar to that at the First Floor, and includes such delicious concoctions as red beet soup with chilli vodka or pork chops with garlic mash and tamarind gravy. It's unlike many other new Soho restaurants because it's not saying, 'Look, I'm here, I'm hip' – with the Dog House it's more a case of finding the place and enjoying the feeling of being somewhere odd and special. The other important thing is that you don't have to eat here; the bar is open and is better for a drink than most Soho joints.

Ed's Easy Diner
12 Moor Street W1
071-439 1955

Open: Mon–Thurs
11.30 a.m.–midnight;
Fri-Sat,
11.30 a.m.–1 a.m.,
Sun
11.30 a.m.–11 p.m.
No credit cards
Average: £12

A small hamburger bar with seating around the counter, Ed's is a slice of not-quite-authentic fifties America which has at least made the effort to make the place efficient and fun. A steady flow of American beer such as Budweiser or Michelob is the best way to drown the very large hamburgers which come plain or with a generous amount of melted cheese on top. The coffee is the American variety which means vast quantities served up in mugs but incredibly weak. If the burgers are not enough – and they should be, I can assure you – their chocolate brownies will definitely anchor you to the spot. And if that happens, then right in front of you at the counter is your own personal slot machine which will pour out the best of fifties music for a mere 10p.

The staff here have that American familiarity and friendliness which is so foreign to Britain, but if you can suffer through the bullshit the burgers are worth it.

The French House

49 Dean Street W1
071-437 2799 (bar),
071-437 2477
(restaurant)

Open: pub – Mon–Sat
midday–11 p.m.,
Sun midday–3 p.m.,
7–10.30 p.m.;
restaurant – Mon–Fri,
lunch 12.30–3 p.m.,
dinner
6.30–11.30 p.m.,
Sat dinner
6.30–11.30 p.m.,
Sun lunch 1-3 p.m.
Credit: A, DC, V
Average: £40

This famous pub has as long a history as Soho and as big a reputation. During the war it was the home for the Free French and de Gaulle spent a considerable amount of time there.

Gaston Berlemont, who was the last of the family who originally owned the pub, recently retired back to France, but the pub has kept its spirit. Through the years it as been a popular haunt of artists and writers. Brendan Behan and Dylan Thomas drank till they dropped here and the Scottish painters Colquhoun and McBryde made it their second home. What attracted them to this small smoky room? Was it the photographs of past patrons, including boxers and criminals, or the French aperitifs and half-bottles of champagne, or the lack of any kind of draught beer? The clientele is still made up of artists and actors and the odd bookie waiting for a nod. It's quite simply one of the best bars I have been in anywhere in the world, but it does seem to encourage you to drink too much.

The recently opened first-floor restaurant is an absolute must if you intend to eat either lunch or dinner in Soho. The menu, mainly of the Modern British school, offers delightful soups such as wild mushroom, and the main courses include grilled swordfish and boiled beef and dumplings. It's small, intimate and popular with Soho's old crowd, who know what they like – you'll need to book if you want to be sure of getting one of the eight tables.

Outside the pub is an area known as McEwan's terrace, a small step where drunks and down-and-outs – who for some reason all seem to be Scottish – gather. Sometimes it can be difficult distinguishing them from the pub's customers. However, regulars of the quality who used to frequent the place – Vivien Leigh, Wyndham Lewis, Aleister Crowley, Salvador Dali – no longer hang around in such numbers. Stars these days tend to drink water and eat bits of rice; gone are the days when they got drunk with us mere mortals.

The Gay Hussar

2 Greek Street, W1
071-437 0973

This East European restaurant is a favourite with political powerbrokers from both sides of the House – Roy Hattersley sits at the same table every time he comes here, as does broadcaster/journalist Derek

Open: Mon–Sat –
lunch, 12.30–2 p.m.,
dinner 5.30–11 p.m.
Credit: Amex
Average: £40

Jameson. The food is essentially a meat-meets-meat affair, influenced by countries as diverse as Austria and Serbia. There are dishes, such as spinach pancakes, which are suitable for non-meateaters, but you do get the feeling that the Gay Hussar is aimed at sharp-toothed carnivores. Thick, rich Hungarian wines complement the food exactly.

Hazlitt's Hotel
6 Frith Street W1
071-434 1771

Credit: A, Amex, DC,
MC, Visa
Average: £89 + VAT
for a single room, £105
+ VAT for a double.
Breakfast £5.95

Built in the eighteenth century, this was once the home of reactionary and author William Hazlitt, and is now popular with publishing types and people from the nearby CBS Records. The rooms are small but the management prides itself on the fact that they have kept the building's period charm. Prices are reasonable for the centre of London, and although the staff are very friendly they never ask questions and if you need to be out later than midnight they supply you with your own front-door key. In many ways the hotel is a sophisticated bed and breakfast which offers little more in the way of food and drink than the teapot and kettle in the room – presumably they have never felt the need to compete with the many cafes, bars and restaurants within walking distance.

Kettner's
29 Romilly Street W1
071-734-6112

Open: restaurant,
11 a.m.–midnight;
champagne bar,
Mon–Fri
11.30 a.m.–3 p.m.,
5.30–11 p.m.,
Sat 5.30–11 p.m.
Credit: A, Amex, DC, V
Average: £20

You get a strange feeling in here that the ghosts of a grander past are looking down in scorn at what Kettner's has become. Once an elegant brasserie and champagne bar, Kettner's was taken over by the Pizza Express chain who, to their credit, have maintained the elegant bar though they have changed the brasserie over to a pizza-based menu. That's not a bad thing; in fact I can't recommend it enough – where else can you eat a Four Seasons pizza for £6 in such exotic surroundings? The service is always friendly and the bill is always surprisingly low, which makes for a big change from the Soho norm. Upstairs in the Oak Room pianist Alan Clare, who has played with everyone from Billie Holliday to Sinatra, plays once or twice a week. He's one of the jazz greats.

Afternoon tea is served up in the Edwardian grandeur of the bar next door which, once the scones are taken away, plays host to the media moguls who might be celebrating a good day but who nowadays are more likely to be drowning their sorrows. The champagne here is reasonably priced – a bottle of

Charles Heidsick is available at £10, less than it'll cost in any rival establishment – and there is a variety of champagne-based cocktails, such as Bellinis at £4, which do the job in a most pleasant way.

Maison Bertaux
28 Greek Street W1
071-437 6007

Open: Mon–Sat
9 a.m.–7 p.m.,
Sun 9 a.m.–1 p.m.,
3–7 p.m.
No credit cards
Average: £8

From a distance you wouldn't think twice about this place, but as soon as you see the window with its fresh array of newly baked cakes from the upstairs bakery, it all becomes much more exciting. Coffee and chocolate eclairs or strawberry tarts are just the thing for tea, and enormous croissants are wonderful in the morning. Maison Bertaux is a great place for an intimate chat or, even better, a discreet eavesdrop on the table next to you – very naughty but very entertaining. The decor is simple and the tables sparse, but if you want grandeur head for Fortnum's. This is the real Soho, with all its history and eccentricity under one roof.

Mildred's
58 Greek Street W1
071-494 1634

Open: Mon–Sat
12–11 p.m.
No credit cards
Average: £20

Mildred's is Soho's most popular vegetarian hangout, not just for the obvious eco-friendly types but also for besuited business people and local residents who have become regulars because the food is fresh, cheap and never boring. The place is run entirely by women – only because they can't find men who will work hard enough – and over the last four years they have done well enough not to need any male assistance. It's small and slightly cramped and more often than not you have to share a table with other hungry faces. The soups are a good bet and the regular stir-fry vegetables with rice, shrimps and cashews are a must. Mildred's has recently been awarded a licence, which makes it a more comfortable place to go in the evening. It has a no-smoking policy and the mixture of professionals and idealists makes for a tempestuous atmosphere worth dropping in for.

Patisserie Valerie
44 Old Compton Street
W1
071-437 3466

Open: Mon–Sat
8 a.m.–8 p.m.,
Sun 10 a.m.–6 p.m.
No credit cards

Patisserie Valerie is one of Soho's most famous cafes, and for that reason one of its most popular. The cake display in the window is formidable and you can be assured that they are all fresh and perfectly baked. Film, art-school and theatrical folk are all treated with equal disdain by the staff, who seem to think that the world is against them. It is always crowded, except perhaps when it first opens in the morning, so getting a seat is difficult. If you do manage to get

Average: £8

a seat you can have a toasted sandwich or a hot croissant before you devour a big cream cake, but you'll have to share with Soho's homegrown coterie of oddballs. It all really depends on how you feel – if you're in an adventurous mood this place is ideal, but if you want to read a book and enjoy a cake then it's not for you.

Pizza Express
10 Dean Street W1
071-437 9595

Open: 10 a.m.–midnight
Credit: A, Amex, V
Average: £25

The Pizza Express chain remains London's most successful quality fast-food empire. Everything served here is prepared in an open-plan kitchen which enables you to see how clean and efficient the whole operation is. Instead of making you feel that you must rush out of the door as soon as you've devoured your meal – which arrives very quickly – the staff here make you feel welcome and you can stay as long as you like, even if there is a queue waiting for tables. Downstairs in the basement is regular live music which, depending on the night, is either trad jazz or some souped-up modern improvisation which in a sense reflects the food – fast, furious and with a memorable aftertaste.

I recommend the Neptune, which consists of ample amounts of anchovies, olives, capers and tomatoes, or the American Hot, which is a mixture of pepperoni sausage, hot green peppers, mozzarella and tomato. The only disappointment are the sweets, which seem a bit boring and production line, but the coffee is fine and the house wine is a reasonable frascati, though I suggest you suck on a cold Peroni beer which compliments the food perfectly.

Presto
4 Old Compton Street
W1
071-437 4006

Open: Mon–Sat
11.30 a.m.–11.30 p.m.
Credit: V
Average: £20

The old-style restaurant/canteen atmosphere here encourages people to wander in throughout the day to enjoy a quick plate of home-made pasta or a basic plate of gnocchi at around £3. A special mention must be made of the crumble and custard which is on the menu most days. It may not be good for the belly but it's a sensual experience. Presto is a Soho experience where the food matches the varied custom, the prices are kept low and the food decent. It even manages to keep the price of its best Italian wine down to £7.25.

The owners are Romans who enjoy having a chat with the regulars, who include everyone from film-maker and writer Derek Jarman to fashion students

from St Martins, which is only around the corner. Presto, with its unpretentious atmosphere, hasn't changed in years and is all the better for it.

The Red Fort

77 Dean Street W1

071-437 2115

Open: lunch,
midday–3 p.m.,
dinner 6–11.30 p.m.
Credit: A, Amex, DC, V
Average: £40

The best Indian restaurant in Soho is a bit on the pompous side, but the food when it comes makes up for any airs and graces you might have endured before its arrival. The Bangladeshi specialities such as roop chanda are heavily spiced and delicious to boot. There's a more than decent selection of vegetarian dishes which combine raita and sag (spinach) with some of the best rice I have tasted. The best of the large choice are the chicken korma and the keemas, which are on the expensive side at £10 but are worth it – though usually I think that Indian food should never cost too much as it is available all over Britain at such good prices. But here the great setting and the good reputation put a couple of extra pounds on the bill.

Signor Zilli

41 Dean Street W1

071-734 3924

Open: lunch, Mon–Fri,
Sun midday–3 p.m.;
dinner, Mon–Sun
6–11.30 p.m.
Credit: A, Amex, Visa
Average: £40

Do not let its over-the-top exterior put you off this remarkably good little restaurant which is the pride and joy of Venetian Signor Zilli. The murals are somewhat oppressive, but the food is liberating. Surprisingly, considering the history of the area, Italian food in Soho tends not to be that good, but here an emphasis has been put on simple fish dishes which are quite a surprise. Grilled swordfish or fresh salmon or a plate of spaghetti vongole are all served up without much ado, complemented by a rocket salad lightly coated with a balsamic vinegar dressing. The people who work here know what they are doing and leave you to get on with it, but always seem to appear as if by magic when you are thinking about asking for something.

Soho-Soho

11–13 Frith Street W1

071-494 3491

Open: rotisserie –
Mon–Fri 8 a.m.–1 a.m.,
Sat midday–1 a.m.;
restaurant – lunch,
Mon–Fri
midday–3 p.m.,

The upstairs room at Soho-Soho is enlarged by the big bright windows which give the place a sense of space rare in an area where most places are small and cramped. The food here is a sort of modern French embracing the exotic and the simple. The wines are pricey but the free parking in the nearby NCP in Wardour Street lightens the pain a little. The chef, Tony Howorth, came from the Ivy in Covent Garden and has brought its high standards with him. Although the menu sounds grand the place is

dinner, Mon–Sat
6 p.m.–midnight;
wine bar – Mon–Sat
11 a.m.–11 p.m.
Credit: A, Amex, V
Average: downstairs,
£28; upstairs, £60

in fact quite laid back and definitely has no dress codes.

Downstairs in the multi-functional cafe/bar/rotisserie, the atmosphere from late morning, when breakfast is available, to late afternoon, when the place is recovering from another packed day, is one of the best in Soho. Omelettes, grilled baby chickens or skewered aubergine, courgette, pepper and fennel come to the aid of the hungry and harried. It's much cheaper than upstairs, but you cannot book and it gets so busy that if you don't get there early you will have to wait.

Star Cafe
22 Great Chapel Street
W1
071-437 8778

Open: Mon–Fri
7 a.m.–5 p.m.
No credit cards
Average: £14

Breakfast here begins at 7 a.m., offering anything from healthy muesli to a pair of Scotch kippers. Every combination of the traditional breakfast is available. Most dishes include toast and coffee or tea, and the names of the set combinations speak for themselves: 'The Terminator' is two sausages, egg, bacon, potatoes and beans, and the 'Veggy Grill' is two eggs, mushrooms, tomatoes, beans and potatoes. One of the breakfast dishes – smoked salmon and scrambled eggs – is named after local advertising mogul Tim Mellor.

If you've missed breakfast but are looking for a budget lunch, then home-made soups and various pasta dishes will always fill the hole without making you feel that you need surgery to get out of the chair. Never leave here without going for the hot chocolate fudge cake. The restaurant is licensed and has a fine takeaway service. The people who work here are fast-talking joke-cracking wiseguys who will always cheer you up, even if they have to tickle you to get a smile on your face. The Star Cafe has also won a *Time Out* award for best basic food in a central cafe.

Yung's
23 Wardour Street W1
071-437 4986/4566

Open: midday–4 a.m.
Credit: A, Amex, V
Average: £20

Yung's was the first place I ever went to have a Chinese meal and it remains one of my favourites. They call it 'Dancer's Delight' in the clubs and at the weekend it is impossible to get a seat here at 3 a.m. Again, it's not particularly glamorous – but this is irrelevant as the food is always good and fresh. Yung's is a few doors down from the Wag Club and successive generations have come here after a night of sweating and dreaming. The waiters here never ask questions and never look strangely at the odd

night creatures who come back so regularly, but make you feel at home as much as a Chinese restaurant can – which admittedly is not much.

SHOPPING

Algerian Coffee Shop
52 Old Compton Street W1
071-437 2480

Open: Mon–Sat
9 a.m.–7 p.m.
Credit: A, Amex, DC, V

Since so many of the good delis and patisseries which made Old Compton Street special have been forced out by high rents and rates, the Algerian Coffee Shop is a beacon in the desert. It specialises in both coffee and tea and carries on its shelves some of the strangest and most exotic-smelling Arabic teas and South American coffees, and many of the local restaurants come here for their supplies. I find normal Algerian and Turkish coffees too strong and go instead for the excellent Algerian Special (£4.20 a pound), which is well worth a try. Yummy chocolate-covered beans cost £1.30 for 100g, and teas average £1.20 for a quarter of a pound.

Ally Cappellino
95 Wardour St W1
071-494 0768

Open: Mon–Fri
10.30 a.m.–6 p.m.
Credit: A, Amex, V

A mixture of formal and very comfortable-looking clothes by the designer Ally Cappellino sit side by side in this large Soho store. I have never quite understood what it is all about here, but the window displays are encouraging and a recent attempt to design clothes for kids looks like being a success. The prices are a wee bit high – around £60 for trousers and £160 for good cotton jumpers with navy design – but you are paying for a name and the certainty that there will not be many people selling the same thing, as most of the designs are made only in limited numbers. The customers are the usual Soho mix of advertising and film people who like the idea of something slightly different from the norm and which is subtle rather than loud.

American Retro
35 Old Compton Street W1
071-734 3477

Open: Mon–Sat
10.15 a.m.–7 p.m.
Credit: A, Amex, V

This store started out selling secondhand clothing, but has now started manufacturing its own products with an emphasis on clothing which has definitely nothing to do with the retro Americana stock it once sold. Fifties watches, lighters and sunglasses are about all that is left of this.

Upstairs there is a good mix of the best recent publications in the art world, an eclectic collection of postcards (from 60p), and every little attachment you might possibly want to put into your inside pocket, your trouser pocket, or around your wrist or neck. Downstairs is a selection of smart Smedley underwear which hangs beside AR's own, cheaper version. Own-brand sportwear and bags are also available. There's also just about everything from polo shirts at £40 to jeans at £60, but Sea Island cotton briefs, however well designed, are overpriced at £25 per pair. Classic matelot shirts are always in stock and are very popular.

The whole ethos of the shop is to stock classic clothing with a twist. There's an eye to natural fabrics here, and they are concerned to buy recycled products and jewellery. This is the kind of shop where you'll find things you never knew you wanted. It's also the perfect place to buy a present but be sure it's for someone special as you will certainly be spending money.

Anything Left-handed
57 Brewer Street W1
071-437 3910

Open: Mon–Fri
9.30 a.m.–5 p.m.;
Sat 9.30 a.m.–2 p.m.
Credit: A, V

This shop sells over a hundred items specifically designed for the five per cent of the population which is left-handed.

Left-handed playing cards, corkscrews and scissors (invaluable) all make life much easier, and there's also a lot of information on left-handedness available. Scissors cost £5.95, a potato-peeler is £1.95 and a tin-opener £3.95. On a more frivolous note, a left-handed boomerang is £12.95.

Ben de Lisi
8 Silver Place W1
071-734 0089

Open: Mon–Fri
10 a.m.–6 p.m.,
Sat by appointment
Credit: A, Amex, V

When he moved to London American-born designer Ben de Lisi brought with him an idea of the kind of woman he would like to design for: of no particular age group or nationality, she is a modern woman between twenty and fifty who wants to feel easy and comfortable about her clothing.

Velvets, crepes, patchworks, heavy damasks and brocade are all worked into his collections, which include day and evening wear without ever overstating the case. His choice of colours is simple and the versatility of his clothes is obvious. Prices range from £130 for a top to £300 for an evening dress which would look right in any company. His shorter black dresses cost around the £220 mark. If you are not a showy person but like wearing something very beautiful, this is the place for you.

Berwick Street Market

The shouting, chanting and banter which lasts from early morning to late afternoon, six days a week, in

Central SOHO

Berwick Street W1

Open: 9 a.m.–5 p.m.

this market is an unmissable part of Soho life. The stalls specialise in fruit, which is of better quality than that in most London markets. They're not as cheap as they might be but they're still a better deal than supermarkets or fruit and veg shops. The best times to do business here are early in the morning, when all the best produce is available, or late in the afternoon when all the bargains come up for grabs. Prices and quality vary from stall to stall. If the traders sound aggressive don't worry – they are probably all from the same family. As well as fruit and veg there's a decent cheese stall around Walker's Court, and halfway up is one of the cheapest flower stalls in London. It's all supposed to start at 9 a.m., but if you're desperate for a banana or a piece of Emmenthal you can find certain stalls open at four.

Black Market Records
25 D'Arblay Street W1
071-437 0478

Open: Mon–Sat
10 a.m.– 7 p.m.
No credit cards

If you are interested in what is going on in clubland then this is the place to find out. Morning to evening the music pours out of this place, which is probably the most popular underground record store in London, and the guys who run it have a pretty good feel for what is going to be happening in the near future. It sells specifically imports from America and Europe – if a record is good enough it only takes a day for the shop to get copies over. This is definitely a place for vinyl junkies and is always seething with DJs who want to get the most current grooves before their rivals. Fights have been known to break out as enthusiasts wrangle over the one remaining slab of essential plastic, and once you get in the door the music is so loud that it is impossible to think. Upstairs they deal with Techno and hip-hop, downstairs it's the cooler sound of Garage and House.

The shop has branched out recently and started its own label, which deals mostly in House, much of it recorded in back bedrooms for very little money and sheer love of the music.

Record prices vary according to what you are looking for. The new imports can range from £30 to £100 just for a twelve-inch single. Dave, who owns the shop, tells me that his best clients are his own staff.

Duffer of St George
27 D'Arblay Street W1
071-439 0996

The men behind the Duffer were well aware that there was a gap in the market where elegance meets cool. They found it, nurtured it, and now dictate in

Open: Mon–Sat
10 a.m.–6.30 p.m.;
Thurs 10 a.m.–7 p.m.
Credit: A, Amex, DC, V

their own language what is going to be the look for
the year. Their knitwear, which is beautifully made
and starts at £65 for a linen sweater, has been a
constant success because of the simple designs, often
borrowed from the sixties, and the fact that they are
so easy to wear. They now also do their own range
of denim (from £65) which is cut generously around
the groin, a rarity in jeans. There's also a good
selection of leather waistcoats and jackets which start
at £75 for a denim jacket and then skyrocket into the
land of no return. Their attempts to get into the world
of tailoring have not been so successful, but the
designs, which are a cross between the hustler and
the pimp, have at least got a sense of humour.

Duffer goods can now be found in other stores, but
this shop always has the items first and often they
will include some of their classic designs which are
very difficult to get hold of elsewhere.

Janet Fitch
25 Old Compton Street
W1
071-287 3789

Open: Mon–Sat
11 a.m.–8 p.m.,
Sun 1.30–7 p.m.
Credit: A, V

Janet Fitch opened her first store, in Percy Street, just
north of Oxford Street, in the eighties and quickly
built up a following for her selection of art jewellery
and funky clothes. This new shop is the perfect place
to pick up an interesting and wearable gift. Selling
such things as Michael De Nardo's beautiful jewellery
made from silver, chrome and found objects (£20–
£100) and silk scarves, Fitch has found a niche in the
overcrowded accessories market and has miraculous-
ly managed to keep her prices reasonable.

W & G Foyle Ltd
113–119 Charing
Cross Road WC2
071-437 5660

Open: Mon–Wed, Fri,
Sat 9 a.m.–6 p.m.,
Thurs 9 a.m.–7 p.m.
Credit: A, V

Foyle's is an institution in the book world. Floor after
floor of shelves are packed with books on everything
from psychology to romance. The problem with the
place is its rather laborious system of payment: once
you take your book to the counter you have to leave
it and take the receipt you're given to a cashier who
will stamp it for you before you can go back and
claim your book. It is all a very long, boring process.
Nevertheless, Foyle's is a great place to shelter from
the elements and wander round looking at what is
on offer, and there is a terrific bargain basement.

John Pearse
6 Meard Street W1
071-434 0738

Meard Street is an odd little street, which was built
by the carpenter John Meard in 1718 and was famous
for being the home of the drunken prostitute Bet
Flint, who was much admired by Samuel Johnson. It

Central SOHO

is easy to imagine all kinds of goings-on in this pedestrian precinct, but nowadays it is mostly populated by drunks and homeless people who sleep in doorways. In the middle of all this is John Pearse's tailor's shop, which always looks fantastic. It is possible to buy an off-the-peg garment such as a linen or flannel jacket for around £400, but it is Pearse's bespoke suits which make him stand out from his competitors. It is said that Jack Nicholson flies in especially to be fitted by Pearse, whose clients are a mixture of the rich and famous and people who just love clothes. Pearse himself looks slightly deranged but his advice on clothes will always be good and sound. And remember that once he has cut a pattern for you life becomes a simple matter of choice of colour for ever more.

John Richmond

'Destroy, Disorder, Disorientate' is the anarchic motif chosen by this very popular designer. His attempts to do something newish with leather and anything else, from rubber to Lycra, have made him the darling of the pop/rock world and he is now probably on the verge of superstardom. His clothes are expensive, but his new Destroy label, sold from his Neal Street shop in Covent Garden, is supposed to make the clothes more accessible to younger patrons.

The famous leather jackets with the tattoo down the side of the arm retail at £500 and his long dresses, which could be worn as formal evening wear, start at around £160 and then spiral upwards. His 3D vision is paying off and Richmond, who remains a very nice unassuming man, is on the verge of stealing the mantle of Britain's most successful and famous designer from Vivienne Westwood.

Liberty

Nineteenth-century entrepreneur Arthur Lasenby Liberty was astute enough to realise that there was a growing market for silks and various goods from the East, especially Japanese prints and fans, and in 1925 his Regent Street empire was gathered under one roof when he had this store built in an amalgam of styles. The entrance on Great Marlborough Street is the most dramatic, with its fake Tudor front and interior built from the remains of two men o' war ships. Liberty's influence on fashions, especially in the late nineteenth and early twentieth centuries, is

Open: Mon–Fri
10 a.m.–6.30 p.m., Sat
by appointment
Credit: A, Amex, V

John Richmond
2 Newburgh Street W1
071-734 5782

Open: Mon–Sat
10.30 a.m.–6.30 p.m.
Credit: A, Amex, V

Liberty
210–220 Great
Marlborough Street W1
071-734 1234

Open: Mon–Sat
9.30 a.m.–6 p.m.;
Thurs
9.30 a.m.–7.30 p.m.
Credit: A, Amex, V

unquestionable, and it was during this period Ruskin, Burne-Jones, Rossetti and Whistler were regular customers.

This magnificent store always leaves me feeling exhausted; though I have been there enough times to know the shop backwards, I still get lost. But that's one of the best things about the shop as it means that there is always something new to discover: designer clothes, porcelain and glass, oriental carpets, rugs, books and, best of all, their furniture department, which mixes old and new designs very successfully.

The furniture leans heavily towards the Arts and Crafts Movement, which in many ways is in a sadly kitschy state. If you're interested, though, they have an exhibition of authentic Arts and Crafts furniture here every May.

It is possible to find a bargain amongst the vast quantity of objects available, but this takes time and it can be depressing to find that what you really want is out of your price range. In January and July they have regular sales, and these might be the perfect time to buy a roll of Liberty furnishing fabric or a Jasper Morrison sofa bigger than most apartments. The way to shop at Liberty is to make a day of it and fuel yourself from their cafes and restaurants where nothing is particularly great but is always adequate. It is a better store than the bigger Harrods precisely because of the nooks and crannies which just might have that something you never knew you were looking for. They also have a well-organised export and delivery system which makes life easier if what you buy has to travel.

Lina Stores
18 Brewer Street W1
071-437 6482

Open: Mon–Fri
6 a.m.–6.30 p.m.,
Sun 6 a.m.–5 p.m.
No credit cards

This Northern Italian deli supplies the best range of Italian foodstuffs in the neighbourhood. The owners come from a small village and have brought that rural gentleness with them. Every day they make fresh pasta, including ravioli filled with pumpkin or cheese, which are delicious and cheap at the price, starting at about £2.90 per pound. They also have a fine selection of cheeses. The hams, olives and salami are all delicious and it's probably a good idea to ask one of the family to tell you what is the best buy. Focaccia and ciabatta breads are available every day – with a small piece of gorgonzola they make a perfect lunch.

Lonsdale Sports Equipment Ltd

19–21 Beak Street W1
071-437
1526/3375/1741

Open: Mon–Fri
9 a.m.–6 p.m., Sat
9 a.m.–5 p.m.
Credit: A, Amex, V

Crammed with every conceivable boxing accessory, Britain's most famous boxing store is heaven for the enthusiast, but strangely enough it is not only lovers of the Sweet Science who come here – Lonsdale's own brand of sports clothing is extremely popular with clubbers and fashion victims. Sparring gloves are available at around £40 to £100, punch bags begin at £45 and there is a good range of books which might help you if you are considering a career as a pugilist. I suggest you begin timidly and treat yourself to one of the many different sweatshirts or T-shirts displaying the Lonsdale name – as recently seen on the usually naked chest of Mr Miserable Morrissey. The wool or cotton shorts with the name down the side are fantastic looking but they tend to shrink, so buy big no matter what they tell you. Satin shorts also look good and come in at £21.

The men in the shop are the same ones you see in the corners during the big fights, throwing water on the fighter or shouting some kind of optimistic advice in his cauliflower ear. They really know their stuff and are patient and helpful to novices.

Mark Powell

Above Duffer of St
George, 27 D'Arblay
Street W1
071-287 5498

Open: Mon–Fri
10.30 a.m.–7 p.m.,
and by appointment
No credit cards

One of the great Soho characters, tailor Powell has had shops, lost them, opened others and closed them the next day due to dodgy landlords. He has now tightened up his operation and has moved it to a small room on D'Arblay Street, where he will measure you up for one of his suits. He prefers an Edwardian cut which means narrow trousers amd thin, high lapels which give the shirt and tie a dignified appearance. The suits, depending on the fabric, start at about £300, which is pretty good going considering that an off-the-peg suit will cost much the same.

Powell's tough East End image adds to his mystique – he is said to have been personal tailor to the Kray twins. He is fact a very soft and nice man, and is tailor to the likes of Jonathan Ross, Vic Reeves and many more media celebs who enjoy what they reckon is a flirtation with danger.

Pam Hogg

5 Newburgh Street W1
071-287 2185

Open: Mon–Sat

The eccentric Scottish woman designer transcends any period or location. She is unique. Her face tells the story of a woman who has taken life to every extreme and still landed on top. Each year her designs become even more uninhibited and uncompromising

10 a.m.–6 p.m.
No credit cards

as she flaunts sexuality and invites the eye to roam the body with her bodysuits, which hug and cling like a second skin. Her clothes are not for the shy or demure but they are a relatively inexpensive way in which to feel liberated for an evening. Her catsuits start at around £100 and shirts and velvet tops are about £60.

Randall and Aubin
16 Brewer Street W1
071-437 3507

Open: Mon–Fri
8 a.m.–6.30 p.m.,
Sat 8 a.m.–6 p.m.
Credit: A, V

Soho's most famous butcher shop has been trading in quality meat and game for over a hundred years. Sadly it closed for a while after the owner Roma Galer died, but it has recently been bought by Rod Lane, owner of the exotic members' club 2 Brydges Place, who intends to refurbish in the same style of old. Although butchers' blocks have now been outlawed by the EEC, the effect of the marble tops and the wooden floor remains, as do the choice cuts of meat available. It's a bit more expensive than most, but they offer a large choice of organic meat and their Christmas hampers are mouthwatering. Specialities include pâtés, sauces and mustards from France.

**Shipley Specialist
Art Booksellers**
70 Charing Cross Road
WC2
071-836 4872

Open: Mon–Sat
10 a.m.–6 p.m.
Credit: A, Amex, V

Ian Shipley's specialist shop is a joy to rummage through – the books are very beautiful, always expensive but very difficult to resist. If you're a student of modern art or design this wall-to-wall chamber of knowledge will almost certainly have anything you want – if not, they'll gladly order it for you. They also stock new exhibition catalogues, including those from good shows in the States and in Europe. The window arrangements deserve a special mention: each month they are based around a different theme, from sex to industry, and the results are always remarkable.

**Silver Moon
Women's Bookshop**
68 Charing Cross Road
WC2
071-836 7906

Open: Mon–Sat
10.30 a.m.–6.30 p.m.
Credit: A, Amex, V

Silver Moon is devoted to books concerning women; there is a strong feminist bias and a man wandering in might feel a little unwanted. From Vita Sackville-West to Jeanette Winterson, women's writing is comprehensively covered, and there is a very good selection of books on female artists and political activists. If you need to know more about women's issues in the twentieth century, look no further.

Downstairs there is a cafe, an old-style bookish place where the coffee is less important than the surrounding library.

Central SOHO

Soccerscene
30–31 Great
Marlborough Street W1
071-439 0778

Open: Mon–Wed, Fri,
Sat 9.30 a.m.–6 p.m.,
Thurs 9.30 a.m.–7 p.m.
Credit: A, Amex, DC,
Switch, V

Every football fan who visits London comes to this specialist football shop at some point in their stay – probably during the first five minutes. It's always full of fans grabbing at everything to do with their team, be it Bayern Munich or Liverpool – there's a vast selection of shirts for just about every club or national team. At the back of the shop it's possible to find older, obsolete designs such as old tracksuits or football tops. As clubs change their strip every season, it can become difficult to find a replacement once your favourite has worn out, and Soccerscene is your best bet. The prices of the tops vary, as some have obviously been imported, but will always be around the £29 mark. Also on offer is a wide range of goods, including mugs, pens, bags and hats. They have a wide selection of videos as well.

Sports Pages
Caxton Walk, 94-96
Charing Cross Road
WC2
071-240 9604

Open: Mon–Sat
9.30 a.m.–7 p.m.
Credit: A, Amex, V

This specialist sports bookshop was opened in September 1985 and after a difficult beginning (nobody could find it), it is now one of the best of its kind in the world. Everything published about sport is available here, from banal biographies of famous cricketers to brilliant reissues of classic sports books such as Moynihan's *The Soccer Syndrome* and A. J. Leibling's *The Sweet Science*. The shop is the obsession and passion of John Gaustad, who'll spend as much time as you need finding rare treasures or pointing you in the right direction. There is a comprehensive selection of sports videos to help you relive England's footballing successes or their inglorious failures. Boxing's finest moments, from Sugar Ray to Ali's best fights, as well as those of motor racing, martial arts and equestrian memorabilia, are all available on tape as well as on the printed page. Gaustad has allowed a terrific selection of football fanzines to take over a huge amount of space though they really can't bring much profit to the business.

Tin Pan Alley
Denmark Street WC2

Musicians from all over the world come here to buy their guitars and drum kits. All through the day, but especially in the afternoon, the air is full of the sound of budding guitar heroes trying out some classic or ridiculous effect at peak volume.

All of the shops specialise in some type of instruments or can repair almost anything, but for its sheer sense of fun go to Andy's at number 27, which is a favourite with fast-fingered thrash-metal fans who like to throw shapes as well as sounds.

Unity Records
47 Beak Street W1
071-734 2746

Open: Mon–Sat
10 a.m.–7 p.m.
Credit: A, Amex, MC, V

There's been a proliferation of shops in Soho's square mile recently, all dealing with fragmentations of what was once quite simply dance music. Most of the shops will not see the end of their first year, mainly because they are run by enthusiasts who don't have the organisation or the muscle to keep bang up to date with this ever-changing scene.

The store is divided into three parts. The first is loud and deals with head-breaking European techno music as well as hip-hop and rap. The atmosphere of the sound-proofed back section, home to the sound of sweet soul, is smoother than baby cream. It's worth a trip just to see how different the people here look from those in the front of the shop.

Downstairs Unity markets its own goods such as hats, shirts and jackets, all well made and carrying as good a price for this clubby type of clothing as you will find anywhere else.

ENTERTAINMENT

Apollo Theatre
26 Shaftesbury Avenue
W1
071-494 5070

Open: bookings,
Mon–Sat
10 a.m.–8 p.m.
Credit: A, Amex, V

Above the photographs and notices and the neon board, two angels perch on the domed towers of this Edwardian theatre, designed in a French Renaissance style. The Apollo is the smallest of the six theatres on the Avenue, and has built a sturdy reputation for itself as a home for West End comedy. From Margaret Rutherford and Sybil Thorndike to Kenneth Williams and Albert Finney, this intimate theatre, which seats just over 700, has been a place for audiences to watch performers sweat and triumph at occasionally uncomfortably short range.

In recent years the successful team of Peter O'Toole, writer Keith Waterhouse and director Ned Sherrin has brought laughter and tears to the venue with their productions of *Jeffrey Bernard Is Unwell*, the story of a Soho drunk, and *Our Song*, the story of a Hampstead drunk.

Cafe de Paris
3-4 Coventry Street W1
071-437 5534

Cafe de Paris was once the place where Mayfair's high and mighty, including kings and princes, danced, watched cabaret stars such as Marlene Dietrich and Maurice Chevalier and drank gallons of

Open: Tues–Sat
10.30 p.m.–6 a.m.
No credit cards
Admission: £10,
Sat £12

champagne. Its interior was based on the luxurious Palm Court on board the fated SS *Lusitania*, and the glamour of this era is now recreated during after-noon tea dances.

At night, the Cafe de Paris is London's most fashionable hangout. Each night is different – Tues-day evening is called Cafe Society and is dedicated to ballroom dancing; Wednesday and Thursday fea-ture various one-offs such as Venus Rising (women only) and Uptown (soul and funk music); Friday is Sex, attracting a mixed/gay crowd into erotic go-go dancing, and Saturday is Merry England, run by the team responsible for the highly successful Love Ranch. At the bottom of the stairs is a bar where people who would never come here to dance talk and do deals. Once past that you come to a balcony which is the place to be, or if you don't want to dance you can go and find the downstairs bar which is hidden in a maze of corridors. This is where London's beautiful and glamorous congregate to bitch about everyone else. Love affairs begin here and end in a day. It's an experience which you must have once. You can face the consequences later.

The Globe Theatre
Shaftesbury Avenue W1
071-494 5065

Open: bookings,
Mon–Sat
10 a.m.–10 p.m.
Credit: A, Amex, V

Built in 1906 by the eminent theatre designer W. G. R. Sprague, the Globe's over-the-top neo-classical façade dominates Shaftesbury Avenue. Inside, the theatre – probably the best-preserved in London – is even more lavishly ridiculous, with Louis XVI or-namentation and columns framing the boxes. Some people think the decor is beautiful and some ridicu-lous, and though I am from the latter school I do have a sneaking regard for the theatre's history.

Jill George Gallery
38 Lexington Street W1
071-439 7343/7319

Open: Mon–Fri
10 a.m.– 6 p.m.;
Sat 11 a.m.–4 p.m.
No credit cards

This is a spacious two-floored gallery which specialises in comtemporary painting both figurative and abstract. Its size lends itself to big works but in fact smaller pieces look just as good here. It's a wonderful space for paintings, which look beautiful with the rays of light shooting over the Soho skylines through the many windows – it all makes for the right atmosphere.

Each show tackles the frustrations of contemporary painters who are being ignored in favour of new conceptualists of theorists. The gallery represents the Scottish artist Martin Kane, who has never failed to sell any painting he shows here. Other artists of note are Harry Holland, David Hosie, Crawford Adamson and Peter Kenneally, all of whom show at least once a year. The downstairs gallery is much more subdued and perfect for showing drawings or prints. George has somehow managed to maintain a policy of keeping her prices within reach of the public, which in a greedy art world is a great thing.

The Lyric Theatre
Shaftesbury Avenue W1
071-494 5045

Open: bookings,
Mon–Sat
10 a.m.–8 p.m.
Credit: A, Amex, V

The Lyric is the oldest of Shaftesbury Avenue's six remaining theatres. Built in 1888, it initially featured mainly operettas, though Sarah Bernhardt arrived for a series of plays in 1898. However, it was in 1902, when Forbes-Robertson repeated his performance of Hamlet, thought to be one of the greatest ever, that the Lyric gained a reputation for serious theatre. The list of actors who have trod the boards here is impressive: Tallulah Bankhead, Leslie Howard, Noël Coward, Ralph Richardson and Laurence Olivier all performed at the Lyric. The theatre continues to attract the best writers and actors – Joe Orton, Alan Ayckbourn, Alec Guinness, John Malkovich and Glenda Jackson have all performed or had their work performed here.

Madame Jojo's
8–10 Brewer Street W1
071-734 2473

Open: Mon–Sat
10 p.m.–3 a.m.
Credit: A, Amex, V
Admission: £8-£10

Madame JoJo's is an upmarket piano/cabaret bar where all the tables are served by very tall and oddly beautiful transvestites. It can be a rather intimidating place to enter but after that it's fun all the way – the staff have very hilarious put-downs for any rude customers, so be warned. There is a cabaret spot at midnight, featuring anything from Marilyn impersonators to transvestite magicians. Madame JoJo is host for the evening, and presides over events clad in the kind of outrageous sequinned dresses no woman would ever wear.

If you're in a decadent mood, Madame JoJo's is definitely worth trying out – the drinks are a bit expensive but you are paying for very distinctive service.

The Marquee
105 Charing Cross
Road
071-437 6601

The Marquee started life as a jazz club, hidden under the Academy Cinema on Oxford Street. It moved to Wardour Street in 1964, and became Britain's foremost rock venue, attracting the likes of the Yardbirds, Jimi Hendrix and The Who, who would all play in

Open: 7–11 p.m.;
club nights
7 p.m.–3 a.m.
Credit: A, V (charge fee)
Admission: £1–£6

front of the hot, cramped audience. Any band worth their salt played this place and the Wardour Street venue saw many of the very best punk performances of all. The club always seemed to be able to get the best from musicians, who never held back here and seemed to enjoy every minute of their gigs.

The Marquee outgrew its premises and moved to its current venue on Charing Cross Road, where each night's music attracts a different type of person, all of whom share the same love of live music. The drinks are reasonably priced and the new venue does not smell as bad as the old one.

Palladium Theatre

8 Argyll Street W1
071-494 5020

Credit: A, Amex, DC,
MC, V

Until 1865, when it became a circus and then a skating rink, this theatre, known to all as the London Palladium, was a grand mansion belonging to the Duke and Duchess of Marlborough. Variety became the speciality of the house and nothing seems to have changed much since it opened in 1910 with a bill topped by Nellie Wallace. The Palladium became the place all acts dreamed of playing – from Gracie Fields to Ivor Novello, from Ken Dodd and the Crazy Gang to Americans such as Danny Kaye, Frank Sinatra and Judy Garland, the Palladium has witnessed the world's biggest stars rise or fall on its revered boards. More recently Jason Donovan and then Philip Schofield filled the 2,300–seater theatre every night with their performance of Andrew Lloyd Webber's *Joseph and the Amazing Technicolor Dreamcoat*.

Ronnie Scott's

47 Frith Street W1
071-439 0747

Open: Mon–Sat
8.30 p.m.–3 a.m.
Credit: A, Amex, DC, V
Average: £30
Admission: £12

This legendary jazz club moved to this address from a Gerrard Street basement in 1965, at a time when Soho had gone crazy with the new sounds of pop and jazz. It's a period that's long gone but Ronnie Scott's remains as popular as ever. It's a perfect venue for jazz – it's intimate and informal and it gets very hot and steamy. Every big jazz name has played here for a night or a season, including Nina Simone, Art Blakey and Chet Baker. Ronnie himself is a saxophonist and his own band often plays here. Check what's on before you arrive as the policy can be erratic and the music varies between salsa and modern jazz. Food consists of snacks or more substantial dishes – steak, chicken or burgers will cost around £9 – and the drinks prices are reasonable, but you come here for the music first and foremost.

The Wag Club
35 Wardour Street, W1
071-437 5534

Open: Mon–Thurs
10 p.m.–3 a.m.,
Fri–Sat 10 p.m.–6 a.m.
No credit cards
Admission: Mon–Thurs
£3–£5, Fri–Sat £6–£9

The Wag has been pumping out up-to-the-minute dance music since the sixties, through the soulful seventies and eighties and up to the frenetic nineties, and is still popular despite its rather heavy-handed door policy.

During the eighties, under the guidance of a few knowledgeable heads, the Wag became the favourite hangout of people like George Michael and Sade. This cool period was taken over by the advent of acid house and techno.

Before going it's probably best to call them first to find out just what's going on that evening; the prices on the door vary according to how popular each night is. Membership, which you can get at the door, costs a couple of pounds. Inside there are two bars on two levels, as well as a small cafe/restaurant where burgers, chips, lasagne et cetera are available at around the £2–£4 mark.

ALLY CAPPELLINO

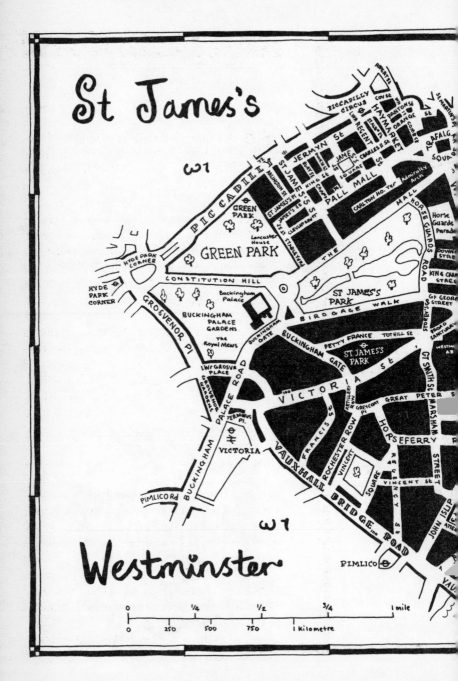

St James's

Westminster

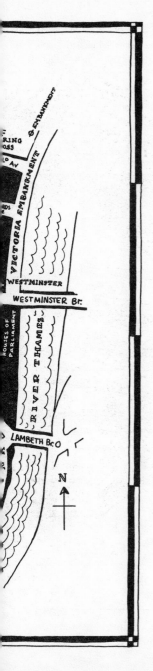

*W*estminster, with the Houses of Parliament, Whitehall, Westminster Abbey and Westminster Cathedral within a gentle shout of each other, is where power in this country has been concentrated since the eleventh century and the days of King Canute. It is here that the history of Britain has been shaped. Edward the Confessor changed the shape of London when he decided to move the main Royal residence upstream from the City, then, as now, the centre of business in London, to the new church, soon to become an abbey, at Wesminster, separating the seat of government from the commercial centre of London. William Caxton, the man who created a revolution in printing, lived here and printed his first edition of Chaucer's *The Canterbury Tales* and Malory's *Morte D'Arthur* from a small shop in the grounds of the Abbey.

However, during the fifteenth century the streets around the Abbey and the new seat of power fell into disreputable hands and were considered highly dangerous – thieves and pickpockets mingled with merchants and the wealthy, creating a volatile atmosphere which often exploded. The original palace of Westminster was burned down in 1834 and the current Victorian-Gothic building built in its place. Nothing much else has changed since then other than that the dangerous types are now confined to the Houses of Parliament.

Integral to this area, which is the powerhouse of the country, is Whitehall, running north from

Central

Parliament Square and up to Charing Cross. Off the main road is a complicated warren of buildings housing the civil servants who run each government department. There are over 12,000 of these grey specialists roaming the corridors of these magnificent buildings, ensuring that the status quo of British politics is maintained no matter who is in power. Whitehall is the home of officialdom. Scotland Yard, the headquarters of the police force, sits on the site of the one-time official residence of the Kings of Scotland, who stayed here before paying homage to their English fiefs. The whole area is a bit of a bureaucratic nightmare and it's very difficult to walk around without worried-looking policemen or security people looking at you or asking questions. It is no longer possible to walk along Downing Street, where the Prime Minister and the Chancellor of the Exchequer live at numbers 10 and 11 respectively, as Margaret Thatcher, conscious of various attempts on the lives of prime ministers, had gates erected to shut the street off from the public.

As this is the seat of government, the civil servants are well looked after in private bars and clubs where many a political decision is made over a bottle of claret. As a result the area is not well served with cafes or restaurants and is very much a place which is abandoned at night.

Inspired by Inigo Jones's piazza in Covent Garden, the grand houses of St James's Square were the first to be built in this part of London: until the arrival of the aristocracy in 1660, the area around St James's Palace was little more than fields and a few hills. Developers realised the potential of building big houses around Charles II's newly restored home and St James's became the most fashionable spot in London. By the end of the eighteenth century the elegant squares and houses of St James's had been substantially altered and it had become a place for foreign embassies and consulates. The large, opulent homes of St James's and Mayfair have mews lanes running behind them, where their horses and carriages would be kept; now converted, these mews houses are some of the most desirable residential properties in London.

The wealth of the people who lived in St James's attracted high-class shops such as art dealers, jewellers and very special delicatessens, as well as a string of nightclubs. St James's Square and St James's Street were the central part of the area and clubs such as the Army and Navy, the Oxford and Cambridge, the Wyndham and the Caledonian all based themselves alongside the coffee and chocolate houses where the leisured and monied classes would gather.

Today the buildings of St James's house, for the most part, assurance and media-based companies, as well as the London Library. It is no longer as grand as it once was, but there are still a few good specialist shops and galleries worth visiting. A walk around the streets gives you a faint whiff of how things must have been in the heady, post-Waterloo days of the eighteenth century.

HOW TO GET THERE

Tubes
- Bond Street
- Green Park
- Hyde Park
- Marble Arch
- Oxford Circus
- Piccadilly Circus

Buses
- New Bond Street: 8
- Oxford Street: 2A, 2B, 6, 7, 8, 10, 12, 13, 15, 16A, 23, 25, 73, 53, 53X, 55, 74, 82, 88, 94, 98, 113, 135, 137, 137A, 139, 159, 176, 274, C2
- Park Lane: 2A, 2B, 10, 16, 73, 74, 82, 137, 137A
- Piccadilly: 8, 9, 14, 19, 22, 38
- Regent Street: 12, 13, 15, 23, 36, 53, 53X, 88, 94, 139, 159

SIGHTS AND SITES

Albany House
Albany Courtyard W1

On the southwest side of Piccadilly Circus is Albany House, named after George III's favourite son, Frederick, Duke of York and Albany. It was sold in 1800 and converted by Alexander Copeland into apartments intended mainly for wealthy bachelors. It's very difficult to get an apartment here as it's very like the co-operative New York apartment blocks where any prospective tenant is vetted. The policy here is one of no estate agents, journalists, small children or animals. The blocks have always been popular with the literary crowd and William S. Burroughs, Graham Greene, Aldous Huxley and J. B. Priestley have all lived here at one time or another.

Buckingham Palace
Queens Gardens SW1

When George IV came to the throne he decided that his home in Carlton House was not big enough, and that a more imposing building was required for a ruling king. John Nash was brought in to build a 600–room palace – most of the rooms are used by staff and as offices, and the Royals themselves use very few. The building is not one of Nash's greatest achievements but the gardens, where regular tea parties are held in the summer, are very grand, with expansive lawns and a wide variety of trees and flowers. When the Queen is home you can see the Union Jack flying above Buckingham Palace.

On most mornings crowds gather to watch the Changing of the Guard or to catch a glimpse of a member of the Royal family, who seem to have something of a hunted look about them these days.

The Cenotaph
Whitehall SW1

This plain, stark memorial, designed in 1920 by Sir Edwin Lutyens, the influential Edwardian architect, was originally intended as a monument to the dead of the First World War. It is now seen to honour the dead of the Second World War as well and is the focus of attention on Remembrance Sunday, the second Sunday in November. The Cenotaph is a timeless piece of sculpture and shocked many when it was first unveiled. The bold geometry of its shape goes beyond any religious reference and in its time served as an indication of what was to come in the art world. It is one of very few pieces of public art to take risks and still be accepted by the public.

Cleveland Row, SW1

South of the neo-classical splendour of architect John Vardy's Spencer House, once owned by Princess Diana's family and now by the National Trust (the furniture is in Kenwood House in Hampstead; see Hampstead) is a contrasting block of split-level flats. Built in 1960 and designed by Sir Denys Lasdun, they incorporate the simplicity of modern design without ever upsetting the visual balance of the neighbouring houses and apartment blocks. The block caused a scandal when it was first put up but has been accepted since as part of London's reluctant lurch into the modern world.

The Economist Building
25 St James's Street
SW1
071-839 7000

The Economist Building stands out against the clubland comfort of St James's. It is an astonishing grouping of three towers of unequal height, compensating for the slope of the street, and in many ways is more eye-catching than the Regency buildings all around. The building was designed by Alison and Peter Smithson in 1962 and the world-renowned *Economist* magazine, Britain's nearest equivalent to the American *Newsweek*, is based there. There are sculpture exhibitions in the Plaza, and these tend to change every ten weeks or so.

Green Park, W1

Open: 7 a.m.–dusk

Charles II transformed this rough plot of land, notorious as a place where people were attacked and robbed, by planting it with new trees and flowers. During the eighteenth century it was a popular spot for gentlemen to fight duels and during the reign of Queen Victoria several attempts were made on her life as she drove through the park. After walking through the shops and the arcades of Piccadilly, Green Park is a great place to go for a stroll down to the southern end, where you come out at Buckingham Palace and St James's Park (see separate entries).

Houses of Parliament
Westminster SW1
071-219 3000

In 1834 the Palace of Westminster, with the exception of the Great Hall, was burnt to the ground, and a competition was organised to find an architect to take on the responsibility of building a new seat of power in the Elizabethan or Gothic style. This was won by Sir Charles Barry. With the help of superbly imaginative drawings from Augustus Pugin, the building was completed in 1860. Frescos by artists such as Frederick

Watts and William Dyce captured historic scenes from Britain's literary and political past.

The House of Lords and the Commons are both scenes of great political activity. The Lords have the best room in the building and it is from here that they review, revise and amend legislation. They have less power than the Commons, but they are an important body nonetheless.

Beyond the House of Lords is the Peers Lobby and the Central Lobby, where the public can enter to listen to debates in the Strangers Gallery or meet their MP. A debate in the Commons can provide some of the best theatre in London. The best time to come is at Prime Minister's Question Time, and it can be painful to watch the Opposition hammer home a point. The two sides are separated and may not cross the red line between them, originally drawn to prevent arguments from becoming fights. Prime Minister's Question Time begins at 3.15 p.m. on Tuesdays and Thursdays. Tickets can be obtained from MPs or from the consulate or high commission of your own country if you are a non-resident, and ticket-holders are allowed in first. Apply two to three months in advance. Non-ticket-holders might get in once things have quietened down but that might not be until most of the real action is over. For a guided tour apply for a permit to the Public Information Office.

The formidable clock tower houses the famous bell Big Ben, which arrived here in May 1858, carried by sixteen horses. Originally known as Victoria, legend has it that the bell got the name by which it is now known from the famous boxer Benjamin Court, who in September 1857 fought 60 rounds with Nat Langham. Before automatic winding was installed, it would take two men 32 hours to wind up the clock. In the basement of the tower is a cell in which those agitating in the area of the Palace of Westminster would be incarcerated – the last person to spend time there was Emmeline Pankhurst, leader of the Suffragette movement, who was imprisoned there in 1902.

Jermyn Street, SW1

Tucked away parallel to Piccadilly, there is not much left of the original Jermyn Street, which was developed in the seventeenth century. The main attraction is Wren's St James's Church (see separate entry), but the street still has a certain charm and has made its name as a shopping area for quality goods. However, things are all very expensive here and in some cases very old-fashioned. Worth a visit are the cheese merchants Paxton & Whitfield at number 93, the shoeshop New & Lingwood at number 53, and the hatters Bates at number 21 (see separate entries). There's a few good buildings worth a look, and at number 40 there's a notorious nightclub called Tramp, very popular during the seventies and early eighties with the likes of Jackie and Joan Collins and now favoured by people like Andrew Neil, the editor of the *Sunday Times*.

The National Gallery
Trafalgar Square WC2
071-389 1785

Open: Mon–Sat
midday–6 p.m.,
Sun 2–6 p.m.
Admission free to main
collection

A site for the National Gallery was found on the north side of Trafalgar Square in 1832. The building was designed by William Wilkins and has been added to ever since it was completed – the newest addition is the controversial Sainsbury wing. This came about as the result of an architectural competition in which Prince Charles took great interest, criticising any attempts at anything modern. What we have now is a post-modern palace designed by the husband-and-wife team of Robert Venturi and Denise Scott-Brown.

The gallery's first director was Sir Charles Eastlake, who travelled widely in Italy every year, looking for good Renaissance pictures to add to the gallery's collection, now one of the most extensive in the world. In the main collection every European school of painting is well represented. There is so much to see here that it's worthwhile planning your trip carefully and taking in only a few rooms rather than trying to fit everything in in one day. Be warned, though – the Impressionist and Post-Impressionist pictures always attract large crowds and noisy coach parties, so try to come either early in the morning or later in the afternoon.

There is a new exhibition space in the basement but it is too dark to be a really suitable space for paintings. Recent exhibitions have shown the work of tortured Norwegian artist Edvard Munch, as well as a large selection of Rembrandt's work. There's an admission charge payable for special exhibitions – check for details. The new wing does have an advanced micro gallery – a computer information

system with pages of historical and other information on all the paintings.

The cafe in the main building is very poor and it might be a better idea to walk down the Mall to the ICA cafe (see separate entry) or go round the corner into Soho where there is a decent choice of places to eat and drink. The cafe in the new wing is sadly no better, but it does have a great mural by Portuguese artist Paula Rego. There's also a bookshop which sells catalogues, slides and prints.

National Portrait Gallery

St Martins Place WC2
071-306 0055

Open: Mon–Fri
10 a.m.–5 p.m.,
Sat 10 a.m.–6 p.m.,
Sun 2–6 p.m.
No admission charge to
main gallery and most
shows

This gallery was established in 1856 at the suggestion of the fifth Earl of Stanhope, who thought that the country needed a place where the most famous and eminent faces in British history could be seen by the public. The gallery has over 8,000 portraits in its collection, which is constantly updated – not all of these are on display but they can all be seen on request. Those portraits on display are arranged chronologically and a walk around the various rooms will take you through the history of Britain.

As well as paintings, the gallery has a formidable collection of photographs – supposedly more than 500,000 of them. There are regular exhibitions of the work of photographers as established as Helmut Newton as well as portraits by up-and-coming new photographers. These shows are always well thought out and hung in a good space upstairs, which suggests that the gallery takes photography seriously.

Piccadilly, W1

The name of this grand street comes from 'picadils', a kind of stiff collar sold by Robert Baker, a seventeenth-century tailor who had a shop on the Strand. Baker bought up the property around the north of the Circus and built himself a grand mansion which was derisively nicknamed Piccadilly House. Despite the authorities' best efforts the name stuck.

After the Restoration of Charles II, widespread building took place and mansions were built to stand beside the inns and small shops of the area. Up until the Victorian era buildings were constantly being demolished and rebuilt, and used as houses, hotels or clubs. The hotels in Piccadilly are the grandest and most expensive in London, but if you do stay here you get the best service in the world and the feeling that everywhere in London is within reach. The area is renowned for its private clubs, where the members, usually men, sit around pretending to be more powerful than the rest of us humans. If you're not a member, I don't think you're missing a great deal. Much more exciting is the variety of shops, among them Fortnum and Mason (food), Hatchards (books), and Simpsons (clothes) which offer a vast selection of the best of British goods. It's here that the few remaining British aristocrats do their shopping – but if you look hard enough there are bargains to be had.

Piccadilly Circus, W1

I always feel sorry for people who arrive in London and head straight for Piccadilly Circus looking for something magical. It's a huge disappointment as it is in fact an ill-conceived spot with very little to offer other than neon signs and poor shops. The hoardings surrounding Eros have only recently come down, and the statue itself is, at the time of writing, undergoing repair – in fact, it's unlikely that it will ever again stand in Piccadilly Circus. The fountain was designed by Alfred Gilbert and erected by public donations in memory of the seventh Earl of Shaftesbury. Until the 1940s flower girls stood underneath the fountain selling their wares, but nowadays it's a place for punks from all over the country to sit and drink warm beer.

The Queen's Gallery
Buckingham Palace,
SW1

Open:
March–December,
Tues–Sat
10 a.m.–5 p.m.,
Sun 2–5 p.m.
Admission: £2.50,
concessions £1.80

Along with the Royal Mews, where the Queen's much-loved horses are kept, this is one of the two sections of Buckingham Palace open to the public. Here are shown paintings selected from the Queen's formidable collection which is remarkable for its diversity. Much of the work was inherited but she supposedly takes an active interest in what is shown to the public. One of the treats of this place is that the displays are constantly changing.

The Queen's Gallery can become very busy and crowded but it is worth a visit, if only to see some unique examples of Renaissance work. It's infinitely more rewarding than time spent gawping at Buckingham Palace or the Changing of the Guard, both of which tend to attract coach parties by the bucketload.

St James and Pall Mall Clubs

In the mid-nineteenth century the gambling houses and coffeeshops of St James's and Pall Mall were transformed into more substantial home-from-home

clubs for gentlemen. Most of them are exclusively male hangouts where politicians and old-school-tie businessmen mix in private and enjoy the use of swimming pools, restaurants, libraries and reading rooms away from their families and in the company of their kindred brothers. It's impossible for us mere mortals to gain access to these places unless accompanied by a member, but if you are a bit cheeky you can take a look through the window and you might see a famous parliamentarian asleep on a leather sofa or engrossed in the *Financial Times*.

At 71 Pall Mall is the United Oxford and Cambridge University Club and the Royal Automobile Club, founded in 1897, is at number 89. The RAC has its own post office, Turkish bath and very large swimming pool. At numbers 104-5 is the Italianate palazzo, designed by Charles Barry, of the Reform Club, one of the few established clubs to accept women as members. At number 106 is the Travellers' Club; during the nineteenth century, when travel was still very dangerous, people about to embark on a trip would gather here to discuss and plan their voyage. At number 107 is the Athenaeum, one of the most famous clubs in the world. It is here that the major power-brokers of church and state converge for a sherry or two and a chat about the state of the nation. Named after Emperor Hadrian's famous university in Rome, it is considered a highly intellectual if boring club. The Army and Navy Club is on the corner of Pall Mall and St James's Square. It has a bar and drawing room where women are allowed – army wives stop here for a quick change on the way to summer garden parties at Buckingham Palace.

The St James's Club on Park Place has recently started taking new members and allowing people to use their rooms. It's a perfect base from which to see London – it's expensive, around £150 a night, but the service is second to none and the restaurant has become very good.

St James's Church
197 Piccadilly W1
071-734 4511

Open: 8.30 a.m.–7 or

Built by Sir Christopher Wren on an original site in 1676-84, everything about this church is beautiful, from its typical seventeenth-century interior with Corinthian columns to the limestone carvings which sit comfortably alongside the elaborate plasterwork.

8 p.m., depending on
the programme

The marble font is the work of Grinling Gibbons.

The church has recently become a venue for chamber-music performances, as well as a concert by Siouxsie and the Banshees. The Centre for Health and Healing is based in the church and offers a whole range of alternative health services (071-437 7118), and the Rebecca Hossack Gallery is underneath the church. The cafe, the Wren at St James's, is good (see separate entry).

St James's Park
St James's Park SW1
071-930 1793

Open: dawn to dusk

This is the oldest of London's royal parks and in many ways the most beautiful; it is next to Buckingham Palace so it is maintained especially well. It was once a marshy field where lepers at the nearby hospital fed their hogs. Henry VIII turned it into one of his hunting fields and William III enjoyed sitting in his watchtower on Duck Island, smoking his pipe and watching the many species of bird living here. Today the park has over 30 species of bird, including pelicans, ducks, geese and gulls. During the summer it never seems to be particularly busy here, and so is a perfect place to go if you want a quiet breathing space in the city. The view across the lake is particularly beautiful.

Overlooking the pond there is a cafe which is all right for tea and a pastry, but forget about the meals.

The Tate Gallery
Millbank SW1
071-821 1313

Open: Mon–Sat
10 a.m.–6 p.m.,
Sun 2–6 p.m.
No admission charge
for entrance to
collections; major
exhibition £4.

Sidney Smith's Tate Gallery was built on the site of a penitentiary demolished in 1890, and is so good that it is almost as hard to leave as a jail. It was presented as a gift to the nation by the sugar magnate Sir Henry Tate and houses a collection of international modern art and a national collection of historic British art. The earliest painting in the collection is John Bettes's 'Man in a Black Cap' (1545). All main British schools are well represented here and included are works by Hogarth, Stubbs and Reynolds. The most important section is the impressive Turner collection, a new gallery paid for by the Clore foundation.

The Tate is without a doubt the best gallery in London and is particularly good for viewing sculpture, as the use of natural light is tremendous. It has been criticised for buying work late and therefore not acquiring the best pieces from contemporary artists – its buying is curtailed by its limited government grants – and to some extent this failing is borne out by the rather poor selection from the American

Abstract Expressionists. Recent shows have included work by the German avant-garde artist Otto Dix, the founder of British pop art Richard Hamilton, and sculptor Richard Long, and the collection has recently been entirely rehung.

The bookshop is well stocked and illuminating, and the Tate Restaurant (see separate entry) is worth a visit in its own right.

Westminster Abbey

Westminster Abbey
SW1
071-222 7110

Open: except during
special services,
Mon–Fri
9.20 a.m.–4 p.m.,
Sat 9.20 a.m.–2 p.m.,
4–5 p.m.,
Sun services only
Admission: £3,
concessions £1.50

Since William the Conqueror's coronation in Edward the Confessor's church in the eleventh century, 39 monarchs have been crowned and sixteen buried in Westminster Abbey. Its beauty and monarchical significance ensured that it was left undamaged during the Reformation. Nothing remains, however, of the Confessor's church, which was pulled down in the thirteenth century by Henry III, who had a much more magnificent building constructed in the style of the recently completed Rheims Cathedral. The King's connections with France (through his French wife) and his use of French masons influenced the style of the building considerably. However, the Abbey was not completed until 1734, when Hawksmoor designed two square towers with a gable between them in the style of the first master mason. Shaped like a Latin cross, the Abbey is built from stone quarried in Caen and shipped at great expense and with great difficulty across the channel.

When you visit, enter by the west porch so that you can immediately see the cross formed by the outer walls. You can see the French influence in the nave, the highest in England, which is 35 feet wide and has twelve bays. Things to look out for are the white marble monuments which line the walls and which chronicle the changing styles of each period. There is also an anthology of thirteenth-century sculpture and pre-Reformation religious art which is probably the best in the country. There are also monuments of Churchill and Pitt the Younger, as well as a good portrait of Richard II by the French artist Andre Neauneuve de Valenciennes.

The most popular part of the Abbey is known as Poets Corner where there are tributes to Dryden, Drayton, Beaumont, Milton, Sheridan, Burns, Coleridge, Wordsworth, Byron, Tennyson, Browning, Dickens, T. S. Eliot, Dylan Thomas, W. H. Auden and, of course, Shakespeare, many of whom are actually buried here as well.

There are so many interesting historical artefacts that I recommend you join one of the daily tours – you could easily lose yourself here. There's four tours a day and they cost around £6 – call for details.

EATING AND DRINKING

Balls Brothers
20 St James's Street
SW1
071-321 0882

Open: Mon–Fri
11 a.m.–10.30 p.m.;
restaurant –
midday–2.30 p.m.; bar
buffet – 5.30–8.30 p.m.
Credit: A, Amex, DC, V
Average: lunch
£37.50, buffet £18

This very upmarket wine bar caters to the local art dealers belonging to the Pall Mall clubland, and lots of dark oak panelling and intimate booths give the bar an air of subdued calm that they seem to like. The restaurant's menu is principally made up of fish dishes, including sole, salmon and a delicious and fresh seafood salad, as well as a range of starters and puddings.

However, it is the selection of wines that give Balls Brothers its credibility. Decently priced Bordeaux and clarets, both very popular with the regulars, are well selected and surprisingly drinkable even without food.

Cafe Figaro
6 Lower Regent Street
SW1
071-839 1765

Open: 7 a.m.–midnight
No credit cards
Average: £12

This small Italian cafe in the heart of St James's and Piccadilly opens early for breakfast and serves up very good spaghetti and tagliatelle dishes at lunchtime. It's one of the cheapest eateries in the area and therefore attracts a lot of local office workers who tend to gulp their food down and disappear as quickly as they arrive. Next door to the cafe are the offices of *Elle* magazine, whose staff tend to use the place as their second home. Cafe Figaro does a variety of Italian-style sandwiches, ranging from focaccia and mozzarella to salamis and Parma ham on ciabatta. The cappuccinos and espressos are good but the prices for both are above what you would expect to pay in a central London cafe.

The Caprice
Arlington House,
Arlington Street SW1
071-629 2239

Open: lunch
midday–3 p.m.,

With its sister establishment, the Ivy in Soho, the Caprice is probably still the most fashionable restaurant in London, attracting the cream of London's glitterati – unless you're Michael Caine or some other such person it is next to impossible to get a table here. It's not clear why the place should be so popular – the food is simple and the decor, which features

dinner 6 p.m.–midnight
Credit: A, Amex, DC, V
Average: £60

David Bailey's photographs of famous regulars, is pleasant enough, but neither is a great deal out of the ordinary. I put the attraction down to the charm of owners Christopher Corbin and Jeremy King, who have the rare ability to make you feel at ease with your surroundings – whenever I have managed to get a table, by booking months in advance, I have always found this calm establishment very relaxing. The style rather than the menu is what's important here, but the best dishes are always the really simple ones such as the salmon fish cakes or chicken fried in soy sauce. You can sometimes get seats at the bar, which are bookable and are fine – as long as you don't mind having your back to the action.

The Criterion Restaurant
220 Piccadilly Circus
W1
071-925 0969

Open: Mon–Sat
midday–midnight,
Sun midday–10.30 p.m.
Credit: A, Amex, DC,
Forte, MC, V
Average: £35

Theatre designer Thomas Verity built the Criterion in 1870 on the site of the notorious White Bear pub. The mosaic tiling is breathtaking and the long bar is probably the most beautiful in London. For a long time it was a forgotten spot, though at one time it was the decadent hangout of the Mayfair set who would move between here and the Cafe Royal (see Soho), and it was here that Oscar Wilde would spend his royalties on his favourite young man of the moment. This very British establishment is serviced almost exclusively byAntipodean and American waiters.

The drinks are reasonable here at £2.50 for a glass of wine or £1.50–£2.50 for a beer. It has just reopened however after a period of refurbishment, which probably means that the prices will escalate and the bar be taken over by City folks – we wait with baited breath. The food is American-influenced Italian fare and is not great in my experience, though presumably the new management will be looking to change things. In the evenings you can come just for a drink, although there is limited space, and it's a good place to come for tea – cucumber sandwiches, scones, cakes and tea cost £6.50 a person. At the back there is an extraordinary ballroom which has been left untouched since World War II but is about to reopen as a function room unmatched in London.

The Fountain
Fortnum and Mason Ltd,
181 Piccadilly W1

A visit to the Fountain is a kitsch delight. The people who come here make you feel as if you are sitting in the middle of a Noël Coward comedy. Pink dresses,

071-734 8040

Open: Mon–Sat
7.30 a.m.–11 p.m.
Credit: A, Amex, DC,
MC, V
Average: £30

The Morpeth Arms
58 Millbank SW1
071-834 6442

Open: Mon–Sat
11 a.m.–11 p.m.,
Sun midday–3 p.m.,
7–10.30 p.m.
Credit: A, V
Average: £10

Quaglino's
16 Bury Street SW1
071-930 6767

Open: lunch
11.30 a.m.–3 p.m.,
dinner 5.30–11 p.m.
Credit: A, Amex, DC, V
Average: £40

sports jackets and very loud voices are the order of the day, and make for a very entertaining afternoon. The food is actually very good – the game pies come from the store's own selection and the fresh fish dish of the day is usually faultless. There's a very British if limited feel to the menu, which is not much more than pies and veg if truth be known, but this can sometimes be a delight as a lot of fancy stuff can take its toll after a while. The Fountain is also the best place in London to have afternoon tea with the family as they don't really mind noise here.

Not quite on the river but on the opposite side of the road at a very busy junction, the Morpeth is a comfortable and traditional pub which has a history all of its own. The cellars are connected to an old tunnel which was used by prisoners to escape from the Millbank penitentiary where the Tate Gallery now stands. There are rumours that the pub is haunted by the ghosts of those prisoners who died in the tunnel.

If you are looking for a quiet spot to mull over what you have seen in the Tate, this is ideal: it's popular with the curators from the gallery as well as with students who come here for divine inspiration but settle for a pint of Young's bitter. If you're peckish you can have some good, basic pub food such as a toasted sandwich or a bowl of homemade soup. There are three specials a day such as shepherd's pie and lasagne, which cost a reasonable £3.

The original Quaglino's was opened in 1929 by Giovanni Quaglino, who came to London from the Grand Martinez Hotel and quickly established the capital's most fashionable restaurant, which became the darling of the beau monde. So successful was the restaurant that in 1935 it was launched on the Stock Exchange, but unfortunately it was burned to the ground in 1975.

In came the king of redevelopment, Terence Conran, who has not tried to recreate the old Quaglino's but instead created something entirely new. The interior of this enormous restaurant is truly stunning. Eight columns have been painted by famous artists, and the menu is projected on to the wall. The atmosphere is similar to Conran's riverside 'Gastrodome' (see Thames) and the entrance is packed full of teas, coffees, pastas, jams and chocolates. The food could never be described as cheap but it can be wonderful – the menu covers everything from oysters to gnocchi and various risottos. Better still, there's no minimum charge.

The Red Lion Inn

23 Crown Passage
SW1
071-930 8067

Open: Mon–Fri
11 a.m.–11 p.m.,
Sat 11 a.m.–9 p.m.,
Sun midday–3 p.m.;
restaurant – Mon–Fri,
lunch midday–2.30,
dinner 5.30–9 p.m.
Credit: A, Amex, V
Average: £20

The Red Lion Inn is one of the oldest licensed houses in the West End and it is said that Charles II would come here through a secret passage from St James's Palace to meet his orange-seller mistress Nell Gwynne. It's quite small and smoky but it is a very good example of an old English pub. The windows and bar look Victorian and the bar is a great favourite with local art dealers and lawyers. Apart from its location, though, there is nothing particularly remarkable about the pub but it's at least as good as any other in the area for a swift half, and typical bar snacks are available. Food is available in the restaurant and is fairly traditional – steak and kidney pudding or steak and mixed grill is £9.95. Puddings include trad jam roly-poly.

The Ritz

Piccadilly W1
071-493 8181

Open: cocktail bar –
Mon–Sat
11 a.m.–11 p.m.,
Sun 11 a.m.–3 p.m.,
7–10.30 p.m.,
cocktails from 6 p.m.;
Palm Court – Mon–Sat,
11 a.m.–11 p.m.,
Sun 11 a.m.–3 p.m.,
7.30–10 p.m.
(coffee from 8 a.m.);
Louis XVI restaurant –
lunch, 12.30–2.30 p.m.,
dinner Mon–Sat
6–11.15 p.m.,
Sun 6–10.30 p.m.
Credit: A, Amex, DC, V
Average: £220 for a
double room; afternoon
tea £27; lunch £52;

The Ritz has a reputation as a home for the elite and the very well off, but in fact it can be quite reasonable and offers the best of everything without too much ado. There's nowhere else in London you can sit, sip and be happy surrounded by such a lush history and grandeur. The hotel was built to the specification of Cesar Ritz and opened in 1906. My friend and mentor Philip Core, now sadly dead, painted a beautiful mural depicting the famous people who since then have used the hotel as a home from home. The Louis XVI interior leaves nothing to the imagination but the Ritz, after all, is really a kind of theme park. Treat yourself to a bottle of house champagne at £25 and enjoy what is going on around you.

While it used to rest a little on its formidable reputation, the Ritz has recently successfully relaunched its grill room, which is now very special indeed. You have to wear a tie, but it can be nice to dress up sometimes. Afternoon tea is available in the Palm Court from 3 p.m., and you can have a set lunch in the restaurant, which costs £26 for three courses.

The last time I came here the artists Gilbert and George were sitting here sipping drinks with their

dinner £70
Restaurant and bars
open to non-residents

Simply Nico
48a Rochester Row
SW1
071-630 8061

Open: lunch
midday–2 p.m.,
dinner 7–11 p.m.
Credit: A, Amex, DC, V
Average: £60

Tate Gallery
Restaurant
Tate Gallery, Millbank
SW1
071-821 1313 ext 279

Open: Mon–Sat,
lunch midday–3 p.m.
Credit: A, V
Average: £30

The Wren in St
James's
197 Piccadilly W1
071-437 9419

Open: Mon–Fri
8 a.m.–7 p.m., Sat,
Sun 10 a.m.–5 p.m.
No credit cards
Average: £10

Bates
21a Jermyn Street SW1

influential dealer and gallery-owner Anthony D'Offay. Even they seemed overawed by the beautifully vulgar interior.

Famed as the rudest chef in the world, Nico Landenis has no qualms about throwing out any customer who offends him, but his temper does not affect the harmony of his dishes, which are second to none in London. His superb goats'-cheese or deep-fried squid salads alone are worth a visit, but it is meat dishes which are his speciality. The ten desserts include a hot banana charlotte with caramel sauce and creme anglaise and are all good. The wine is expensive and exclusive but the house wine is good enough to get you through the evening.

The menu of this basement restaurant has a British feel to it and includes such savoury delights as beef tartlets or beef in madeira sauce, as well as an over-the-top Stilton and apple strudel for veggies. Desserts include a steamed ginger pudding and a good lemon tart. There's a far-reaching wine list which offers an extensive selection of Bordeaux and clarets with a good range of prices. The mural 'Expedition in Pursuit of Rare Meats', by Rex Whistler, is the perfect backdrop to this strangely little-known restaurant. It's open for lunch only and it's necessary to book.

Named after the great architect Sir Christopher Wren, who took such great pride in building St James's Church, this clean-looking unlicensed cafe is not a quiet, pious, church-going person's place to eat but a target for back-packing tourists who have heard about it in the Andes, the Rockies and the Alps. It has a good reputation as a place to get a good, wholesome vegetarian meal at a decent price. Vegetable flans and bakes are not particularly memorable but are all very filling, and they open in the morning for coffee and a croissant. I recommend that you have an early lunch here and then go into a free classical recital in the church at 1 p.m.

SHOPPING

Bates is where gentlemen come to buy their hats. Panamas, bowlers and cricket caps are all available

071-734 2722

Open: Mon–Fri
9 a.m.–5.30 p.m.,
Sat 9.30 a.m.–4 p.m.
Credit: A, Amex, DC, V

**The Economist
Bookshop**
23a St James's Street
SW1
071-839 7000

Open: Mon–Fri
9.30 a.m.–6 p.m.
Credit: A, Amex, DC, V

J. Floris Ltd
89 Jermyn Street SW1
071-930 2885

Open: Mon–Fri
9.30 a.m.–5.30 p.m.,
Sat 10 a.m.–5 p.m.
(December
9 a.m.–6 p.m.)
Credit: A, Amex, MC, V

New & Lingwood
53 Jermyn Street SW1
071-493 9621

Open: Mon–Fri
9 a.m.–5.30 p.m.,
Sat 10 a.m.–5 p.m.
Credit: A, Amex, DC, V

here, and the shop itself looks as if it hasn't changed in decades. If you want to get a sense of old retailing style in London, put your best clothes on and come here. The walls of the shop are adorned with photographs of famous people such as James Mason wearing the hats, which are the finest of their type and cost between £40 and £400. A Panama hat, for example, will start at £60.

This shop, underneath the modern Economist Building (see separate entry) is the place to come if you want to learn how to manage your finances or learn about the world of money and economics, and also serves up a mixed bag of in-house advertising. An Economist Diary should be part of any money person's portfolio, and if you really want to identify with the magazine there are pens, notebooks and various knickknacks with the name spread all over them.

The smell of jasmine, rose and various herbs greets you as you walk in the door of this upmarket perfumery, which is very English but not as twee as many of its competitors. Their soaps, oils and bath essences are delicious and the packaging alone is enough to make you buy something as a present for someone else. I have used their shaving soaps and brushes for as long as I can remember and have never wanted to change. Prices begin at £6 but can go up alarmingly, depending on what you're after. Floris has enough to keep you browsing for hours, and in the run-up to Christmas there's a uniformed doorman to usher you in, which is a nice touch.

If you're a men's shoe fetishist this shop, which doesn't seem to have changed at all since the thirties, is the place for you. Unfortunately it will not be cheap, as prices start at £175, but they use the best leather and suede and, even more adventurously, lizard and crocodile skin, cut to fit even the oddest feet. The staff are wonderfully helpful, even if you have holes in your smelly socks as I did when I first went in; they might advise you to get a foot mould made so that your shoes will be designed especially for your own feet and not some imaginary ideal. The footwear you get here are shoes for life. Downstairs there is a selection of shirts and accessories for sale at the going Jermyn Street price, which is high, but the goods are of the highest quality and will not fall apart once you get them home.

Oshushi No Yoshino

212 Piccadilly W1
071-287 1733

Open: Mon–Sat
10 a.m.–7.30 p.m.,
Sun 10 a.m.–6 p.m.
No credit cards

Right in the front of the Japan Centre, a specialist shop serving mainly London's large Japanese population, Oshushi No Yoshino is a revelation. It is an excellent place to get beautifully prepared and presented takeaway Japanese food. They serve only sushi, but it is the cheapest in London and, if not the best, it is good enough for the home crowd and will certainly please the uncritical. Depending on how hungry you are, a portion will cost between £4 and £7. The food is so well packed that when you unwrap it you'll find that nothing has been disturbed. Wash down the whole experience with their special Japanese green tea at £1 a serving.

Paxton & Whitfield Ltd

93 Jermyn Street SW1
071-930 0259/9892

Open: Mon–Fri
9 a.m.–6 p.m.,
Sat 9 a.m.–4 p.m.
Credit: A, Amex, DC,
MC, V

The oldest cheese shop in London, Paxton & Whitfield offers over 300 variations of the weight-watcher's nightmare, and it's impossible to go for a look without at least tasting the goods – the staff here would never allow a potential customer out the door without getting them to munch on some special once-in-a-lifetime experience. If you don't know anything about cheese, don't worry – they'll help you to find something you might like. The shop itself looks incredibly posh but the people who work here are much too involved with the produce to care about intimidating the customer.

Simpson

203 Piccadilly W1
071-734 2002

Open: Mon–Wed, Fri
Sat 9 a.m.–6 p.m.,
Thurs 9 a.m.–7 p.m.
Credit: A, Amex, DC, V

Simpson's, which has been around since 1936, consists of seven floors of quality fashion for men and women. The store has its own line of clothes, called Daks, which is more reasonably priced than some of the other labels available here, including Valentino and Armani. If you find yourself in instant need of a good suit, this store will have something for every occasion and to fit every size. You will need a fat wallet – a man's suit will cost anything between £275 and £800, and in autumn 1993 they will be launching a new range of suits at £199. They also sell casual leisurewear at more bearable prices, and at the January sales here you can find some fantastic bargains, especially accessories. The building, designed by Joseph Emberton, was the first welded-steel structure in London and is now listed.

Thomas Heneage
42 Duke Street SW1
071-930 9223

Open: Mon–Fri
10 a.m.–6 p.m.
Credit: A, Amex, DC, V

In the heart of the high-brow St James's art world lies this elegant bookshop. Every shelf holds a fantastic selection of art books, both rare and new. The catalogues of most major shows around the world can be found here; if they don't have what you want the shop will gladly order it for you. They pride themselves on their fine selection of reference books on subjects as varied as porcelain, sculpture, ancient art and contemporary pieces. Prices tend to be high here, but it is a dream collection.

Tower Records
1 Piccadilly Circus W1
071-439 2500

Open: Mon–Sat
11 a.m.–midnight,
Sun 11 a.m.–10 p.m.
Credit: A, Amex, DC, V

Tower Records is one of the biggest megastores in London and you should be able to find any sort of music on one of its four floors. They have a fantastic jazz section here which is soundproofed off from the rest of the shop, and which has a huge selection of old and new releases. The store also sells American and Japanese imports, and there is a theatre and concert booking office, open from 9 a.m. to 9 p.m from Monday to Saturday, and from 11 a.m. to 8 p.m. on Sunday. There are constantly new events to keep the punters entertained, whether it's Guns 'N Roses popping in or the Brodsky Quartet playing live.

ENTERTAINMENT

The Comedy Theatre
Panton Street SW1
071-867 1045

Credit: A, Amex, V

The Comedy is a Haymarket theatre, although the spirit of the place is firmly within Soho. It was once considered a place of ill repute, mainly because of the local 'roisters' and 'doubtful resorts' opposite, and the building itself has changed very little since it was designed by Thomas Verity in 1891. Pillars hold up the dress circle, obscuring the view from some seats, so you should always ask if your view is going to be obstructed. The Comedy is one of the oldest theatres in London and its dimly lit gold interior gives you the feeling that you have stepped back in time.

Of all the West End theatres, the Comedy is probably the one which has done the most interesting work and which takes the most chances. Thankfully most of the risks are worth it and the productions and the intimate atmosphere of the theatre have succeeded in attracting a new and fresh audience. It was at the Comedy that Arthur Miller's *A View from a Bridge* and Tennessee Williams's *Cat on a Hot Tin Roof* were premiered, and in recent years the theatre has seen successful revivals of modern comedies by the likes of Harold Pinter.

The Institute of Contemporary Art
Nash House, The Mall
SW1
071-930 0493

Open: midday–11 p.m.
Credit: shop and
restaurant, A, Amex,
DC, MC, V
Day membership: £1.50

The concept behind the ICA is to introduce new and exciting forms within the arts, which looks wonderful on paper but which in practice can make for quite a harrowing evening. Events here change very quickly which means that it's a worthwhile place to keep coming back to. Some of the most interesting and some of the most ridiculous moments I can remember have been spent in the ICA. Because of its policy of encouraging diversity, events can be pretty much hit-or-miss, but three things are consistently good: the bar, the bookshop and the high-quality cafe. It can be worth coming here just for these alone and by-passing the cinema, galleries and performance spaces.

To get through to the various events you will need to be a member. The ICA has become popular with a mixed bag of people – once the home of the radical intelligentsia, now a mixture of high- and low-art lovers use the facilities.

The cafe is worth a special mention as it changes its menu daily and there is always a good vegetarian dish at around £4 and a brilliant tiramisu – you have to try it.

Paris Studios
Lower Regent Street
SW1
071-580 4468 ext.
3387

The Paris Studios are used by the BBC to broadcast live shows or to try out new ideas on an audience. It's a small, intimate theatre, ideally suited for the fast, language-based game shows and quizzes which are usually made here, and anything on Radio 4 that has ever made you and the studio audience laugh has probably come from here. To get a seat you have to apply to the BBC or go to the Paris Studios and pick up a ticket application form. Entry is free, and you can apply to watch as many different shows as you like. Tickets for popular shows may well be in limited supply, though. Write to: Radio Ticket Unit, BBC, London W1A 4WW, and ask for coming attractions. Shows usually begin at around 7.30 p.m.

Plaza Cinema

17–25 Piccadilly Circus
SW1
071-930 0144;
071-240 7200
(bookings)

Credit: A, V

Like most West End cinemas, this four-screen complex offers a selection of big new commercial movies. The screens are quite big and the cinema comfortable, though the food and drink on offer is no better than one has learned to expect in London. If you want to see the new Arnie flick or the latest Sly Stallone, this is probably the best bet. There's late shows on Friday and Saturday nights, and the programme changes each Friday. During the week matinees cost £4, and in the evenings and on weekends this rises to £6.50.

Robin Symes Ltd

94 Jermyn Street W1
071-930 9856

Open: Mon–Fri
10 a.m.–5.30 p.m.
No credit cards

This beautiful small gallery deals in authentic pieces from Roman, Greek and Western antiquity, as far back as the second century BC. The window displays are among the best in London, with armlets, stone engravings or seal boxes, all lit to best effect. The prices are very high for this type of work as it is so rare – but then again, you are buying a piece of history. An armlet, for instance, can range in price from £50 to £50,000.

St John Smith Square

Smith Square SW1
071-222 1061

Credit: A, V

Originally built in a baroque early eighteenth-century style and designed by Thomas Archer, this church, with its four spectacular columns, has always been a popular piece of architecture, though through the years it has suffered badly from the worst kind of criticism. The church has twice been gutted by fire and it was badly damaged during World War II, but was rebuilt by Marshall Sisson, who ensured that the acoustics were up to scratch. It is now a popular classical music venue, with concerts every Monday lunchtime, costing £5, as well as most evenings. It's difficult to come here without thinking of Dickens's description of the church in *Our Mutual Friend*: 'A very hideous church with four towers at the corners, generally resembling some petrified monster, frightful and gigantic, on its back with its legs in the air.'

Theatre Royal Haymarket

Haymarket SW1
071-930 8800

Credit: A, Amex, V

This theatre, designed by John Nash, has a colourful history. Oscar Wilde's *A Woman of No Importance* and *An Ideal Husband* were first produced here in 1893 and 1895, though the theatre now has a reputation for being the most traditional of all London's theatres. From John Gielgud's repertory season during World War II to recent triumphs by Hollywood stars such as Jack Lemmon's performance in O'Neill's

A Long Day's Journey into Night, the emphasis has always been on quality rather than innovation.

From the outside the theatre is very beautiful but inside it is difficult to be comfortable in the poky stalls, and the bars and foyer are major disappointments. But these gripes aside, the theatre reeks of history and for some reason seems to win better performances from actors than many other West End stages.

Recently the Theatre Royal has been used by a new school of comic writing, led by Ben Elton, who has written two hits for the stage and succeeded in attracting a new television audience.

J. FLORIS LTD

West

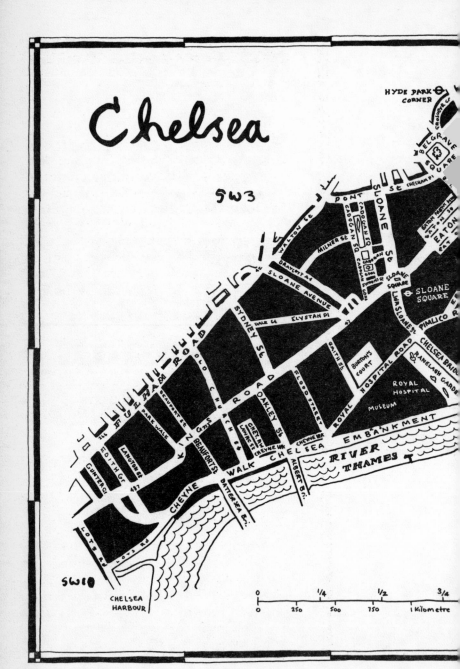

Chelsea

SW3

HYDE PARK
CORNER

SW1

VICTORIA

NOR PL.
GROS. GORE
ROAD
BUCKINGHAM PALACE
TON ST.

N

1 mile

*i*t was the arrival of Sir Thomas More, Henry VIII's Chancellor, in 1520 that put Chelsea on the map. More built himself a country-style mansion on the banks of the river and the aristocracy followed the great man in moving outside of the city walls and building grand houses on what had until then been little more than pastureland. The area became known as the Village of Palaces. In the seventeenth century Nell Gwynne, favourite mistress of Charles II, was one of the many benefactors who helped to create the inspiring Royal Hospital at the Sloane Square end of the King's Road, built by Christopher Wren as a home for old soldiers (see separate entry). Later, the arrival of writers such as Swift and Leigh Hunt cemented the area's reputation as a place suitable for the literati, who were followed by the artistic establishment such as England's most famous painter Joseph Mallord William Turner, who lived at 119 Cheyne Walk, and later Augustus John. Though you would be hard put to find such talent there now, Chelsea has never lost its reputation as a home for intellectuals.

Chelsea became the new home of the beau monde during the sixties and of the hippies in the early seventies. It was the stomping ground of the punks during the late seventies, and now all these tribes tend to come back to Chelsea to search out a little piece of their history. Recently Chelsea has been taken over by the new English upper-middle classes, who have been renamed Hoorays or Yahs.

In recent years Chelsea has yet again become a quiet provincial part of London; although there are thousands of shops and cafes on the King's Road, there aren't many that are particularly good. The main trendy shopping centre has moved to Covent Garden (see Covent Garden), which has succeeded in making its streets and services far more attractive than the tired zone of Chelsea. It sometimes feels as if everyone in Chelsea is waiting for something to happen rather than trying to make anything happen themselves, and the rents and rates are so high here that if there is not an instant return on an investment shop owners get scared off.

The history of the place can be read in its buildings, so explore the streets, especially those toward the river – it is well worth while.

HOW TO GET THERE

Tubes
- Hyde Park Corner
- Knightsbridge
- Sloane Square
- South Kensington
- Victoria

Buses
- Beaufort Street: 19, 45A, 49, 249, 349
- Brompton Road: 14
- Ebury Bridge Road: 11, 239, C10
- Fulham Road: 14, 45A
- Grosvenor Place: 2A, 2B, 8, 16, 36, 38, 52, 73, 82
- Kensington Road: 9, 10, 14, 19, 22, 52, 74, 137
- King's Road: 11, 19, 22, 49, 249, 319
- Sloane Street: 19,22, 137, 137A, C1

THE MAN IN THE MOON

Belgravia, SW1

Before the nineteenth century this area was known as the Five Fields, an area crisscrossed with paths where donkeys and sheep were put to graze. Until a couple of hundred years ago it was a very dangerous area where people wre often robbed and cut up by attackers, and until the last century it was a favourite dwelling place for young knaves and aristos who took great pleasure in killing each other. With Bloomsbury and Islington, Belgravia was among the great developments of the early nineteenth century and was mainly the work of Thomas Cubitt. Belgravia is the most impressive and best preserved of this Nash-influenced Regency-style architecture.

The three principal squares are Eaton, Belgrave and Chester. All have central gardens and they are connected by wide streets, something rare in London. Belgrave Square is the most spectacular, with its stuccoed houses decorated by porticos and columns. The area is now a home for the likes of ex-prime minister Margaret Thatcher, and the streets which were once the home of donkeys are now bumper-to-bumper full of Range Rovers.

Chelsea Physic Garden
66 Royal Hospital Road
SW3
071-352 5646

Open: closed winter; summer, Sun, Wed 2–5 p.m.; Chelsea Flower Show week midday–5 p.m.

The Chelsea Physic Garden was established in 1673 by the Worshipful Society of Apothecaries of London, and is the oldest botanic garden in England, after Oxford's. Despite suffering severe storm damage in the late 1980s, its herb, water and rock gardens still boast many rare and unusual plants and trees. The Physic Garden is a favourite haunt for the serious gardener and, on Sundays, for those in search of a quiet haven for afternoon tea. Sitting on the lawn with a cup of tea in one hand and a newspaper in the other, it's hard to believe that you're in the centre of London.

Occasionally on Thursdays there are lectures here on subjects such as Medicinal Plants in the Montpelier Jardin des Plantes – they start at 6.30 p.m. and admission is £2.

Cheyne Walk, SW3 and SW10

Chelsea's reputation as a place much loved by artists is borne out by the impressive list of people who have lived on this small riverfront street. England's greatest artist, Turner, lived at the beginning of the street, though his house has since been knocked down. He loved the ever-changing river light which had such an influence on his work. James Abbott McNeill Whistler shared number 36 with his collection of precious Chinese porcelain. The poet Swinburne lived alongside the pre-Raphaelite artist Dante Gabriel Rossetti at number 16 and the novelist Mrs Gaskell was born at number 93. In recent years pop stars have moved into these beautiful bohemian properties – Mick Jagger is rumoured to own one of the beautiful riverside apartments with a spectacular view over the Thames.

Also on Cheyne Walk is Crosby Hall. A fifteenth-century dining hall with a timbered roof, it was moved from Bishopsgate in the City and reconstructed here in 1910. Since 1992, however, it has been a private residence, and it is not open to the public. However, any planning permission given to the new owner will be subject to an agreement that the Hall will be open to the public at least 60 days a year.

Royal Hospital Chelsea

Royal Hospital Road
SW3
071-730 0161

Open: Mon–Sat
10 a.m.–midday,
2–4 p.m.; Sun 2–4 p.m.
No admission

This institution for veteran and invalid soldiers was founded by Charles II and designed by Christopher Wren in the style of the Hotel des Invalides in Paris. The building was completed in 1691 and was one of the last secular buildings Wren was involved with. For a military structure it has a remarkable lack of pomp and the brick buildings are grouped around homely open courtyards. The old men who walk with great dignity up and down the King's Road, wearing blue uniforms with scarlet greatcoats in the winter, live here in this beautiful building. They are war veterans and some of the older ones actually faced the horror of World War I.

There is much to see here, including Soane's Stables, added later by Sir John Soane. The view from here extends all the way down to the Thames and it is worth taking a look at Grinling Gibbon's bronze of Charles II dressed as a Roman soldier. The Great Hall is also worth a look, if only for Verrios's large canvas of Charles II.

Every May sees the opening of the Chelsea Flower Show, one of the highlights of London's calendar, when this place is transformed into a colourful haven for garden enthusiasts. Flowers and dogs are about the last remaining passions of Brits, who see this show as a very important event.

There is no admission charge to the Royal Hospital; if you want a guided tour contact the Adjutant at the number above.

EATING AND DRINKING

The Argyll

316 King's Road SW3
071-352 0025

Open: lunch, Tues–Sat
midday–12.45 p.m.,
Sun midday–4 p.m.,
dinner, Mon–Sat
7–10.45 p.m.
Credit: A, Amex, DC, V
Average: £60

The idea behind this swish Chelsea restaurant is to keep the surroundings simple and leave the mind free to concentrate on the food. The decor here is as plain as a working-man's cafe, and the only decoration comes from the clientele. Chelseaites swear by the chef Anand Sastry, who learned his stuff at Marco Pierre White's Harvey's (see Battersea and Clapham). He brought with him from Wandsworth a creative presentation which borders on the sculptural, and some of his spectacular dishes include wild mushroom ravioli and crispy duck and lentils on potato rosti. The wine is slightly more pricey than the food but the house wine is a good Bordeaux (£11), which goes rather well with most dishes.

La Bersagliera

372 King's Road SW3
071-352 5993

Open: Mon–Sat, lunch
midday–3 p.m., dinner
6 p.m.–midnight
No credit cards
Average: £25

It's impossible for this place to have a bad night – the food is so simple that it could never disappoint. Freshly cooked pizzas (about £5) and brimming plates of seafood pasta, with a carafe of cold white wine, are brought to your table minutes after you ordered them, and suddenly you are in heaven. Puddings are standard Italian restaurant fare – my beloved tiramisu is available here, as well as a good slice of pure chocolate cake.

It's a small place and always busy as it is a favourite with the locals. There is always a mixture of people here – not just those Nice Folks From Chelsea but other, less typical, types too. For some reason it's always been popular with musicians, so don't be surprised to see a famous bunch of hairy heads slobbering over a piece of garlic bread.

Deal's Restaurant

Harbour Yard, Chelsea
Harbour SW10
071-376 3232

Open: Mon–Thurs

Chelsea Harbour can be a strange and ghostlike place. It often feels as if there is a high-security presence keeping you out. It's the new dwelling place of the home-in-two-cities brigade – LA and Chelsea Harbour. Most of the people who use this restaurant live here or have a friend who does. The food is a mixture

midday–11 p.m.,
Fri, Sat
midday–11.30 p.m.,
Sun midday–10 p.m.
Credit: A, Amex, DC, V
Average: £32

Ebury Wine Bar
139 Ebury Street SW1
071-730 5447

Open: bar – Mon–Fri
11 a.m.–11 p.m., Sat,
Sun midday–3 p.m.,
6–10.30 p.m.;
restaurant – Mon–Fri,
lunch
midday–2.45 p.m.,
dinner 6–10.30 p.m.,
Sat, Sun lunch
midday–2.45 p.m.,
dinner 6–10 p.m.
Credit: A, Amex, DC, V
Average: £30

The English House
3 Milner Street SW3
071-584 3002

Open: lunch, Mon–Sat
12.30–2.30 p.m., Sun
12.30–2 p.m.; dinner
Mon–Sat
7.30–11.30 p.m., Sun
7.30–10 p.m.
Credit: A, Amex, DC, V
Average: £60

La Famiglia
5–7 Langton Place
SW10
071-351 0761

Open: lunch

of Modern British and American, which really means anything you want, and also includes dishes such as spring rolls, Thai curries and satays. The view over the river gives the place a certain appeal. I find the whole complex quite odd and a bit ugly, but there are many rich people who think otherwise. If you want a high-security meal with a nice view, this is the safest place in London.

This wine bar is heavily populated with Hoorays, that strange breed of upper-middle class English men who seem to see life as an extension of their privileged schooldays. If you can fight through them and get yourself a table, it's a perfectly fine place to sample a few nice wines and have a snack. The food has improved here recently and they have begun to offer various pasta dishes as well as their normal grilled meats. Fillet steak is £10.95, and entrecote steak £9.50. Vegetarian and fish dishes are available and grilled plaice with parsley butter is £7.75. The wine list is extensive and the selection of house wines is reasonable and affordable.

The last time I was here was Beaujolais Nouveau day and I'm afraid I got so drunk I can't remember what I had to eat. I just hope it was better than the wine.

This place is Englishness taken into camp tweedom but for all that the food is quite good. The setting is a quiet-looking house on the border of Chelsea and Brompton Cross, Knightsbridge (see Knightsbridge) and its chintzy curtains and carpets appeal to an assortment of people, including bankers and locals. The secret of the place is the simplicity of the British traditional food, which includes peppered duck, lamb or home-made sausages.

The desserts (£5–£6.50) are definitely the thing to try, though, as they include an assortments of steamed puddings and a fantastic bread-and-butter pudding.

Since the 1960s, when it was the hippest hangout in Chelsea and Fulham, La Famiglia has been consistently successful and is a very popular meeting place for members of the publishing, newspaper and film worlds – editors and ageing financial types all seem to enjoy afternoon rendezvous here with members

midday–3 p.m., dinner
7 p.m.–midnight
Credit: A, Amex, DC, V
Average: £40

**The Ferret and
Firkin**
114 Lots Road SW10
071-352 6645

Open: Mon–Sat
11 a.m.–11 p.m., Sun
midday–3 p.m.,
7–10.30 p.m.
No credit cards

Olivo
21 Eccleston Street SW1
071-730 2505

Open: lunch, Mon–Fri
midday–3 p.m.; dinner,
Mon–Sat 6.30–11 p.m.
Credit: A, Amex, V
Average: £40

Picasso's
127 King's Road SW3
071-352 4921

Open: Mon–Sat
7.30 a.m.–midnight,
Sun 9 a.m.–11 p.m.
Credit: A, Amex, DC, V
Average: £25

of the opposite sex. Alvaro, the owner, is very relaxed about the various stars and Royals who eat here almost every day. The food is always exciting and perfectly cooked. You have to book well in advance to come here, but it's well worth visiting.

This is the best real-ale pub in Chelsea and despite the fact that it's completely jammed at weekends, it has quite a nice atmosphere. They brew their own beers here, and they seem to be getting stronger and stronger. This kind of stuff is the only type of beer the British brew which could compete with Belgian or German beers. The Ferret and Firkin also sell traditional pub grub such as pies and pasties.

They often have some kind of live music in here, be it a piano player or a collection of drunken Hoorays on a stag night. This is not a pleasant sight.

This recently refurbished restaurant has captured the imagination of local hipsters and grey-suited politicians alike. Rough, yellow-plastered walls stencilled with blue give the place a light, breezy feel which suits the food, into which they have put just as much effort. Ruccola and shaved parmesan salads, followed by char-grilled chicken with herbs – or a fresh piece of red mullet with olives and tomatoes are all perfect and make Olivo one of the best finds in the district. Starters average £5 and mains around £10. Puddings such as chocolate and almond tart average £3-£4. It's an unpretentious place where the owner has really tried to keep the prices down and the quality up – you can get a three-course lunch for £15, which is a bargain.

This cheap Italian cafe-restaurant has long been a popular rendezvous with people either going to the cinema across the road or out for the night. In the morning it opens for breakfast, and does a very good cup of coffee. The main menu is very simple and cheap. You can fill a hole in here quite easily without spending more than a fiver. If you feel the need to wash your spaghetti carbonara down with something, it is licensed.

In the summer the front doors are opened, tables and chairs are put outside, and the place becomes a favourite haunt of the Chelsea cruisers, young men and women who seem to do nothing but flirt with their friends on the street.

San Frediano

62 Fulham Road SW3
071-584
8375/071-589 2232

Open: Mon–Sat, lunch
12.30–2.30 p.m.,
dinner 7–11.30 p.m.
Credit: A, Amex, DC, V
Average: £40

Situated in the middle of the Fulham Road, this Italian restaurant has survived the fickle foodies who move from place to place as each fashionable critic points the way to the next slice of hype. It serves traditional Italian food which is a bit expensive but always reliable. Featuring pasta and other dishes such as risotto with wild mushrooms, the menu only occasionally wanders into new approaches to Italian food. The waiters are charming and, to be honest, a bit overbearing. It's better here at lunchtime than in the evening.

SHOPPING

American Classics

400–404 King's Road
SW10
071-351 5229

Open: Mon–Sat
10 a.m.–6.30 p.m.
Credit: A, V

If you need a real pair of 501s with the genuine stitching and washed-out feel, this is probably the best place in London to try on a pair. Over the past ten years the capital has been hit by a deluge of fifties Americana, but this place is one of the very few to have consistently come up with the goods. Finding the right pair is often a matter of timing, though. Apart from denims, American Classics has a brilliant collection of thick alpaca cardigans and kitsch fifties Hawaiian shirts, all at decent prices – everything here is negotiable.

Antiquarius Antiques Market

131–141 King's Road
SW3
071-351 5353

Open: Mon–Sat
10 a.m.–6 p.m.
Credit: ask

There are over 150 stalls in this indoor market, which has been here since the early sixties. Each stall on this site has its own character and it seems that almost anything you might want to buy is here in some shape or form. There's a brilliant section dealing with old Victorian lace clothing, with reasonable prices for dresses and shirts. The jewellery stalls have the rare and collectable as well as relatively recent pieces, and the watch stalls are said to be particularly good. Some stalls will take credit cards, but most won't – check.

Boy

153 King's Road SW3
071-351 1115

Open: Mon–Sat
10 a.m.–6.30 p.m.

This shop made its name during the punk period when it aped the designs of Vivienne Westwood and made them very commercial. The clothes are all much of a muchness in the sense that they all have the Boy slogan plastered over every available square inch. In recent years they have also started doing very clubby

Credit: A, JCB, V

clothing, coming up with sportswear lines and the obligatory woolly or baseball hats. They have a classic range here which means that if you have always wanted a pair of bondage trousers you're likely to be able to find them on a rail at the back. Prices are around the £30 mark, though trousers can go up to £100. The quality is not particularly wonderful, but the name has a nostalgic ring to it.

**Chelsea Antiques
Market**
245-253 King's Road
SW3
071-352
5689/071-352 1424

Open: Mon–Sat
10 a.m.–6 p.m.
Credit: ask

This market has everything from a clairvoyant to second-hand jewellery stalls where it is possible to pick up an emerald or diamond at some of the most reasonable prices in London. Each stallholder is as much an expert on life as he or she is on the goods for sale. Most of the stalls will deal only in cash, and it's worth getting a second opinion on what you're planning to buy.

The market is a bit dark, but is nevertheless well worth a visit.

**Chelsea Farmers
Market**
Sydney Street SW3

On the corner of Sydney Street and the King's Road, these very Chelsea, very twee wooden buildings house a mixture of food and garden shops. The market is a useful and welcome alternative to a footsore trek up and down the King's Road, especially when it's crowded with out-of-town wannabee hip kids at the weekends. Shops include a branch of Neal's Yard Wholefoods (see Covent Garden), Pet Care of Chelsea, which doesn't sell animals but which has a vast array of accessories and pet foods, and the Chelsea Gardener. This last shop has a terrific selection of outdoor plants, seeds, tools and other bits and pieces for the garden, as well as an 'Instant Garden' service for any size patch of land you happen to have. At the back is a large garden beautifully set out with plants and shrubs, and a huge bed of universal pansies, a glowing tapestry of colour. There's also Balloon and Party Gifts, where you can get your balloons printed, and Neal's Yard Remedies, which sells indulgent creams and lotions in the famous blue glass bottles. Guillotine boasts that it is London's most eccentric wine merchants, and I'd be hard pushed to disagree – see for yourself.

If the shopping is too much for you, the Chelsea Farmers Market also has a selection of cafes and a pizza place where you can rest up for a while.

The Flower Stand
Old Church Street
(outside Queen's Elm
Pub), 241 Fulham Road
SW3
071-351 7996

Open: 8 a.m.–6 p.m.
No credit cards

Situated in an expensive stretch of the Fulham Road and on the corner of the busiest junction in the neighbourhood, this very colourful flower stall is perfectly placed to pick up passing trade. A variety of popular flowers, from tulips to roses, are not too heavily priced and the flowers tend to be fresh and in good condition – not always the case with street stalls. Lilies cost £10 for five stems, tulips and chrysanthemums are £5 a bunch, freesias £4 a bunch and roses £1 a stem.

The Garage
350 King's Road SW3
071-351 3505

Open: Mon–Fri
10 a.m.–6 p.m., Sat
10 a.m.–6.30 p.m.
Credit: ask

Located in a spectacular building that was an old ambulance station until the developers got a hold of it, the Garage is the latest attempt by lovers of the King's Road to relaunch the street with a new zing and zap. Unfortunately it doesn't quite deliver, though it is worth a visit. There are various stalls here which have attempted to capitalise on the designer boom of the eighties and create their own labels and designs. The clothes are clubby, if a bit tired-looking.

Grey House Books
12a Lawrence Street
SW3
071-352 7725

Open: No set time –
ring first
No credit cards

It's probably best to phone here for an appointment as there is no telling when the shop opens or closes. This bookshop is for lovers of the crime novel and especially for those who admire Conan Doyle's Sherlock Holmes. It doesn't look or feel like a bookshop but more like a small house, set in the picturesque part of Chelsea Village so loved by the likes of the painter Whistler. The shop stocks a comprehensive selection of hard- and soft-back crime fiction and the staff have an incredible knowledge of the subject.

Harts The Grocer
248 Fulham Road
SW10
071-351 7031

Open: 24 hours, 365
days
Credit: A, Amex,
Switch, V

This supermarket is clean, well lit, not badly designed and sells fresh fruit and beautifully prepared food around the clock. They seem to have everything you might possibly need here, from a bottle of booze to a great selection of goodies at the delicatessen counter. Their barbecue chicken and salad bar is very popular.

Harts is another sign that London has at last begun to wake up to the idea of all-night shopping, something America has enjoyed for years.

Manolo Blahnik
48-51 Old Church
Street SW3
071-352 8622

Manolo Blahnik is probably the most stylish man in London. The shoes he sells are handmade to his own exquisite designs, and his shop is a treat to visit as it sits snugly down in one of those little Chelsea back

Open: Mon–Fri
10 a.m.–6 p.m., Sat
10.30 a.m.–5.30 p.m.
Credit: A, Amex, V

Patrick Cox
8 Symons Street SW3
071-730 6504

Open: Mon–Sat
10 a.m.–6 p.m.
Credit: A, Amex, V

Peter Jones
Sloane Square SW1
071-730 3434

Open: Mon, Tues,
Thurs, Fri
9 a.m.–5.30 p.m.,
Wed
9.30 a.m.–7 p.m., Sat
9 a.m.–6 p.m.
No credit cards

Suzanne Ruggles
90 Fulham Road SW3
071-584 3329

Open: Mon–Sat
9.30 a.m.–6 p.m.
Credit: A, V

streets. He is miles ahead of most other shoemakers, and his shop has been copied all over the world. A pair of Blahnik shoes will set you back anything from £150 to £600, though the average price for a pair is £230, which is steep, but the shoes are hand made and very special.

There's not a lot which can be done to change shoe design without the footwear becoming an unwearable piece of art or an uncomfortable toe-pinching mistake. But some people have succeeded in gently bringing in new shapes and ideas. One such is Manolo Blahnik (see separate entry above); the other is Patrick Cox. Cox has spent a lot of time moving around the fashion world as well as clubland, and he has kept abreast of the changing times. The soft buckled loafers, which come in anything from alligator to snakeskin, are the best-looking shoes I have ever seen and feel like leather socks. The prices vary, as do the materials, but there's nothing for under £100.

When it was first built by Crabtree, Slater and Moberly in 1936, this building was regarded by Londoners as the height of avant-garde taste. The sister store of Oxford Street's John Lewis, Peter Jones is famous for its policy of matching any price you can get for its goods – 'Never knowingly undersold' is its motto. They cater for every domestic need, from carpets to curtain material and from school uniforms to wedding dresses. It's a busy and efficient place which, although popular with the Chelsea and Fulham upper-middle classes, known as Sloanes, is also very easy-going and shows no snobbery towards anyone. There is a cafe and restaurant here, both of which are very popular with mums and daughters out on a shopping spree – the restaurant is on the fourth floor where there is a brilliant view of London across the Belgravia rooftops.

The elegant wrought-iron furniture designed by Suzanne Ruggles catches the spirit of the neo-Gothic style which so dominated Victorian architecture and interiors. The iron may not look very comfortable but her chaise-longue, upholstered in green and costing around £400, is not only incredible to look at but actually very relaxing to lie on. This shop also stocks bookshelves and a good selection of quarry tiles which would make even a bedsit look baronial. Neo-classical chairs and glass-topped tables and coffee tables fit in very well with the fashion for salvaged metal, but Ruggles's work goes beyond fashion and will continue to look good for years to come.

World's End

430 King's Road SW10

071-352 6551

Open: Mon–Sat
11 a.m.–6 p.m.
Credit: A, Amex, V

During the seventies Vivienne Westwood's shop Let It Rock sold classic fifties clothing to enthusiasts until she married her strange ideas with Malcolm McLaren's ability to sell practically anything to anybody and together they opened the shop Sex. Suddenly rubberwear was the thing to be seen in, and astutely seeing the potential of blending all their influences, McLaren created the Sex Pistols, a group of wayward musicians who sparked off the movement known as punk. Over the years Westwood designed clothes and supplied McLaren with ideas, but eventually she set off in new directions on her own. Her shop Seditionaries sold bondage fashion clothing and was visited by people from all over the world; it's now called World's End and is her sole remaining outpost in the area.

Westwood's individual style and attitude towards clothes have made her Britain's premier designer, though while some people see her as a genius, others see her as a crazy eccentric making unwearable clothes. Her clothes, however, are always worth looking at, and every season she comes up with a new theme, which can be anything from Pagan Britain to Baroque France. Somehow she always manages to translate period to garment and then make it all over for the twentieth century.

ENTERTAINMENT

Chelsea Arts Club

143 Old Church Street

SW3

071-376 3311

Members only

In the late nineteenth century so many arty types lived in Chelsea that a gathering place was long overdue. In 1891 Whistler, Wilson Steer and Co. moved to a house at 181 King's Road. It proved too small for them so they moved to the above address, which now holds one of the most popular arts clubs in the world. The bar is dowdy and tired-looking but suits the crumpled faces of the hungover artists looking for inspiration. Snooker tables supply the entertainment and are normally played on with unsteady hands. The back room holds a decent restaurant which specialises in simple meat and fish dishes.

To get in in you need to know a member and to become a member you have to be proposed and accepted, which I am told is very difficult. It's a funny place to watch serious people become ridiculous through drink. It has a sizeable garden at the back.

Embargo
533b King's Road
SW10
071-351 5718

Open: Tues–Sat
8 p.m.–3 a.m.
Credit: A, Amex, DC, V

When it opened this was going to be the bar which finally attracted people away from the clubs of Notting Hill Gate and Soho and back in the direction of the once wonderful King's Road set. The idea was for Embargo to be a members-only bar and dining club serving Italian food, but for a time it seemed that people preferred the lowlife of Soho to the very, very expensive world of SW10. In recent months a new policy of allowing most reasonable people in has lifted the club out of the doldrums but unfortunately it has attracted a singularly unexciting clientele.

**The Man in the
Moon Theatre Club**
392 King's Road SW3
071-351 2876

No credit cards

This small theatre pub is situated in the heart of the area known as World's End. The theatre space is often used by up and coming actors and writers to try out new material, giving them the chance to do things which they will never get to do on the commercial circuit. This doesn't mean that the public doesn't have to pay to see grown-ups do silly things in the name of art – but then somebody always has to pay. In my experience the work done here varies between very awful and very average, but I keep going back because I like to see actors take risks before they hit the big time. The theatre is always worth a try, though – it's cheap and you can always go back down to the pub if things get too bad.

**The Royal Court
Theatre**
Sloane Square SW1
071-730 1745

Credit: A, Amex, V

Built in 1887 by Emden and Crewe, the building in which the Royal Court has been burnt, bombed and rebuilt throughout its illustrious history. In the fifties, after it was taken over by the English Stage Company, the theatre became an international home for new plays, though before this Shaw had used the venue to rehearse and stage many of his new works, including *The Philanderer*. But it was the ESC's production of John Osborne's *Look Back in Anger* which set the theatrical world alight in a period of post-war disillusionment when a new and angry voice used the stage here as a platform to shout at the sleeping establishment. The Royal Court had found a radical voice, and it was here that people came to taste a bit of what the future held.

Since those heady days the Royal Court has continued to put on radical work, although it has continually also been threatened with closure, and is the country's most important theatre outside the national institutions such as the RSC and the RNT. Caryl Churchill's satire on City brokers, *Serious Money*, was a huge hit here in the 1980s and moved up to the West End, and one of the most recent successes at the Royal Court has been the production of Ariel Dorfman's *Death and the Maiden*, which was a great success in the West End and also opened on Broadway.

The small space upstairs is more experimental and therefore cheaper. New things are often tried out here first and brought into the main house if they work – Death and the Maiden is a good example of this.

606 Club

90 Lots Road SW10

071-352 5953

Open: Mon–Sat
8.30 p.m.–2.30 a.m.,
Sun 8.30 p.m.–midnight
Credit: A, V

The people who run this place have made a genuine attempt to capture a little piece of the smoky live jazz atmosphere. It kind of works in a nostalgic way and, more importantly, it stays open into the small hours when most good Chelsea folk are sleeping snugly. Live bands play here every night and a lot of musicians turn up from other gigs to jam with whoever is playing. They do food, but mostly it is a music and drinking venue. Membership is not required, and it's as good as any place you might find in Chelsea or Fulham. There is a music charge of £3.95 from Sundays to Thursdays, and £4.20 on Fridays and Saturdays.

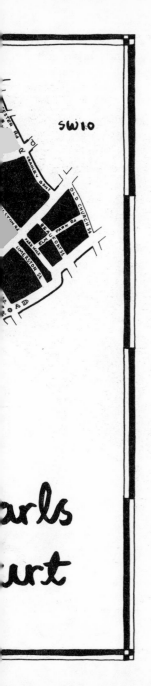

SW10

arls

urt

EARLS COURT

Originally a small hamlet, Earls Court gets its name from the earls of Warwick and Holland, who had their courthouse here. Much of the development of the area took place during the nineteenth century, and it wasn't until 1880 that farmland was bought up and used to build large homes for minor traders and importers. After World War I many of the big houses were converted into hotels or subdivided into those sad, lonely places called bedsits. The area is now nicknamed Bedsit Jungle or Kangaroo Valley because of the large numbers of Australians and New Zealanders who live here.

The abundance of cheap hotels and different cultures should make Earls Court one of London's most exciting areas, but exciting it is not. Earls Court Road is a major through road to South London and is constantly seething with aggressive traffic. The top corner of the road, where it meets Old Brompton Road, is the most interesting part. The pub on the corner is a favourite with skinheads and punks, two tribes long out of sync with the rest of the world, who tend to stand outside looking for attention.

In the sixties, when Earls Court was still a satellite area, my grandmother had a shop here. She used to know her customers by name and gave credit to many of them. I used to visit here as a kid and would walk quite freely down the Old Brompton Road talking to the Irish builders working on the new hotels. It was a time that saw great changes in the area – young swingers, groovy, hip and with a pocketful of cash took

full advantage of the sexual revolution sweeping the country. While London's police were kept busy with the vice and gangland feuds of Soho, drugs were easily available in Earls Court, where cheap hotels sprang up, providing rooms for prostitutes and rent boys, and gay men claimed the area as their own.

Now Earls Court is still very much the area where time stood still, though with the advent of AIDS the nightlife is less free and easy than it once was. A network of bars and cafes catering to the gay community has sprung up, and droves of backpacking Australians on their trips around the world stop off here. Earls Court's reputation as a cosmopolitan stronghold isn't really justified, though. There are no particularly good restaurants, cafes or bars here, though the banner of free love still flies, rather limply, over the district. For the purposes of this book, therefore, I've looked further afield into Fulham and the borders of Chelsea for more exciting places.

HOW TO GET THERE

Tubes
- Barons Court
- Earls Court
- Fulham Broadway
- Gloucester Road
- West Brompton
- West Kensington

Buses
- Chelsea Harbour: C3
- Cromwell Road: 74
- Earls Court Road: 31, 74
- Finborough Road: 31, C3
- Fulham Road: 14, 45A
- Fulham Palace Road: 11, 74, 190, 220, 295
- Northend Road: 28, 391
- Old Brompton Road: 74, C1
- Queen's Gate: 70
- Redcliffe Gardens: 31, C3
- Warwick Road: 31, 74, C3

BROMPTON CEMETERY

SIGHTS AND SITES

The Boltons SW10

The crescents off Old Brompton Road known as The Boltons get their name from the family who owned most of the land here during the nineteenth century. The two facing crescents were built in the 1850s by George Godwin and the vast houses here have always been highly sought after as residences, though the prices are extremely high even for this area and can run into millions. The prices have never deterred the likes of Douglas Fairbanks Jr. Beatrix Potter, the creator of Peter Rabbit, lived here and had her house on the site where the Bousfield Primary School now stands. In 1956 the school won an architectural award for the designers, Chamberlin, Powell and Bon, who also designed the Barbican complex (see The City).

Brompton Cemetery
Finborough Road SW10
071-352 1201

Open: winter
9 a.m.–4 p.m., summer
9 a.m.–7 p.m.

The first cemetery to be run by the state, this graveyard was built in 1840 and bought by the General Board of Health in 1852. The Brompton Cemetery has all the qualities of London's other Victorian new-Gothic graveyards, such as Kensal Green (see Notting Hill) and Highgate (see Hampstead and Highgate) cemeteries, and is a fascinating insight into the way our ancestors regarded death. It's one of the few quiet public spots in Earls Court, and is not at all a bad place to read the paper in peace and quiet. My grandmother's newspaper shop was opposite the Brompton Cemetery and as a kid I would stare from my bedroom window at the tombs and catacombs – not the most cheery of sights in the morning. The cemetery is a popular hangout for the local gay community.

Earls Court
Exhibition Centre
Warwick Road SW5
071-370 8011

This immense building is used for a variety of purposes, including rock concerts, operas and boxing fights. The London Boat Show takes place here each January, the Royal Tournament in July and the Ideal Home exhibition is held at the Exhibition Centre each March and April. At one time Cruft's, the famous dog show, was held here. Times and prices of each show vary, so it's best to ring first for information. The façade of the Exhibition Centre is very ugly and I think the place lacks any real atmosphere, but it seems that if you want to see a

successful act these days you have to come to some place with the warmth and charm of an aircraft hangar. The Exhibition Centre is so big that during concerts they put up screens so that you can see what is happening on stage – which seems like a waste of money to me.

St Cuthbert's Church

Philbeach Gardens SW5
071-370 3263

Open: services,
Mon–Sat 6.30 p.m.,
Sun 10 a.m., 11 a.m.;
viewing by appointment

This church, situated behind the Cromwell Road, comes as a pleasant sight with its surprisingly subtle Art Nouveau style. The building, which seems to hang in the air without the dark dominance of other Anglican churches, was designed by H. R. Gough in 1884. Look out for the lectern and the organ, beautifully crafted by Bainbridge Reynolds. The church is one of the few buildings of note in this dreary area where the ugly Exhibition Centre dominates.

EATING AND DRINKING

Ambrosiana Creperie

194 Fulham Road
SW10
071-351 0070

Open: midday–midnight
Credit: A, V
Average: £18

The people who run this place have definitely made an effort to relaunch the crepe as an ideal bite to eat on a night out rather than just French fast food. There are 25 different crepe on the menu here, including cheese, mushroom, chicken and fish fillings.After a crepe the best thing to go for is a galette, and there is a selection of 41 to choose from. The prices are low – around £5 for a crepe and £3-£4 for a galette. More and more people have been encouraged to come and try this kind of food which was so popular in London in the days of the Obelisk chain.

The Blue Elephant

4–6 Fulham Broadway
SW6
071-385 6595

Open: lunch – Mon–Fri,
Sun midday–2.30 p.m.,
dinner
7 p.m.–12.30 a.m.
Credit: A, Amex, DC, V
Average: £56

The interior of the Blue Elephant is reminiscent of a jungle landscape, and this upmarket Thai restaurant has become the darling of the Chelsea and Fulham set who think it's as close to Phuket as 'one' needs to get. The focus here is definitely on presentation, and an army of waiters will carry sculpted fruit dishes and trays of exquisitely arranged noodles, rice, fish and meat concoctions to your table. The food is authentically Thai but the prices are definitely British, averaging out at about £28 a head – £27 more than it would cost in Bangkok.

Bonjour Vietnam

593 Fulham Road SW6
071-385 7603

Like its stablemate Teppanya Kisan (see separate entry), this Vietnamese restaurant looks like a relic of the design-conscious eighties, when great emphasis

Open: Mon–Sat,
lunch 12.30–2.30 p.m.,
dinner 6.30–11.30 p.m.,
Sun midday–11.30 p.m.
Credit: A, Amex, DC, V
Average: £25

Caruso
585 Fulham Road SW6
071-381 3422

Open: lunch, Mon–Fri
midday–2.30 p.m.,
dinner Mon–Sat
6.30–11.30 p.m.
Credit: A, Amex, DC, V
Average: £30

Eleven Park Walk
11 Park Walk SW10
071-352 3449

Open: Mon–Sat,
lunch 12.30–3 p.m.,
dinner
7.30 p.m.–midnight;
Sun, lunch
12.30–3 p.m.
Credit: A, Amex, V
Average: £30

The Jolly Maltster
17 Vanston Place SW6
071-385 3593

Open: Mon–Sat
11 a.m.–11 p.m., Sun
midday–3 p.m.,

was put on things like colour-coordination, weird-shaped tables and chairs, and uniformed staff. However, it does serve up good Vietnamese food such as Hanoi beef soup, stuffed squid and lamb covered in ginger. The menu is long and detailed and somewhat confusing to those unfamiliar with South-East Asian cooking, but despite the overpowering look of the restaurant the food is good and not too expensive. There are set menus at £12.50 and £14.50 for four courses, or £9.90 for three, which certainly seems a bargain in an area that can prove expensive.

Selected as one of London's best restaurants by the weekly listings magazine *Time Out*, Caruso is a simple and very unpretentious Italian restaurant where people come to eat rather than to sit in some architect's fantasy or an interior designer's showroom. Mussels, crostini with chicken livers, roast quail and salmon with zambucca are just some of the dishes featured here, and are all good. The wine list is both good and approachable, with house wine costing £10 for a litre flask. It's an older crowd which comes here, and the good food and service ensure that they keep coming back.

This Italian restaurant is one of Fulham's most popular restaurants, especially with the glitterati who enjoy preferential treatment here. When I visited Eleven Park Walk I was treated quite badly by the staff and found the pomposity of the place overbearing. Nevertheless, people keep coming back here, which says a lot for the food, which is not cheap but is very good indeed: risotto with lobster, seafood salad and the duck and chicken dishes are all wonderful. House wine is £7.50. The atmosphere is light and there is enough room for everybody to spot any arriving celebs – but try to ignore the flash waiters and the rude barmen.

This Courage pub does decent bar food, including hot meals such as lasagne and steak and kidney pie, costing around £3. It's also a good place to meet up with friends before going to watch some football at nearby Stamford Bridge, and fills up very quickly at the end of a match. No one particular group of people frequents the pub, but it does seem to attract

7–10.30 p.m.
No credit cards
Average: £10

Kramps
6 Kenway Road SW5
071-244 8759

Open: midday –11 p.m.
Credit: A, V
Average: £11

Luigi's
359-361 Fulham Road
SW10
071-351 7825

Open: Mon–Fri
8 a.m.–8 p.m., Sat
8 a.m.–6 p.m.
No credit cards
Average: £8

The Navigator Restaurant
The Polish Air Force
Club, 14 Collingham
Gardens SW5
071-370 1229

Open: Tues–Sun, lunch
midday–3 p.m., dinner
6–10.45 p.m.
No credit cards
Average: £15

Stamford Hill Cafe
466 Fulham Road SW6

locals of all sorts, who have been coming here for years. They do a good Sunday roast here, cooked that day on the premises, which will not cost more than £5.

Earls Court must be the only area in London where you can still find creperies, which went out of fashion everywhere else in the late seventies, when people started taking an interest in strangely presented foods in odd restaurants.

Kramps isn't as elegant as its nearby rival Ambrosiana (see separate entry), but they do try to offer every possible combination of the savoury and the sweet, all wrapped up in a pancake. A bottle of the house wine is £6.95.

This cafe is owned by the same people who run the delicatessen at number 349. In its early days Luigi's was a deli selling fresh pasta and ice creams, as well as home-cooked meals. The owners would occasionally give some of their home-cooked food to friends and children, and as word of how good the grub was got around, more and more customers demanded to be able to sit and eat. Now you can have a plate of penne, spaghetti or chicken here for under £4. They also do very good cappuccinos and espressos, and you can buy any dish you particularly fancy and take it away to eat at home later. The cafe is unlicensed, but you can bring your own wine and they don't charge corkage.

The crumbling walls and the faces of the people who practically live in the Navigator seem to be the restaurant's main attraction. Polish World War II veterans and refugees from years of Communism gather daily to sup on thick meat and vegetable soups. Dishes such as lamb and cabbage seem to arrive on your table almost before you've ordered them, which makes the place all the more exciting.

Do not expect people to speak English to you here, and try – if you can – to keep off the flavoured vodkas which will show you about as much pity as Vlad the Impaler.

Just around the corner from Stamford Bridge football ground, home to the Chelsea football club, is this cafe, painted in the Chelsea colours and obviously

No credit cards
Average: £10

Teppanya Kisan
593–599 Fulham Road
SW6
071-386 7728

Open: Mon–Sat, lunch
12.30–2 p.m., dinner
6.30–11.30 p.m.
Credit: A, Amex, DC, V
Average: £40

The White Horse
1-3 Parsons Green SW6
071-736 2115

Open: Mon–Fri
11.30 a.m.–3 p.m.,
5–11 p.m.,
Sat 11 a.m.–3 p.m.,
7–11 p.m.,
Sun 11 a.m.–3 p.m.,
7–10.30 p.m.
Credit: A, Amex, V
Average: £14

The Wilds
356 Fulham Road
SW10
071-376 5553

Open: lunch, Fri–Sun
12.30–3 p.m.,
dinner, Mon–Sat
7–11.30 p.m.
Credit: A, V
Average: £30

aimed at the home crowd. The menu offers a variety of dishes such as liver and onions and steak and kidney pie, all of which come with chips; for dessert try traditional jam pudding. The cafe is a must for breakfast and has no pretensions whatsoever, unlike some of its more glamorous neighbours.

This Japanese restaurant boasts a large mock lobster in the window to indicate the delights waiting inside. Lobster is of course on the menu, but traditional Japanese dishes such as tappanaki, sliced beef and yakitori – skewered and grilled chicken – are all available. You can have sushi here, but you have to book and order ahead. The food is all fresh and beautifully presented, and the prices are more reasonable than those charged by many of London's Japanese restaurants.

This pub gets absolutely packed – and not just because of the fantastic food or the drinks, but more because it tends to attract and keep people of a certain wealthy type. The staff here could be of the same clan as the clientele, and at times can be fantastically rude. Rudeness, in fact, is very much on the agenda here, which is a shame, as the pub looks like it might be a very nice place. If you want a peek at London's good-looking middle classes having fun, this is the place to start. The food varies from burritos and enchiladas to Barnsley chops, but is always very good. The White Horse has an extensive range of foreign beer such as Framboise, and is the only pub to carry Traquair house ale. Be warned – this delicious dark brew is wickedly potent.

This is a new and relatively upmarket restaurant on the Fulham Road, a stretch crammed full of places to eat. The Wilds is good for a long, expensive evening spent trying a few new dishes – as long as you are prepared to pay for them. I don't know what it is that makes the public take to some places, but whether it's social cachet, good food, plush interior or bad manners, the Wilds has it all. The food falls into the Modern British category, and they have a good but limited selection of French wines plus some South African ones. House wine is a reasonable £8 a bottle.

Windmill Wholefoods
486 Fulham Road SW6
071-385 1570

Open:
10.30 a.m.–11 p.m.
Credit: A, V
Average: £8

Though there are still lots of greasy spoons and tacky second-hand furniture shops on Fulham Broadway, things are changing and more and more interesting places are beginning to open up. Windmill Wholefoods is a small wholefood deli and takeaway, as well as a cafe. The menu here changes daily but there are a few regular dishes such as butterbean and broccoli or carrot and cashew soup. The cafe is patronised by typical veggies as well as New Agers who spend a lot of time here gazing at each other. The goods on sale include almost everything necessary for a veggie casserole or pie; tea and coffee, but no alcohol, are available in the cafe.

The Wine Gallery
49 Hollywood Road
SW10
071-352 7572

Open: Mon–Sat
midday–3 p.m.,
6.30 p.m.–midnight,
Sun 7–11.30 p.m.
Credit: A, V
Average: £15

This wine bar features an extensive wine list as well as a reasonable menu. The selection of wines leans heavily towards the French, but doesn't ignore the popularity of New World wines with the British. On the few occasions I have been to the Wine Gallery it has been too busy to sit down and enjoy a glass of wine and a chat, but the food was not at all bad – small and nibbly, just what you want in this kind of place. They insist that you eat with your drink and will offer you crudites at about £2 if you're not that hungry, but deep-fried mushrooms or potted shrimp seem to be the best bet, along with a glass of the house Bordeaux – very reasonable at £1.75.

SHOPPING

Le Boulevard
178 Fulham Road
SW10
071-370 1338

Open: Mon–Sat
9.30 a.m.–5.30 p.m.,
Sun
9.30 a.m.–5.30 p.m.
No credit cards

This small French patisserie takes great pride in offering up such delights as nougat pastries and chocolate croissants and there is a wide selection of elaborate flans and cakes which can be iced to your own requirements. The birthday cakes and decorations are done downstairs and the smell of the place is very definitely Paris rather than Fulham Road. Delicious small cakes cost between 70p and £1.50. Shops like Le Boulevard are an indication that the Fulham Road is embracing village life.

Cannelle
166 Fulham Road
SW10
071-370 5573

Canelle's frosted window gives no clue, other than a small, beautifully arranged display, that there is a patisserie here. The place is as expensive as it looks, but then a lot of preparation has gone into the elegant cakes and pastries, as well as the deliciously fresh breads, that adorn the counter here. Beautiful little cakes and larger cakes and tarts to serve six are all delicious, as are the breads. The patisserie has caught the imagination of the local people, who see it as very much part of social life. Cannelle is all about quality, style and modernity.

The CCC is very much part of Chelsea and Fulham village life, and sells everything from Italian salami and sauces to a variety of different breads and tinned foods which you could never buy in a supermarket. It's best known, however, for its fine selection of cheeses, meats and smoked salmon. The staff are all helpful and they can provide delicious and beautifully presented food for any size party you may be having in the home, garden or office. A London institution.

For as many years as I can remember, this shop has been selling second-hand junk a cut above your ordinary tat. The shop's window display always looks amazing, packed full of stuffed bears, paintings, golf clubs and old cameras – anything that could conceivably find a buyer. I don't think it's possible to come here without buying something. The prices vary according to the quality of each item, but they are all very reasonable and, better still, negotiable.

In recent years men's and women's bespoke tailoring has become very popular; there is now a new breed of tailor, less greedy than the old, who have moved away from the high-rent high-rates of Savile Row and its environs. These new young tailors are not attempting to compete with the old school; rather they are attracting a new type of customer who not only wants a couple of suits at around the £650 mark but also the shirts and accessories to match. Davies will also make women's clothes – a beautifully cut dress will cost £175 excluding fabric. The overall look is stylish but just a touch unconventional.

The smell of joss sticks hits you as soon as you walk through the door of this shop, and in fact all the goods on sale here have a faint seventies hippyish quality about them. Crystals, lotions, creams and Hindu icons create an atmosphere which is obviously attractive to local young hippies and their bearded, balding,

Open: Mon–Sat
9 a.m.–6.30 p.m., Sun
9 a.m.–6 p.m.
Credit: A, Amex, DC, V

**Chelsea Catering
Company**
305 Fulham Road
SW10
071-351 0538

Open: Mon–Fri
8 a.m.–6 p.m., Sat
8 a.m.–1 p.m.
No credit cards

A. Clarke and Sons
340 Fulham Road
SW10
071-352 0615

Open: Mon–Fri
8.30 a.m.–4.30 p.m.
No credit cards

**Douglas George
Davies**
300 Fulham Road
SW10
071-352 5180

Open: Mon–Fri
8.30 a.m.–6 p.m., Sat
10 a.m.–1 p.m.
No credit card

Ganesha
8 Park Walk SW10
071-352 8972

Open: midday–7 p.m.
Credit: V, A

tired-looking parents. Ganesha is also known for its Indian silver jewellery and incense. This is the other side of Fulham life, and has nothing to do with smart restaurants and German cars. If you need a bit of spiritual guidance, Ganesha could well be your new home.

Hackett
65a/b New King's
Road SW6
071-731 7964

Open: Mon–Fri
10 a.m.–7 p.m., Sat
9 a.m.–6 p.m
Credit: A, Amex, V

The best menswear shop in London, Hackett's has always had a timeless approach to tailoring and men's ready-to-wear clothes which makes things very easy for the man without the time or the taste to organise his own wardrobe. The second-hand clothes with which Hackett made its name have now gone, replaced by Hackett's own-label garments, all of which are made in Britain. The tweed jackets, Prince of Wales suits, brogues, city-slicker chalk stripes, and evening wear are all perfect and should suit every occasion in town or country, and all at a good price.

Lea and Sandeman
301 Fulham Road
SW10
071-376 4767

Open: Mon–Sat
9 a.m.–8.30 p.m.
Credit: A, V

This old-style wine merchants easily competes with successful chains such as Oddbins, making it very simple for you to find something you'll like. They have a vast selection of vintage and non-vintage wines, all very well chosen. There is a discount for those who buy cases and they also have a delivery service, which is free anywhere within the UK. The staff here are helpful and friendly, and will take the time to discuss your choice – there's no need to feel intimidated if you feel you don't know much about wine.

Luigi's Deli
349 Fulham Road
SW10
071-352 7739

Open: Mon–Fri
9 a.m.–9.30 p.m., Sat
9 a.m.–7 p.m.
No credit cards

Fulham's best deli is owned by the same family who run Luigi's cafe further along the Fulham Road (see separate entry). There's a good mix of cheese and pasta available as well as fresh breads and coffees. Dried wild mushrooms, normally quite difficult to find in London, are relatively cheap here, as are the various types of pasta and sauces, all of which are freshly prepared each day. Most of the Italian restaurants in the Fulham area get their bits and pieces from here, and no wonder.

Over the Moon
460 Fulham Road SW6
071-381 0210

Tucked in between football souvenir shops and cafes is this shop selling everything to do with the psychic and the supernatural. There are tapes here to help you to diet, get closer to your soul or have an out-of-body experience, and if you need to know what the future holds, you can even a have Tarot reading done here. I'm totally cynical about everything to do with the supernatural, but I do enjoy the theatre of it all – and you should be able to find every prop you need in Over the Moon.

Phase Eight
345 Fulham Road
SW10
071-352 9025

Open: Mon–Sat
9.30 a.m.–6 p.m.
Credit: A, Amex, V

This shop is part of a successful chain of fifteen stores dotted around the capital and as far north as Scotland. The women's clothes it sells are both practical and stylish enough for the office and for big occasions, and they also do their own range of clothes which starts at £40 and goes as high as £200. There are also clothes available from designers such as Patsy Seddon and the excellent Nicole Farhi. Their understated elegance looks very comfortable.

Reno's Barber Shop
31 Jerdan Place SW6
071-381 9927

Open: Mon–Sat
9 a.m.–6 p.m.
No credit cards

Reno's is an old-style barber shop, where you won't ever find copies of Vogue or expensive treatments lining the shelves. I wouldn't come here for anything too elaborate, but for a short back and sides this place is perfect. Reno's was once very popular with the skinheads who enjoyed the barber's no-nonsense technique as he swept their locks off, though most of the customers seem to be part of Fulham and Chelsea's large Italian contingent. Reno's is a good place to catch up on local gossip, which always seems to include a death, a marriage and a divorce.

ENTERTAINMENT

Chelsea Football Club
Stamford Bridge Ground
SW6
071-385 5545

Formed in 1905, Chelsea was once London's most fashionable soccer club – its popularity received a boost recently when the ex-Minister of Fun David Mellor allegedly wore a Chelsea shirt to make love, prompting the remark that it was the first time in ages anyone in the Chelsea strip had scored at all. Prime Minister John Major is also a fan. The best place to watch the game is at the Shed End, behind the goal at the Fulham Road end of the pitch – however, this is also where the die-hard fanatics go, so you might be more comfortable in the stand. Not being a Chelsea supporter, I can't get too excited over the football – I'll leave you to decide.

The Double Bass

This club for sweating young ravers perfectly suits Earls Court's feeling of being caught in a time warp.

Open: Mon–Sat
9.30 a.m.–5.30 p.m.
Credit: A, V

162 Earls Court Road
SW5
071-835 2021

Open: 10 p.m.–5 a.m.
No credit cards
Admission: £12

Hurlingham Club
Ranelagh Gardens SW6
071-736 8411,
bookings 071-731
3691

Open:
9 a.m.–10.30 p.m.,
Sun 9 a.m.–9 p.m.
Credit: A, Amex, DC,
Switch, V

MGM Cinema
142 Fulham Road
SW10
071-373 6990

Credit: A, V

Queen's Club
Palliser Road W14
071-385 3421,
membership queries
071-385 5162

Open: 8 a.m.–10 p.m.
Credit: A, V

Prerequisites are sequinned vests, plastic boots, heavy make-up and a knowledge of sixties soul music. Fab, hip and happy, this venue has weathered recession, transient tastes and heavy policing and somehow its retro swinger clientele still manage to shake their ever-so-fashionable long hair and let loose.

Built in 1760 for a government specialist, Dr William Cadogan, Hurlingham House has been altered and enlarged on numerous occasions by its subsequent owners. At one time it was a pigeon-shooting club – and not the clay variety. In 1905 the pigeon-shooting club was replaced by a polo club – the game, was first played here in 1874. In 1945 the polo grounds were bought by London County Council and turned into Hurlingham Park. The club is steeped in sporting tradition and anything from croquet to cricket is still played here. Each year before Wimbledon a reception is held here for tennis players and officials. The local Chelseaites use the club as a place to shed some pounds or to entertain their friends. It's expensive to join and there is a five to six-year waiting list.

The centre of most Chelsea and Fulham people's nightlife, this five-screen cinema complex concentrates on big commercial Hollywood-style films. It is always busy here, especially on a Monday when there are cheap tickets to all the films, but it can be quiet and peaceful for the early afternoon show. The people who come here tend to be ever so trendy, and a lot of the younger boys and girls are obviously home from boarding school and are trying to make as much of their freedom as possible. The bar and the food counters are average, but there are plenty of other places on the Fulham Road to grab a bite to eat before or after the film.

Each June before Wimbledon, the big event of the tennis year, Queen's have their own tournament, the Stella Artois, which allows the big stars to warm up and get used to playing on English grass courts rather than the more internationally common clay courts. However, tennis in London is very much a social occasion and it seems that only the rich can afford the prices charged by clubs such as this one. Membership of the Queen's Club is about £700 a year, and court fees vary from £6 to £10, depending on the time of day. However, many parks in London have tennis courts which cost little or nothing to use and which are probably the best bet for if you want a game rather than a chat and a drink.

The Troubadour
265 Old Brompton
Road SW5
071-835 1434

Open: Mon–Sun
8.30 a.m.–11.30 p.m.
No credit cards
Average: £12

This coffee house has managed to survive changing fashions and attitudes and looks stuck in a sixties time warp. Folksy and hippyish customers recite their poetry here to a tolerant clientele and management, so if you have a masterpiece you feel like trying out there is no better place in London to guarantee you a hearing. The food is unspectacular – pasta, omelettes and other snacks – and they do not serve alcohol, but the coffee makes the trip worthwhile.

CHELSEA FOOTBALL CLUB – PETER
OSGOOD IN HAPPIER TIMES

Holland Park

*i*t is over 300 years since William III gave Kensington its royal status, and this posh suburb still thrives as a much sought-after address for London's rich and famous. The arrival of the Princess of Wales added a desperately needed touch of glamour to Kensington Palace, though the constant snooping and prying by the tabloid press has caused the security around the Royals to be tightened up to a degree that it is no longer possible to see Diana driving around Kensington in a convertible.

Kensington Gardens are the main attraction of the area and the sight of nannies, drunks, writers and musicians walking around talking to themselves is a daily event. The houses around the Gardens and Kensington backstreets are without doubt the homes of the privileged. Every car seems to be a Mercedes or Jaguar, and every front room is decked out in the best but not always the most tasteful that money can buy. Kensington's not the most eventful area because of the type of people who live here; they prefer the streets to be quiet and their sons and daughters to be home early rather than raving in a local bar or club. There is in fact a dearth of nightlife here – there's no local theatre or central point other than the park to bond the locals together. It's a very private and discreet world – there are a few choice restaurants and bars, but nothing in comparison to areas to the north, where the beginnings of Notting Hill wander into the bohemian quarters of Ladbroke Grove. The two areas could not be more

different – I have spent time in both and found Kensington a very sobering experience.

In the sixties Kensington High Street was the site of Biba, the extraordinary store for new dazzling fashions which cocked a snook at the Establishment. Kensington Market and Hyper-Hyper (see separate entries) are now the only areas of Kensington where anything new is produced, and the heady days of the Regine club, once the most fashionable in London, are also over. However, in many ways Kensington High Street is a more comfortable version of Oxford Street – it's just as well served by a diversity of shops and cafes but is more pleasant and less tiring to walk up and down. Every good high street chain is here, including Marks and Spencer, Dillons, Tower Records and Jigsaw.

The area known as Holland Park is where London's art dealers and media folk love to live. It's clean, wealthy and seemingly approachable, but the streets and squares are hidden behind fences and walls which immediately tell you to keep your distance. It's largely residential and there's little of interest here apart from the houses themselves, which of course are not open to the public. Certain streets, such as Portland Road, still have a quaint seventies feel where ex-hippie types mingle with the old-boy school of the art world, but in the eighties new wealth moved in. There are a few remnants of more picturesque times but most of the families who have been here for generations have pulled down the blinds and are busy ignoring the outside world.

HOW TO GET THERE

Tubes
- Gloucester Road
- Holland Park
- High Street Kensington
- Notting Hill Gate
- Shepherd's Bush
- South Kensington
- West Kensington

Buses
- Cromwell Road: 74
- Holland Park Avenue: 12, 94
- Holland Park Road: 49
- Kensington Church Street: 27, 28, 31, 52, 70
- Kensington High Street: 9, 9A, 10, 27, 28, 31, 49, 52, 70, C1

SIGHTS AND SITES

The Commonwealth Institute

Kensington High Street
W8
071-603 4535

Open: Mon–Sat
10 a.m.–5 p.m., Sun
2–5 p.m.
No admission charge

The Commonwealth Centre was founded in 1887 to commemorate Queen Victoria's Golden Jubilee. Originally based in Imperial College Road, it moved here in 1962 when this new building, designed by Sir Robert Matthew – who also designed the Royal Festival Hall – was opened by the current Queen. The galleries are funded by the Foreign Office and every inch of wall and floor space is packed with interesting items given as gifts from every corner of the Commonwealth. The Institute is best known for its educational policy: kids can come along here to be shown everything from costumes to cookery in the activities department. Live drama performances and poetry recitals are often held here and the galleries, which show a healthy mixture of fine art and tribal art, are often and undeservedly neglected by the public. It's their loss, for the shows here can be as good as in any other London gallery.

Edwardes Square, W8

On the southern tip of this magnificent square at the western end of Kensington High Street, laid out in 1819, lies a small Tuscan temple which was originally a miniature summer house. The square is surrounded by artists' studios and beautiful houses. There is a famous story that this was the place where Napoleon's spies were based during the wars with Britain. It is now the London base for a number of international arts people including David Hockney, who normally lives in LA. You cannot gain access to the gardens in the square unless you get a key from someone who lives there, but it is worth walking past anyway as it shows nineteenth-century planning at its best.

Holland Park, W11

Open: summer
7.30 a.m.–9.30 p.m.,
winter
7.30 a.m.–4.30 p.m.

Holland Park is one of London's best-kept secrets. The streets and squares surrounding the park huddle together concealing most of the entrances and making sure that it remains well maintained and well hidden from those who do not live in the area. It's all on a hill, and though the Kensington High Street end is open, the Holland Park end is wooded. At the Abbotsbury Road entrance there is a car park which gets very crowded after midday. The best time to go is about 9 a.m., just before the locals bring their

strange-looking dogs into the park – it's not unusual to see Yorkshire terriers and shitzus with curlers around their ears and small boots on to keep their feet warm.

For children there are two play areas, one on either side of the car park. One is a one o'clock club, with a grassy area and sandpits, open on weekdays from 1 to 4 p.m. It's intended for children under five and their carers, and the club is supervised by experienced child leaders. It's free, as is the play park, set in a sheltered site and open daily from 10 a.m. to 6 p.m. Here there are swings, double towers, fire poles and a large slide and ramp, all built especially for those between five and sixteen who see themselves as small Schwarzeneggers. It could be a good place to rid yourself of troublesome kids – for ever.

At 10 a.m. the park cafe opens and is the perfect place for breakfast. It is run by an Italian family who take great pride in their selection of pastries and incredibly good cups of cappuccino. You can also get hot meals such as spaghetti bolognese or chilli and baked potato. Locals play chess here from early morning until late in the afternoon. They never seem to speak to each other and I have seen one bring an acoustic guitar to while away the time as his opponent plans his move. On these occasions it's probably better to stay inside, where the more tuneful Van Morrison can often be seen looking for inspiration in the shape of a cake. If another rendition of 'Mr Tambourine Man' is really getting you down there is always the Japanese garden through the woods at the top of the park. It genuinely captures something of the tranquillity and simplicity the Japanese find so important in their gardens, and if you do take children put them on a lead.

There are three walks through the woods – Chestnut, Lime Tree and Rose Walks – which will give you the chance to see some of the fifty or so different types of birds living here.

Most facilities in the park are free and the energetic can choose between a football pitch, tennis courts, putting green, golf nets and a cricket pitch, and in the summer there is also an open-air theatre.

Of the other things to see, Holland House, the only surviving example of a Jacobean house in London, is now a hostel for backpackers, and the Orangery occasionally puts on exhibitions by local artists.

Kensington Church Street, W8

This long winding street, one of London's most quaint and elegant, was once a country lane between Notting Hill and Kensington and was divided by a toll gate until 1864. You used to be able to walk around the original Kensington barracks but they were recently knocked down and replaced with the hideous shopping precinct which stands without much character at the Kensington end, and there are now few eighteenth-century houses along the street. Also at the Kensington End, however, is the Carmelite church of Our Lady of Mount Carmel and St Simon Stow, which was built in 1865 to the design of Pugin but bombed in 1944 and rebuilt by Sir Giles Gilbert Scott.

The shops along this street have a reputation for selling the very best antiques and fine art. There are a few choice restaurants but they tend to be at the Notting Hill end of the street (see Notting Hill), which seems to have a very different atmosphere.

Kensington Gardens, W8

William III and Queen Mary were responsible for creating Kensington Palace and the Gardens, which stretch all the way along Bayswater and along the boundary of Hyde Park. The Gardens are not what they were but the pond and the view of Kensington Palace are still worth walking to see. They are open to the public now but that was not always the case. In the eighteenth century George II opened the park to respectably dressed people and there is a famous story of his being robbed as he walked alone one morning. Apparently he needed to have one of the seals on his watch returned, so the robber duly brought it back to him the next day.

Close to the part of the Serpentine which comes under the bridge into the gardens are a few pieces of sculpture worth seeing – 'Peter Pan' by Sir George Frampton, and G. F. Watts's 'Physical Energy'. To the north there is a small children's playground with swings donated by J .M. Barrie, the creator of Peter Pan, and there is a beautiful oak carving by Ivor Innes, dating from 1928, in which elves and small children mingle.

The Orangery next to Kensington Palace is open

West

from May to October for afternoon tea and light meals.

Kensington Palace
Kensington Gardens W8
071-937 9561

Open: 1 October–31
March, Mon–Sat
9 a.m.–4.15 p.m., Sun
11 a.m.–4.15 p.m.; 1
April–30 September,
Mon–Sat
9 a.m.–4.45 p.m., Sun
11 a.m.–4.45 p.m.
Admission: adults
£3.90, children £2.50,
concessions £2.80

This was originally a Jacobean house dating from the mid-seventeenth century and purchased by the Earl of Nottingham who named it Nottingham House. In 1689 it was sold to William III and Queen Mary, who thought that the supposedly clean air of Kensington might help the King's asthma. England's most famous architects, Wren and Hawksmoor, were employed to rebuild the house and create a palace which the Queen was impatient to have finished very quickly. The King and Queen enjoyed the splendour of Kensington Palace, again employing Hawksmoor to change the Dutch-style gardens and the orangery back to a more English design.

Though Queen Anne allowed the place to fall into great disrepair, royalty has continued to live here. The Hanoverian line of Georges spent much of their time between trips to Germany at the palace, but the monarchy eventually settled into the even bigger and more splendid Buckingham Palace. Kensington Palace is now the home of the Princess of Wales, the Queen's sister Princess Margaret, Prince and Princess Michael of Kent and the Duke and Duchess of Gloucester. The state apartments are worth visiting and you can also get a sense of how royalty lived from the display of court dress from the seventeenth century to the 1920s. The winter cafe inside the apartments is open to the public from October to March, and in the Orangery is a restaurant which opens from April to September.

Kensington Palace Gardens, W8

This private road was laid out in 1843 by James Pennethorne and is lined with the most beautiful private mansions, which were most sought after by London's wealthy. The houses are now mainly embassies – the Lebanese, Nepalese, old Soviet Union and Czechoslovakian governments are, or were until recently, represented here; the road is a safe haven from potential extremists. Unauthorised vehicles are barred from the road but you can walk down it, though there is a checkpoint at each end and the entrances to each building fairly bristle with armed guards. The road itself, though, is still very quiet and mysterious and is a pleasant route by which to enter or leave Hyde Park or Kensington Gardens.

Kensington Town Hall

Hornton Street W8
071-937 5464,
071-937 2542 (library)

Open: library: Mon,
Tues, Thurs, Fri
10 a.m.–8 p.m., Wed
10 a.m.–1 p.m., Sat
10 a.m.–5 p.m.

This odd-looking building, the adminstrative centre of the Royal Borough of Kensington and Chelsea, was designed by Sir Basil Spence and completed in 1976. I lived opposite it for many years and after a period of hating everything to do with it grew to admire it greatly. There are pieces of sculpture lying all around this brick complex, including such works as 'River Form' by Barbara Hepworth and 'Worshipper' by Jacob Epstein. The camp-looking gilded figure on top of the adjoining library was made by William Mac-Millan to serve as a lightning conductor. The library has a big bright room which you don't have to join to use, so if you're in the mood for a quiet read in studious conditions, use this place.

Kensington Village, W8

Kensington Village is the name given to a very small area just off the beaten track, behind Barkers department store. Surrounded by leafy plane trees, it has a few shops and restaurants and it gives you an idea of what Kensington used to be like.

Kensington is small enough to walk around in a couple of hours, and the walk from the park through De Vere Gardens – named after the original owners of the land around Kensington – takes you past the London home of American writer Henry James and into the narrow lanes of the old village. None of the shops is too exciting, but the walk is pleasant enough. Walking around St Alban's Grove takes you back up through Kensington Square, which has had a whole host of famous residents, including the pre-Raphaelite painter Burne Jones, Hubert Parry – who composed the music for 'Jerusalem'. The great William Makepeace Thackeray, who wrote *Vanity Fair* and Pendennis, lived at Number 16.

Leighton House

12 Holland Park Road
W14
071-602 3316

Open: Mon–Sat
11 a.m.–5.30 p.m.
Admission: donations
welcome

Built in 1866, Leighton House was once the home of Lord Leighton, who was one of the most fashionable painters of his time. While on his travels he discovered a taste for the exotic and would return home laden down with the ceramics and textiles from North Africa which he preferred to the stuffiness of English Victoriana. Although he was very hospitable he always chucked friends out by bedtime – he built only one bedroom and so never had room for any guests to stay. Presumably breakfast in Leighton House was a quiet affair. The Arab Hall was added in 1876/7.

The house itself has beautiful mosaic fountains and pre-Raphaelite paintings from the likes of Burne-Jones and Millais, and small concerts regularly take place in the music rooms upstairs where Leighton entertained his many friends, and for a few moments you can feel yourself taken back in time as you enjoy the magnificence of the house and its garden. Leighton House is one of London's forgotten treasures and its doors are open to everyone and anyone willing to make the effort to come. Guided tours are available and cost £1.50.

Linley Sambourne House
18 Stafford Terrace W8
081-994 1019
(Victorian Society)

Open: Mar–Oct, Sun
2-5 p.m., Wed
10 a.m.–4 p.m
Admission: £2,
concessions £1

Linley Sambourne, the Punch cartoonist, lived here from 1874 to his death in 1920. The house was presented to the nation in 1980 and the Victorian Society is now responsible for it. Everything, from the decoration, the wallpaper and the layout of furniture is the way it was in the 1890s, when Punch was the best magazine in London. The magazine finally folded in 1992, when the readership fell to an all-time low and the biting satire of the past turned into something much softer and unwanted. The house gives you an idea of the style of the time and of the way a cultured and artistic family home looked.

Melbury Road, W8

It's worth taking a walk down this small street just to peer into the huge houses which were once bohemian retreats for Victorian artists, though few artists could afford to live here now. These days the interiors of the houses have changed a good deal but the look of the street is really no different. Aleister Crowley, the occultist and black magician, lived in the sinister neo-Gothic house at number 29 which now belongs to Led Zeppelin guitarist Jimmy Page, who is obsessed with Crowley. Next door lives the filmmaker Michael Winner, who told me that each room in Page's house has a different theme, though the closest I have ever got was a quick look over the garden wall.

St Mary Abbot's Church
Kensington Church
Street W8
071-937 5136

Located on the corner of Kensington Church Street and Kensington High Street, this church was founded in the twelfth century. It was rebuilt in the fourteenth century and again in the seventeenth, and was finally restored in 1869 by the great architect Sir Giles Gilbert Scott. Behind the church is a charming little street,

Kensington Church Walk, which runs to the west of the church. It's approached via the church grounds, or you can go up Kensington Church Street, take the first left and go left again down a little path. There are a few shops here, none of which is particularly interesting, but the walk itself and the small garden area are very tranquil and suitable for getting away from the hubbub of the High Street.

The Serpentine Gallery
Kensington Gardens W2
071-723 9072

Open: 10 a.m.–6 p.m.
No admission charge

Situated in the middle of Kensington Gardens, this small gallery is one of the most radical in London. The Serpentine works superbly because the space is stimulating and always well used, and the setting is magnificent. From the abstract landscapes of Ivor Hutchins to Andy Warhol's photographs, it has seldom failed to capture the critics' imagination. Each year in January and February it shows a selection of work from the Barclays Young Artist Awards, and in early May there's Broken English, a show of work by young British artists.
The bookshop here is a small but very good.

EATING, DRINKING AND SLEEPING

The Ark
35 Kensington High Street W8
071-937 4294

Open: lunch, Mon–Fri midday–3 p.m., dinner, Mon–Sat 7–11.15 p.m.
Credit: A, Amex, V
Average: £35

The Ark was the first proper restaurant I ever went to. I was taken by a girlfriend who knew all about this type of thing, and I remember feeling embarrassed as I couldn't speak French and had never chosen wine other than cheap rubbish. But in a matter of seconds the people here made me feel totally at ease. The food was delicious and a bottle of house wine served me well. That was over fifteen years ago and today the Ark looks as if very little has changed. There's no need for this kind of place to change as the interior is classically elegant and the menu has enough changes to last a lifetime. The trad French dishes here such as champignons de campagne and grilled steak are magnificent.

The Belvedere
New Lodge, Holland Park W8
071-602 1238

Open: lunch, Mon–Sun

Though there has been a restaurant here for some time, it's never really caught the public's imagination, which is strange as the setting is perfect and the building, which looks like an old country house, is welcoming. However, in 1991 new management took over the restaurant and this old ballroom of the house

midday–3 p.m., dinner,
Mon–Sat 7–10.30 p.m.
Credit: A, Amex, DC, V
Average: £50

has been transformed into a fashionable place attracting the local glitterati as well as foodies. As the park looks well all year round, there's always a romantic atmosphere. The food falls into the rather nebulous category of Modern British, and though the results are patchy there are some very special dishes to be had here. On Sundays they provide brunch and children are very welcome. The Belvedere will give you a great meal in a terrific setting – what more could you ask?

Cafe Gstaad
Kensington Shopping
Mall, Kensington High
Street W8
071-938 1110

Open: Mon–Sat
7 a.m.–6.30 p.m., Sun
9 a.m.–4 p.m.
No credit cards
Average: £10

Tucked between the shops in the arcade leading towards High Street Kensington tube station is this little open-plan cafe, which is a big favourite with local office workers and tourists. The sandwiches range from egg mayonnaise to Italian salami and watercress (£1.70), and the coffee is good enough to warrant a visit. You can have hot meals such as lasagne or cottage pie at £3.30 or chicken risotto at £2.80, but I feel that the cafe is too much part of the station complex to make me want to spend too much time here.

Church's
20 Kensington Church
Street W8
071-938 2336

Open: Mon–Fri
11 a.m.–11 p.m.
Credit: A, Amex, DC, V
Average: £30

This small basement wine bar is popular with local students, especially English-language students, and rag-trade people, who seem to spend half their time here. Though I lived nearby for several years I never once came in the door until very recently, when I found it perfectly pleasant, although some of the clientele were a little flash for my liking. The food varies between standard British fare such as pie and chips to home-made pizzas and fish dishes. A good place for a drink or a meal.

Cibo
3 Russell Gardens W14
071-371 6271

Open: Mon–Fri, lunch
midday–2.30 p.m.,
dinner 7–11 p.m., Sat
dinner 7–11 p.m., Sun
lunch
12.30–3.30 p.m.,
dinner 7–10.30 p.m.
Credit: A, Amex, DC, V
Average: £50

The small area between Shepherd's Bush, Kensington and Holland Park is one of the most expensive places in London to live, which makes it surprising that there has for so long been such a shortage of good places to eat here. Cibo, however, is changing all that. The food includes dishes such as scallops or risotto with wild mushrooms as starters. For a main course you could try the very special sea bass or the sauteed calves' liver with aubergines, peppers and courgettes. I have found, however, that the fish dishes tend to be even better than the meat, which sometimes disappears beneath various sauces. Their two-course 'lunch for a tenner' is an absolute bargain. The wine list features a good selection of Italian wines but is a bit on the expensive side.

The Greyhound
1 Kensington Square
W8
071-937 7140

Open: Mon–Sat
11 a.m.–11 p.m., Sun
midday–3 p.m.,
7–10.30 p.m.
Credit: A, Amex, DC, V
Average: £18

This pub is a favourite with the people from Kensington Market, which means that it gets a very mixed bag of very different-looking folks drinking and playing snooker in the back room. It's a decent, clean bar and the beer is not overpriced considering the exotic location of Kensington Square, but don't ask for something difficult like a cup of coffee. By bar standards the food is adequate, and they do various home-made pies at lunchtime. Try a steak and kidney pie with veg, and for dessert chocolate fudge cake or apple and sultana sponge.

Halcyon Hotel
81 Holland Park W11
071-727 7288

Credit: A, Amex, DC, V
Average: £235 for a
double room

After years behind scaffolding this hotel, situated on the corner of Holland Park Avenue and Abbotsbury Road, surfaced and immediately became the latest darling of visiting film and pop stars. There are 43 rooms here, a mixture of rooms and suites. It is very informal and yet retains a plush atmosphere in which deals can be struck over power breakfasts and lazy pop stars can plot ways in which to spend lots of money. It just manages to avoid pomposity, but if you can afford it better service will not be found in London. The only problem or benefit, depending on how you want to look at it, is that you might have to sit at a table beside the likes of Jim Kerr or Matt Dillon. The restaurant and bar are open to non-residents.

Hiroko
Kensington Hilton, 179
Holland Park Avenue
W11
071-603 5003

Open: Tues–Sun, lunch
midday–2.15, dinner
6–10.15 p.m.
Credit: A, Amex, DC, V
Average: £70

The restaurant is always busy and is very popular with visiting or resident Japanese, which is something I've never understood as the service is slow, the atmosphere sterile and the prices very high. It is close to the BBC and to its many satellite production companies, and that also gives it a good deal of custom, but I think it's one of those places where you go mainly to be seen. Hiroko is a favourite with record-company people who probably feel that sushi leaves you feeling about ready for the next line or two. Pop stars come here in numbers and table-hop at an alarming rate in their bid to be noticed. It can be a very sad sight.

The pine loving room serves up good portions of sushi and sashimi, but as is usual in Japanese

Julie's Wine Bar
137 Portland Road
W11
071-727 7985;
restaurant 071-229
8331

Open: wine bar, lunch
11.30–2.45, tea
4-6 p.m., dinner
7–10.45 p.m.;
restaurant – lunch,
Mon–Fri
12.30–2.45 p.m., Sun
12.30–3 p.m., dinner,
Mon–Sat
7.30–11.15 p.m., Sun
7.30–10.15 p.m.
Credit: A, Amex, V
Average: £60

Launceston Place
1a Launceston Place W8
071-937 6912

Open: lunch, Mon–Fri,
Sun 12.30–2.30 p.m.,
dinner Mon–Sat
7.30–11.30 p.m.
Credit: A, Amex, V
Average: £50

Maggie Jones
6 Old Court Place,
Kensington Church
Street W8
071-937 6462

restaurants there is not a lot available for vegetarians. Set lunches and dinners are available.

Of the downstairs restaurant and upstairs conservatory here, both are reliable but up is better than down. In the conservatory at about 3.30 p.m. afternoon tea is served complete with freshly baked scones, cream, jam and all those heart-attack-inducing goodies nobody in their right minds should eat. I always have a problem with jam as I used to pick fruit as a child working in the Perthshire area of Scotland and saw terrible things added to the berries to increase their weight. I am positive that Julie's jam is free of Scotsman's jam thickener.

The place itself plays on its Englishness a bit too much for me, but its mixture of Victorian gentility and seventies hippie gothicness makes it worth a trip. The people who manage the bar have a decent attitude and don't aspire to any kind of snobbishness. You can sit here quite comfortably for an hour over a cup of tea, reading one of the newspapers which they supply. The food in the downstairs restaurant is mainly English with a hint of French, and is always good.

This is the quiet cousin of the *très* fashionable Kensington Place, but is a better place to go for various reasons, including the service and the lack of a pecking order in deciding who sits where and who is able to get a table. The menu concentrates on solid dishes which are well tested and tasted here by a steady local clientele. The chef, Charles Mumford, knows exactly who he is catering for and always comes up with the goods. The menu is varied enough to appeal to most people but, unless you are a vegetarian of course, I recommend you try his meat dishes. Otherwise, go for the grilled liver or the poached salmon which not only taste wonderful but are good for you as well.

This restaurant is rumoured to be named after Princess Margaret who lives in the nearby Kensington Palace and whose married name was Armstrong-Jones. The touch of Englishness in the name is reflected in the menu – everything is cooked in ye olde style. Fish pies, steak and kidney pies, rack of

Open: lunch
12.30–3 p.m., dinner
6.30–11 p.m.
Credit: A, Amex, V
Average: £50

lamb, and rabbit and mustard casserole are all available at a main-course price of about £11. The wine comes in huge bottles and at the end of your meal is measured by a stick so you pay only for what you had. Upstairs the seats are in booths surrounded by hunting pictures and dripping candles. It's a great place to go with a bunch of people – try to take the big table in the middle which sits about twelve people.

The Muffin Man
12 Wrights Lane W8
071-937 6652

Open: Mon–Sat
8 a.m.–5.30 p.m.
No credit cards
Average: £10

This busy little breakfast and tea cafe caters well for the tourists in the nearby hotels. The waitresses wear rather traditional uniforms and dish up helpings of cream and scones and pots of English Breakfast or Indian teas. It's quieter in the mornings and they do a good cooked breakfast. Try a cream tea – £3.80 per person for a pot of tea, two scones, jam and cream. The traditional set tea is even yummier, with tea, cucumber and tomato sandwiches and a choice of cake, all for under a fiver.

Palms
3 Campden Hill Road
W8
071-938 1830

Open:
9.45 a.m.–midnight
Credit: A, V
Average: £25

Palms is an example of how good fast food can be served up night after night. On Saturdays it's always packed, with a mixed clientele of tourists, shoppers from the nearby Kensington High Street and local regulars. The menu is based on grills, salads and pasta dishes – grilled salmon steak is £7.45, goats'-cheese salad is £6.50 and for starters (average £3) you could try whitebait or minestrone soup. The place has a very light feel to it, and is full of palms and other plants.

Phoenicia Restaurant
11–13 Abingdon Road
W8
071-937 0120

Open:
12.15–11.45 p.m.
Credit: A, Amex, DC, V
Average: £28

Lebanese restaurants have sprung up all over Kensington since the early seventies, when a community of Lebanese people settled in West London. Phoenicia, situated in a small, leafy street, is one of the few which have managed to withstand the test of time and it's one of the most popular Lebanese restaurants in London. The afternoon menu offers a set buffet lunch (£8.95) with a selection of traditional dishes such as okra with tomatoes and hummus, as well as the delicious tabouleh, a mixture of chopped parsley, tomatoes, crushed wheat, olive oil and lemon juice. A meze (set meal with many small courses) costs about £15 per person, and the buffet is a real bargain.

La Pomme d'Amour
128 Holland Park
Avenue W11
071-229 8532

Open: lunch, Mon–Fri
12.30–2.15 p.m.,
dinner, Mon–Sat
7–10.45 p.m.
Credit: A, Amex, DC, V
Average: £45

This extremely old-fashioned French restaurant has a pleasant conservatory at the back, and the front is hidden from Holland Park by thick curtains which look more Louis XIV than nouvelle cuisine. The food has not changed an iota over the years and neither has the clientele, which is mainly made up of Holland Park swells or BBC executives having secretive meetings. In the evenings it's a place to go for an old-style, quiet, romantic evening, but don't expect to try out new ideas in French cooking. Their set menus are reasonably priced and much more economical than going à la carte.

The Prince of Wales
14 Princedale Road
W11
071-727 0045

Open: Mon–Sat
11.30 a.m.–11 p.m.,
Sun midday–3 p.m.,
7–10.30 p.m.
No credit cards
Average: £16

The locals like to play games in this pub, which has survived the wear and tear of its punters and changed hardly at all over the years. In the late seventies and early eighties it was a favourite with up and coming young pop stars but has now returned to a kind of Holland Park gentility where nothing much ever happens apart from arguments about the prowess of the women's darts team compared with that of the men, or some such matter of local importance. Although a bit dowdy, the pub has pretensions to olde-worlde charm. Food in the ground-floor restaurant is a mixture of French, English and Italian cooking.

The Stick and Bowl
31 Kensington High
Street W8
071-937 2778

Open:
11.30 a.m.–11 p.m.
No credit cards
Average: £10

This small Chinese restaurant lies next door to Kensington Market. The food comes from the same kitchen as the more upmarket restaurant next door but is less than half the price. The place is very popular with West London's Chinese students and is always busy at lunchtimes and during the evenings. The restaurant is very small and not very well known but once you go there you'll be hooked, as the egg fried rice and duck dishes are as good as any I have had in Chinatown. All the dishes are available to take away and there's beer or house wine, as well as traditional Chinese tea, to drink.

Wodka
12 St Alban's Grove
W8
071-937 6513

Open: lunch, Mon–Fri
12.30–2.30 p.m.,

As soon as you get in the door try a glass of honey vodka (£2.25) or a half-bottle of frozen Zubrowka, which is bison-grass vodka – either one will sort you out for a very special evening.

Wodka is different from other Polish restaurants in that it is aimed at a younger market. Most of the people who come here end up drinking a lot, which

dinner, Mon–Sun
7.15–11 p.m.
Credit: A, Amex, DC, V
Average: £40

must be hard work for the people who have to serve them, but they never seem to complain. It's a great place to get drunk and stick your face into some northern Polish cuisine. I recommend the golabki – cabbage stuffed with minced pork, rice and cranberry sauce.

SHOPPING

Amazon
22 Kensington Church
Street W8
071-376 0630

Open: Mon–Sat
10 a.m.–6.30 p.m.
Credit: A, Amex, DC, V

If the world looks gloomy and you're fed up with London's weather one solution is to spend, spend, spend. Amazon is a good and not too expensive place to head for if you're in that kind of mood. There are five shops all virtually next door to each other on Kensington Church Street, and in the main shops they have almost permanent sales, where you can get a jacket reduced from £69 to £35, and silk shirts at about £15. Because the clothes seem such bargains, there's always the chance that you could come out of here with more than one outfit, which is something you could never do on the over-zealous trap of Sloane Street. Amazon also stocks the stunningly cut clothes of Nicole Farhi and Matinique for both men and women.

In the men's section, trousers range from £30 to £80 and shirts, depending on the material and the pattern, could leave you with change out of £50. Women's clothes range from very cheap seconds and end of ranges (In-Wear, French Connection) to more expensive lines, but are always good value. All considered, this makes Amazon one of the few clothes shops in the area outside Hyper-Hyper and Ken Market really worth a visit.

Anta
141 Portland Road
W11
071-229 5077

Open: Tues–Sat
10 a.m.–5.30 p.m.
Credit: A, Amex, V

Every conceivable tartan – though barely a single authentic one – is on show here, used for carpets, curtains, wallpaper, cups, plates, salad bowls and kimonos. Like traditional tartans themselves, the stock here is funny, useful and kitsch, and you can decorate your home from top to bottom in a way that will make you step a-gaily as soon as you wake.

The brains behind Anta are Lachie and Annie Stewart, who live with their family on the wild northeast coast of Scotland, past the Black Isle. They are currently redeveloping a twelfth-century castle overlooking the sea and hope to have put their

pinks, purples and greys all over the old limestone by the turn of the century. They use local craftspeople to realise their designs and although their main showroom is here in Holland Park, the best place to see what they have to offer is up north.

Barkers of Kensington
63 Kensington High Street W8
071-937 5432

Open: Mon–Wed, Fri 10 a.m.–6.30 p.m., Thurs 10 a.m.–7 p.m., Sat 9.30 a.m.–6.30 p.m.
Credit: A, Amex, DC, V

Until recently this was where Kensingtonians bought their household appliances, makeup and bits and pieces for the garden. However, during the design boom of the eighties Barkers began to look a bit tired and dowdy. Part of the ground-floor section of the store was sold off – now the Barkers Arcade, it is home to several high-street shops such as the very successful chains Jigsaw, Hobb, Principles and Warehouse, all of which have benefited from having such a prestigious shopfront in what is the main part of Kensington High Street. Barkers alone could never have managed to give a fresh and younger look to what is essentially a quiet and middle-class area. The department store still thrives, though, and on its four floors sells everything you'd expect a department store to sell. It also has a restaurant and a coffee shop.

Bernard J. Shapero
80 Holland Park Avenue W11
071-493 0876

Open: Mon–Fri 10 a.m.–7 p.m., Sat 10 a.m.–5 p.m.
Credit: A, Amex, DC, V

During the summer the congestion along Holland Park Avenue can be poisonous as cars, buses and taxis race towards the M4 and Heathrow, or the M40 and Oxford, shrouding the grandeur of the houses in a polluted mist. Relief can be found in the antiquarian world of number 80, where books on travel, art and architecture mix happily with history and fiction. It's a spacious shop where delightful surprises can be found. Forgotten books take pride of place here and first editions in great condition are always available – at prices ranging from £12 to £20,000.

Crabtree and Evelyn
6 Kensington Church Street W8
071-937 9335

Open: Mon–Wed, Fri, Sat 9.30 a.m.–6 p.m., Thurs 9.30 a.m.–7 p.m.
Credit: A, Amex, V

Crabtree and Evelyn is, funnily enough, an American company which has made a great success out of selling a slightly phoney Englishness back to the English. Bath gels, powders, creams, ointments, baskets of soap and old English teas are all for sale here and give you something of an idea of the image they have manufactured for themselves. However, the scented soaps here are superb, ranging from avocado to strawberry, and the range of Beatrix Potter-type accessories are so twee that they're forgivable – a Peter Rabbit bowl is a good gift. I only make the effort to come here at Christmas, but it's worth more visits than that.

Cullens
112 Holland Park
Avenue W11
071-221 7139

Open: 8 a.m.–10 p.m.
Credit: A, V

Cullens is a chain of delis which has recently sprung up all over London, offering late-night shoppers a better chance of getting something palatable to eat. They have attempted to offer a range of cheeses, breads and pastas which all require little or no effort to serve up once you get them home, and they also have a range of frozen menu dishes which cost between £2 and £4. The bread is baked on the premises. The shops are all licensed and they also stock 'emergency' goods such as toothpaste and washing-up liquid. It's a little more expensive than most local stores but the quality is good and you can depend on them to be open when they say they will.

Early Learning Centre
225 High Street
Kensington W8
071-937 0419

Open: Mon–Fri
9 a.m.–6 p.m.
Credit: A, V

Whether you have children or not, this store is well worth a visit – the books and toys on sale here have all been thoughtfully designed so that the kids who receive them get maximum educational benefit from them. From My First Sony – a small, own-make karaoke machine costing £19.99 – to plastic fruit which you can cut and put together again, the toys are marvellous. There are books available to suit the youngest babies and children up to about nine years old. There's a section of the shop set aside for children to play with the toys and basically run riot. A terrific shop you'll enjoy as much as the kids.

Frog Hollow
15 Victoria Grove W8
071-581 5493

Open: Mon–Sat
9 a.m.–5.30 p.m., Sun
11 a.m.–5.30 p.m.
Credit: A, Amex, V

This is my favourite kids' shop in London; it sells an enormous range of items related to frogs, as well as what is supposedly the largest collection of soft toys in London. The frogs pulled me in as my daughter reminded me of one when she was small, as she never crawled but pushed herself around on her bottom and leapt from place to place. Here you can get frog soap which wears away to reveal a little prince hiding inside (£4.99) or great bobbing frog bathplugs. There are lots of other novelties here which make Frog Hollow a delight for kids and possibly even more of a delight for adults.

Hyper-Hyper
26 Kensington High
Street W8
071-938 4343

Unlike the traders in Kensington Market, many of whom concentrate on cheap and cheerful tat, the stallholders here (about 65 of them) are trying to sell upmarket goods at cheaper prices. Young designers

Open: Mon–Wed, Fri,
Sat 10 a.m.–6 p.m.,
Thurs 10 a.m.–7 p.m.
Credit: ask

ignored by the fashion magazines – Pam Hogg started here before she moved to Newburgh Street (see Soho) – sell their wares to a strange collection of shoppers, some of whom are only here to look at the rather odd-looking people who work here. It looks like the designers do their apprenticeship in the cheaper Kensington Market and then move over here when they feel the time is right to climb the ladder. Trousers cost on average £40 to £90, jackets are between £60 and £200 and a dress will cost you anything from £40 to £200.

At the back of the basement in Hyper-Hyper there is an old pullman railway car which is now used as a restaurant and cafe. The food is nothing special but the coffee is good and they have a decent selection of pastries.

Kensington Market

Kensington High Street
W8
071-938 4343

Open: Mon–Sat
10 a.m.–6 p.m.
Credit: ask

When I was in a punk band in the late seventies and early eighties, I spent half my life in this place. It is very easy to get lost in this never-ending tunnel of stalls (about 100 in all). The market has three levels where you can buy anything from an old biker jacket to a good pair of second-hand jeans, get your hair done or have a tattoo. Some stalls – such as retro specialists Johnsons on the first floor – have been there for years but each new trend brings an onslaught of backroom designers trying to sell their wares. Some of the goods on sale are not good quality-wise, but the prices are reasonably low for most items of clothing. There are a few places to have your hair cut or have a cup of coffee and a sandwich – all of which are pretty basic – and a couple of specialist record stalls in the basement dealing in old punk records and new dance labels.

C. Lidgate

110 Holland Park
Avenue W11
071-727 8243

Open: Mon–Fri
7.30 a.m.–6 p.m., Sat
7.30 a.m.–5 p.m.
No credit cards

In my time I have lived all over London, and once ended up next door to this old-style butcher's shop, which could easily give you the impression that you are in a rural village rather than a huge city. Though I'm not a vegetarian I've never been a great meat eater, and eventually found living here too much to deal with. However, the herb sausages and the cuts of meat are so exceptional that I'm sure even veggies stare jealously in the window at times. You can get organic and grass-fed beef and lamb here, as well as pork and a whole range of game, including venison and wild boar. They also stock free-range eggs, olive oils, cheeses and chutneys and oils, and the incredibly helpful staff will give you advice on how best to cook the meats you have chosen. It's the best butcher's in London.

Maison Blanc
102 Holland Park
Avenue W11
071-221 2494

Open: Mon–Sat
8 a.m.–7.30 p.m., Sun
8.45-5.40 p.m.
Credit: A. V

This authentic French patisserie is the brainchild of the ex-wife of the famous chef Raymond Blanc and is a welcome addition to Holland Park's eateries. The idea behind Maison Blanc is simple and very French: a selection of fresh breads and pastries which change subtly from day to day but which are all delicious. Campaillou and pain de campagne are highly recommended, as are the delicious religieuse chocolat and tarte aux poires. Gorgeous.

D. Mellor and A. L. Baxter
121 Kensington Church
Street W8
071-229 2033

Open: Mon–Fri
10 a.m.–6.30 p.m.,
Sat 10 a.m.–4 p.m.
Credit: A, Amex, DC, V

This antiquarian bookshop deals in the sciences, literature, medicine, travel, history and medieval manuscripts. It has recently been expanded to take in two shopfronts and has books pouring out of the walls on four floors. The less expensive books are in the basement, but their incredible selection of first editions are all on the first floor. They also restore books, which is done in front of you and adds to the interest of the visit. Prices for the books start at around £5 and go up into the thousands.

Russell's Nursery
80 Earls Court Road
W8
071-937 0481

Open: Mon–Wed, Fri,
Sat 9 a.m.–5.30 p.m.,
Thurs 9 a.m.–6.30 p.m.
No credit cards

It's difficult to imagine finding a cheap garden centre with a good selection of plants in the middle of London, but that's exactly what this small, family-run business is. The people here take great pride in offering advice on perennial plants as well as the problems of planting new ones, especially in a city garden. Miniature pine trees, clematis (from £6) and traditional Japanese paeonia shrubs (from £5) are available here, as well as tree paeonias, which start at £9–£10.

Snow and Rock
188 Kensington High
Street W8
071-937 0872

Open: Mon–Fri
10 a.m.–8 p.m., Sat
9 a.m.–6 p.m., Sun
11 a.m.–5 p.m.

When this place first opened I felt that surely there couldn't be enough skiing and mountain climbing enthusiasts in London to support such a huge specialist store. I obviously never realised just how popular these activities are.

Everything you could ever need for the slopes is available here, from fashion accessories to harnesses and boots that could take you to the summit of Mont Blanc. Ski suits cost between about £150 and £600,

(winter only)
Credit: A, Amex, V

and there is a very comprehensive selection of climbing gear for everyone from the casual hill walker to Chris Bonnington.

Trailfinders
194 Kensington High
Street W8
071-938 3444

Open: Mon–Wed, Fri,
Sat 9 a.m.–6 p.m.,
Thurs 9 a.m.–7 p.m.,
Sun 10 a.m.–2 p.m.
Credit: A, Amex, DC, V

This travel agency can sort out any obscure holiday you can think of. They specialise in walking trips over the Andes or Himalayas, as well as trips into the depths of the rainforests or the jungle, and they can plan the cheapest way around the world for you, however long or short you want your trip to be. Although they are primarily a travel agency for the independent long-haul traveller, they also carry a comprehensive book and map section with an emphasis on Africa and Australia. Linked to the agency is the very useful Trailfinders travellers' clinic, where you can get your jabs and so on before heading off – call 071-938 3999 for details. Many of the Australians who arrive in England are on a Trailfinders package of which London is one stop in many.

Waterstone's
193 Kensington High
Street W8
071-937 8432

Open: Mon–Fri
9.30 a.m.–9 p.m., Sat
9.30 a.m.–7 p.m., Sun
11 a.m.–6 p.m.Credit:
A, V

There are three levels to this branch of Waterstone's, which is one of the best in London. In the basement are books dealing with subjects such as sociology and history; on the ground floor is fiction, old and new, as well as a good travel section; and the first floor holds a large art section with a huge selection of beautifully put together and very expensive books. The staff here definitely know what they are doing and are very helpful, whether it's the works of Barbara Cartland or Martin Amis you're trying to find.

ENTERTAINMENT

Kensington Odeon
263 Kensington High
Street W8
071-371 3166
(bookings), 0426-914
666 (programme details)

Credit: A, V

This complex houses six large cinemas, all offering up the latest Hollywood commercial films. It's not a bad place to come and see epics, as the sound quality and the screens are quite good, but it's a pity the management hasn't realised that cinema-goers are no longer happy with only popcorn and hot dogs. New complexes up and down the country offer up good food and bars, yet the Odeon resists change and has stayed the same year after year.

On Fridays and Saturdays there are late-night showings which are very popular with the local lovers who snog their way through the evening, which can be unfortunate for you if you end up beside them – especially if the film is terrible.

THE COMMONWEALTH INSTITUTE

KNIGHTSBRIDGE

*t*he name Knightsbridge comes from the bridge that crossed the Westbourne river around the spot at the southern end of Hyde Park where the Albert Gate now stands. Since the eleventh century this stretch was known as a place where knights and young blades would duel or fight, giving the area a dangerous reputation made worse by a rash of hold-ups by highwaymen. The tradition of highway robbery remains today, carried on by Knightsbridge's outrageously expensive shops which supposedly offer the best of everything but at a price which would intimidate most of us. The military connection also remains, with the barracks designed by Sir Basil Spence dominating the horizon by Hyde Park in a much unloved manner.

Knightsbridge changed dramatically after the Great Exhibition of 1851, the brainchild of Queen Victoria's husband Prince Albert. A cathedral-like glass building, housed over 100,000 exhibits from all over the world, and before it was taken down 6,000,000 people had visited this celebration of art and invention. The areas known as Knightsbridge and South Kensington would never again be quiet and rural; the exhibition had brought wealth and gentrification to rough fields and quite dangerous spots. I think Knightsbridge lacks soul, but what it does have are three of the best museums in Europe, all sitting next to each other. The Victoria and Albert Museum, the Natural History Museum and the Science Museum (see separate entries) look awesome and a bit intimidating, but they

are worth discovering. Don't wander in at random, as they are too large to cover in a day, but choose certain specific parts to visit.

Knightsbridge's main street of shame has to be Sloane Street, where high-fashion shops sell their bits of cloth for the price of a home. This long avenue, which joins Knightsbridge to Sloane Square and Chelsea, was planned by Henry Holland in the late eighteenth century. Edgar Allan Poe went to school here and Oscar Wilde fell from grace as a consequence of his afternoons of pleasure at the Cadogan Hotel.

Along the top end of Queen's Gate and the southern stretch of Hyde Park is the Royal College of Art, whose degree shows in June and July are always worth a visit – try and see if you can spot the next David Hockney or Frank Auerbach. It sits in the shadow of the enormous Royal Albert Hall, an ugly building much loved by the British, in which the annual Proms concerts take place from the end of July until mid-September and where the likes of Eric Clapton play regular concerts.

Hyde Park is the largest of London's parks, and was used as hunting grounds by Henry VIII. It was first opened to the public in the seventeenth century, and today wealthy Knightsbridge residents use it as their back garden, walking their dogs and children and indeed horses through it, often in the early hours.

HOW TO GET THERE

Tubes
- High Street Kensington
- Hyde Park Corner
- Knightsbridge
- Sloane Square
- South Kensington

Buses
- Brompton Road: 14
- Cromwell Road: 14, 74, C1
- Gloucester Road: 49
- Grosvenor Place: 2A, 2B, 8, 16, 36, 38, 52, 73, 82
- Kensington Road: 9, 9A, 10, 52, C1
- Sloane Street: 19, 22, 137, 137A, C1

EMPORIO ARMANI

SIGHTS AND SITES

All Saints Church
Ennismore Gardens
SW7
071-584 0096

Open: before and after
services
Services: Sun and Great
Feast Days, Divine
Liturgy 10.30 a.m.; Sat,
vigil service 5.30 p.m.;
eves of Great Feasts,
vigil service 6 p.m.
More frequent services
on Feast Days and
during Lent (ring for
details).

Built as a 'weekday' church by Lewis Vuilliamy in 1846 for the local gentry, who disappeared to the country at weekends, All Saints gradually fell into disuse in the 1930s and 1940s. In 1953 it was taken over by the Russian Orthodox Church who have made it their Cathedral for Great Britain and Ireland and have dedicated it to All Saints and of the Assumption of the Mother God. Vuilliamy, who also built St Michael's Chapel in Highgate, modelled the Church on St Zeno's in Verona, and the West Front, added in 1896 by Cecil Harrison Townsend, is absolutely identical to St Zeno's. The murals of biblical saints inside, designed by Heywood Sumner, are a wonderful example of the Arts and Crafts style so popular in Britain in the late nineteenth century. The tall iron Corinthian columns, a gallery running on three sides and a small clerestory make All Saints one of the prettiest churches in this part of London. Go to one of the wonderful choral Orthodox services and take in the atmosphere.

**The Natural History
Museum**
Cromwell Road SW7
071-938 9123

Open: Mon–Sat
10 a.m.–5.50 p.m.,
Sun 11 a.m.–5.50 p.m.
No credit cards
Admission: adults £4,
children £2,
concessions £2.30

Designed in 1873 by Alfred Waterhouse, who also designed Strangeways prison, to house the natural history collection of the British Museum, the Natural History Museum is a very beautiful building. The elaborate terracotta decoration by Sir Richard Owen, the first museum superintendent, is specially worth a look. As soon as you enter the museum itself you are faced with a 150-million-year-old diplodocus dinosaur, and its 26-metre-long body is truly awesome. Its brothers and sisters are now housed in a special permanent dinosaur exhibition, stunningly designed and featuring animatronic dinosaurs sure to delight the kids, as well as interactive displays and astonishing models. Also worth a special look is a cross-section of a Sequoia redwood tree, with dates such as the birth of Christ and the Norman Conquest marked on its rings – the sight gives you an incredible sense of the passage of time.

The collection here is so huge that the museum can only display a small part of it at any one time, and it really is impossible to take in everything at one visit – much better to see one or two sections at a time. The ground floor has a very good information desk where you can get a good plan of the museum –

places worth a special mention include the Darwin Room and the Mammal Room. The Natural History Museum repays any amount of visits. There is a gift shop and a cafe which is only average but which can be a very welcome place to rest your feet.

Oratory of St Philip Neri (Brompton Oratory)
Brompton Road SW7
071-589 4811

This is without doubt one of London's most beautiful churches. It was designed in 1884 by Herbert Gribble and until Westminster Cathedral was built in 1903 it was the chief place of worship for London's Catholics. Because it is so beautiful it is still popular, especially for weddings and baptisms. Inside, the triptych depicting Thomas More and John Fisher at their Tyburn execution was painted by Rex Whistler, the lady altar is from Brescia and St Winifred's chapel is Flemish. The Church is known to Londoners as the Brompton Oratory, but it is actually named after St Philip, who founded the institute of the Oratory in Rome. Its location was unpopular at first, as Brompton was then seen as a rural neighbourhood of second-rate gentry and second-rate shops. Sunday Mass here, however, is an experience beyond such things as class and shopping, and the choir would make even an atheist's heart melt. Live classical performances have also proved to be very popular here.

The Science Museum
Exhibition Road SW7
071-938 8000

Open: Mon–Sat
10 a.m.–6 p.m., Sun
11 a.m.–6 p.m.
Credit: A, V
Admission: adults £4,
children £2.10

The Science Museum was founded in 1864 to give a permanent home to the science and education collections of the Victoria and Albert Museum. With over 10,000 exhibits illustrating in depth the developments in science, technology and medicine, the museum can at first appear somewhat intimidating – but it is in fact a fascinating way of getting to understand the modern world.

On the ground floor is the Apollo 10 command mobile, a V2 rocket and a 1905 Rolls-Royce – a display that introduces everything from basic power to land travel and the exploration of space. But it's the first-floor launch pad and the third-floor flight lab which are the most exciting sections of all – they're instructive for kids and embarrassingly good fun for adults, and there are lots of interactive displays to help the children understand the scientific principles involved.

The museum is vast and can be rather exhausting, so it's best to plan your visit first at the information desk on the ground floor. There are lectures and films here every day, and as these change constantly it can be worth while revisiting to catch something particularly interesting. There's also a small cafe on the fourth floor where you can sit and mull over what you've seen, and a gift shop where you can buy anything from an Escher jigsaw to a pair of socks with an astronomical motif.

Victoria and Albert Museum

Corner of Cromwell Road and Exhibition Road SW7

071-938 8500

Open: Mon–Sat 10 a.m.–5.50 p.m., Sun midday–5.30 p.m. Admission: voluntary donation

Created when Prince Albert and his sidekick Henry Cole decided after the Great Exhibition of 1851 that something was needed to stimulate the minds of young students, this massive collection – the largest decorative arts museum in the world – is housed in seven miles of gallery space spread over six floors. Don't even try to wander around aimlessly as taken at once it is all too much. You can see some of the most beautiful jewellery and glass in the world here, as well as Raphael's tapestry cartoons. The Indian section is quite breathtaking and there is a terrific selection of British watercolours. The recent twentieth-century wing holds everything from a set of odd-looking drawings by designer Nigel Coates to wallpaper by Joan Miró.

Perhaps one of the most interesting sections of the entire museum is the twentieth-century wing. With displays of from arts and crafts to Psion organisers and T-shirts, it also features 'Design Now', a regularly changing exhibition of contemporary design, and has had increasingly brilliant photographic shows over the past couple of years. New to the V&A is the Frank Lloyd Wright gallery, opened in January 1993 and a must for anybody interested in architecture.

Next door to the twentieth-century wing, a very nice advertising campaign recently relaunched the V&A cafe, which is independent of the museum and has created an imaginative self-service menu which is a vegetarian's delight. Mountains of salad and a daily fish platter have always convinced me that sitting in here is much more enjoyable than aimlessly wandering the corridors, though it's not terribly cheap.

EATING AND DRINKING

Bill Bentley's
31 Beauchamp Place
SW3

This place is part of the chain of Bill Bentley's restaurant and oyster bars around London. The restaurants made their name and kept it by mixing fresh

071-589 5080

Open: Mon–Sat, lunch
midday–2.30 p.m.,
dinner 6.30–10.30 p.m.
Credit: A, Amex, V
Average: £40

Bibendum Oyster Bar

Forecourt, Michelin
House, 81 Fulham Road
SW3
071-589 1480

Open: Mon–Sat
midday–10.30 p.m.,
Sun midday–2.30 p.m.,
7–10 p.m.
Credit: A, V
Average: £30

Blake's Hotel

33 Roland Gardens
SW7
071-370 6701

Credit: A, Amex, DC, V
Average: £150 for a
double room

La Bouchée

56 Old Brompton Road
SW7
071-589 1929

Open:
9.30 a.m.–11 p.m.
Credit: A, DC, V

fish dishes with traditional English fare such as pies, served with glorious helpings of mashed potatoes and mushy peas. The dishes of the day are usually well put-together salads or fish dishes, which, considering the location, are all reasonably priced at between £6 and £10. The cuteness value of Bentley's is high, especially in the oyster bar downstairs.

The Oyster Bar is situated at the front of one of London's most beautiful buildings, which used to be an old garage before it was converted into a store, a restaurant, a bar and a publisher's office. It's difficult to get a seat here as the place is quite small and popular, especially at lunchtime, with the Conran Shop brigade. There's an emphasis on seafood here (it's as good as you'll get anywhere in London) but there's also a choice of simple salads. Half a dozen oysters cost £7.50 and a Caesar salad is £5.50. The food is a simpler version of that available in the upstairs restaurant, which is supposed to be one of the finest in London. Bibendum upstairs is big on etiquette and downstairs is big on cool, and I think you'd be better off trying downstairs first.

Blake's Hotel is the creation of Anouska Hempel, an English celebrity who once acted at something or other. It is very popular with old rockers and fashion folks who have never quite had their finger on the pulse. I have never quite seen its attraction myself, but its reputation is legendary and its mixture of the camp, the gothic and the hippie makes the visitors very happy. The rooms all have themes – though they may have changed since, they were Mediterranean, with a mix of dark, sensual colours, the last time I was there. There's even a library where you can sit and ponder, and the bar and restaurant are good enough to try even if you're not a guest here.

This small restaurant has made a genuine attempt to reproduce the atmosphere of a brasserie on the boulevard St Germaine in Paris. Outside there is a small oyster stall, and the restaurant itself has a good menu offering unpretentious French food at a reasonable price. La Bouchée is always busy as the word has got out about what a good little place it is, but the service is so quick that you'll probably get a seat

Average: £20

very quickly. Goats'-cheese salad at £3, or mussels at £4, or even six oysters for £5 are all bargains to start your meal with, and main-course dishes are simple affairs such as steak and chips or turbot grilled and served up on a salad – perfect. Before 8 p.m. you can have a set meal for £4.95, and between midday and 3 p.m. there is a set lunch for £5.95 – a good deal. The house wine is a good, cheap Bordeaux. La Bouchée has a brilliant atmosphere, but do try to get a table upstairs as the basement can be a little noisy.

Daquise
20 Thurloe Street SW7
071-589 6117

Open:
10 a.m.–10.30 p.m.
No credit cards
Average: £20

The South Ken area has been heavily influenced by Polish culture ever since the first Poles fleeing Nazi occupation landed in England. Throughout the day this restaurant-cafe serves food which is Polish through and through, and if you have never eaten this kind of fare before Daquise is a great place to start. Thick beetroot or cabbage soups followed by a main course of marinated pork or sausages are the order of the day and should be tried at least once. I have been coming to this secret little spot for years, if not to be sated by their food, then to eat the delicious cream cakes and coffee. The people sitting around here not only look interesting but sound it.

Emporio Armani Express
Emporio Armani, 191
Brompton Road SW3
071-823 8818

Open: Mon, Tues,
Thurs, Sat
10 a.m.–6 p.m., Wed
10 a.m.–7 p.m.
Credit: A, Amex, V
Average: £30

Looking out over Knightsbridge, this cafe on the first floor of Giorgio Armani's diffusion store (see separate entry) was designed by the maestro himself. Like L'Express in the basement of Joseph Pour la Maison (see separate entry), Emporio Armani Express is a good place to have a snack or to contemplate what it is you need to change or improve your image. The food is expensive for what it is: ravioli with wild mushrooms, which makes a very small plateful, costs around £10. A coffee is £2, but at least it is the real thing. The waiters are dressed in white linen uniforms which are better, in my view, than anything on the rails of the store, and their attitude is defiantly that of the school which does not like serving people. The best thing about this place is the coffee and the view, both of which might entice you to spend too much time here.

L'Express
Joseph, 16 Sloane
Street SW1

The eighties saw the introduction of a new style of having a snack, the brainchild of Joseph Ettedgui. He singlehandedly introduced Londoners to things that

071-235 9869

Open: Mon–Sat
9.30 a.m.–6 p.m.
Credit: A, Amex, DC, V
Average: £30

The Fenja Hotel
69 Cadogan Gardens
SW3
071-589 7333

Credit: A, Amex, DC, V
Average: £130–£195
for a double room

L'Hotel
28 Basil Street SW3
071-589 6286

Credit: A, Amex, V
Average: £125 for a
double room

Joe's Cafe
126 Draycott Avenue
SW3
071-225 2217

Open: Mon–Fri – lunch,
midday–3.30 p.m.,
dinner
7.30–11.30 p.m.; Sat
– breakfast
10 a.m.–midday,

the rest of Europe had been enjoying for years – somewhere decent to sit and have a good cup of coffee. The long elegant bar with its black leather stools is a chrome-clean example of industrial elegance. The food is simple cafe-bar food such as goat's-cheese salad or chicken mayonnaise sandwiches at £5, or hot dishes such as penne with a pesto sauce – all unremarkable but cleverly filling. I have only come here to drink the coffee, which is very good, eat mountains of chocolate cake and waste away another afternoon. It's a great place to have Sunday brunch, and now that it is licensed you can spend long enjoyable afternoons here.

This place is like a small stately home – all very, very English and quaint with rich carpets and walls of prints. It's Olde England with a modern sense of management – all modern amenities and 24-hour room service are available. The fourteen bedrooms all have full decanters in them, which is a nice touch. Breakfast is served in your bedroom and costs £7.25 for the Continental or £11.25 for the full English version. The Fenja Hotel has no restaurant, but there are a host of places worth visiting within walking distance.

This hotel, with its eleven small rooms, has a rural French feel. There is no restaurant, but you have access to its sister hotel, the Michelin-starred Capitals, next door. The rooms are beautifully put together, though there's only just enough room to swing a cat. The French flavour comes from the rustic wallpaper and bed coverings which look as if they are straight out of a Provençal farm. The wine bar, Le Metro, is open to non-residents.

This is where you can try the famous Porkinson's sausages, the invention of the late photographer Norman Parkinson, who had a great sense of humour and loved his sausages. The link with fashion does not end there: Joe's Cafe is is one of the many ideas from the nimble brain of Mr Fashion and Lifestyle Joseph Ettedgui.

The bar is open to non-diners and the mix of black and chrome sets the tone for the rest of the place. It looks a bit eighties but it can only be a matter of time before this particular style is again fashionable. The

lunch midday–3 p.m.,
dinner 7.30–11 p.m.,
Sun – breakfast
10–11 a.m., brunch
11 a.m.–3.30 p.m.
Credit: A, Amex, DC, V
Average: £60

bar is very popular with the fashion crowd, who seem to enjoy the eclectic menu which shifts from chicken teriyaki to fish cakes without much problem. Joseph himself can often be found here watching what is going on and making sure that his machine is kept rolling. I do think that Joe's Cafe is a bit pricey for what it is, especially since Brompton Cross has so much to offer at the moment – like the Oyster Bar in the Michelin Building. But it is a good place to go for Sunday brunch.

Joe's Cafe

Harvey Nichols, Sloane
Street SW1
071-235 5000

Open: Mon, Thues,
Thurs, Fri 10 a.m.–7
pm., Wed
10 a.m.–8 p.m., Sat
10 a.m.–6 p.m.
Credit: A, Amex, V
Average: £20

Also part of the Joseph empire, this cafe is the younger cousin of the upmarket Draycott Avenue branch. Its decor is very much in keeping with the Joseph lifestyle philosophy – there's a mixture of chrome and black and white, and a clean simplicity which has made it a popular haunt with shoppers and fashion aficionados.

The cafe gives these people exactly what they want after a hard day's shopping: a decent cup of coffee and a snack such as the dried tomato and prosciutto salad, which comes in at £8. It's not cheap, but it is enjoyable.

Le Metro

28 Basil Street SW3
071-589 6281

Open: Mon–Fri
11 a.m.–11 p.m., Sat
11 a.m.–7 p.m.
Credit: A, Amex, DC, V
Average: £24

Set in the basement of L'Hotel behind Harrods, this is the place to come for breakfast (£4) in Knightsbridge – the chefs are on rotation from the main kitchen, so they know how to knock up something special at this time of the morning. The food at lunchtime can be as simple as a plate of pasta or a salade niçoise at £3, or a warm chicken-liver salad at £5.40.

The evening menu changes daily but there is often a good plate of risotto to be had, as well as perfect pasta dishes which will leave you with change from a tenner. Another plus is that a large portion of the formidable wine list can be had by the glass.

Minema Cafe Bar

43 Knightsbridge SW1
071-823 1269

Open: Mon–Sat
11 a.m.–midnight, Sun
11 a.m.–7 p.m.
Credit: A, Amex, DC, V

This very modern cafe has had quite a lot of money spent on it to make sure that the place looks very special. Despite the steady stream of traffic passing outside, the view over Hyde Park adds to the attraction of this non-nostalgic coffee house. Croissants, brioches and pains au chocolat are all £1.25, and for those who need refuelling before a Knightsbridge shopping trip or a movie there are larger

Average: £18

snacks such as carpaccio at £7 or focaccia bread with a variety of fillings at £5. For dessert try the delicious Tartofo Visconti. The bar menu is very decently priced: a Rolling Rock, Becks or Sol is £1.95 and a bottle of good Chilean Cabernet Sauvignon is under £7. The place is a new experience for art-movie lovers, who are usually more used to sitting in fleapits and being treated quite badly – it's one of the very best places in London to snack and to see something very special.

190 Queensgate
190 Queensgate SW7
071-581 5666

Open: bistro – breakfast
9–11 a.m., lunch
midday–3 p.m., dinner
6 p.m.–12.30 a.m.;
restaurant –
7 p.m.–midnight
Credit: A, Amex, DC, V
Average: restaurant
£70, bistro £40

Tony Worrall Thompson has taken all the experience he gained running Ménage à Trois, the Knightsbridge restaurant which made his name, and created a gem here in an area of London where there is very little activity. The restaurant downstairs is very grand and has prices to match, but the place to be is up in the Brasserie, which is lively, comfortable and at the same time a bit rough.

The food is a blend of Italian and what is now called Modern British. There are rocket salads at £2.95 and interesting fish-based starters which are never far off £8; the main dishes will leave you with little change from £15. This is expensive for brasserie food but you are getting the best. The wine is a good mixture of New World and French, all arranged at a level that never aims too high. The painter Peter Blake is very fond of sitting in one of the corners with his family and friends such as Pete Townshend of The Who. Various Rolling Stones often roll in during the evening. It's a great place and I can't recommend it enough – if only to have a look and see which old celeb has had a tuck or two.

Star of India
154 Old Brompton
Road SW5
071-373 2901

Open: Mon–Sat, lunch
midday– 3 p.m., dinner
7–11.30 p.m.; Sun,
dinner 6 p.m.–midnight
Credit: A, Amex, V
Average: £40

I spent one of the worst days of my life here once trying to interview the French prima donna Vanessa Paradis, who did not want to be there and who did not want to talk. As conversation struck a new low the food arrived. Vanessa didn't want to eat either, so I gave up on her and tucked in. After a few minutes of seeing the pleasure on my face she couldn't stop herself trying the spinach dish and then the chicken, and then she had a nibble of the nan bread and became much more agreeable. The food here is incredible and the people who work here are very funny and enjoy making you laugh. The chicken marinated in yoghurt and cooked with fresh chillies is exceptional, as are the dhansak dishes – a hot and sour mixture of meat and vegetables.

It's slightly more expensive than ordinary Indians, but the atmosphere – the place is painted with classical imagery – verges on the spectacular. It's very popular in the evenings, so book.

The Stockpot
6 Basil Street SW3
071-589 8627

Cpen: Mon–Sat
8 a.m.–11 p.m., Sun
midday–10.30 p.m.
No credit cards
Average: £12

The Stockpot – and the people working here – look exactly the same as they did when I first came here in 1977. Then it was a cheap cafe in an expensive neighbourhood, and it's still totally predictable, rather ugly and always busy. It's also good value, with main dishes available under £3. There's a scattering of Stockpots between Chelsea and the West End, and they're all perfect when you get fed up with the nonsense and rigmarole associated with more fashionable food.

Le Suquet
104 Draycott Avenue
SW3
071-581 1785

Open: lunch
12.30–2.30 p..m.,
dinner 7.15–11.30 p.m.
Credit: A, Amex, DC, V
Average: £70

If ever a London restaurant evoked the feeling that you're in the south of France, this is the one. The fish comes in fresh from France each day and you can see the lobsters banging into each other in the main-room tank, waiting to be chosen by some hungry and callous diner. If you eat here you simply must have the seafood platter (£15), a combination of nearly everything on the menu. It's the most expensive dish available in the place, but washed down with a bottle of Sancerre it will take you into another dimension. Get a seat at the bar, a carafe of wine and your fruits de mer and concentrate on every magnificent taste.

Turner's
87–89 Walton Street
SW3
071-584 6711

Open: Mon–Sat, lunch
12.30–2.30 p.m.,
dinner 7.30–11 p.m.
Credit: A, Amex, DC, V
Average: £80

Brian Turner's restaurant has become a big favourite with the foodies of SW3. His experience of French cooking has given him the confidence to start his own establishment and take on the big guys of haute cuisine. He's more than likely to appear at your table and ask you in his no-nonsense York-shire manner what you thought of the food, and though his cooking is not too elaborate it is always interesting. Set menus at £18–£26 per person are highly recommended. Specials include the unlikely-sounding brandade de haddock aix concombres a l'Aneth.

SHOPPING

Agnès B
111 Fulham Road SW3
071-225 3477

Open: Mon
11 a.m.–6 p.m.,
Tues–Sat
10 a.m.–6 p.m.
Credit: A, Amex, V

French fashion designer Agnès B has managed to combine chic and practicality in her designs for men, women and children under eight. Her cotton shirts (from £60) are wonderfully comfortable, and lately she has attempted to marry flared trousers with tight tank tops. This seventies revivalism has been a disaster for most fashion houses but it seems to work here. Her men's clothes are not as distinctive as the women's, but they have a loyal following of pop stars and club people. The kids' clothes are cute but, unlike the adults', expensive for what they are.

Azagury
50 Knightsbridge SW1
071-235 0799

Open: Mon–Sat
9.30 a.m.–6 p.m.
Credit: A, Amex, V

This is the showroom from which designer Jack Azagury shows his grand evening wear; though he never boasts of it, Princess Diana has been seen wearing his clothes, which are definitely aimed at the top end of the market. They begin at £500 and head up and up, but are very beautiful. Down the road at 38 Knightsbridge is Azagury Fleurs (071-259 5141), which sells flowers arranged by the master himself. You'll pay more than you would in the florist's on the corner but you will be getting something very special indeed.

Bonham's Auction House
Montpelier Street SW7
071-584 9161

Open: Mon
8.45 a.m.–7 p.m.,
Tues–Fri
8.45 a.m.–6 p.m., Sun
11 a.m.–4 p.m.
No credit cards

Bonham's is the smallest of the major London auction rooms, and for that reason is slightly more relaxed. If you're a collector of good contemporary painting or ceramics, this is a great place to find out more about what you like and there's a good chance you'll get it for less than you'd pay in a gallery. They also have furniture sales occasionally, which can be very exciting if you're after something that you've waited a long time to see. Bonham's also hold more wacky auctions – recently they held two sales of Doctor Who props which were a great success. There are as many as seven sales a week so it is probably worth calling or writing to them and finding out what is coming up.

Christian Lacroix
Sloane Street, SW1
071-235 2400

Open: Mon, Tues, Thurs,
Fri 10 a.m.–6.30 p.m.,

The golden boy of haute couture, Lacroix has just about conquered the universe. His designs are extravagant, and the elegant brocade he uses so well has now become his signature. Each season he seems to become even more popular with the press – maybe this is because he is the nice one out of a pretty

Wed 10 a.m.–7 p.m.,
Sat 10 a.m.–6 p.m.
Credit: A, Amex, DC, V

The Conran Shop
Michelin Building, 81
Fulham Road SW3
071-589 7401

Open: Mon, Wed–Sat
9.30 a.m.–6 p.m., Tues
10 a.m.–6 p.m., Sun
midday–5 p.m.
Credit: A, Amex, V

Cutler and Gross
16 Knightsbridge Green
SW1
071-581 2250

Open: Mon–Sat
9.30 a.m.–6 p.m.
Credit: A, Amex, V

unpleasant bunch of designers. The most basic of dresses will take your breath away, but cost £1,500 – it's an enormous amount of money to spend on something so memorable that you only dare wear it once or twice. Day dresses are around £400 and an evening gown can cost anything up to £4,000. I found the small shop quite intimidating, but maybe that's because I was a poor man in a rich woman's shop.

The magnificence of the old Michelin garage, decorated throughout with glazed tiles and looking as if it comes from a painting by Toulouse-Lautrec, was where more adventurous car lovers would once have brought their beloved Renaults or Citroëns and Mercedes to be serviced. Inside the building, where there are the Bibendum restaurant and oyster bar, offices, flower stalls and fish shops, is the remarkable Conran Shop, the brainchild of Sir Terence Conran, whose taste and experiences of other countries created a design revolution in this one. Everything you could ever want to make the perfect home is here. From the garden to the bedroom, every elegant new idea in home furnishing can be seen, often for the first time in Britain, in this store. There is a definite quality stamp to the goods – the only thing that worries me is that £2,000 is a large amount to pay for a sofa that is probably going to end up in a lot of other houses. The basement is the best part – here the goods, such as kitchenware, lamps, kidswear and stationery, are smaller and more affordable. They also do a wedding-list service. It's my favourite shop in the whole of London.

While other shops attempting to sell designer spectacles have fallen by the wayside, Tony Gross has kept his eye on the changing times and subtly adapted his shop, which has been around since the seventies, to suit the market. I bought my first pair of what I would call real sunglasses from here – they were all silver and blue tint, a hint of Americana meets fifties Paris. They cost me £50, which in 1981 was a fantastic sum of money. The shop is still trading, dealing only in Cutler and Gross products which are as popular as ever. In a tiny little alleyway, you could easily blink and miss it, but once there, the service is second to none.

West KNIGHTSBRIDGE

Emporio Armani

191 Brompton Road
SW3
071-823 8818

Open: Mon, Tues,
Thurs–Sat
10 a.m.–6 p.m., Wed
10 a.m.–7 p.m.
Credit: A, Amex, DC,
JCB, Switch. V

This store stocks the master designer's diffusion line – less formal and cheaper outfits than those sold under the famous Black Label in Armani's other shop around the corner (see separate entry). The ground floor sells leisurewear, all with the Emporio slogan in some form, and there is also a small section for kids from about three to twelve years old. Again, this is mostly sportswear, though a bit too nice for jumping around a field in. Upstairs is the womenswear, which moves elegantly between English-style country wear and smart office outfits for the professional woman. A man's or woman's jacket here will cost around £300, and a suit between £400 and £500. The clothes all have the style, the cut and the label, which is so important to some people, but I think they are always something of a disappointment. More affordable are caps at £20, and there is also a range of interior accessories.

Giorgio Armani

178 Sloane Street SW1
071-235 6232

Open: Mon, Tues,
Thurs–Sat
10 a.m.–6 p.m., Wed
10 a.m.–7 p.m.
Credit: A, Amex, DC, V

This magnificent-looking shop is a showcase for everything good about Armani's designs for men and women. A woman's suit comes in at £995, and that's a simple black wool two-piece; a man's jacket will not leave you with much change out of £700. The difference between this shop and the Emporio store is huge. Here you will leave feeling that you've seen something special, and anything you do buy will repay you in many ways over the years, while the other shop is really a good place to buy a label and not much else.

Harrods

Knightsbridge SW1
071-730 1234

Open: Mon, Tues, Sat
10 a.m.–6 p.m.,
Wed-Fri 10 a.m.–7 p.m.
Credit: A, Amex, DC, V

Harrods was founded in 1849 by Henry Harrod, a greengrocer from Stepney in East London who had come west to avoid the cholera epidemic of 1848. Staffed at first by two shop assistants (it now employs 3,500 people) and offering cheaper goods to those who paid cash, Harrods was immediately successful, making vast profits which were all ploughed back into the store. In 1883 the building was burnt down but the indefatigable Harrod had it rebuilt on five floors to the design of architect Alfred Williams. Amongst the first people to open an account here were Ellen Terry, Oscar Wilde and Lillie Langtry.

Since then Harrods (now owned by Mohamed al Fayed) has carved itself an international reputation based on its ability to supply almost anything. An apocryphal story tells of a gentleman who, doubting the store's reputation, rang the pet department to order an elephant. Unperturbed, the salesman asked, 'African or Indian, sir?' The five floors of goods, food and restaurants take in around a million pounds a day. Best place of all, I think, is the sumptuous food hall: 500 different cheeses and 130 different types of bread and scones are available, and the confectionery department sells in excess of 100 tons of chocolate each year. The charcuterie counter is a dream and you can buy any type of ready-made meal, from sushi to fresh pasta, to take away with you.

(See also separate entry for Oliver Sweeney.)

Harvey Nichols
109–125 Knightsbridge
SW1
071-235 5000

Open: Mon, Tues,
Thurs, Fri
10 a.m.–7 p.m., Wed
10 a.m.–8 p.m., Sun
10 a.m.–6 p.m.
Credit: A, Amex, V

The most seductive things about this department store are the window displays. They change each month and increasingly look like works of art. From the elaborate warren of make-up counters to the higher floors where rails of clothes are separated by designer, the names come flying as you come up the escalators. I've always found the place to be a claustrophobic nightmare, but I've only ever gone at the weekend, which is probably a mistake.

They have recently opened up the fifth floor as a foodmarket, and there is also a bar, cafe, wine shop and restaurant here. The foodmarket, which is not exactly cheap, sells everything from charcuterie to fish and chocolates. The emphasis is on dairy produce, though they stock 175 different cheeses from all over the world, as well as specialty foods from Mexico, Japan and Thailand. Much of the food on sale has been selected by Henry Harris, the chef in Harvey Nichols's restaurant.

Jasper Conran Shop
303 Brompton Road
SW3
071-823 9134

Open: Mon–Sat
10 a.m.–6 p.m.
Credit: A, V

The beau monde's favourite women's designer, Jasper Conran has gently created an instantly recognisable look. It's a very classy mix of soft expensive wools, especially cashmere, and tailored dresses and suits which float around the body rather than cling to it. Powdery colours emphasise the statement. His clothes are for working women who unashamedly want to look and feel sexy. While prices for some outfits can rise as high as £800 or more – and an evening dress will definitely cost at least that much – some items carry (slightly) more affordable tags of around £200.

Jigsaw
31 Brompton Road
SW3
071-584 6226

Open: Mon, Tues,
Thurs–Sat
10 a.m.–7 p.m., Wed
10 a.m.–8 p.m.
Credit: A, Amex, V

Jigsaw's shopfront, the most dramatic of any in Knightsbridge, was designed by Nigel Coates, who was also responsible for Katherine Hamnett's shop on Sloane Street (see separate entry). It adds glamour to a stretch of shops which should all have attempted to do something with their façades and interiors but which have sadly allowed cheap conversions to ruin them or have simply allowed the cobwebs to gather. Inside the clothes on the rails mix classic designs with comfort and just a tweak of fashion. This store is part of a small London chain, which means that prices have been kept down as far as possible and there are bargains to be had. A dress will cost over £80, but a good pair of trousers need not be more than £40. As far as women's high-street chains go, Jigsaw is by far the best in both quality and design.

Joseph
21 Sloane Street SW1
071-235 9868

Open: Mon, Tues,
Thurs, Fri
10 a.m.–6.30 p.m.,
Wed 10 a.m.–7 p.m.
Credit: A, Amex, DC, V

The Joseph empire, which stretches from South Molton Street to Knightsbridge and Chelsea, is the most extraordinary success story in fashion. Joseph introduced names like Hamnett, Miyake, Yamamoto and Alaia to the fashion-conscious and his stores are style leaders and never follow fashion. The Joseph look changes each season but always combines softness with sexiness. His own line of clothes includes his brilliant Joseph Tricot range of knitwear, which has continually adapted itself to changing fashions and even created a few of its own – including the shorter skirt, which Joseph did long before anyone else.

The shops are a blend of space and tasteful design, and this relatively new store incorporates everything good about his philosophy. Furniture from the likes of sculptor Tom Dixon and Mark Brazier Jones dominates the ground floor, and this mixture of art and fashion alludes to the complete Joseph lifestyle, which is second to none in terms of beauty.

Katherine Hamnett
Sloane Street SW1
071-823 1002

Open: Mon, Tues,
Thurs–Sat
10 a.m.–6.30 p.m.,
Wed 10 a.m.–7 p.m.

The most interesting thing about this shop is the actual design. Fish tanks bubble away in a transcendental blue light in the window, designed by Nigel Coates, and in many ways the window and the space inside overshadow Hamnett's clothes. Once upon a time, when she was using drill cotton, parachute silk and rough linen in military-style designs, she was two steps ahead of the pack: her prices were about right and

Credit: A, Amex, DC, V

every musician, actor, model and advertising man seemed to be clad head to toe in Hamnett clothes. Things change very quickly at the house of Hamnett, however. Her recent drop in popularity can be seen as either the pack catching up and doing what she did but at a more affordable price, while hers hit the roof, or as the result of opening expensive shops like this one. The clothes themselves are very much a reflection of what's going on in the rest of the fashion world. Jeans here are around £60 and a man's shirt will cost about £75.

Margaret Howell
29 Beauchamp Place
SW3
071-584 2462

Open: Mon–Sat
10 a.m.–6 p.m.
Credit: A, Amex, V

Beauchamp Place was one of London's coolest streets in the late seventies and early eighties, but it has failed to keep its reputation from being tarnished by the arrival of very cheap discount shops and places selling expensive rubbish. Margaret Howell's shop, however, sells individual and elegantly cut clothes for women. From office to home and evening wear, Howell caters for every need and her clothes are priced accordingly – a good suit will definitely set you back £200 or £300. Her look is a mixture of the tough and the feminine – chalkstripe suits and leather jackets are placed beside simple brogues and thick leather shoes. She should be Britain's answer to Armani but somehow she hasn't received the necessary financial backing and media support. If you want to start looking a bit more serious about how you dress, this is not a bad place to start.

Oliver Sweeney
Men's shoe department,
Harrods, 87–135
Brompton Road SW1
071-730 1234

Open: Mon, Tues, Sat
10 a.m.–6 p.m., Wed,
Thurs, Fri
10 a.m.–7 p.m.
Credit: A, Amex, DC, V

Oliver Sweeney's shoes mix the elegant with the robust and practical. From walking boots to evening wear, the character of the shoes remains consistent and worth every penny of the £199 to £215 a typical pair costs. The shoes are named after famous British actors – the Olivier is a delicate brogue, the Redgrave is a heavy walking shoe and my favourite, the Guinness, comes in burgundy and black and has the kind of thick black sole that seems to be impossible to find nowadays. Sweeney was the man who told me that I had been wearing the wrong size shoe for the last ten years and that it would be in my interests to move up a size. Since then my poor battered feet have been enjoying a more comfortable and happy existence.

Rigby and Peller
2 Hans Road SW3
071-589 9293

Open: Mon–Wed, Fri
9 a.m.–5.30 p.m.,
Thurs 9 a.m.–7 p.m.,
Sat 9.30–6 p.m.
Credit: A, Amex, DC, V

This shop has the reputation of being invaluable to women in search of the perfect fit in bra and knickers. It's undoubtedly the place where the smart ladies of Chelsea and Kensington head for when they're in need of a bit of a lift. The place specialises in helping women who have either no bust or an extremely large one, and as well as underwear they also stock a range of swimwear for those with the same problem. A bra custom made to fit you exactly will set you back about £200. It's a classy joint with a royal warrant.

ENTERTAINMENT

Minema
45 Knightsbridge SW1
071-235 4225

Credit: A, V

A smallish cinema overlooking Hyde Park, which generally shows high-quality art-house movies such as anything by Woody Allen or a new Bertolucci. The seats are very comfortable and the size of the place makes it very intimate. It tends to attract the local 'toffs', who walk about the cinema as if it were their own front room. Despite this, the Minema is still one of the best places in London to see a good film. They have recently refurbished the cafe (see separate entry), which is a fantastic success and well worth visiting.

Pizza on the Park
11–13 Knightsbridge
SW1
071-253 5550

Open:
8.30 a.m.–midnight
Credit: A, Amex, DC, V
Admission for music
evenings: £12–£15
Average: £20

Part of the Pizza Express chain, this restaurant has an awful lot more going for it than the other high-street pizzerias. It opens at 8.30 a.m. for breakfast and from 11.30 a.m. starts serving a range of sixteen delicious pizzas, all costing around £5.

Pizza on the Park is most famous, however, for the quality of the live music played in the basement every night. They have monthly seasons featuring everything from trad jazz to cabaret, and recently had a 'Lady of Broadway' season. Admission is £12 to £15, depending on who is playing, and as the venue attracts some very fine musicians it is extremely popular. Give them a call to find out who's playing, and it might very well be a good idea to book yourself a table.

Notti Hil Ba

n otting Hill can be loosely defined as the area immediately north of Kensington, and it is believed that Saxon settlers known as Cnottingus, or Sons of Cnotting, gave the district its name around AD 700. The Portobello Road, the epicentre of Notting Hill, takes its name from the famous battle of 1739 at Puerto Bello in the Gulf of New Mexico, when the Spanish were beaten by Admiral Vernon's fleet.

Up until the nineteenth century Notting Hill consisted mostly of farmlands and a settlement known as the Kensington Gravel Pits. The toll gate separating Notting Hill from Kensington and from which Notting Hill Gate gets its name was built in the eighteenth century and it is thought that the road (Bayswater Road/Holland Park Avenue) stretching through the area from Bayswater and on to Shepherds Bush was originally a Roman road.

On 3 June 1837 a Mr John Whyte of Brace Cottage, Notting Hill, opened what he described as a Racing Emporium. Called the Hippodrome, it overlooked Ladbroke Grove and had three tracks, one each for racing, steeplechasing and exercise. The enterprise was doomed, however, due to the reluctance of the locals to accept the blocking of their rights of way and the invasion of their district by the hawkers, thieves and gypsies who flocked to the racecourse. The new gentry were unable to accept the influx of what they described as the scum and the offal and had the place closed after Whyte ran into debt.

The course buildings were renovated and the houses still stand today.

Only a stone's-throw away, surrounding the area where Kensington Sports Centre now stands on Whymer Road, a settlement of a few cottages and a piggery developed into a slum. The main source of employment here was brick-making, at which a family could earn £2 to £3 a week; the men were said to drink at least seven pints of beer a day to quench the thirst of this exhausting work. By 1849 there were a thousand people and over 3,000 pigs living in some 200 hovels. Charles Dickens wrote of the area that 'Notting Hill, in the Parish of Kensington, is a plague spot, scarcely equalled for its insalubrity by any other in London'. However, it was in the next twenty years or so that the famous Portobello Road market began to develop. Towards the end of the century literary, professional and military men, along with their families and servants, began to move into Notting Hill and several private, middle-class schools opened, among them an Academy for Young Gentlemen. After World War II and with the arrival of Asian, Chinese and West Indian immigrants, London began to embrace a whole new culture. Immigrants from the Caribbean settled in the relatively cheap housing of the Notting Hill and Ladbroke Grove areas, and their influence on the street life of this period was dramatic and can still be clearly seen. The August Bank Holiday each year brings thousands of people into the Notting Hill area to celebrate Carnival, bringing a taste of the Caribbean to West London with steel bands, floats and food stalls.

During the Thatcher years of the 1980s the comparatively low rents (which have since gone up) of the area attracted a number of art galleries to Notting Hill. A now annual summer arts festival grows bigger each year and the galleries, which once catered to locals, are now more like their Cork Street brothers – people are vetted on entry and prices have risen dramatically. The rise of the gallery scene was undoubtedly linked to the influx of new money into Notting Hill during the 1980s, when cheap apartments were still available and the middle classes flocked to an area which they saw as offering a sense of danger as well as good shopping.

The main focus of the area is Portobello Road (see separate entry for Portobello Road Market). As well as tourists, it attracts young trendies and eagle-eyed antique hunters. Notting Hill is still one of the hippest areas in London. It even has its own recognised tribe, known as the 'Nottinghill-billies' – youngish bohemian types who inhabit its world of bars and restaurants.

Though Bayswater was known between the eleventh and fifteenth centuries as a resting and drinking place for horses, the history of this central area really begins only in the last 150 years or so. Throughout the Victorian era the hotels which line Bayswater's streets were large, fashionable houses, many of them modelled after John Nash's magnificent Regents Terrace (see Oxford Street and Marylebone). Bayswater was never able to compete with Belgravia (see Chelsea) as a home for the wealthy, but it did hold great appeal for the middle classes.

Since the beginning of this century, many of Bayswater's buildings have been rebuilt in a hotchpotch of styles. One of the few interesting buildings here is the Inverness Court Hotel, built in 1912 and with a magnificent baroque-rococo frontage. Bayswater is no longer as magnificent as it once was. Cheap bedsits and hotels attract a mixed crowd and there seem to be people hanging out on every corner. However, some of the best apartments in London, overlooking Hyde Park, are to be found here, and the Bayswater Road is a good place to look for a mid-priced hotel, including the rock 'n' roll hangout The Columbia.

HOW TO GET THERE

Tubes
- Bayswater
- Holland Park
- Ladbroke Grove
- Lancaster Gate
- Notting Hill Gate
- Paddington
- Queensway
- Royal Oak
- Westbourne Grove

Buses
- Bayswater Road: 12, 70, 94
- Bishop's Bridge Road: 7, 15, 23, 27, 36
- Chepstow Road: 7, 28, 31, 70
- Elkstone Road: 23, 31
- Great Western Road: 28, 31
- Kensal Road: 23
- Ladbroke Grove: 7, 15, 23, 52, 70, 295, 302
- Pembridge Road: 27. 28, 31, 70
- Queensway: 70
- Westbourne Grove: 7, 15, 23, 27, 70

KENSINGTON PLACE

SIGHTS AND SITES

All Saints Road,
W11

The All Saints, or the Front Line as it is known locally, has been a gathering place for young Afro-Caribbeans for the last thirty years. It's lined with a mixture of small shops selling anything from musical instruments to West Indian food, as well as dub reggae stores, all of which give the street a reputation as a happening place. The late-night blues clubs which once took place in every basement are now sadly long gone. The street used to have a reputation as a drug haven, but that now seems to be a thing of the past. In recent years a heavy police presence has done a lot to change the atmosphere of the street, but not really for the better. Nowadays you are as likely to see young trendies trying out the restaurants that now open and close along the street with alarming speed as the cool dudes of former years. During the Notting Hill Carnival on the August bank holiday weekend, the Front Line regains its high profile as steel bands play up and down the length of the street.

Bayswater Road,
W2

Every Sunday along the Bayswater Road, from Marble Arch up to about Lancaster Gate, artists hang out hundreds of paintings on the park railings and wait for a sale. Most of the work consists of pretty mediocre drawings and paintings of clichéd London scenes. It can be worth taking a walk up and down the long street, however, as somewhere tucked in among the tourist bait might be something which really appeals to your taste.

The buildings overlooking the park are a mixture of grand eighteenth-century villas and terrible new hotels. Turn into the cosmopolitan stretch of Queensway and take a walk past the ice rink (see separate entry), Lebanese restaurants, Chinese cafes and the shopping centre Whiteley's (see separate entry).

Kensal Green All
Souls Cemetery
Harrow Road W10
081-969 0152

Open: Mon–Fri, winter
9 a.m.–4.30 p.m.,

This was the first commercial cemetery to be opened in London. A Gothic design by H. E. Kendall was the winner of an architectural competition to design the graveyard, but it was eventually decided to build it in the Greek revival style.

The cemetery flourished throughout the Victorian era, and the Victorians' morbid fascination with death

summer
9 a.m.–5.30 p.m., Sat,
Sun 10 a.m.–4 p.m.

can still be seen in the many tombstones and urns here. The cemetery gained social acceptance when the Duke of Sussex and his sister Sophia were buried here. Other famous 'residents' include the poet Thomas Hood, Sir Marc Isambard Brunel, the actor Charles Kemble and the great writer Thackeray, who was buried here in 1863.

The Friends of Kensal Green run guided tours (Saturday and Sundays at 2.30 p.m., from March to October; from November to February the tours take place one Sunday in four only). They cost £2 and leave from the cemetery chapel steps – any queries should be addressed to the cemetery.

EATING, DRINKING AND SLEEPING

L'Artiste Assoiffé
122 Kensington Park
Road W11
071-727 4714

Open: 7.30–11 p.m.
Credit: A, Amex, DC, V
Average: £70

Stuffed to the barrels with bric-à-brac probably found on the Portobello Road, this place has a timeless quality which is preserved at all costs by the management, who have managed to keep their parrot and dog alive for years, though the beasts always look as if they are about to pop it – the parrot is said once to have told a member of the Royal Family to fuck off. The food is French country cooking, which basically means thick soup and lots of heavily sauced meats, followed by sorbets and tarts. It's got a lot of distractions and is very frivolous – the perfect place to go to cheer yourself up or to break some bad news to someone.

The Brasserie Du Marché
349 Portobello Road
W10
081-968 5828

Open: Mon–Sat
10 a.m.–11 p.m., Sun
11 a.m.–4 p.m.
No credit cards
Average: £35

Of all the bars and restaurants in the Notting Hill this is the least pretentious. It has been influenced to a certain degree by the successful Kensington Place, where the owners once worked, but has carved itself a creditable reputation for decent food – the fresh salmon is always perfect – at modest prices.

They open early for coffee and pastries, and do a special brunch menu on Sundays. You can also come here at any time just to sit and read a book over a cup of chocolate, a relative rarity among London restaurants.

Cafe Grove
253a Portobello Road
W11

Situated on the first floor of an indoor market, and offering a perfect view of goings-on below, this place was started up by a mad combination of

071-243 1094

Open: Mon–Sat
9 a.m.–6 p.m., Sun
10.30 a.m.–5.30 p.m.
No credit cards
Average: £20

The Canal Brasserie
Canalot Production
Studios, 222 Kensal
Road W10
081-960 2732

Open: Mon–Fri
9.30 a.m.–10.30 p.m.
Average: £28

The Churchill Arms
119 Kensington Church
Street W8
071-727 4242

Open: Mon–Sat
11 a.m.–11 p.m.,
Sun midday–3.30 p.m.,
7–10.30 p.m.
No credit cards
Average: £25

Clarke's
124 Kensington Church
Street W8
071-221 9225

Open: Mon–Fri, lunch
12.30–2 p.m., dinner
7–10 p.m.

Italians and an Australian. Fights were known to happen in the kitchen, with pots and pans flying over who burnt the toast. It now runs like a well-oiled machine, catering for vegetarians and serving up a decent pasta dish each day for £4, including salad. The cafe con leche is superb and worth the visit and on Sunday mornings they serve up a big breakfast to the hungover masses.

You could easily miss this restaurant as it is hidden away in the middle of a studio complex housing a number of media businesses. Originally a bookcase factory, the building has now been turned into a production house where TV, film and advertising people 'create' new ideas, though they seem to spend a lot of their creative time here in the brasserie – and who can blame them? The food has an Italian feel to it, with starters (around £4) such as chicken livers with bruscetta, capers and ham, or Russian salads with parmesan. Especially good is the pan-fried duck breast with blackberry sauce and vegetables. There are fish and vegetarian dishes available every day. The atmosphere here is very relaxed – it's a big, spacious and airy room and the back wall overlooks the canal.

They like to play games in this bar, especially psychological games. The barman is alleged to be the rudest man in London, which seems to be a major attraction in a strange kind of English way. Any time I've been here I've wanted to headbutt the barman but the food is good enough to eat and the chess opposition is formidable. The pub itself is clean and pleasant and is a decent place to meet friends for a few drinks. It's nothing out of the ordinary, though.

They serve a mixture of Thai and English food and a main course here should cost you about £4.50.

Much favoured by people in the know, this is a place you should go to at least once if you are really interested in food. The Californian-influenced menu, featuring a lot of char-grilled fish and meat, is a mixture of styles and tastes that places chef Sally Clarke in a league of her own. As it's a fixed menu it's a good idea to phone ahead in case they're serving something that will have you running into

Credit: A, V
Average: Dinner £74,
lunch £50

Costas
18 Hillgate Street W8
071-727 4310

Open: Tues–Sat, lunch
midday–2.30 p.m.,
dinner 5.30–10.30 p.m.
No credit cards
Average: £16

The Earl of Lonsdale
277–281 Westbourne
Grove W11
071-727 6335

Open: Mon–Sat
11 a.m.–11 p.m., Sun
midday–3.30 p.m.,
7–10.30 p.m.
No credit cards
Average: £12

First Floor
186 Portobello Road
W11
071-243 0072

Open: Mon–Sat
7.30 p.m.–1.30 a.m.,
Sun 11 a.m.–6 p.m.
Credit: A, Amex, V
Average: £40

the street. The restaurant gets very busy and is quite small, so it's wise to phone ahead and book.

Next door is & Clarke's deli which has an assortment of beautifully shaped breads as well as cheese and wine, all of the very highest quality.

A fish and ship shop which is not so well known as Geales (see separate entry) around the corner in Farmer Street, Costas nevertheless has its own very strong identity, forged by its Greek owners (who also run the Greek restaurant a few doors down). The Greek influence is apparent in the starters, which include taramasalata and humus, but it is the main courses which are of most interest. Cod, haddock, rock salmon or plaice is the order of the day. Puddings include banana fritters in melba sauce and peach melba.

At one time the Lonsdale was the centre of London's rock 'n' roll industry, and saw more deals being made than many record company offices. During the seventies and eighties rock and punk bands used the bar as an information centre. Who was working with who? Who had signed a deal? Who had been dropped? What concert had bombed? Today it remains popular, but the rock gods have disappeared to the LA sun or just dropped out of sight as the 'greebo' rockers were replaced by dance-band DJs or musicians who aren't into the pubs and this kind of lifestyle. Proper food has now replaced the crisps of olden times – there's a lasagne-type dish and a vegetarian dish every day. It's a Samuel Smith pub and sells the normal beers as well as Pure Brew, a natural lager, and the very trendy pint bottles of Strong Pale Ale.

Located above a pub which has a rather dubious reputation, the First Floor is so hip it can be confusing. Though it's meant to be Modern British, the food varies from Japanese to Jamaican, but always seems to work. Salmon with a sun-dried tomato and herb crust served with glazed chicory and salsa verde, or lamb accompanied by roast parsnips and vegetables, will set you back £15. It's better here in the evening than it is at lunchtime; candlelight makes the setting perfect. The wine is never too expensive, but finding

the right thing to drink with the rather unusual food can occasionally be a problem. Book the upstairs room for your birthday – it's beautiful and cheap and the terrific food makes for a successful evening.

The Fortune Cookie
1 Queensway W2
071-727 7260

Open: midday–11 p.m.
Credit: A, V
Average: £20

This is one of the many Chinese restaurants which have moved to Bayswater from the fierce competition of Chinatown. It opens at noon and serves up delicious piles of Chinese food for the rest of the day. Sweet and sour pork, noodles and perfectly concocted special fried rice are as popular with the many local Chinese who use this place as they are with the new inhabitants of Bayswater. A set menu for two costs £20.

Galicia
323 Portobello Road
W10
081-969 3539

Open: Tues–Sun, lunch
midday–3 p.m., dinner
7–11.30 p.m.
Credit: A, DC, V
Average: £30

This is the place to go after a long Saturday trawl through Portobello market. It's situated at the northern end of the Portobello Road and is extremely popular with the local Spanish community. The bar is a fog of thick tobacco smoke and guttural Galician dialect and is not immediately inviting, but it's worth persevering – eventually they'll get around to serving you in that cool, indifferent manner which lets you know that you had better have your order ready as these guys are not going to help you decide. The bar food is better than that in the restaurant in the back room. Everything you would expect from a tapas bar is here, including spiced sausage and potatoes as well as squid in blue-black ink, which is delicious. Wash it all down with dry sherry, or some beer which, unusually for London, is always served cold here.

Geales
2 Farmer Street W8
071-727 7969

Open: Tues–Sat, lunch
midday–3 p.m., dinner
6–11 p.m.
Credit: A, V
Average: £25

This busy backstreet restaurant has taken fish and chips upmarket and by doing so has hit on a very successful formula. Fresh cod, haddock, plaice and rock salmon are cooked the way they ought to be, in the beef dripping that gives the batter such a distinctive taste. The fish all comes with chips and mushy peas or a gherkin and they do a good deal on fish, chips and champagne here, which is very well put together. The wine list is small and good, and there is a choice of bottled beers or draught lager. Geales is an odd restaurant with rather strange customs, such as making you pay the drinks bill up front, but it is one of the best places in London to try classic English fish and chips.

Kensington Place

201–205 Kensington
Church Street W8
071-727 3184

Open: lunch, Mon–Fri
midday–3 p.m., Sat,
Sun midday–4 p.m.;
dinner, Mon–Sat
6.30–11.45 p.m.,
Sun 6.30–10.15 p.m.
Credit: A, V
Average: £45

Sitting in here is the closest you will ever get to being in a fish tank. Passing faces stare in the huge windows at the happening people who make up Kensington Place's clientele. It's very popular with media people and minor pop stars and was very successful in the affluent eighties when new money was looking for a new home. Despite the recession, though, it's usually still packed as the food is actually very good. The simple things here are always the best – try the chicken and goats' cheese mousse or the fish dish of the day, and follow it up with some home-made ice cream or baked tamarillos served with vanilla ice cream. There's a set lunch menu which is very good value, as indeed is the restaurant as a whole – the problem is getting a table.

The Ladbroke Arms

54 Ladbroke Road W11
071-727 6648

Open: 11 a.m.–3 p.m.,
5.30–11 p.m.
Credit: A, V
Average: £15

The bar food at this small pub at the Holland Park end of Ladbroke Grove is good and worth coming for – fresh prawns and good slices of steak are always available and the rest of the menu changes daily. It's an attractive place, with lots of flower baskets hanging outside and an open fire and well-stocked bar inside. It's probably not a good idea to get drunk here, however, as the clientele are for the most part off-duty policemen from the police station across the road.

Lisboa

57 Golborne Road
W10
081-968 5242

Open: 8 a.m.–8 p.m.
No credit cards
Average: £4

Apart from the people, everything you see here is as fresh as it can be. The pastries are baked downstairs and a constant stream of warm Portuguese croissants and cakes are eagerly consumed by a bizarre pot-pourri of people from all different walks of life who find themselves sharing a table and listening to each other's nonsense. Throughout the day media, fashion and art-world folk gather to discuss projects which will probably never come to fruition. I have heard more bullshit in this cafe than anywhere else in the world. It is wonderful. The coffee is served in a tall glass and is exceptionally good, especially in the morning; to complement it try a small rice cake, called a bolo, which is a meal in itself. The local Portuguese community uses this place a lot and all their wedding and christening cakes are made here, and at Christmas and Easter special festive cakes are made.

Maison Bouquillon

45 Moscow Road W2
071-727 4897

Open: Mon–Fri
8.30 a.m.–9 p.m., Sat,
Sun 8.30 a.m.–8 p.m.
No credit cards
Average: £5

After a walk through Hyde Park this is a perfect place to have a cake, a coffee and a long chat. They never hurry you out of this place and at times are so friendly that they look as if they're about to join in your conversation, however intimate it may be. The coffee is excellent and the cakes are outrageously good, especially the eclairs, which have so much cream in them that it takes an afternoon to get through one. One of their ham and cheese croissants is perfect in the morning and fills you up for the rest of the day.

Maison Pechon

127 Queensway W2
071-229 0746

Open: Mon–Sat
7 a.m.–7 p.m., Sun
9 a.m.–6 p.m.
No credit cards
Average: £5

Everything you see in this patisserie is made downstairs in the bakery. The smell of almonds, jams and chocolate hits you as soon as you walk in the door and immediately makes you feel starving. The cakes and pastries and the coffee are as good as you'll get anywhere else in London; there's also a selection of very sinful ice cream (£1.60). The best time to go is for Sunday breakfast, when the groggy heads of Bayswater are getting themselves together after a long night.

Makan

270 Portobello Road
W10
081-960 5169

Open: Mon–Sat
10.30 a.m.–9 p.m.
No credit cards
Average: £14

Located in the heart of all the noise and business around Portobello Market, Makan is owned by a husband-and-wife team who spend a great deal of their time by the ocean in Malaysia, though the restaurant remains open when they are away. Why they come back to England is a mystery but we should be grateful, because their food is magical. Though I have been eating their squid and rice for years and would be reluctant to change to something else, the sweet potatoes and noodles are impossible to ignore. It's strictly non-smoking, and all their dishes are available to take away. Makan is unlicensed but has a good range of soft drinks.

Malabar

27 Uxbridge Street W8
071-727 8800

Open: Mon–Sat, lunch
midday–2.45 p.m.,
dinner
6.30–11.15 p.m.; Sun,
lunch
midday–2.45 p.m.,

This two-floored Indian restaurant has become something of an institution in Notting Hill. It always seems to be very busy and the smallish, cosy rooms are more intimate than the Indian restaurants in the nearby Westbourne Grove.

The menu features unusual dishes such as grilled marinated chicken livers as well as the more traditional pasandas, dhals and dhansaks. A terrific vegetable thali costs about £12 including dessert and coffee, and comes highly recommended. The food is

dinner 6–11 p.m.
Credit: A, V
Average: £35

Micro-Kalamaras
66 Inverness Mews W2
071-727 5082

Open: Mon–Sat
7.30–11.30 p.m.
Credit: A, Amex, DC, V
Average: £18

Mike's Cafe
12 Blenheim Crescent
W11
071-229 3757

Open: Mon–Sat
7 a.m.–6 p.m.
No credit cards
Average: £6

192
192 Kensington Park
Road W11
071-229 0482

Open: Mon–Sat, lunch
12.30–3 p.m., dinner
5.30–11 p.m.; Sun
lunch 1-3.30 p.m.,
dinner 7–10.30 p.m.
Credit: A, Amex, V
Average: lunch 20,
dinner £40

fantastic but it does tend to be a little expensive – but then you are in the upmarket section of Notting Hill.

This Greek restaurant sits next door to its big sister, Mega-Kalamaras, which is plusher, more expensive and licensed. Mega may have the looks, but Micro definitely has the atmosphere. The menu has a selection of good, authentic Greek vegetarian and meat dishes and my favourite is the baby squid, which comes deep-fried and piled on a plate. The seemingly unending set meal is £12 a head and definitely worth a try if you're feeling hungry. The restaurant is not licensed, but you can take your own wine which they will open for you without charge. Many people feel that this is one of the best Greek restaurants in London. It certainly has the nicest staff, who will always do their best to find you a seat in this busy, successful little place.

Mike has been opening his doors to the real workers every morning at 7 a.m. since time began. All day he serves heavy plates of bacon, beans, chips and two toasts, washed down by big mugs of tea. They never get an order wrong in here, even though the caff is always packed with big hungry men in a hurry. You often see models stopping off here on the way to appointments, slurping their tea and stuffing their faces with stodge and not putting on an ounce of weight. Mike's Cafe is cheap, warm and clean, and that's everything you need from a caff.

This wine bar/restaurant is a favourite spot for local art dealers and people from the publishing and music businesses. It's owned by the same people who own the Groucho Club in Soho, and tends to attract a similar clientele of celebs as well as locals. Various members of Pink Floyd are often to be seen here, as is Jason Donovan, nibbling on a seasonal salad which is one of the many consistently good things about this place. The modern European cuisine here is quite decently priced and the menu very sensibly blurs the line between starters and main courses. The atmosphere is always worth sampling, as is the extensive wine list – the house wine is a bit of a disappointment but everything else is good.

The Portobello

22 Stanley Gardens
W11
071-727 2777

Open 24 hours
Credit: A, Amex, DC,
MC, V
Average: £120 for a
double room including
breakfast

This is a sexy but increasingly tired-looking hotel set in the nice part of Notting Hill. Unfortunately it has become increasingly popular with rock people, who are normally overweight, overwrought and over-demanding and who tend to take advantage of the 24-hour breakfast service in the basement restaurant just as you're planning a quiet drink. It overlooks the quiet and well-kept gardens behind where local residents including Tina Turner do their sunbathing. The prices are high and the 25 rooms can be small, though every one is different. If you're in the mood for a saucy weekend try to get the room with the fourposter bed or the round room, complete with round bed and Victorian stand-up bath. The hotel is not open to non-residents.

The Portobello Star

171 Portobello Road
W11
071-229 8016

Open: Mon–Sat
11 a.m.–11 p.m., Sun
12.30–3 p.m.,
7–10.30 p.m.
No credit cards

A small, uncomfortable bar, the Portobello Star is popular with the supposedly real people of the area who see it as too old and dingy for the new inhabitants or even the drug dealers, who have moved into so many of the local pubs, to move into. The Star has taken over from the Warwick Castle down the road as the home of the 'Roughler' fraternity of Notting Hill old-timers, who take their name from the Rough Trade shop (see separate entry) and whose occasional home-produced magazine takes an irreverent look at the new people who regard Notting Hill as their own. You can get bar snacks here, but food isn't really their thing. A Whitbread pub, they also serve the excellent Castle Eden and Flowers Original.

The Uxbridge Arms

13 Uxbridge Street W8
071-727 7326

Open: Mon–Sat
11 a.m.–11 p.m,, Sun
midday–3 p.m.,
7–10.30 p.m.
No credit cards

In the heart of Notting Hill Gate's backstreets, Uxbridge Street boasts a healthy selection of small, good restaurants, but its main attraction is undoubtedly the Uxbridge Arms. With its low beams and open fire, it has a great atmosphere and serves as a traditional local to the residents of Notting Hill village. It's a Whitbread pub and serves a good selection of real ales as well as the usual lagers. The back bar is the most relaxing place to go. The Uxbridge Arms serves no food, but it doesn't have any music or machines either, and is certainly one of Notting Hill's best bars.

The Warwick Castle

This was once the place to feel the vibrations of the real Notting Hill, but the grubby interior that was once

225 Portobello Road
W11
071-221 5140

Open: Mon–Thurs
midday–11 p.m., Fri,
Sat 11 a.m.–11 p.m.,
Sun midday–3 p.m.,
7–10.30 p.m.
No credit cards

much loved is now merely unsavoury and uncomfortable. The place was, admittedly, never much more than a pool table and a few stools in the first place, but the rumour that there was a decent pint of Guinness to be had here was enough to keep them coming. People actually used to travel to get here, which could only be because it had a reputation for being cool, and West London is obsessed with being cool. It can be strange when you realise that the person talking to you in some kind of New York street vernacular was actually brought up as a lord. Some would argue that the Warwick hasn't changed. Don't believe them, and don't touch the bar food unless you're desperate.

SHOPPING

Aero
96 Westbourne Grove
W2
071-221 1950

Open: Mon–Fri
9.30 a.m.–6.30 p.m.,
Sat 10 a.m.–6 p.m.
Credit: A, V

Aero has attempted to push the case for modernism in quality furniture design. There's a lot of chrome and glass here, as well as good, interesting lighting, and they display the conical furniture of Matthew Hilton and the sculptural pieces of Henry Moore to good effect. The vast majority of the furniture available in Aero, however, is made to their own in-house designs.

You need to be careful when shopping in places like this, as modern pieces tend to be expensive due to the high quality of the materials used, and you cannot always be sure that your sofa or sideboard will become a collectors' item. Also, London homes, especially apartments and flats, tend to be on the smallish side and much of this furniture demands a big, airy space in order to be seen to its best effect.

**The Bicycle
Workshop**
27 All Saints Road W11
071-229 4850

Open: Tues–Sat
10 a.m.–6 p.m.
No credit cards

The Bicycle Workshop is where most people in this part of town come to get their bicycles repaired. It's always busy here and it can often be difficult to get your bike in for a service and have it back on the same day. They will also make bicycle frames to order – racing and touring bike frames cost from £200 to £500. Repairs are very cheap here and the store also offers a limited selection of spare parts, as well as bags and fashion wear. Outside there is a selection of very old bikes which are for sale, though some of them are used for spare parts.

Books For Cooks
4 Blenheim Crescent
W11
071-221 1992

Open: Mon–Sat
9.30 a.m.–6 p.m.
Credit: A, Amex, DC, V

Probably the best cookery bookshop on the planet where you can find anything from a recipe for the most obscure Peruvian dish to the truth about haggis. This homely, welcoming shop even has a cafe at the far end. It's a place for the beginner as well as the expert, and it seems that they are constantly helping people who come and describe a dish they had in a restaurant the night before and now want to make at home. The owner is highly knowledgeable and kind to a degree but please don't try her patience too much.

Ceramica Blue
10 Blenheim Crescent
W11
071-727 0288

Open: Tues–Sat
10.30 a.m.–6.30 p.m.
Credit: A, V

This building was home to one of the first art galleries to come to Notting Hill in the eighties, but when that world turned upside down Ceramica Blue opened here overnight and has been a great success. The frontage and the shop itself have a very Sicilian feel enhanced by the use of carved wood and an explosion of colour inside. Large and small bowls and vases from Italy, France, Wales and England, all of which are very brightly coloured, stand on the shelves. Tiles cost from £5, mugs start at £8, and you can also get signed one-offs from famous Sicilian potters – prices for these range from £25 to £80.

Cheeky Monkeys
202 Kensington Park
Road
071-792 9022

Open: Mon–Sat
9.30 a.m.–5.30 p.m.
Credit: A, V

Cheeky Monkeys sells a mixture of second-hand designer and practical clothes, priced between £5 and £50. Some of the dresses are a bit over the top and the amount of pink on show was a bit much for me, but there's a great selection from sources as varying as Yves St Laurent and Mothercare. As well as clothes, the store stocks new shoes and accessories, and has the only fitted shoe department for young children in West London. The most popular part of the shop, though, is a playgroup for kids between two and five years old, which costs £3 an hour and is supervised by two Montessori teachers. They have also opened a children's hairdressing area, with cuts costing from £5, which just might stop parents doing it themselves.

David Wainwright
251 Portobello Road
W11
071-727 0707

Open: Mon–Sat

This store has found itself a comfortable niche in the market for authentic Asian artefacts and furniture. David Wainwright regularly visits Thailand and India, bringing back with him high-quality wooden and metal pieces which would look good anywhere. Mirrors cost from £60 to £200, small tables begin at

9.30 a.m.–6.30 p.m.,
Sun 11 a.m.–5 p.m.
Credit: A, Amex, V

£150 and go up to £750, and there's a variety of candlesticks which range from £20 to £200, making Wainwright's one of the most popular shops in West London – most of the local trendies seem to have furnished their flats from here.

Decorative Parlour Pieces
82 Golborne Road
W10
081-969 6262

Open: Tues 1–5 p.m.,
Wed, Thurs
10 a.m.–5 p.m., Fri,
Sat 9 a.m.–5 p.m.
No credit cards

Most of the items on sale here come from France, and the enamel painted boxes and tins, as well as the decorative iron and wooden beds would look completely at home in a chateau in deepest Provence. This highly respected shop sells only good, authentic pieces at reasonable prices. The last time I was there they had just sold all their enamel tins and kitchenware to a Japanese collector who had wandered in off the street. It's that kind of place – if you like something snap it up as quickly as possible before it goes. Beds range from £250 to £800, candlesticks are around £15 and sets of enamel pots £45. There's also a great selection of lamps – hanging lamps cost from £120 upwards.

Dub Vendor
150 Ladbroke Grove
W10
081-969 3375

Open: Mon–Sat
9.30–6.30 p.m.
No credit cards

The heavy, heavy sound of reggae put through the echoes and repeats is what dub is all about, and here rare and unheard-of records can be found which, when played with the right emphasis on the bass, can make your knees tremble and your trousers fall down. From I Roy to V Roy, all the original cuts can be found here in this shop which has recently moved from a tight little space underneath the flyover. The shop is usually packed full of local Rastas who treat the place as their second home.

Elgin Books
6 Elgin Crescent W11
071-229 2186

Open: Tues–Sat
10 a.m.–6 p.m.
Credit: A, Amex, V

This old-style village bookshop has a generous range of new hardback and paperback books with a table of newly published recommendations in front of the till. It's a lot friendlier and more intimate than the high street chains, and doesn't try to compete with them in terms of range; if they don't have what you want they will gladly order it for you. Many writers, such as Martin Amis and Emma Tennant, live locally, and this shop will always have their books in stock.

Fiddles and Sticks
13 All Saints Road W11
071-221 4040

This musical instrument repair shop has a team of professionals who can mend anything from flutes and saxophones to guitars and even harps, though they specialise in stringed instruments. It's a small shop which has recently been done up, and now looks

Open: Mon–Sat
10.30 a.m.–6 p.m.
No credit cards

**The French Kitchen
Company**
42–44a Westbourne
Grove W2
071-221 2112

Open: Mon–Fri
9 a.m.–5.30 p.m.,
Sat 10 a.m.–5 p.m.
Credit: A, V

R. Garcia and Sons
250 Portobello Road
W11
071-221 6119

Open: Mon–Wed, Fri,
Sat 9 a.m.–6 p.m.,
Thurs 9 a.m.–1 p.m.
No credit cards

**Golborne Road,
W10**

Open: market, Fri, Sat
8 a.m.–5 p.m.

very Victorian, as does the character who owns the place and does most of the repairs. When I bought a balalaika here recently, he was able to show me how to tune and play it.

If you're looking to stock your kitchen with pots and pans which not only look good but which are also practical working tools, this should be your first stop. Everything you could ever need for the home – or indeed the restaurant – is available here. Heavy, enamelled metal Le Creuset cookware is available here and is perfect for Agas or country houses but perhaps a little bit specialist for small London flats. Plates, cutlery, thousands of pots and pans (from £20 for a heavy-based saucepan) and every ladle or scoop that has ever been designed can all be had from here, at very good prices.

This Spanish store can be disappointing on a first visit but if you take the time to examine the various shelves you will find the most extraordinary bottles and cans of squid, sun-dried tomatoes, artichokes and the like. Garcia's also sells pasta and meats such as hams and salamis. The shop also stocks an amazing selection of around twenty different types of olive. There is also an excellent selection of Spanish wines. Garcia's caters mainly to the local Spanish community, but the people here are always willing to spend some time telling you what's what.

The Golborne Road crosses the Portobello Road (see separate entry for Portobello Road Market), its more famous cousin, towards its northern end, and with its large market on Fridays and Saturdays, selling fruit, veg and junk, it is in many ways an extension of the Portobello. In fact, many of the more interesting stalls, selling anything from a Jim Reeves record collection to an original art-deco bookshelf, can be found here. As well as the weekend market there are shops – open every day – selling antique furniture which, again, tends to be relatively cheap. The Golborne Road also boasts a strange mix of cheap cafes – there are Moroccan, Algerian, Portuguese, Spanish and Irish cafes dotted here and there.

Overshadowing the area like a watchful giant is Trellick Tower, a block of council flats with an incredible view of London, though it is also thought to have a dangerous side which I have never come across. Behind the tower is the Grand Union Canal, and a walk along the towpath will take you as far as Camden Town and, beyond that, to Islington, Hackney and Limehouse.

Graham and Green

4, 7 & 10 Elgin
Crescent W11
071-727 4594

Open: Mon–Fri
10 a.m.–6 p.m., Sat
9.30 a.m.–6 p.m.
Credit: A, Amex, V

The ubiquitous G&G sell anything from a well-strapped leather bag to a length of colour-printed Indian linen. The various branches are like smaller versions of Liberty, and charge similar prices. Number 4 specialises in arty, ethnicky knickknacks for the home, number 7 in more modernistic accessories and kitchenware, and number 10 in expensive but classy women's clothing. The chain has spawned a number of imitations such as Verandah on Blenheim Crescent. The staff are very Notting Hill and are definitely not as polite as the customers, who nevertheless keep coming back.

Harper and Tom's Flowers

13 Elgin Crescent W11
071-792 8510

Open: Mon–Sat
9 a.m.–7.30 p.m.
Credit: A, V

Harper and Tom's started out as a small street-corner stall. They now also have a large shop which will put together a beautiful arrangement for you, as well as supply you with plants and dried flowers. You'll find that Tom has the ability to sell you just about anything, though it's hard to resist any of the flowers and plants on sale here. Deliveries within the local area are free. The corner stall continues to sell a good mix of irises, hydrangeas, sunflowers, eucalyptus and chrysanthemums, as well as houseplants, all at reasonable prices.

Honest Jon's

278 Portobello Road
W10
081-969 9822

Open: Mon–Sat
10 a.m.–6 p.m., Sun
11 a.m.–5 p.m.
Credit: A, Amex, V

From Blue Note to the new sounds of British jazz, this ragbag of a store has a wide choice and a decent selection of second-hand and reasonably priced records. They specialise in rare and deleted jazz and also jazz fusion and soul. The people who work here are very well informed but have a tendency to let you know it. It's a very well-established place and a favourite with local jazz bands, who tend to listen to more than they buy here. There's another branch in Camden.

Low Pressure

186 Kensington Park
Road W11
071-792 3134

The first place in London to sell authentic and practical surfing gear, Low Pressure stocks all the most popular labels such as Life's A Beach, Stussy and Hot Tuna. The shop itself is run by real surfers who take

Open: Mon–Sat, winter
10 a.m.–6 p.m.,
summer
10 a.m.–8 p.m.; Sun,
winter midday–6 p.m.,
summer 10 a.m.–6 p.m.
Credit: A, V

a tremendous pride in their attitude towards the environment. Everything here, including the interior fittings, made from wood from ships, is either recyclable or already recycled. At the back of the store, where the boards are stored, is a large mural of whales and dolphins, and video displays reflecting campaigns such as Surfers Against Sewage and the Clean Water Initiative. Here you can pick up a second-hand board at prices which start at £150. New boards cost between £200 and £300. Clothing prices start at £15 to £20 for a T-shirt and go up as high as £100, and there's also a wide range of swimwear costing in the region of £20–£30. Low Pressure also stocks a wide range of accessories and specialist magazines.

Mr Christian's
11 Elgin Crescent W11
071-229 0501

Open: Mon–Fri
9a.m.–7 p.m., Sat
9 a.m.–6 p.m., Sun
9.30 a.m.–2 p.m.
No credit cards

This delicatessen is situated comfortably in an elegant little street which attracts the wealthier clientele of the Portobello market. Rolls filled with anything from brie and salami to curried chicken are available every day and a decent selection of bread and cheese is always on display. Hot food made on the premises, such as stuffed pimentos, costs from £1.50 upwards. It's a bit on the expensive side, but it's great when you are in a rush. There's a delivery service available, and on Saturdays they have a stall outside selling filled rolls and salt beef.

Music and Video Exchange
28–30 Pembridge Road
W11 (records); 36
Notting Hill Gate W11
(clothes); 38 Notting Hill
Gate (records); 56
Notting Hill Gate
(musical instruments and
computers); 64 Notting
Hill Gate (books)
071-221 1075

Open: 10 a.m.–8 p.m.
Credit: A, V

This place started as a second-hand record and tape exchange that would take anything that wasn't scratched, but will now buy anything from an old bicycle to a second-hand novel and sell it at a decent price. As regards music, times have changed, and they are now more interested in the CD market than they are in LPs, which they tend to look on with scorn. They still do have an incredible selection of old records, all of which are in good condition, and it's a great place to go if you're feeling nostalgic. The bookstore is a wonderful place – it seems to specialise in modern fiction, and as the price of a book is reduced every fortnight or so it remains unsold, you can pick up quite new novels very cheaply indeed. Lots of unwanted review copies are sold here, so you can sometimes get a newly published hardback for the price of a paperback.

No. 80
80 Golborne Road
W10
081-960 5531

Open: Mon–Sat
10 a.m.–5.30 p.m.
No credit cards

In amongst the junk heaps and the fruit stalls lining the Golborne Road, which is often considered a poor relation of the Portobello Road, lies No. 80, which stocks a strong mix of decorative antique pieces from many different sources and periods, as well as a wide range of iron beds, pine shelves, art-deco lamps and old wrought-iron lamps, all of which would look good somewhere. It's the kind of store where the more you look the more likely you are to find something interesting hidden behind what looks like junk. Prices are all reasonable – a French table lamp I liked cost £60, though prices go as high as £1,000 for a chandelier.

Pau Brasil
282 Portobello Road
W10
081-964 2290

Open: Tues–Sat
10.30 a.m.–6 p.m.
Credit: A, DC, V

In its time this place has been a record store, an antiques market and a squatter's flat, but it is now the proud possession of a young Brazilian who has transformed it into a mixture of a deli and a curio shop. Everything on sale here comes from Brazil: the walls and shelves are lined with wooden artefacts and the fridge is ablaze with differently coloured food and drinks. Try guarana, a drink made from crushed seeds and said to be a sort of natural speed – it's very popular in high-energy clubs. Brazilian tapas cost about 60p a portion, and gifts range in price from £1 to £10. There's also a range of women's swimwear (around £40) in fluorescent colours, and Brazilian musical instruments (also around £40). There's also a selection of leaflets about Brazil, as well as imported newspapers to cater for the large Brazilian population attracted to the Portobello Road area by the well-established Portuguese community.

Portobello Road Market, W10 and W11

Open: fruit and veg,
Mon–Wed, Fri, Sat
8 a.m.–1 p.m., Thurs
8 a.m.–1 p.m. (limited
selection); junk, Fri
8 a.m.–3 p.m., Sat
8 a.m.–5 p.m.;
antiques, Sat
8 a.m.–5 p.m.

This long street stretches northwards from Pembridge Villas, very close to Notting Hill Gate, towards Ladbroke Grove, and was once a rough track leading to Portobello Farm. Towards the end of the eighteenth century and all through the nineteenth century revellers would gather on what is now known as the Westbourne Grove Junction to sell their wares, drink and eat at the many food stalls that sprang up. Two hundred years later very little has changed.

The official Portobello Road market was established in 1870, with dealers selling everything from herbs to horses. It wasn't until the next century, when the Caledonian market closed, that antique dealers came here in any numbers, to be followed by hordes of people looking for a bargain.

Early on Friday mornings you can buy cheap clothing from the covered section underneath the Westway, where you can buy a pot-pourri of items such as picture frames, buttons, beads, books and herbs. Further on up the road you come to junk stalls selling the strangest selection of knickknacks at very low prices, giving this area of the market an authentic scrapyard feel.

The main antiques market takes place on Saturday, when the antique dealers come out in force. The road is packed with people from early morning to late afternoon, and is an eccentric mixture of different stalls and cultures. In recent years the council has toyed with the idea of making Portobello a cobble-stoned pedestrian precinct, but the idea was decided-ly unpopular with the fruit-and-veg stallholders who are here five or six days a week, and with the local people who manage to live perfectly normal lives in the middle of all this mayhem.

Mainly young people, the residents of the Portobel-lo Road area are well served by the variety of bars and cafes here, which include Portuguese, Spanish, Irish and West Indian establishments as well as traditional greasy spoons. The social novelist George Orwell lived at 10 Portobello Road, and the writer Martin Amis has often used the street as a setting for his novels about the indiscretions of the eighties.

BOOKS FOR
COOKS

Rough Trade
130 Talbot Road W11
071-229 8541

Open: Mon–Sat
10 a.m.–6 p.m.
Credit: A, V

The most independent record shop in Britain, Rough Trade was the place where the alternative music scene born off the back of punk really matured. Under the guiding light of Geoff Travis a record label was formed and a network of distribution contacts ensured that new, independently made records were available all over the country. The label had some financial difficulties but has now re-emerged with its base on the Golborne Road.

Covered with posters from seminal punk and post-punk releases and gigs, the Rough Trade shop is the meeting place for people interested in new music and the creation of a live scene, and was the best place to find out what was happening. That scene has shrunk but Rough Trade now have their own label, WIIIJA, on which lots of hip new groups such as Huggy Bear and Silverfish started. The shop will take indie groups' first singles on a sale or return basis and now that CDs seem to have taken over completely, it's one of the few places where you can get new releases on vinyl. There's another branch opened below Slam City Skates in Covent Garden's Neal's Yard (see separate entry), and Rough Trade also has branches in Tokyo and Paris. Don't annoy the owners by asking for original pressings of 'Anarchy in the UK', though – they only sell current releases.

Themes and Variations
231 Westbourne Grove
W11
071-727 5531

Open: Mon–Sat
10 a.m.–1 p.m.,
2-6 p.m.
Credit: A, V

The owners probably regard this place as a gallery but I prefer to call it a shop, dealing specifically with fifties and sixties art objects such as ceramics, furniture and lighting. Everything you could ever want to decorate a home can be found here but at prices which go as high as £1,500 for a chair. There's no doubting the taste of the French owners, who were the first to give a showcase to now very successful designers such as Tom Dixon, and the shop is always an explosion of colour. Everything here is authentic but demands a certain type of home – big.

Tom's
226 Westbourne Grove
W11
071-221 8818

Open: Mon–Sat
8 a.m.–8 p.m., Sun
10 a.m.–2 p.m.
Credit: A, V

This beautifully designed shop, heavily influenced by Italian and French delicatessens, offers a wonderful range of fresh goods and a helpful, knowledgeable service. From wild mushrooms to cheese so soft it's practically running out of the door, this culinary treasure chest is a delight just to smell. You can have a coffee and a multi-layed baguette at a decent price here while you decide what to buy. The owner is Tom Conran, son of Habitat founder Terence Conran, and he has obviously learned all his father knows about taste. It's a bit on the expensive side but the food is really good.

The Travel Bookshop
13 Blenheim Crescent
W11
071-229 5260

Open: Mon–Sat
10 a.m.–6 p.m.

In ten years of coming here I have never left this shop empty-handed, and several times an hour spent browsing and leafing through some odd publication has inspired me to take a cheap holiday in some remote zone. The shop sells both the old and the new, so it is possible to find a classic work of travel writing hidden among the Rough Guides and the photo books. Travel catalogues are arranged by

Credit: A, Amex, V

Whiteley's
Queensway W2
071-229 8844

Open: 10 a.m.–8 p.m.

continent and are free, and they also have an invaluable mail-order service.

Towards the end of the last century an ambitious young Yorkshireman called William Whiteley came to London in search of fame and fortune. Six years later he opened a small shop in what was then the very unfashionable Bayswater. 'Everything from a pin to an elephant' was his slogan; he was a natural businessman and Whiteley's prospered – so much so that ten years after his arrival in London he realised his dream by opening the most comprehensive store London had ever seen. The first department store in London and the model for others such as Selfridge's, in its heyday Whiteley's employed 6,000 people. Tragedy struck, however, when William Whiteley was shot dead by a young man claiming to be his illegimate son. The store went into decline; not even Whiteley's sons could summon up anything like their father's entrepreneurial spirit and enthusiasm for selling. After World War II the big stores in the West End made Bayswater once again a forgotten part of London and the store eventually closed its doors in 1981.

Eight years later, however, the Edwardian grandeur of the store was revived when Whiteley's was reopened as a modern shopping complex, catering to the new type of young person who had moved into the area. It now provides for virtually every need – books, groceries, furniture and clothes are all on sale here and there are restaurants, coffee bars and a multi-screen cinema complex. The first two floors are where the shops are, and the second floor is the food section. The Italian Mamma Amalfi looks as if it has come straight from a Tuscan village, the French wine bar goes for a very Parisian look and the American cocktail bar is a blaze of neon and hamburgers. Poon's Chinese restaurant is also very good. The restaurants take their last orders at around 10.30 p.m., and the building itself opens at 8 a.m. and closes at midnight. The American-style cinema complex (see separate entry for Whiteley's UCI) shows the latest releases.

ENTERTAINMENT

Anderson O'Day
255 Portobello Road
W11
071-221 7592

Open: Tues–Fri
10.30 a.m.–5.30 p.m.,
Sat 11 a.m.–4 p.m.
Credit: A, Amex, V

Gallery owner Pru O'Day has had enough sense to realise that the art market is the most volatile of them all and as a result has concentrated on a few select artists, slowly building up a reputation for dealing in beautifully constructed modern pieces. Her belief in her artists' ability has made her the most successful of all gallery owners in the area. From the Glaswegian Mario Rossi to Birmingham's Ian Jones, as well as Londoner Maria Chevska, Anderson O'Day has shown itself able to find and develop painters from all over the country and from all different backgrounds. It's also a very friendly place which encourages you to come in and have a look.

**Cobden Working
Men's Club**
170 Kensal Road W10
081-969 0584

Open: Mon–Sat
midday–11 p.m., Sun
midday–3 p.m.,
7–10.30 p.m.
No credit cards

This space is to be found above a bar popular with some of the roughest-looking people you're ever likely to encounter. They never seem to blink as hordes of trendy locals make their way up the stairs for a a live performance by local talent. It's an amazing venue which was once a Saturday-night variety spot until it fell on hard times and was rescued by one of London's many entertainment entrepreneurs. The trendy part of the club is not open every night, so ring first to check. You can hire the hall for functions, but there is no food.

The Coronet Cinema
Notting Hill Gate W11
071-727 6705

Credit: A, V

The most magnificent of all the Notting Hill cinemas dates back to the late nineteenth century, when it housed a mixture of music hall and variety. It has now sadly fallen into some disrepair and looks quite sad – the changing peoples of Notting Hill village have failed to protect this building and there is a rumour that it is soon to be a McDonald's. It would be a shame to see it go as it's a great Saturday-night venue, just like you imagine cinema used to be. It doesn't take bookings, but despite its old-fashioned feel it still manages to put on popular films almost contemporaneously with the West End cinemas.

The Electric Cinema
191 Portobello Road
W11
071-792 2020

More than any other building, the Electric has caught the spirit of the district. It's been threatened with closure for years and at the time of writing is in receivership, but somehow it has always managed to survive, showing European art movies to a contented

Credit: A, V

few. Recently developers tried to transform the cinema into an indoor market but were defeated by local residents, who now unfortunately seem to sit at home watching videos rather than come here. The Electric refuses to give up though, and recently has been the venue not only for film premieres but also live concerts. The programme changes daily but leans heavily towards the artier side of things, offering some excellent double bills.

Gate Cinema
Notting Hill Gate W11
071-727 4043

Credit: A, V

When they used to put on late-night films here – European art house and gay movies were especially popular – this cinema would be full of couples snogging and sometimes doing a bit more than that. It no longer opens so late but does still promote the more interesting movies currently being made, and occasionally hosts premieres. The programme changes every month unless demand justifies a longer period for a film. The interior is very plush and comfortable – almost too much so, which of course is fatal if you have to concentrate on subtitles.

Gate Theatre
The Prince Albert, 11
Pembridge Road W11
071-229 0706

No credit cards

This successful small fringe theatre has consistently put on topical plays dealing with local issues as well as the universal. It is all done on the cheap but somehow usually comes off well, and it gives new writers a chance to show their work. It is the only performance space of its type in the neighbourhood and suffers from the same problems as other pub theatres – principally lack of money, lack of space and noise. But they make do and they do it well.

Porchester Centre
Queensway, W2
071-792 2919

Ring for details of times
for various activities
No credit cards

If your body is in desperate need of tightening up the Porchester baths and steam rooms and the gym are all decently priced. The pool is exceptionally clean and large enough to accommodate the good as well as the bad swimmers, and next door is a smaller pool which is ideal for kids. Connected to the pool by an adjoining door are the Turkish baths, where they provide towels and so on and where there is a small snack bar, and for the one price you can also use the pool. It doesn't work the other way round, unfortunately. The steam rooms have alternative days for men and women, except on Saturdays, which are mixed. On the men's days the place is full of taxi drivers swapping stories and having their backs beaten with an old rug rope. Monthly and yearly membership is available.

Queens Ice-Skating Club

17 Queensway W2
071-229 0172

Open: Mon–Fri
11 a.m.–4.30 p.m.,
7.30–10 p.m., Sat, Sun
10 a.m.–12.30 p.m.,
2.30–5 p.m.,
7.30–10 p.m.
Credit: A, V for large parties and in shop only
Admission: £4–£5

I have never enjoyed this place as I have no natural rhythm and find that falling on cold, hard ice tends to hurt rather a lot. Other people tell me that it can be great fun for novices as well as the highly skilled. All the necessary equipment is available for hire, but I think that there's a certain attitude needed to skate well and that can't be rented – but there is enough going round here for everybody to share. There are a bar and cafe here which are adequate, but Queensway is full of many more interesting places to eat and I would recommend you try one of these instead. At the weekend it's impossible to move here, let alone get on the ice, but everybody looks as if they are having a good time.

Todd Gallery

1–5 Needham Street
W11
071-792 1404

Open: Tues–Fri
11 a.m.–6 p.m., Sat
11 a.m.–5 p.m.
Credit: A, V

Probably the most ambitious of all the local gallery owners, Jane Todd experimented with conceptual and abstract work in her smaller gallery at the top of the Portobello Road before moving to these much grander surroundings, which are an indication of how seriously she takes the gallery.

Todd's is rumoured to be backed by musician and artist Brian Eno – whose judgement is not to be taken lightly.

The Special Photographers Co.

21 Kensington Park Road W11
071-221 3489

Open: Mon–Fri
10 a.m.–6 p.m., Sat
11 a.m.–5 p.m.
Credit: A, Amex, V

This gallery was an early success in the art world simply because it opened at a time when there were very few spaces dealing exclusively with photography. There has been a consistently good series of exhibitions here which all concentrated on the beauty of the photograph rather than on abstract themes or the never-ending debate on photography as art. They look after the great jazz snapper Herman Leonard, and it's always worth a visit just to see his prints of Nina Simone or Miles Davis.

Subterrania

12 Acklam Road W10
071-963 0940

Open: Mon–Thurs
8 p.m.–2 a.m., Fri, Sat
11 p.m.–3 a.m.,
Sun 7–11 a.m.

At one time this was a popular reggae and punk venue known as Acklam Hall. When it gave up trading there was a definite lack of nightlife in Notting Hill. Though it looks like nothing from the outside, Subterrania can, at its best, be one of London's greatest venues, featuring good garage and house nights, with guitar bands earlier in the evening. Some bands think it is the worst venue in the world to play,

Credit: A, V

Admission: £5–£10

as you have to use the house PA, but it's possible to create a terrific atmosphere here. It's on two levels, with a balcony overlooking the stage – I prefer downstairs, as there is a good bar there and a decent-sized dancefloor. The strange tension created by the Westway, a huge road which runs overhead, adds to the atmosphere. I've spent some of the best nights of my life here, and used to love it when I lived locally in Cambridge Gardens, as I only had to fall out of the door to get home. Queues start to form outside at around 10 p.m. They have quite a heavy door policy here, which can be a bore but which does at least help to prevent any trouble.

Whiteley's UCI

Whiteley's, Queensway
W2
071-792 3324
(bookings), 071-792
3332 (programme
details)

Credit: A, V

The cinema section of Whiteley's is responsible for making the shopping centre such a success. The eight screens, all of varying sizes, show commercial, Hollywood-style films and the individual cinemas are all very comfortable, with little places on each chair for you to stow your drinks. You can leave your car in Whiteley's car park, which is very expensive but safe and convenient, but the real selling point of the cinema complex is its proximity to Whiteley's various bars and restaurants, all of which open late.

North

Camden

NW1

CAMDEN

Camden Town's origins date back to the late eighteenth century when the former Lord Chancellor, Charles Pratt, Earl of Camden, started developing his estate of rough farm land around the area now known as Camden High Street. The layout of the quarter today follows the original coach routes which ran through Camden High Street on their way to the North before dividing, as the underground system does today, in the direction of Highgate or Hampstead. When the Regent's Canal was completed in 1820 it opened the area to industry and schemes of wharfs and warehouses were developed alongside it, as well as new businesses as varied as breweries and piano manufacturers. Edwardian times saw Camden Town develop into a network of small family businesses including everything from herbalists to saddlers and from tripe dressers to picture-framers. Horse buses carried visitors, shoppers and people looking for entertainment at one of Camden's many public houses or the Bedford Theatre of Vanities on the High Street, which featured performances by stars such as Marie Lloyd, Vesta Tilley and George Robey. It is now a branch of the Abbey National.

The Victorian railway lines cutting through Camden were built by Irish navvies who brought their families and a taste of Ireland to the area, though Camden's Irish feel has been usurped by the Greek Cypriot community who arrived between the wars and in the midfifties, transforming areas such as Pratt Street into

a home from home. Today there is a healthy variety of Greek-Cypriot restaurants and shops here.

In the sixties local authority housing schemes destroyed the old Camden and left it with housing estates and blocks of flats which, while they do provide homes, are so close together that they are now showing signs of inner-city squalor and decay.

Camden is renowned for its weekend market, where thousands of people of all age groups gather to rummage around looking for a bargain or to watch the variety of tribes who come to congregate in the many bars and cafes which seemed to appear from nowhere over the last few years. Here Saturday is calm compared to Sunday, when the market is a mass of seething bodies which occasionally stop to buy or look at something. You can find anything from a mohair coat to a pair of good worn Levi's here – as well as every conceivable knicknack you could want for your home, from candlesticks to curtain fabric.

Camden is home to media people and writers. During the week it is quieter, and has a villagey atmosphere not unlike that of Notting Hill and Islington. The writer Alan Bennett lives here, as well as musician Jazzie B of Soul II Soul fame and the actor/writer/director Simon Callow. The borders around Camden Town are leafy and green enough to separate it from the West End but it is still incredibly close to central London, making it an expensive but mixed area to live in.

HOW TO GET THERE

Tubes
- Baker Street
- Caledonian Road
- Camden Road
- Camden Town
- Chalk Farm Road
- Edgware Road
- Euston
- Kentish Town Road
- King's Cross
- Marylebone Road
- Mornington Crescent
- Regent's Park
- St Johns Wood
- St Pancras
- Swiss Cottage

Buses
- Adelaide Road: 31, C11, C12, N31
- Albany Street: C2
- Camden Road: 29, 253, N9, N29, N90
- Camden Street: 44, 214
- Chalk Farm Road: 31, 68, 168, N5, N31, N93
- Euston Road: 10, 14, 14A, 18, 27, 74, 135
- Eversholt Street: 68, 168
- Finchley Road: 13, 46, 82, 113
- Hampstead Road: 24, 27, 29, 134, 135
- Kentish Town Road: 46, 134, 135, 214, C2, N1, N2, N93
- Marylebone Road: 18, 27, 74
- Park Road: 13, 82, 113, 274
- Prince Albert Road: 274
- Regent's Park Road: 274
- Royal College Street: 46
- St Pancras Road: 46, 214
- York Way: 10, C12

SIGHTS AND SITES

Arlington House

1 Arlington Road NW1

This huge red-brick building, financed by the nine-teenth-century philanthropist L. Rowton, opened in 1905. It once housed over a thousand homeless men but now provides four hundred beds for London's lost and forgotten people. At night, when it lights up, it becomes one of the saddest sights in the city. The small windows which hide the people inside are like those of Victorian prisons, and the building is a macabre and awful place which should remind us of the people who suffer every day in this great big city.

London Zoo

Regents Park NW1
071-722 3333

Open: winter
10 a.m.–4 p.m.,
summer
10 a.m.–5.30 p.m.
Credit: A, V
Admission: £6 (children
£3.70)

Founded in 1828, London Zoo immediately caught the public's imagination when the Zoological Society of London's collection of zebras, monkeys, bears and many other animals, including turtles, were put on display here in Regents Park. In 1832 the animals of Kew's Royal Menagerie and the king's animals, which used to roam freely around the Tower of London, were moved here – the royal family had then in their collection an alligator, an anaconda and an Indian elephant. Improvements were made to the place throughout the twentieth century, and additions in-cluded a futuristic penguin pool by the great architect Lubetkin and the Mappin Terraces, built to house the bears and designed by Belcher and Joan, who also designed the aquarium.

During the Second World War many animals had to be destroyed to prevent them escaping should the zoo be bombed. The snakes were decapitated and the fish were eaten. In 1958 Chi-Chi, the world's most famous giant panda, arrived from China, and attracted millions of visitors to the zoo.

Due to a lack of adequate funds, the zoo has had serious financial problems over the last ten years, and has faced closure on a number of occasions. It's also under threat from the growing idea that zoos are not an acceptable way of keeping animals who would be better in their natural environment, although this argument does not take into account the fact that many species survive in zoos which would otherwise have been hunted into extinction. It's a vexed ques-tion, and a difficult one, but there is no doubting the pleasure that London Zoo has given to millions over the years, and the great loss its closure would mean.

Madame Tussaud's Waxworks and The London Planetarium

Marylebone Road NW1
071-935 6861

Open:
10 a.m.–5.30 p.m.
No credit cards

Madame Tussaud made wax figures at the court of the French king Louis XVI, and specialised in models of the heads of those about to go to the guillotine. At the turn of the century she took her work to England and toured her models around the country, where they met with great success. Her trick was always to update her models and to keep them topical, and she would go to enormous expense to buy authentic robes and gowns from famous figures – George IV was paid £10,000 for his coronation robes.

The best of the wax models do have an uncanny resemblance to the originals, and a tour through here will take you past historical figures from Lord Nelson to the wild-eyed Picasso. Royals are much in evidence, and after the separation of the Prince and Princess of Wales, their models were moved a discreet three inches apart. By far the most popular room, though, is the chamber of horrors. You're allowed to take photographs, but you'll be hard pushed to find the room.

Next door is the London Planetarium, opened in 1958, which is a far, far better place to go. A visit here will take you on a journey through the cosmos with the help of a Zeiss projector. It's a brilliant way to try to understand the magnitude of the universe. The Lasarium show is definitely worth its extra charge: it combines a laser show with up-to-date dance music and looks like a giant, amazing pop video. You can get a combined ticket that allows you entry into both the Planetarium and the waxworks, or you can go to either one separately. The choice, as they say, is yours – but I'd go for the Planetarium every time.

Primrose Hill, NW1

071-486 7905 (Royal Parks)

Open: 5 a.m.–30 mins before dusk

Up until the reign of Elizabeth I, Primrose Hill, which gets its name from the abundance of primroses which grow here in spring, was a forest alive with bucks, boars and wild bulls. The main hill, which is 206 feet high, has been a popular place to view the city since the eighteenth century, and in the nineteenth century young bucks would come here to duel and settle their scores. The 112 acres of land, officially part of Regents Park, remain a popular walking place for Londoners seeking a breath of fresh air at the weekend, but during the week it's very quiet and peaceful. On a clear day the view of the capital is magnificent. During the winter Primrose Hill is one of the few places in London where you can do some sledging, although you may have to wait several years in between trips with your sleigh.

Regent's Canal Tow Path, NW1

The English have a very special talent for hiding wealth, and the rather ramshackle facades of some of the houses along this tow path are more than likely to be hiding well-kept, impressive Victorian interiors and that particular mixture of high-tech consumerism and fake-rustic decor. Though the houses might not look great from the front, the gardens at the back are the great English giveaway – they are gorgeous and as private as a St James's club, often hidden behind trees and high fences.

At weekends the section of canal around Camden Lock is jammed with tourists and shoppers seeking bargains among the dozens of stalls in the one-time haylofts and stables, but during the week the whole area is blissfully quiet and peaceful. A walk eastwards along the towpath will take you towards Islington – where there's a small nature reserve well worth visiting with kids, though at the time of writing it's under threat from the Channel Tunnel – and eventually through Bethnal Green and Limehouse to the Thames. Westwards will take you to Little Venice – quite unlike any other part of London – and Kensal Green, going through London Zoo on the way.

Regent's Park, NW1

071-486 7905 (Royal Parks)

Open: 5 a.m.–30 mins before dusk

This large tract of land, one of the many hunting grounds owned by Henry VIII, was largely undisturbed up until the early nineteenth century when George III, then the Prince of Wales, asked architect John Nash to develop it, linking it to Westminster with a new street, Regent Street. Nash was nearly 60 when he took on this project in 1811 and completed it in only fifteen years. It's an astonishing example of good town planning. In Park Village West Nash created one of the first garden cities, beautiful villas surrounded by greenery, but the white stuccoed terraces of the area are all worth looking at, particularly the magnificent Chester and Cumberland Terraces. Also worth a look is the Macclesfield Bridge over the canal, with its three brick arches resting on a cast-iron Doric column. The Nash sweep carries on

down through Regent Street (see Oxford Street and Marylebone) and on to Piccadilly, where it curves towards Haymarket and St James's Park.

Somers Town, NW1

This often forgotten-about area lies between St Pancras Station and Hampstead Road, with Crowndale Road to the north and Euston Road to the south. It was once the site of Totenhall Manor, a medieval house surrounded by a moat and by rough farmland. The house belonged to the Somers family – Baron Somers of Evesham was Lord Chancellor in 1697. The unstoppable growth of London spread into Somers Town in the eighteenth century, when the house was demolished and replaced with many more dwelling places, used to house the poor. People fleeing the French Revolution arrived here in numbers, and in 1808 St Aloysius Church in Phoenix Street was founded to serve a new congregation of French immigrants. During the rest of the nineteenth century the area became home to various groups of refugees. Spaniards fleeing the political turmoil in their own country settled alongside the French; Somers Town became ever more squalid and degenerated into a slum and a ghetto. Throughout the Industrial Revolution, labourers and workers on the new buildings and the canals lived in Somers Town, which by now was a high-density area and thought to be very dangerous.

Today Somers Town remains dangerous to walk through at night. For a hundred years it has been synonymous with vice of all sorts, and though there has been campaign after campaign to stamp out prostitution, drugs and crime, they still thrive in the backstreets and alleys.

The TV-AM Building
Hawley Crescent NW1

Not open to the public

This building replaced the Camden Brewery which once specialised in a brand called Elephants Pale Ale which I am led to believe was delicious. The odd construction there now comes from the mind of Terry Farrell, who designed it in 1982 for the new independent breakfast-television company TV-AM. This jaggedy mixture of studios and offices, with symbolic boiled eggs standing on the roof, brought Camden firmly into the high-tech production world of the media, and is regarded as an eyesore by many people, including lovers of modern architecture.

Across the road is MTV, the all-day and all-night music channel which shows non-stop videos introduced by rather silly people called VJs. TV-AM lost its franchise in 1992. The building is now a home for various TV production companies.

EATING AND DRINKING

Bar Gansa
2 Inverness Street NW1
071-267 8909

Open: Mon
midday–11.15 p.m.,
Tues–Sun
10.30 a.m.–11.15 p.m.
Credit: A, V
Average: £20

This cleverly marketed menu offers a selection of traditional Spanish tapas such as squid and lots of garlic bread, all of which seem to be under £5. Everything is hot and spicy, which of course calls for lots of cold San Miguel and Dos Equis to wash it all down. It's a favourite with the local media types such as the crowd from MTV. It can be difficult to get a table but it's worth the effort just to check out the VJs and their fan clubs. Funny and fulfilling – what more could you want?

Belgo
72 Chalk Farm Road
NW1
071-267 0718

Open: Mon–Fri,
lunch 11 a.m.–3 p.m.,
dinner 6–11.30 p.m.,
Sat 11 a.m.–midnight,
Sun
10 a.m.–10.30 p.m.
Credit: A, Amex, V
Average: £40

Don't be put off by the Belgian theme, which to most people (rightly) means fish and beer, or mussels and chips. Belgo looks like a post-modern larder, all clean and spacious, and the waiters float around the room dressed like Trappist monks in long habits. The walls are adorned with Rabelaisian words carved above the ash tables. The food is a mixture of the odd – wild boar sausages, or rabbit cooked in cherry beer – and the delightful – large dishes of moules biere et lardons followed by lobster, all accompanied by frites and a dish of mayonnaise. There is a set course meal which includes mussels, salad and beer for £8.95. Belgo has the widest choice of hoppy Belgian beers in the UK, from Leffe blonde at 6 per cent to Corsendonck Agnus at 8 per cent – the fruity yeasty tastes are a joy.

Cafe Delancey
3 Delancey Street NW1
071-387 1985

Open: 8 a.m.–midnight
Credit: A, V
Average: £30

Cafe Delancey has become something of a Camden institution as one of the few places in this cosmopolitan area where you can get a good breakfast from early in the morning, or can come in to for a snack and a coffee at any time during the day. Meals are served from 8 a.m., and you can have a veggie breakfast, a full English breakfast or a Continental breakfast at £3.50. The service is quite laid back, but the cafe is a good place to hang out. Steaks, fish and salads are all available throughout the day, but I think it's in the mornings that this place is at its best. It's a good place for a quiet snack and a glass of wine before a movie or a night at the Jazz Cafe (see separate entry).

Camden Brasserie
216 Camden High Street NW1
071-482 2114

Open: Mon–Sat, lunch midday–3 p.m., dinner 6–11.30 p.m., Sun, lunch midday–4 p.m., dinner 5–10.30 p.m.
Credit: A, V
Average: £40

The Camden Brasserie is a big favourite with local thespians and media folk who see it as a decent sort of place to spend a decent amount of money on a decent meal. A big steak served with salad, chips and mustard is perfect, and they do good calf's liver and char-grilled chicken; vegetarian dishes are also available. They have a large selection of French and New World wines which start at about £10 and go as high as £50. The decor is that of an upmarket American diner with lots of checked cloth and smiling staff, and the atmosphere is enhanced by an enormous open fire which gives you the feeling that your mum might be cooking in the kitchen. It's a very easy-going place and there is no pressure on you to spend lots of money.

Crown and Goose
100 Arlington Road NW1
071-485 2342

Open: 11 a.m.–11 p.m.
No credit cards
Average: £25

Though this place looks like a private club, it's not – it's a pub which serves good food. The owners have taken the discreet approach to the decor, covering the walls with fine art with a hint of the modern. There's nothing to make you feel uncomfortable in this bar, and the best thing about it is the food, which can be as simple as a steak sandwich or a little more adventurous. Home-made puds such as lemon cheesecake and chocolate mousse all cost £2.50. It's clean and quietly cool in here, and though the bar looks sparse it's actually very well stocked. The tables and chairs are so comfortable that once you sit down you could stay installed there for hours just sitting over a drink if you don't feel like eating.

Daphne
83 Bayham Street NW1
071-267 7322

Open: Mon–Sat, lunch midday–2.30 p.m., dinner 8–11.30 p.m.
Credit: A, V
Average: £20

One of the hippest Greek-Cypriot restaurants in North London, this is not as garish as many of the others and serves up a delightful mix of small dishes which add up to a serious blowout. Feta cheese, aubergines and black-eyed beans are just the beginning and are followed by meatier dishes, but the earlier combination, known as meze and costing £8.25 per person, should be enough to start the night off. Wine and beer are all available. The main courses are all very reasonably priced and the wine, which all comes from Cyprus, does everything it should do.

Diwana Bhel Poori House

121 Drummond Street
NW1
071-387 5556

Open:
midday–11.30 p.m.
Credit: A, Amex, DC, V
Average: £16

This bhel poori house is the original and the best of those to be found on Drummond Street. Diwana is a functional, low-key vegetarian restaurant with shiny pine benches and tables bolted to the floor. All the dishes and jugs are of clinical stainless steel, and the overall impression is one of cleanliness and efficiency. The food, however, is great, and comes as a revelation if you're used only to the heavier, meaty dishes that come from Northern India. The starters are the best, I think – bhel pooris, little wheat snacks, are served with potatoes, black-eyed beans, chick peas and yogurt flavoured with tamarind and spices. They cost about £1.50 each and I always have three different ones – the first as a starter and then two as a main course – as I find the official main courses less interesting. However, they do look spectacular – try a paper dosa, a lightly fried pancake with chutney saubar (hot lentil sauce) and potato filling. Prices are very low – no more than £4 for a main course dish. Diwana is unlicensed but you can take along your own and they don't charge corkage.

El Parador

245 Eversholt Street
NW1
071-387 2789

Open: Mon–Thurs
midday–3 p.m.,
6–11 p.m., Fri
midday–3 p.m.,
6–11.30 p.m., Sat
6–11.30 p.m., Sun
(summer) midday–3 p.m.
Credit: A, V
Average: £20

This tapas bar offers a selection of meat, fish and vegetable dishes, as well as good Navarra and Rioja wines, all of which are decently priced. Downstairs there is a small garden space which is a great place to sit in the summer and fantasise that you're on the Spanish coast rather than in grimy old London. Spanish and Mexican beers such as Ambar and San Miguel are the perfect accompaniment to the delicious small plates of food – try the rosario, spicy Spanish sausage cooked with red peppers and brandy (£2.70).

Quieter during the week than it is on weekends, El Parador is well worth a visit for its good value food and the great atmosphere.

Hamish's Wine Bar

85–87 Parkway NW1
071-267 3591

Open: Mon–Fri
10 a.m.–11 p.m., Sat
6–11 p.m.
Credit: A, Amex, V
Average: £35

I was first attracted to this wine bar during a bout of homesickness when I wanted to hear a Scottish voice shouting drunkenly at me. I had guessed that Hamish was Scottish, but I would never have supposed he would have a long thick beard. This hides the face of a man with superb taste in wine and a way of making you feel that you wanted really to appreciate the stuff. His Czechoslovakian wife helps with the food, which is not quite East European but is heading that way, with dishes such as potato and cabbage soup served with thick white bread. The menu changes daily and includes dishes such as Toulouse sausage with French fries and salad and smoked salmon omelette, also with fries and salad. The wines are a mixture of New World, French and Italian, though I played safe and stuck with a French Chablis which was perfect and reasonable at £11.

Koto
75 Parkway NW1
071-482 2036

Open: Mon–Sat
6–10.30 p.m.
Credit: A, Amex, DC, V
Average: £45

Open only in the evenings, this busy little Japanese restaurant looks anonymous from the street, but once through the door make sure to go upstairs to the cross-legged shoes-off tatami room which has a brilliant atmosphere and is remarkably unpompous for a Japanese restaurant. Eating raw fish and drinking saki (£3 a flask) can be very expensive, but Koto is always very good. The chicken teriyaki (£7.80) and the tempura (£8.80) are splendid, but it's the sushi that are special (£14.50). There are set menus here costing between £19 and £24 a head.

Marine Ices
8 Haverstock Hill NW3
071-485 3132

Open: ice-cream
parlour – Mon–Sat
10.30 a.m.–10.45 p.m.,
Sun 11 a.m.–7 p.m.;
restaurant – Mon–Fri,
lunch midday–3 p.m.,
dinner 6–10.30 p.m.,
Sat midday–10.30 p.m.
No credit cards
Average: £20

For over sixty years the Italian Mansi family has run this successful ice-cream parlour which specialises in home-made water ices and ice creams made on the premises from fresh fruit. It's a place to get fat and fill your face with ingenious frozen concoctions served up in typically over-the-top Italian goblets. The Vesuvius is their speciality – a gigantic sundae that costs £4.85 and includes vanilla, chocolate and masala ice cream, crushed meringue, sponge, cherries, cream and wafers. Cones cost 95p to take away or £1 to eat in and you can take home blocks of ice cream or sorbet for your freezer. The place is a favourite with the local one-child-two-car families, and is still a must with local Italians after Mass on Sunday. Unlike much of Camden Town, it retains a kind of faded glory.

In the restaurant they put together a quick but decent pasta-based lunch or dinner. Other dishes include pizzas and salads, but there is usually no fish on the menu. It's licensed, and they also do takeaway pizzas.

Odette's
130 Regents Park Road
NW1
071-586 5486

For years Odette's has been entertaining NW1's local wealthy and celebs.

This wine bar is not as expensive as it looks. French dishes such as smoked gammon at £8.50 and a perfect

Open: lunch, Mon–Fri
12.30–2.30 p.m., Sun
12.30–3 p.m.; dinner,
Mon–Sat 7.30–11 p.m.
Credit: A, Amex, DC, V
Average: wine bar £30,
restaurant £50

Underground Cafe
214 Camden High
Street NW1
071-482 0010

Open: Mon–Sat
6–11.30 p.m., Sun
11.30 a.m.–4.30 p.m.
Credit: A, V
Average: £20

**WKD Cafe Music
Gallery**
18 Kentish Town Road
NW1
071-267 1869

Open: Wed–Sat
midday–2 a.m., Sun
midday–11 p.m.
Credit: A, Amex, V
Average: £18

white chocolate pudding at £4 are impeccable – and the service is excellent. In the restaurant try the char-grilled tuna with noodles and tomatoes at £11.

The wine list is not spectacular but it is well organised, though unfortunately there is a dearth of French and New World wines at average prices. Worth a try.

It's busy in here during the market days, and even during the week always seems to be crowded. The reason is obvious – ever since it started this place has kept the prices down but has also maintained a decent standard, avoiding falling into the quick-pasta-bar trap which has engulfed the West End. For around £5 you can stuff your face on fresh pasta dishes such as smoked salmon fettucine or linguine with seafood, and there's also fish and meat dishes and salad available. Traditional Italian puddings are also available. Even better, the Underground Cafe is licensed. Definitely one of the best places in Camden to eat and drink good food and wine without having to worry too much about the bill.

This cafe/bar/club, furnished with strange-looking tables and chairs made from a mesh of metals welded together, has made a real effort to look special. It opened in early 1990, when the Mad Max style of sculpture was still popular but on the wane – I tend to think that they have got their timing wrong here and that the place looks dated.

During the day WKD functions as a cafe where you can eat from an odd, international-style menu offering hummus and felafel as well as basic salads. In the evening the bar side of things takes over and the music gets louder and more dance-oriented. It's possible to eat here until 2 a.m., but it seems as if most people come here for the beer. The drinks available are mostly imported lagers, but they've recently started doing cocktails, which are proving to be popular with the regulars.

At the weekends WKD becomes a club which seems to have been adopted by the local gay community, and if you're not in before 10 p.m. you'll have to pay an admission charge.

SHOPPING

Bibendum
113 Regents Park Road
NW1
071-722 5577

Open: Mon–Sat
10 a.m.–8 p.m., Sun
11 a.m.–6 p.m.
Credit: A, V

This enormous warehouse, a cool alternative to traditional wine merchants, stocks the finest and some of the most reasonably priced wines I have encountered in London – prices can range from £2.98 a bottle to £13,000 a case. The size of the place can be baffling at first but everything is laid out in an idiot-proof manner. Most regions of Europe are represented and the New World wines which have made such a dent in the pockets of the French are in good supply. They will put together a mixed case for you. Same-day delivery within the M25 is free and they can also supply all the wine, soft drinks and glasses you need for a party.

Camden Coffee Shop
11 Delancey Street
NW1
071-387 4080

Open: Mon–Wed, Fri, Sat
9.30 a.m.–6.30 p.m.,
Thurs 9.30 a.m.–1 p.m.
No credit cards

The Camden Coffee Shop is one of the smallest and cheapest coffee shops in London, which has nevertheless managed to put together a splendid choice of blends ranging from Continental mild to Kenyan and Colombian. The most impressive coffees here are the Turkish and Arabic types, which are so strong and treacly black that they could keep you going for a week. A pound of Continental blend should set you back no more than £3, which is a rare bargain in London. Very occasionally they will make you a cup of coffee so you can taste what you're buying.

Camden Market
Camden Lock NW1

Open: Sat, Sun
8 a.m.–6 p.m.

The weekend market has become the focal point and main attraction of Camden Town. There's a proliferation of stalls and live music, and nearly every item of second-hand clothing can be bought here at a decent price, as can a huge selection of mostly useless items. Some people say that the market is not what it used to be and that it's gone too far upmarket in search of the monied middle classes. I don't really agree. All that has really changed is that the market has sprawled out of its original starting point in Camden Lock into a number of old warehouses nearby which have now been renovated.

Camden has replaced Portobello (see Notting Hill and Bayswater) as the most popular market in London, though most of the thousands and thousands of people who come here don't really know what they want – it's the activity and the interesting people who make a trip worthwhile. The stalls are a rag-bag of goodies selling anything from new and second-hand clothes to antiques, junk, beds, boats and buttons – some of the things on sale are awful smelly old rubbish and others can be beautiful.

Coming here is a great way to see London at its best, but I think it has become too crowded in recent years, although the mornings and early afternoons can be a little better. Most of the stallholders will only take cash, but some will accept cheques – forget about trying to give them credit cards.

Compendium
234 Camden High
Street NW1
071-485 8944

Open: Mon–Sat
10 a.m.–6 p.m., Sun
midday–6 p.m.
Credit: A, V

The mixture of old and new books in this store is enough to keep you here for most of the day. What works so well about this great shop is the way they mix commercial books from the big publishers with more radical writing from the independent presses. There's a good, comprehensive gay and lesbian section, and areas devoted to women's issues, new age, astrology, and religion. There is also a local history section where Camden's changing history is chronicled, and the staff are all very helpful and make an effort to find what you are looking for. Compendium also imports a wide range of books from American small presses and is often the only place in London to get a particular title. It's good for anything from witchcraft to t'ai chi and is jam-packed with books on every conceivable subject. Badges and postcards are also for sale, and information can be had here as to what's happening on the local literary scene.

Holt Shoes
5 Kentish Town Road
NW1
071-485 8505

Open: Mon, Tues,
Thurs–Sat
9.30 a.m.–5.30 p.m.,
Sun 11 a.m.–5 p.m.
No credit cards

Before Dr Marten's air-sole shoes became fashionable with nearly every tribe of fashion-conscious Londoner, Holt's was one of the few places which actually stocked them: the boys from the band Madness used to come here all the time. The shop certainly doesn't suffer from being overly design conscious, as it hasn't changed to my knowledge in ten years. Shoes with tassels come in at £36, and classic British shoes such as Loake brogues are a bargain at £55 and £65.

**Inverness Street
Market, NW1**

Open: Mon–Sat
9 a.m.–1 p.m.

This street has been the venue for a daily fruit and veg market since 1927. It is an odd street which mixes market stalls with cafes and bars where huddles of men from the nearby Arlington House (see separate entry) sit drinking cheap strong alcohol. Nobody seems to pay much attention to them and the market folk get on with selling their wares. There is a fantastic and cheap cheese stall at the High Street end of the market, selling French delicacies as well as the standard English fare. Always check what you buy in the market before you pay for it, and it might be an idea to choose your own fruit.

Offstage
37 Chalk Farm Road
NW1
071-485 4996

Open: 10 a.m.–6 p.m.
Credit: A, V

Specialising in theatre, film and media books, this shop is so large that you think at first there can't possibly be enough books on these subjects to fill it. It seems, though, that almost every well-known writer has written about or for film at one stage or another, and Offstage is crammed with fascinating books. There are good textbooks available on screenwriting, such as *Screenplay* by S. Field, and copies of original screenplays of classic and popular movies also sell well.

Ron Arad Associates Ltd
62 Chalk Farm Road
NW1
071-284 4965

Open: Mon–Fri
10 a.m.–1 p.m.,
2–6 p.m.
Credit: A, Amex, V

The designer Ron Arad has moved his Covent Garden cavern to North London, where his furniture designs can be seen in a totally new way. They are now situated in an old factory where Ron can keep an eye on his workers from above. His designs are always radical and often uncomfortable, but they are quite something to look at.

A few years ago furniture-making was caught up in the design craze that was sweeping the country, but although Ron has moved on to bigger and better things, he still continues to do what he is very good at – designing wonderful tables and chairs. Metal, plastic or rubber are all bent into contorted shapes which look far more sculptural than functional. Prices are frightening, though, starting at £860 for a tree lamp and going up to £15,000 for a mild steel chaise longue.

Sainsbury's
17 Camden Road NW1
071-482 3828

Open: Mon–Thurs
8.30 a.m.–8 p.m., Fri
8.30 a.m.–9 p.m., Sat
8 a.m.–8 p.m., Sun
9 a.m.–5 p.m.
Credit: A, V

Sainsbury's is a high-street food supermarket which changed the face of British shopping by stocking those items such as good cheeses, olive oils and specialist vinegars which were previously available only in delicatessens and specialist shops.

This high-tech building was designed by Nicholas Grimshaw and is a marvel of beams and taut suspension rods which hold the whole thing together, bringing in as much natural light as possible. Inside, the various food departments in the store are easy to find and the supply of goods is an example of capitalism at its best. There's a fresh fish counter, a delicatessen, a bakery and a counter where you can get a pizza made to order. This consumerist palace offers good parking if you need it, easy access and, most importantly, quality. It works brilliantly.

Swanky Modes
106 Camden Road
NW1
071-485 3569

Open: Mon–Fri
10.30 a.m.–6 p.m.,
Sat 11 a.m.–6 p.m.,
Sun
11.30 a.m.–5.30 p.m.
Credit: A, V

This women's clothes shop has been here for so long that it has become something of an institution. The clothes change each year but they never seem to be in sync with those in other shops as Swanky Modes has always done its own thing no matter what the fashion gurus say. Their swimwear is legendary and their Lycra dresses from the late seventies have become very fashionable again. They also do a made-to-measure service. They have built up a reputation and kept it over such a long period that they have gained regular clients and always seem to be able to attract new people. Clothes are relatively good value but you might not wear them very often. Dresses can vary from £50 to £200, and swimsuits begin at £40.

Tumi
23 Chalk Farm Road
NW1
071-485 4152

Open: 10 a.m.–6 p.m.
Credit: A, V

This South American craft shop sells clothes as well as ornaments and musical instruments. The waistcoats and jumpers (about £50) are made from sheep's or alpaca wool and feature traditional Peruvian designs and colours. The rich texture of Indian history is captured in the garments, which look ethnic enough for the local hippies to adopt them as the latest thing. Authentic South American instruments such as wood pipes, which have a beautiful, haunting sound, are available, and you can also pick up cassettes of the music if you need a little extra inspiration. Pan pipes start at about £9, and there is also a large selection of flutes.

Yellow Jersey Cycles
44 Chalk Farm Road
NW1
071-485 8090

Open: Mon–Sat
9 a.m.–6 p.m., Sun
11 a.m.–5 p.m.
Credit: A, V

This is a great place to buy a bike from as the people here are very willing to spend hours persuading you to feel good about going out there and trying your luck on the London streets, which have never been designed to accommodate cyclists and which are among the most hazardous in the world for them. Camden, however, is one of the few boroughs which have tried to maintain safe cycle routes. I bought my mountain bike from this shop and it cost a reasonable £150, though prices in general vary from £250 to £1,500.

Yellow Jersey Cycles has a full repair shop and as well as cycles sells a full range of associated gear, such as clothing and mountain-bike accessories which are all the rage.

ENTERTAINMENT

Camden Palace

1a Camden High Street
NW1
071-387 0428

Open: Tues–Sat
9 p.m.–2.30 a.m.
Credit: A, Amex, V

Opened in 1904 and originally known as the Camden Theatre, the Palace was designed by the architect W. G. R. Sprague and opened by the legendary actress Ellen Terry. The BBC Orchestra used the building as a recording studio until 1972, when it became listed and was renamed the Music Machine, functioning as a concert hall for the new wave of guitar-based bands such as the Damned and the Vibrators, living out their fantasies of being pop stars. I played there during the seventies when I was the singer in a punk band called the Skids. The first time the entire audience ended up on stage, all trying to fight each other and the band; the second performance was marred by someone being stabbed. It was the kind of palce where this kind of thing happened quite often.

When the bands went back to their day jobs the place became the home of the outwardly flamboyant fantasy figures called New Romantics who enjoyed a brief period of notoriety. Throughout the early eighties velvet-suited men in thick make-up danced the evening away with androgynous women. In the mid-eighties the venue, now known as the Camden Palace, became a refuge for the oddballs from the rave scene who came here to trance, dance and stare at the ceiling.

Nowadays the nights vary between sixties and seventies evenings and rave; admission price depends on how popular each evening is. The ghost of Ellen Terry, which supposedly walks around here at night, must wonder, when she looks down on characters such as Iggy Pop, Steve Strange and the hazy happiness of acid house, what has happened to this good old-fashioned theatre.

**Camden Parkway
Cinema**

14 Parkway NW1
071-267 7034

This beautiful old art-deco cinema has fought a constant battle for survival against the greedy redevelopers who want to do something obscene to the place and turn it into an office suite or a bingo hall.

As I write the fight is going on, supported by local celebrities such as the playwright Alan Bennett, and hopefully the cinema will survive. It puts on General Release films which look perfectly at home in this old picture house which is serving its community in the best way possible.

Camden Plaza

211 Camden High Street
071-485-2443

Credit: A, V

The Plaza is celluloid heaven for art-movie lovers. Unlike its beautiful cousin around the corner in Parkway, which shows more commercial films, this cinema is home to German, French and American films which would never catch the general public's attention. It is indicative of the type of people who live in Camden that this cinema has survived for years and always appears full whenever I go there.

The Falcon

234 College Road
NW1
071-485 3834

Open: Mon–Thurs
11 a.m.–3 p.m.,
5.30–11 p.m., Fri–Sun
11 a.m.–11 p.m.
No credit cards

The Falcon is one of the few venues encouraging live music left in London. When the music scene returned to pop normality, the capital's burgeoning rock scene came to an end. One result of this was that bars which had enjoyed the noise and sweat of live music went thematic as breweries put pressure on their tenants to make their establishments more respectable and profitable. Bands split up and stages were removed and replaced with pots and plants, but not here. The Falcon prides itself on being a live venue and puts on anything from minor heavy metal to serious NME doomhead types who make the most of any opportunity to play in front of a real audience. It's a home for serious grunge music fans who are prepared to watch new bands try out new and quite dreadful tunes, and such stars of the grunge scene as Daisy Chainsaw and the Lemonheads have passed through its grimy portals.

The Forum

9 Highgate Road NW5
071-284 0303

Credit: A, Amex, V

The Forum was originally the Town and Country Club, one of the best live venues in London, especially popular with rock groups who like to build up a sweaty atmosphere. The Marquee Club, when it was still on Wardour Street, was once the place to see real acts play live, but was superceded by the T&C. The bands who played here were, those just about to hit stadium status: Nick Cave, Youssou N'Dour, the Pogues, David Byrne, the Neville Brothers and even David Bowie all played here; Van Morrison played the final gig here in March 1993. The

Forum holds over a thousand people and unusually for London there is enough bar space and staff to cope with the thirsty fans.

It is too early at the time of writing to say whether the Forum will continue the fine tradition established by the Town and Country Club, but we wait with clichéd breath . . .

Hampstead Theatre
Swiss Cottage Centre,
Avenue Road NW3
071-722 9301

Credit: A, V

The Hampstead Theatre is one of the actors' favourite theatres in London. It's intimate, and unlike many fringe venues, the stage is big enough to allow for very physical productions. It has a tradition of using the work of new writers, and in recent years most of the productions – *Someone to Watch Over Me*, *June Moon* – have moved to the West End where they have done very well. *Burn This*, starring John Malkovich, was another recent success. If you're a theatre lover, the Hampstead Theatre should always be on your list.

Jazz Cafe
5 Parkway NW1
071-916 6000

Open: Sun
midday–4 p.m.,
7 p.m.–midnight,
Mon–Thurs
7 p.m.–midnight,
Fri 7 p.m.–2 a.m.,
Sat midday–4 p.m.,
7 p.m.–2 a.m.
Credit: A, V, Switch
Average: £30
Admission: £3–£10

Standing opposite the Camden Parkway cinema and housed in an old Barclays Bank building converted in the late 1980s, the Jazz Cafe provided a North London venue for a form of music which has been undergoing a considerable revival. The new and younger audience attracted by jazz wanted a stylish and comfortable venue to hear the music. The Jazz Cafe was an answer from heaven – it's a modern club with good acoustics and a large bar. There's a table service providing 'modern city cuisine' which includes poached chicken breasts and grilled salmon. Main course dishes range between £6.75 and £10.75, and starters and puddings, including grilled tamarillos, cost about £3. The drinks are a bit on the expensive side and vary from good German beers to New World wines, as well as soft drinks and spirits. But despite the plush interior, this place is all about the music, and especially about giving younger musicians a chance to play in front of a live audience.

Jongleurs
Middle Yard, Camden
Lock NW1
071-267 1999

This comedy club, originally based in Battersea (see Battersea and Clapham), has moved into a building which once was home to the R&B club Dingwalls. Four nights a week at least three stand-up comics come here to do their thing, and obviously thrive on the interaction with the audience. As a result, the live

Open: Thurs–Sun from
8 p.m.
No credit cards
Admission: £5–£8

comedy circuit is booming and Jongleurs is a testament to its success.

Drinks are available at pub prices and you can eat here if you want, though Camden is so well supplied with cafes and restaurants that if I were you I'd go somewhere else before or after the show. If you're of a bashful disposition I'd recommend that you sit well away from the stage, as otherwise you're likely to be picked on by the performers.

MARINE ICES

*S*eparated by the sprawling expanse of Hampstead Heath, these two villages have managed to hold on to their own identities and characters without paying too much attention to the rest of London.

With the astonishing views of the city to be seen from Highgate Hill, and its small streets and village shops, Highgate in many ways has the appearance of a small market town in the north of England. It was from here that in 1937 Richard Whittington was said to have heard the Bow Bells telling him to turn and go back to London, where he would later become Lord Mayor. The original village was centred on the area now known as the Grove, which was the site of many fairs and games in the sixteenth century and which was also believed to be a very healthy place to recover from various ailments. As London expanded the rich flocked to Highgate to build their mansions on the great heights overlooking the growing city. The area is probably best known for its cemetery (see separate entry), which was laid out in 1839 and which remains a tribute to the way the Victorians regarded death. Highgate has always attracted the literary-minded – famous residents have included Lord Byron and Sir John Betjeman – but in recent years it has become home to media types such as TV 'celebrity' Jeremy Beadle and pop star/actor Sting. The area has survived the developers' greed but is now struggling to cope with the sheer volume of traffic that comes thundering through the village towards the North Circular.

North

The houses look as magnificent as they have always done, but the village has lost something of its soul.

If Highgate has lost its soul, then Hampstead has bought a new one. This is the home of London's new monied class who see the village as an important step on the social ladder as well as a nice place to live. It was here that the pagan Queen Boudicca, who fought in vain against the Romans, was buried and here, in AD60, the Roman road to St Alban's began. During the Middle Ages at the time of the Black Death people came to the Heath for sanctuary, and the Great Plague of the seventeenth century saw the village invaded by fleeing Londoners seeking a safe haven. It was during this period that the Gordon Rioters came to attack Lord Mansfield's house at Kenwood, but they were stopped on the way by the landlord of the Spaniard's Inn, who gave the anti-Catholic revolters free drinks until soldiers arrived to deal with them. In the eighteenth century Hampstead became very popular with the arts and literary crowd as a health resort, and the people attracted to the area include William Pitt, the painter Leigh Hunt, H. G. Wells, Sigmund Freud, Robert Louis Stevenson, Anna Pavlova and Ramsay MacDonald. These days Hampstead is a favourite with thespians and media moguls who see it as the perfect place to live. In many ways they're right – Hampstead is well positioned for easy access to central London, and the Heath offers a chance to pretend you're in the country. Although the area has become too expensive for many intellectuals, it remains the home of people like Margaret Drabble, John Lahr and Melvyn Bragg.

HOW TO GET THERE

Tubes
- Archway
- Belsize Park
- Chalk Farm
- Finchley Road
- Golders Green
- Hampstead
- Highgate
- Swiss Cottage
- Tufnell Park

Buses
- Archway Road: 43, 134, 234, 263, N1, N92
- Dartmouth Park Hill: 4, C12
- Finchley Road: 13, 82, 113, N13
- Fitzjohn's Avenue: 46, 268
- Fortis Green Road: 102
- Gordon Ho Road: 46, C11, C12, N93
- Great North Road: 143, 143A, 263, N1, N92
- Haverstock Hill: 168, N5, N93
- Highgate High Street/Highgate Hill: 143, 143A, 210, 271
- Highgate Road: 214, C2, C11, C12
- Muswell Hill Road: 43, 134, 234
- North Hill Road: 143, 143A
- Parkhill Road: 24, 46, N93
- Rosslyn Hill: 46, 268, N5
- Swains Lane: C11, C12

SIGHTS AND SITES

Burgh Museum
New End Square NW3
071-431 2516

Open: Wed–Sun
midday–5 p.m.
No admission charge

This beautiful Queen Anne house is a museum which concentrates on the many exciting developments in Hampstead's history and there is a fine collection of prints by the famous nineteenth-century painter Constable, who was a local resident. Another resident, Dr William Gibbons, was made a very wealthy man by the people who flocked to taste the foul-smelling waters he drew from the local stream and sold as a cure for anything from impotence to death itself.

The museum also puts on very good classical concerts and recitals which always attract good names.

Cromwell House
104 Highgate Hill N6

This remarkable example of a red-brick house which is generous in its proportions while having the minimum of decoration was built in 1638. It has absolutely no connection with the Lord Protector, however, and did not take his name until 1883. Originally a private dwelling, it has been in turn a boys' school, a hospital for sick children and a convalescent home. It used to be occupied by the Montfort Missionary Society who would allow you to have a look at the spectacular staircase, but it is now the Ghana embassy and so is unfortunately closed to the general public.

Hampstead Heath, NW3

Hampstead Heath's 800 acres include Parliament Hill (see separate entry), Golders Hill (between Heath Street, North End Road and West Heath Road) and Kenwood (see separate entry for Kenwood House). Throughout the Middle Ages the Heath was a haven for people escaping plague and disease, and its springs, like those of many uncultivated areas, were supposed to have medicinal qualities – there's an area here still called the Vale of Health. In later times it was popular with writers and poets – the Kit-Kat Club met at the Upper Flask Inn in East Heath Road, and the likes of Steele, Pope and, later, Keats and Shelley became regular visitors. The club was a gathering of influential Whig patriots in the eighteenth century who wanted to make sure that there would be a Protestant succession to the Crown, and was named after the pastry cook Christopher Katt whose house was the venue for the first meeting.

The locals are fiercely proud of the Heath and of

the various facilities on offer, from outdoor bathing (see separate entry for Hampstead and Highgate Bathing Ponds) to fishing and horse-racing. The summer sun seems to bring out the eccentrics in numbers, especially the kind who talk to themselves, and the last time I was there a couple were taking their pet goat for a walk. In the evenings it is a well-known cruising area for gay men, but it's not a good idea to come here at night.

Highgate Cemetery

Swain's Lane N6

081-340 1834

Open: Eastern Cemetery – April-September 10 a.m.–5 p.m., October–March 10 a.m.–4 p.m.; Western Cemetery by guided tour only – Tues, Fri, winter 12, 2, 3 p.m., summer 12, 2, 4 p.m.; Sat, Sun hourly, winter 11 a.m.–3 p.m., summer 11 a.m.–4 p.m. Admission: Eastern Cemetery £1, Western Cemetery guided tours, adults £3, concessions £2, children £1

Established by the London Cemetery Company, whose founder Stephen Geary designed and planned the site, Highgate Cemetery was consecrated in May 1839 by the Bishop of London. The Eastern side, which is the most accessible part of the cemetery, is also the least interesting – the Western side is the bit to see. The landscape gardener David Ramsay designed the serpentine roads and footpaths which lead upwards through the burial area to the church buildings and the terrace. On the other side of the terrace is the Egyptian Avenue, which is entered through Egyptian columns and leads on to 'The Circle of Lebanon'. Here catacombs line either side of a circular passageway, and each tomb has iron doors and stone shelves for coffins. The circle is dominated by a most magnificent cedar tree which rather morbidly stands guard above this strange resting place for the dead.

Among those buried here are Tom Sayers, the last bare-knuckle prize fighter and a nineteenth-century hero, whose tomb is decorated with a carving of his favourite lion. The writer George Eliot also rests in resplendent peace on the Eastern side, and Edward Lutyens's monument to William Friese-Greene, the first man to put moving images on to celluloid in the nineteenth century, who died penniless in 1920, is well worth taking a look at. However, after World War II people's conception of death changed dramatically and the pomp associated with Highgate Cemetery became highly unfashionable. The cemetery duly fell into disrepair until a voluntary body rescued it from obscurity by organising visitors' days when a guided tour of this morbidly fascinating place can be taken. It's very creepy here and looks like the set of a horror film, but it is definitely the real thing. Tours last for about an hour and are limited to 25 people.

Highpoint Flats
North Hill, Highgate N6

Built between 1935 and 1938 by the Tecton group, under the direction of Berthold Lubetkin, these two tower blocks are among the finest examples of this kind of interwar building in Europe. The great Le Corbusier described them as a vertical garden city. They stand on Highgate's highest point and with their panoramic views of London the flats are some of the most sought-after residences in the city. Each of the seven storeys in Highpoint No. 1 contains eight flats, originally built for workers in a local factory. However, the indoor swimming pool and the seminal design make the building an icon for modern architecture lovers. You can't go in, however, unless you're with someone who lives there.

Keats House
Keats Grove NW3
071-435 2062

Open: April–October –
Mon–Fri,
10 a.m.–1 p.m.,
2–6 p.m., Sat
10 a.m.–1 p.m.,
2–5 p.m., Sun
2–5 p.m.;
November–March –
Mon–Fri 1–5 p.m., Sat
2–5 p.m.
Admission: £1.50
voluntary donation

This Regency house, built in 1815, has all the characteristics of the period – white stuccoed facade and arched windows. The house was restored to its former glory in 1974-5 and now looks just how it did when Keats lived here between 1818 and 1820, when he left for Italy and a tragically young death at the age of 26. It was in the gardens of this house that the famous surgeon-turned-poet wrote 'Ode to a Nightingale'. The library is full of his works, including a collection of his first editions and some unpublished poems, and guided tours can be arranged, with commentaries in English, French, German and Japanese. The house sits in one of the most delightful areas in Hampstead – a walk around Keats Grove and the nearby Downshire Hill, with a visit to the small neo-classical chapel of St John, makes a great afternoon.

Kenwood House
Hampstead Lane NW3
081-348 1286;
concert enquiries
071-973 3427

Open: April–September
10 a.m.–6 p.m.,
October–March
10 a.m.–4 p.m.
No admission charge

Kenwood House is a magnificent villa remodelled by Robert Adam from 1764 to 1779 for William Murray, the first Earl of Mansfield and Lord Chief Justice. To the brick house built here around 1700 Adam added the imposing portico on the north front, a third storey, and the wing containing his breathtaking library, or 'Great Room'. He encased the exterior in white stucco and embellished the interior, all in his personal interpretation of the fashionable neoclassical style. The two white brick wings were added in 1793-96 by the architect George Saunders. Most of the furniture Adam designed to complete his decorative designs was sold at auction in 1922, but the furniture collection today includes several of the 'lost' Ken-

wood pieces, discovered in America, as equivalent furniture from other Adam houses.

The Iveagh Bequest Kenwood is internationally known for the collection of paintings formed by Edward Cecil Guiness, first Earl of Iveagh, which he bequeathed to the nation in 1927. Among the many world-famous works are a late self-portrait by Rembrandt, 'The Guitar Player' by Vermeer and a portrait of Mary, Countess Howe by Gainsborough, as well as exquisite paintings by Hals, Van Dyck, Reynolds, Romney, Turner and many others.

In the service wing there is a self-service cafe which is open all year and in the summer a restaurant is also open. Both serve morning coffee, lunches and afternoon teas.

In June, July and August each year there are the well-known outdoor concerts on Saturdays and some Sundays. World-famous orchestras, together with various opera companies, perform contemporary and classical works, and at some concerts there are also firework displays. The idea is to bring a picnic and sit on the hillside by the lake listening to the music coming across the water as the sky changes colour. It's well worth booking in advance as tickets can be very hard to obtain.

Lauderdale House
Waterlow Park,
Highgate Hill N6
081-348 8716

Open: Tues–Fri
11 a.m.–4 p.m., Sun
midday–5 p.m.

This house overlooking leafy Waterlow Park was a favourite with Charles II, who supposedly rented it as a summer residence for his lover Nell Gwynne. In the eighteenth century it became a boarding house and later part of St Bartholomew's Hospital. In 1963 it was badly damaged by fire, but the Lauderdale House Society restored it completely and turned it into a local-history museum and an art gallery showing the work of mostly local artists. The shows put on here are quite good and the house can be rented for private parties. The cafe (see separate entry for Oshobasho Cafe), which looks out towards the park and London, is very good.

**Parliament Hill,
NW3**

Open: 24 hours

Great literary and poetic minds such as Keats, Shelley, Leigh Hunt and Coleridge were all regular visitors to this spot which affords a great view of London as well as of the nearby Hampstead and Highgate. It is supposedly named after the Gunpowder Plotters who planned to watch Parliament burn to the ground from here in 1605. It's one of the most popular parts of Hampstead Heath, probably because of the views, and attracts kite-flyers of all ages who spend afternoons running up and down the hill.

EATING AND DRINKING

Bengal Bertie's
172 Archway Road N6
081-348 1648

Open: Mon–Sat, lunch
midday–2.30 p.m.,
dinner 6 p.m.–midnight
Credit: A, Amex, DC, V
Average: £12

This Indian restaurant doesn't have the best location in Highgate, but if you ignore the traffic and concentrate on the food you will not be disappointed. The waiters here are too nice for words and unusually the piped Indian music seems to suit the atmosphere perfectly. The usual mixture of hot and mild dishes is available and there is a decent selection of vegetable meals to choose from. Chicken and lamb are the specialties and are all priced around the £5 mark. Cold Kingfisher beer is now on draught and goes perfectly with the food, and you also have a choice of booths or open tables.

Cafe Rouge
6 South Grove N6
081-342 9797

Open: Mon–Sat
9 a.m.–midnight, Sun
9 a.m.–11.30 p.m.
Credit: A, Switch, V
Average: £28

I'm not normally partial to nostalgia trips to Paris circa 1930 but in fact the food and atmosphere in this cafe, part of a chain of French bistros popping up all over London, are very good. The young people running the place seem to know what they are doing and the long room is well divided, giving you a place to hide or a long table to share with your loud friends, according to choice. The food is simple enough and surprisingly unpretentious – fish stew, mussels and lamb are all good – and the wine list is comprehensible and affordable. At lunchtimes there's a set menu at about £6. Definitely worth a visit.

Le Carapace
118 Heath Street NW3
071-435 5773

Open: dinner –
7–11.30 p.m. daily,
lunch – Sun
midday–3 p.m.
Credit: A, Amex, DC, V
Average: £50

This French restaurant, set in a Georgian house, is a bit grown-up – as French restaurants in London tend to be – but it can be very enjoyable. The food is quite traditional; there is no à la carte but instead a variety of set menus. These range from about £20 for two courses to £34.50 for a meal which includes wine and an aperitif. House wine is £9.20 a carafe, and half-carafes are also available. There is also an excellent selection of Bordeaux which are a bit expensive, but they have the cream of the crop of St Emilions 1989 in abundance. The restaurant itself is a bit of a fortysomething hangout but can make for a good romantic evening.

Copenhagen Patisserie

196 Haverstock Hill
NW3
071-435 7711

Open: Mon–Fri
7.30 a.m.–7 p.m., Sat
7.30 a.m.–9 p.m., Sun
9 a.m.–8 p.m.
No credit cards
Average: £6

One of the few Scandinavian patisseries in London, this place is worth a visit, if only to try their open sandwiches, which come with a variety of fillings, including sliced egg and herring. They make their own bread here, and it's thick, heavy and delicious. The cafe is near Belsize Park and is a great place to come after a walk on the Heath. Jacket potatoes with filling cost between £2 and £3.50, savoury pancakes are £3.50, large Danish pastries £1.25 and cream cakes £2.

Coffee costs £1, and they have a range of herb teas available at £1.20.

Cosmo Restaurant

4–6 Northways Parade
NW3
071-722 2627

Open: cafe
8.30 a.m.–10.30 p.m.,
restaurant
midday–10.30 p.m.
Credit: A, Amex, DC, V
Average: £15

For years this Central European cafe has been the main meeting point for immigrants to North London, and from morning to evening is busy with local drama students and gossiping regulars. The food is a mixture of basic English cooking and continental fare, such as weiner schnitzel (£7.25) and bratwurst (£4.50) and is always good enough, but the main attraction here is the delicious coffee and the cream cakes. It's the best place in the area for character and cake – I have been coming here for years. Any time of the day is fine, but teatime is best as you can eavesdrop on the complaining locals who drop in.

Everyman Cafe

Hollybush Vale NW3
071-431 2123

Open: Mon–Fri
11 a.m.–11 p.m., Sat
10.30 a.m.–11 p.m.,
Sun
9.30 a.m.–10.30 p.m.
Credit: A, V
Average: £24

Situated in the basement of the Everyman cinema, this is a popular haunt for North London's existentialists and cinema buffs. It has recently been refurbished and now caters for art-movie lovers in a more humane manner – the cafe is now pleasant enough to come to for either a drink or to eat in its own right. Baguettes and bagels are available all day, and there is a hot menu which usually includes a fish dish. The Everyman Cafe is licensed and specialises in New World wines. It's a great place for Sunday brunch and a snack before an early showing.

The Flask

77 Highgate West Hill
N6
081-340 7260

Open: Mon–Sat
11 a.m.–11 p.m., Sun
midday–3 p.m.,

First built in 1663 and rebuilt in 1767, the Flask was a favourite drinking house for the artist William Hogarth, who sketched the drunken scenes here. Nothing much has changed since his day other than the clientele, who are very much the sons and daughters of Highgate's rich and famous. In the summer it is too busy to be comfortable, but in the winter months it's as good as any other pub in London and reeks of

7–10.30 p.m.
Credit: A, V
Average: £17

character and personality. Food is served all day here and the fare, which was once a bit of a nightmare, has improved considerably in recent times.

If you should wish to be granted the ancient right of the freedom of Highgate, all you have to do is to take part in the ceremony of the Swearing of the Horns. You kiss a pair of antlers and swear an oath and are then entitled to various rights – you can kiss the fairest maiden in the room or kick a pig out of the gutter and take his place.

The Flask Tavern
14 Flask Walk NW3
071-435 4580

Open: Mon–Sat
11 a.m.–11 p.m., Sun
midday–3 p.m.,
7–10.30 p.m.
No credit cards
Average: £10

It is a pleasure to find this old-style drinking hole which has a good atmosphere, good food and drink and which is clean. Serving up Young's beer, this is probably one of the very best pubs in the capital – situated on one of the best streets in the neighbourhood it has made a supreme effort to get away from the tawdry image of the London pub. The clientele are old-school Hampstead types whom you might find a bit off-putting, but ignore them and enjoy the surroundings. In the conservatory they serve up food such as very traditional and very good Sunday roasts – a full lunch will cost £4.95 for three courses. There's also a good variety of puddings to fill yourself up with if you need to. If the Flask Tavern doesn't restore your faith in the British pub, nowhere will.

The Horse and Groom (upstairs)
68 Heath Street NW3
071-435 3140

Open: Mon–Sat
5.30–11 p.m., Sun
7–10.30 p.m.
Credit: A, V

This cocktail bar offers a night out which is a bit more special than an evening spent in a smoky pub or cafe with little to offer. Here there is live music from a blues guitarist every Sunday evening and the atmosphere, which tends to attract a slightly older crowd, is very relaxed. There's a list of more than twenty cocktails available, as well as an assortment of good new beers and a strong wine list which leans towards the New World. It's a very comfortable place and unpretentious in the extreme.

Hampstead Tea Rooms
9 South End Road NW3
071-435 9563

Open: 9 a.m.–7 p.m.
No credit cards
Average: £7

This is a great place to refresh yourself after a walk across the Heath, but do not even try to come here at weekends when the place becomes impossibly mobbed. Fruit tarts, croissants and strudels are all good, and home-made lasagne and good omelettes are available at lunchtimes at around £4. Savoury mushroom strudel costs £1.60, fresh cream cakes are £1.50 and a pot of tea is 90p. There is also a long list

of different teas, including the inexplicably fashionable and appalling (to me) fruit teas.

Jack Straw's Castle
North End Way NW3
071-435 8885

Open: Sat, Mon
6–10 p.m., Tues–Fri,
lunch midday–2 p.m.,
dinner 6–10 p.m., Sun
midday–9 p.m.
Credit: A, Amex, DC, V
Average: £30

This pub was built on the site of an old coaching inn and was named after the leader of the Peasant's Revolt of 1381, who was hanged outside in the courtyard. The inn was patronised by Thackeray and by Charles Dickens, who seemed to get all around London in his lifetime. It's a popular pub with people walking through the Heath at the weekend, but is relatively quiet during the week. It serves up a good selection of beers and ales including Highgate Mild. In the winter there's always a welcoming fire blazing, which makes the place seem even more authentic. The upstairs restaurant here serves generous portions of English food, including slabs of steak for less than £10 and delicious prawns at under a fiver.

Lauderdale House Cafe
Waterlow Park,
Highgate Hill N6
081-341 4807

Open: Tues–Sun,
summer
10 a.m.–5.30 p.m.,
winter 10 a.m.–4 p.m.
No credit cards
Average: £17

The owner of this cafe, which looks out towards the park and London, is supposedly the model for the incredibly rude restaurateur in the film *Truly, Madly, Deeply*. It's worth putting up with him, though, as the food is good and is cheap as well. Salmon pancakes or baked stuffed avocados cost £4.50, and you can get a full meal here for less than £10. There's a good selection of vegetarian dishes and at the weekends you can have fresh scones with strawberries for your tea. The high turnover keeps prices low and top whack for a bottle of wine is £6.50. It is an excellent place to bring the kids.

Louis Patisserie
32 Heath Street NW3
071-435 9908

Open:
9.30 a.m.–6 p.m.
No credit cards

The Louis is the best bet in the area for a snack. Steaming hot goulash soup, accompanied by thick crusty bread costs £2.50, perfect frothy coffee £1.20 and Hungarian cream pastries £1.60. These may rot your teeth and thicken your waistline but they will also make you very happy. The cafe is smallish and cosy, and everything is absolutely fresh. The best thing about this place is the piano player who appears here in the afternoons.

Oshobasho Cafe
The Refreshment
Pavilion, Highgate
Woods N10
081-444 1505

When I lived for a while in an apartment overlooking Highgate Woods I was surprised at how few people used them. In the summer there were always foxes in my back garden looking for bins to raid and I assumed that the woods must be a bit wild. During the day, however, they are incredible – the space and

Open: Tues–Sun
8.30 a.m.–park closing
time (summer
9.30 p.m., winter
4.30 p.m.)
No credit cards
Average: £20

the trees are intoxicating to look at and right in the middle is this vegetarian cafe. The Oshobasho Cafe, which has recently been completely refurbished, is the perfect place to stop off and refresh yourself with either their muesli breakfast dishes or a healthy lunch of Spanish omelette, salad and bread at £3.25. If you prefer an unhealthy lunch, the cafe is licensed. It's popular with families walking dogs or babies.

Spaniards Inn
Spaniards End NW3
081-455 3276

Open: Mon–Sat
11 a.m.–11 p.m., Sun
midday–3 p.m.,
7–10.30 p.m.
Credit: A, V
Average: £18

This sixteenth-century weatherboarded house was a favourite haunt of the highwayman Dick Turpin, who stabled his famous horse Black Bess in the toll house opposite, and it is here that Mrs Bardell plots the downfall of Mr Pickwick in Dickens's *The Pickwick Papers*. The Spaniards Inn was also a favourite with Shelley, Keats and Byron. Nowadays, however, it's a favourite with the Hampstead crowd who drive up here at night to look at each other's cars. If this doesn't put you off you could have a very nice time among the ghosts who are meant to walk around the pub. In summer it is one of the few decent places in London where you can sit outside and enjoy the sunshine, and in winter there are big fires in the main bar to keep the cold at bay.

Hot and cold food is available from the buffet at lunchtime (from midday to 3 p.m.) and in the evenings, when there is also a special menu.

Wakaba
122a Finchley Road
NW3
071-586 7960

Open: Mon–Sat, lunch
midday–2.30 p.m.,
dinner 6.30–11 p.m.
Credit: A, Amex, DC, V
Average: £50

This Japanese restaurant is like no other in London – a lot of money has been spent to make it look incredible. From the street you can see little more than a sheet of frosted glass, but the interior is a marvellous celebration of all things Japanese. It's very simple: plain tables line the room and at the top end is a sushi bar where the chef prepares his instruments with loving care before he starts slicing the raw fish. As with all Japanese restaurants in London, Wakaba is quite expensive, but they have made a supreme effort to get the atmosphere right as well as the food.

Zamoyski
85 Fleet Road NW3
071-794 4792

The management has tried very hard to give this place an authentic Polish country feel. Everything has been very simply done – the wooden tables in the bar are bare but for a candle, making the dim basement even

Open: bar – Mon–Fri
midday–3 p.m.,
5.30–11 p.m.;
restaurant – Mon–Sat,
lunch midday–3 p.m.,
dinner 5.30–11 p.m.
Credit: A, V
Average: £30

darker. Between 5.30 and 7 p.m. there is a happy hour when you can get very drunk very quickly on the large selection of frozen Polish vodkas. The Northwest London Polish community comes here in numbers to enjoy the herring and mackerel dishes as well as the stews, which won't do much for anybody on a diet but which really hit the spot during the colder months.

SHOPPING

Beryl Williams
Florist
71 Heath Street NW3
071-435 3876

Open: Mon–Fri
8.30 a.m.–5.15 p.m.,
Sat 8.30 a.m.–5 p.m.
Credit: A, Amex, V

It's usually impossible to park on Heath Street, which always seems to be jammed with traffic, but the displays of exotic and English plants in the window of this florist make you want to stop off and grab something to take home. Beryl Williams caters for weddings, birthdays and christenings, and charges reasonable prices, making everything even more attractive. The shop has been here for generations and it is here that Peter O'Toole buys his carnation each morning. There is an Interflora service, so you can arrange to have your flowers delivered – prices from £15.

Chipie
65 Hampstead High
Street NW3
071-431 4469

Open: Mon–
Wed, Fri, Sat
10 a.m.–6.30 p.m.,
Thurs 10 a.m.–7 p.m.,
Sun 12.30–5.30 p.m.
Credit: A, Amex, DC, V

Selling French versions of 1950s American clothes, Chipie has found a niche in the market for easy-to-wear clothes which are cleverly updated versions of old and classic designs. Their chinos, button-down shirts, cotton jumpers and good leather jackets would look good anywhere.

Like every other big fashion chain, such as Hennes and Gap, Chipie has recently started selling a line of stylish kids' clothes.

Prices here range from £40 for a jumper to £50 for a pair of cotton trousers and £250 for a jacket.

Gap Kids
35 Hampstead High
Street NW3
071-794 9182

Open: Mon–Wed, Sat
10 a.m.–6 p.m., Thurs
10 a.m.–8 p.m., Sun
11 a.m.–6 p.m.
Credit: A, Amex,
Switch, V

Gap Kids is definitely one of my favourite shops in London. This branch, unlike the vast Regent Street store, is on only one floor which makes it easier to find what you want and, more importantly, cuts down somewhat on the temptation. The shop is beautifully designed, and has a huge amount of natural light and a very American feel to it. Everything is very well laid out and you can see at a glance how the various garments mix and match to best effect. Gap have styled these kids in the same successful way they style their adult range – sensible, when it is of course the grown-ups who are doing the buying. The clothes themselves are great, though a little on the expensive side. There's also a full range of hats, gloves and, best of all, tracksuits made in high-quality cotton.

Hampstead Antique Emporium
12 Heath Street NW3
071-794 3297

Open: Tues–Fri
10.30 a.m.–5 p.m.,
Sat 10 a.m.–6 p.m.
Credit: ask

There are 24 specialist dealers in this cosy indoor market, which is all very well organised and polite. There's none of the casbah atmosphere of other London antique markets here, and the stallholders have an air of being quietly informed rather than desperate for a sale. Eighteenth-century mahogany chairs sit alongside Victorian pearl and silver jewellery and beautiful cutlery, and even if you're not interested in buying something it's worth paying a visit just for the atmosphere. If you are a bartering type, try to do it quietly.

Keith Fawkes
1–3 Flask Walk NW3
071-435 0614

Open: Mon–Sat
10 a.m.–5.30 p.m.
No credit cards

Selling a selection of high-quality antiquarian and second-hand books, Keith Fawkes is keeping the tradition of the village store alive in Hampstead. His shop is well organised and there are some gems to be found in his history, literature, travel and theatre sections. The art section is extensive, not expensive and has some great books on the likes of Robert Motherwell, the American abstractionist; when I was there he had a beautiful and very rare book on the sculptor Henry Moore. You could happily spend hours in this wonderful place, where the prices begin at 5p and go up to over £100.

Nicole Farhi
27 Hampstead High
Street NW3
071-435 0866

Open: Mon–Sat
10 a.m.–6 p.m., Sun
midday–6 p.m.
Credit: A, Amex, V

This is the best fashion house in north London, and is the only Nicole Farhi store in London to stock her range of menswear. The cool calm of Farhi's clothes immediately makes the wearer feel a stone lighter and completely in control. They follow a classic line but are suitable for any occasion, and her children's clothes are as big a surprise as her main range. Suits here come in at around £400, and the kids' stuff costs a tidy £30 to £40.

The Pasta Place
42 Heath Street
071-431 0018

Open: Mon–Fri
10 a.m.–8 p.m., Sat
10 a.m.–6.30 p.m.,

Delicious, freshly made pasta and home-cooked sauces are available every day from this new Hampstead deli. Squid, bolognese sauce and pesto all go wonderfully with tortellini, tagliatelle or ravioli (about £2.45 a pound), all of which are as fresh as you could possibly wish for. The Pasta Place also sells just about every other Italian delicacy you could wish for,

Sun 11 a.m.–6 p.m.
No credit cards

including balsamic vinegar and good, authentic parmesan. The prices are slightly above average for this kind of deli, but all the food is extremely well-prepared, clean and fresh. They will also cater for parties at short notice, providing everything from food to wine.

Peppercorns
2 Heath Street NW3
(entrance in Perrins Lane)
071-431 1251

Open: Mon–Sat
10 a.m.–6 p.m., Sun
11 a.m.–5 p.m.
Credit: A, Amex, V

This shop is where North London's macrobiotics come to get their nibbles, and it is as nice as these places ever can be. The staff are helpful and will convince you that a healthier diet will turn you into a nicer person – which can't be bad. Organic wine is also available here at £5 a bottle, and they have a wide range of vitamins and food supplements. Hot or cold food can be taken away. Prices are a little expensive since everything is organic.

ENTERTAINMENT

Andrew Usiskin
11 Flask Walk NW3
071-431 4484

Open: Tues–Sat
10 a.m.–6 p.m., Sun
1–6 p.m.
Credit: A, V

Usiskin's gallery is a mixed bag of sculpture, drawings, crafted boxes and landscape paintings, and it offers contemporary art at approachable prices which begin at £15 and go up as high as £40,000. There's no one particular slant to the work on offer; I think myself that there's a little too much of everything crowded in here to allow you to take it all in. It also perhaps tries a little too hard to please everyone and ends up putting a little too much emphasis on the arts and crafts side of things rather than on the fine art. However, it's a gallery worth supporting as it is one of the few which consistently shows work by new artists.

**The Everyman
Cinema**
Hollybush Vale NW3
071-435 1525

No credit cards

The Everyman Cinema has never bowed to commercial pressure and for years has been showing the most obscure arthouse movies or the most controversial mainstream pictures out at any particular time. Anything David Lynch or Jean Cocteau can come up with will find a home here and it's always worth a visit. The cinema itself is comfortable enough and has the added attraction of a good cafe downstairs.

**Hampstead and
Highgate Bathing
Ponds**
081-348 9908

Situated on the north-eastern side of Hampstead Heath are three bathing ponds – one each for men and women and one mixed. The water is of course absolutely freezing but this does not deter regular

Open: mixed, East
Heath Road –
May–Sept
10 a.m.–6 p.m.; men
and women's pools,
Millfield Lane May–Sept
6 a.m.–9 p.m., Dec,
Jan 7.30 a.m.–3 p.m.,
Nov, Feb
7 a.m.–3 p.m.,
March-April, October
7 a.m.–sunset

K Gallery

101 Heath Street NW3
071-749 4949

Open: Tues–Fri
10 a.m.–6 p.m., Sat
11 a.m.–6 p.m., Sun
2.30–6.30 p.m.
Credit: Amex

New End Theatre

27 New End Square
NW3
071-794 0022

Credit: A, V

users from coming here early in the morning to swim as many lengths as possible.

The settings, in amongst the trees, are beautiful, and in the summer when it is slightly warmer it can be a great place for a picnic.

Unfortunately these places always attract weirdos who want to sit and stare, which can be rather disconcerting, but there are attendants to keep an eye on what is going on.

Admission is free and opening times vary according to season – it's best to ring first to check before packing your towel and heading off.

In amongst the many galleries on the busy Heath Street lies the K Gallery. Unlike many other Hampstead galleries, this one does not rely on twee charm or pastiche to survive but has a policy of showing modern and new art. It's a small but brave space which shows both sculpture and paintings. The abstract work cannot be all that easy to sell in surprisingly conservative Hampstead, but new artists find an outlet for their work here. The prices are kept low – from £150 upwards.

This one-time Victorian mortuary has been turned into one of London's best fringe theatres. It's actually quite comfortable and is well suited to the mixture of revivals and new plays put on. Anything from Shakespeare to Shaw is performed on this stage, without the pressure of looking for a West End transfer, and consequently the work is more interesting and experimental. They sometimes stage matinees on Saturday afternoons, and these finish off a walk over the heath very nicely.

NICOLE FARHI

BALLS POND ROAD

OLD STREET

ISLINGTON

*i*n the days of the Domesday Book, Islington had a population of only 27 householders. It was surrounded by Ken Wood and Queen's Wood and was regarded as a highly dangerous and uninviting place. It was mainly farmlands in the seventeenth century, when the supposed healing powers of the spa waters on the area's hilltops helped create an air of mystery around the sprawling fields, used for little more than grazing. Islington's position, however, meant that farmers and tradesmen coming from the north always went through the area, and people from all over gathered at markets such as Chapel Street market and Camden Passage to exchange and barter goods.

In the eighteenth century Islington became a place of entertainment, when concerts, fireworks, balloon ascents and bear-baiting brought the high and mighty to 'Merrie Islington'. The area remained rural however until the nineteenth century when things began to change very quickly. This period saw the population grow from just over 10,000 to 334,991, and the building of prisons, churches, railways and factories.

The transformation of the land into smart squares and dwellings for successful City merchants turned Islington into a highly desirable area, where houses were much sought after by the new monied classes. But Islington was no Victorian utopia, though the murky poverty of the area did lead it to embrace the sound of the music hall. It was in the now sadly empty-looking Collins' Music Hall on Islington Green that Marie Lloyd sung 'er 'eart out and the young Charlie Chaplin took to the stage. Entertainment, food and alcohol have always been essential ingredients of life on the top of the hill – Mother Redcap's famous cheesecakes from up the Holloway Road, were as famous as Old Mother Pudney's Yorkshire puddings, sold in Exmouth Market (see separate entry). The gin factory on Goswell Road, which transformed the sweet spa waters into what was known as 'mother's ruin', is still there, and is still a great supporter of the local community. I imagine, though, that they're a little less keen than they used to be on the workers enjoying the fruits of their labour – time was when they were paid in liquor.

In recent years Islington has been rejuvenated, with places such as the Old Agricultural Hall (see separate entry) being transformed into a centre of artistic and commercial activity, with annual exhibitions, fairs and performances. It's also a highly sought-after – and expensive – place to live. It's a place of contrasts, and there is something for everybody here, with a choice of restaurants and cafes from all over the globe reflecting the mixture of people who have settled here. Celebs who live in the area include humourist Douglas Adams, performer and writer Stephen Fry and actor Anthony Sher, who are regularly to be seen in choice places in 'the village'. Despite the selling of Islington as a booming home for the stars and a place of upmarket bars and shopping, poverty is still rife here and there's decrepit housing not far from the doors of all the gracious squares so popular with Islington's middle classes. At times the area can feel as dangerous as it did when eighteenth-century mobs ran amok in the streets. It was here, too, that the infamous Dr Crippen cut up and boned his wife Cora. Islington is a place to get a sense of history rather than a fake notion of village life.

The area south of Islington proper and north of the City is known as Clerkenwell, getting its name from the abundance of fresh-water springs in the area, one of which was used in the twelfth century by the clerks of St Mary's Nunnery. Until Henry VIII's dissolution of the monasteries this was a quiet, religious area, but Henry ensured that most of the land and property was given to the new Tudor nobility, who built grand new houses on the outskirts of the City.

In the early seventeenth century, during the reign of James I, London's first piped water supply, known as the New River, was opened here by Hugh Myddleton. During the same period Thomas Sutton, a wealthy philanthropist, created a home and a school for the poor, which became known as Charterhouse, and still looks exactly as it originally did. During the reign of Charles II, however, the nobility moved further west with the king's court to Westminster and St James's, abandoning the areas around the City to tradesmen and merchants, especially after the Great Plague and Fire of 1665 and 1666. Skilled craftsmen who were restricted by various guild regulations within the City set up home in Clerkenwell, which was to become a favourite settling zone for new immigrants such as the French Huguenots, and a centre for watchmakers and jewellers.

As London expanded during the Industrial Revolution, Clerkenwell fell into disrepair and became one of London's most deprived areas, described as a dunghill where children were reared for the gallows. Pickpockets, receivers, coiners and child-strippers ran amok and until the middle of the nineteenth century Clerkenwell was a no-go area for police. It was said of Field Lane that you could have your handkerchief stolen at one end of the street and buy it back at the other. Charles Dickens based Oliver Twist in and around Saffron Hill, where Fagin's academy taught young criminals their trade.

During the nineteenth century Clerkenwell became known as Little Italy due to the number of Italian immigrants who settled here. The Italian church of St Peter's, which still stands on the Clerkenwell Road, witnessed the singing of the great Caruso and Gigli, and the great clown Joey Grimaldi was said to offer up the occasional prayer here. The procession of Our Lady of Mount Carmel takes place each year on the first Sunday after 16 July, and is a feast of colour and food.

The sense of disaffection felt in this poor area made Clerkenwell a centre for radical gatherings, and Clerkenwell Green was the site of pitched battles between the police and angry political movements from the Fenians to the Anarchists. The Green attracted two of socialism's great men – it was here that William Morris founded his socialist press and Lenin studied the works of Marx before the great struggle in his homeland. It's an area well worth visiting, as many of the streets still keep their original layout, but since many communities have moved on, it is quieter than it has ever been.

Finsbury lies east of Holborn, west of Shoreditch and south of Islington. Throughout the twelfth century it was used for sports such as archery and, during the winter, ice-skating. During the seventeenth century the fields were developed into what were thought to be healthy and pleasant gardens, and they were also used as mass graves for plague victims. Those

who lost their homes in the Great Fire of 1666 camped out on Finsbury Fields until they found alternative accommodation. The area was heavily developed in the eighteenth century, when John Wesley took over the old foundry and converted it into a Methodist chapel, preacher's house and school. At times he would preach in Finsbury Fields to as many as 10,000 people. Because of the amount of hospitals in the area the medical profession was based in Finsbury for centuries before eventually moving to the more upmarket district of Harley Street.

In the 1960s and 70s Finsbury was heavily developed to cope with the overspill from the City, caused by lack of office space. Now, the functional and bland office buildings are the most notable thing about the area, though the squares are well worth a walk around.

HOW TO GET THERE

Tubes
- Angel
- Caledonian Road
- Farringdon
- Highbury and Islington
- Kings Cross
- Old Street

Buses
- Caledonian Road: 14, 14A, 17, 259
- Canonbury Road: 271
- City Road: 43, 21, X43
- Clerkenwell Road: 55, 56, 153, 243, 505
- Goswell Road: 4, 56, 153
- Gray's Inn Road: 45. 46
- King's Cross Road: 63, 221, 259
- Old Street: 55, 56, 153, 243, 505
- Pentonville Road: 30, 124
- Rosebery Avenue: 19, 38, 171, 17A, 196
- St John Street: 153, 279
- Upper Street: 4, 19, 30, 43, 279

THE KING'S HEAD

Lubetkin Flats

Rosebery Avenue EC1

It's worth taking a look at the uniform concrete and red ironwork which makes up the blocks of council flats known as the Spa Green estate. At first glance they don't look any different from any other inner city block, but in fact they are surrounded by grass and trees and have an odd sense of beauty about them. Designed by the famous architect Lubetkin, these high-rise apartments are harmonious in their proportions and suit their surroundings. The flats stand on the Spa Fields, the site of 1816's notorious riots against the Corn Laws. Over 100,000 people gathered here to listen to the oratory of the leader Henry Hunt, and a misguided attack by the police left many injured and one policeman dead. Another Lubetkin building, the Finsbury Health Centre, can be found on Pine Street and displays the architect's love of Corbusier-inspired geometric shapes. It's odd to watch people's surprised reaction to the originality of the design.

The Marx Memorial Library

37a Clerkenwell Green
EC1
071-253 1485

Open: Mon 1–6 p.m.,
Tues–Thurs 1–8 p.m.,
Sat 10 a.m.–1 p.m.

The Marx Memorial Library, even in its day as a 'quiet' coffeehouse, was thought by the authorities to be the 'headquarters of republicanism, revolution and ultra non-conformity'. The police supposedly threatened local landlords who rented out rooms for republican gatherings, but what lies behind the ranks of bikes is nothing more dangerous than a collection of some 20,000 books, periodicals and manuscripts relating to Marx and the history of socialism and the working class movement. Now, as Communism falls apart, it is even more interesting to find out how it came about in the first place and why its great promise was so difficult to fulfil. It's worth making the journey to the library just to see the mural. Painted in 1935 by Jack Hastings and recently restored after being discovered behind bookshelves, it tells the story of the workers' struggle through economic turmoil and chaos.

Originally a charity for local Welsh craftsmen, the building became probably the first working-men's club where books and papers could be read over a drink. It was taken over by the London Patriot Society, a radical reform group who supported everything from women's rights to the cause of the Irish Fenians, and in 1892 the Twentieth-Century Press, under the guiding light of writer and painter William Morris, leased the buildings. Lenin was to use the offices of the TCP to produce *The Spark*, the Russian Social Democratic newspaper.

Underneath the library there is a warren of tunnels which are thought to date back to the twelfth century, when Clerkenwell was the territory of the monastic military order the Knights Hospitallers. They may well have been used in 1381 to escape from the fury of Wat Tyler's men, who came up from Essex to revolt against the hated poll tax. In their rage the mob burned much of St John's Priory and took the Tower of London before the king conceded to their demands. As the mob dispersed Tyler died on that small patch of ground in Smithfield which saw so many meet their end.

Royal Agricultural Hall
Upper Street N1
071-359 3535

Open: 9 a.m.–6 p.m.
Credit: A, Amex, DC, V

Islington's liberal zone, home to many a millionaire socialist and patron of the arts, hasn't changed much since Joe Orton and his friend Halliwell were abusing library books, each other and anyone else who crossed their path. The odd sprinkling of eighties design culture lies awkwardly beside the now firmly rooted antique markets and traditional pubs. The major symbol of the affluent eighties is the redeveloped Agricultural Hall, now known as the Business Design Centre, where various fairs are held, including furniture exhibitions and the annual Contemporary Arts Fair. However, the supposed interest in local artists has never shown itself. A strong corporate identity and an inclination toward heavy door policies keep the local community out, and when they are allowed in they are charged more than they might be expected to pay for a new show at the Tate. If it interested itself in promoting and conserving the new the Centre might be of some use to artists but, alas, it is strictly a profit-based centre.

Union Chapel
Compton Terrace N1
071-354 3631

Open: Mon–Fri
9 a.m.–5 p.m.; club,
ring for details

This chapel dates from 1877 and was designed by Cubbitt, who was inspired by the church of Santa Fosca Torcello, near Venice. It houses a piece of the Plymouth Rock upon which the Pilgrim Fathers landed in 1620, which was donated by the Pilgrim Society in 1883. The chapel holds the famous Henry Willis organ played by organists such as Henry Gauntlett, composer of 'Once in Royal David's City'.

Recently revamped, the church is now a club which can hold 1,000 people in an octagonal room surrounded by stained glass windows and vaulted arches. There is a bar in the old Sunday School section but the type of entertainment available here tends to go beyond hymn-singing. A mixture of alternative comedy, live jazz and R&B should see that this new venue is the success it deserves to be. Islington has been looking for a place like this for a long time, but now that it's here, the locals are likely to ignore it – a very London thing.

The Water House
New River Head, 173
Rosebery Avenue EC1
081-689 0171

Open: by appointment

In 1613 water from the Amwell Springs in Hertfordshire was brought 38 miles to London by the engineering skills of Sir Hugh Myddleton, making Islington a significant area for the first time. In 1693 the new River Company built the Water House. Although this was demolished in 1919 the Oak Room, with its bizarre plasterwork, ornate panelling and carved walls, overlooked by a portrait of William III, remains. It's not generally open to the public, but you can ring Angela Howe for an appointment.

EATING AND DRINKING

Alfredo's Snack Bar
4–6 Essex Road N1
071-226 3496

Open: Mon–Fri
7 a.m.–2.30 p.m., Sat
7 a.m.–midday
No credit cards
Average: £6

This place has hardly changed since the 1920s, when it opened as a family-run business feeding the local workers a big breakfast and an even bigger lunch. The art-deco colour scheme gives the caff a sense of grandeur but once you get inside it's down to culinary basics, from bubble and squeak to sausage, egg and chips and a mug of tea. Alfredo's is definitely a traditional caff where anyone asking for a cappuccino and croissant would be shown the exit. The waitress knows the menu off by heart and delivers the goods as soon as you order. For under a fiver you can seriously stuff your face here on home-cooked food – I recommend the boiled bacon or the corned beef, egg and chips. Even better, the place is licensed.

The Angel
65 Graham Street N1

Open: midday–midnight
No credit cards
Average: £12

Formerly the Fallen Angel, this vegetarian gay and lesbian cafe is covered wall to wall with G&L art and a noticeboard advertising homes, meetings and friendship. This relaxed and homely place is a good starting point for an evening's entertainment, and if you're straight it's a very friendly place to come with gay friends, which unfortunately is not always true of gay bars.

Camden Head
2 Camden Walk N1
071-359 0851

Open: Mon–Sat
11 a.m.–11 p.m., Sun
midday–3 p.m.,
7–10.30 p.m.
No credit cards
Average: £12

This busy little pub is set in the heart of Camden Passage antiques market and thus attracts many of the shop owners who sometimes spend more time in here than they do pushing for a sale. It's not unusual for the shops to have a note in the window saying that they're in the Camden Head and are perfectly prepared to do business in there. Apart from the clientele the pub's main feature is the beautiful Victorian etched glass, which gives the place an air of taste and style that lifts it above its rivals. Sandwiches and rolls are served all day and there are hot dishes available at lunchtimes.

Casale Franco
134–137 Upper Street
N1
071-226 8994

Open: lunch, Fri-Sun
midday–2.30 p.m.,
dinner, Tues–Sun
6.30–11.30 p.m.
Credit: A, V
Average: £34

Tucked behind Upper Street's many bars and estate agents, Casale Franco is one of Islington's best kept secrets. It's difficult to find and you may have to wait for a seat, but it's worth it as the mix of simple starters and pizzas is worlds away from the normal unchewable rubbish available on the average high street. The out-of-the-way feeling adds to the appeal. The regulars here swear by the place and wolf down their food as if well aware of the queue outside. Main courses include monkfish or escalopes of veal with wild mushrooms, both at £9.50. Pizzas cost about £6.50 and there is a good selection of wines available.

The Dome
341 Upper Street N1
071-226 3414

Open: Mon–Sat
8 a.m.–11 p.m., Sun
9 a.m.–10.30 p.m.
Credit: A, V
Average: £25

Cafe-bars like the Dome, which arrived on Upper Street after the success of its Kings Road cousin, are quietly trying to fit in these days rather than to take over, as the enormous proliferation of young people in the Islington area prefer to pay pub prices rather than the inflated designer-bar price. However the Dome can be very pleasant for a coffee and a croissant with butter and jam (£1.25) in the morning. In the evening, duck cassoulet or steak will set you back about £8 or £9, puddings such as lemon tart are between £1.95 and £2.50.

The Eagle
159 Farringdon Road
EC1
071-837 1353

The popularity of this large, open-plan bar is largely to do with the fantastic, imaginative food, a mixture of Italian, Catalan and North African cuisine. It's all appreciated by the hordes of arty and journalist types who have made the place their own. The people who work here realise that there are a lot of punters out

Open: Mon–Fri
midday–11 p.m., lunch
12.30–2.30 p.m.,
dinner 6.30–10.30 p.m.
No credit cards
Average: £20

Frederick's

Camden Passage N1.
071-359 2888

Open: Mon–Sat, lunch
midday–2.30 p.m.,
dinner 7–11.30 p.m.
Credit: A, Amex, DC, V
Average: £25

The Hen and Chickens

109 St Paul's Road,
Highbury Corner N1
071-359 1030; box
office 071-704 2001

Open: Mon–Wed
midday–2.30 p.m.,
5–11 p.m., Thurs-Sat
5 p.m.–1 a.m., Sun
7–10.30 p.m.
No credit cards

The Horseshoe

24 Clerkenwell Close
EC1
071-253 6068

Open: Mon–Fri
11 a.m.–11 p.m.
No credit cards
Average: £16

there looking for something a bit more credible price and quality-wise, and who are prepared to journey a few miles to find it. Try to arrive well before 1 p.m., as the place gets very crowded and you can't book. The Eagle Gallery upstairs is free and often shows interesting work.

Chef Jean Louis Polet's range is diverse enough to catch the attention of those experienced in French cuisine and those fresh-faced innocents with a bit of spare money. For the romantics it has all the trimmings – quiet tables, candles and that special French atmosphere which makes you feel you are in the company of someone special, normally the waiter. But never mind the etiquette – it's worth it for the right occasion. Special dishes include rack of lamb served on a bed of spinach with a basil and tomato sauce (£12.75) and the calves' liver with orange sauce. The sorbets are perfect, and other desserts (all £3.45) include an Indian summer pudding served with Chantilly cream.

A famous choice of English beer, the stuff that keeps the country going, is available at this pub on one of the busiest roundabouts in London. The ale is dark and warm and is nothing like that terrible fizzy stuff called lager. It was in the Hen and Chickens that the famous highwayman Dick Turpin spent his ill-gotten gains, but today the atmosphere is all about that rather English way of drinking as if there were no tomorrow. If watching that kind of thing is too much for you, the tiny theatre upstairs, which has improvised comedy on Monday nights, provides a nightly jamboree of twentieth-century pieces. The only food available is doorstop sandwiches, but then the Hen and Chickens is all about drinking rather than eating.

It seems strange that an area as rich in history as Clerkenwell has so few resting places to offer. Clerkenwell Green is one of London's many secret spots which are difficult to stumble across by accident, and is a perfect place to sit for half an hour in peace and quiet. Around the corner in Clerkenwell Close is the Horseshoe, which proudly dates back to 1787 and serves up decent fare and live jazz once a month. It's a gem of a place patronised by both craftsmen and jazz enthusiasts. There's a new bar upstairs where you can get food such as sandwiches and jacket potatoes.

Indian Veg
92–93 Chapel Market
N1
071-837 4607

Open: lunch
midday–3 p.m., dinner
6–11 p.m.
Credit: A, V
Average: £12

Set in the heart of the fruit, veg and cheap clothing market, this place gives you quite a lot for quite a little – and this rare bargain makes it a must. There's a variety of decent dishes which will leave you with a lot of change out of a fiver, and they specialise in bhel poori, exotic little snacks and dosa – stuffed rice-flour pancakes – which make the belly rumble with delight. There's a buffet which gives you the choice of ten dishes and chutneys – it costs £3.50 at lunchtime and £3.75 in the evening, and is amazing value. Unlike many bhel poori houses, Indian Veg even has a licence.

Minogue's
80 Liverpool Road N1
071-359
4554/071-354 4440

Open: Mon–Sat
11 a.m.–11 p.m., Sun
midday–3 p.m.,
7–10.30 p.m.
No credit cards
Average: £30

A pint of real Guinness, a plate of Irish stew and a bunch of fiddles in the background mark Minogue's attempt at Irish authenticity. Local people – mainly Nipples (New Irish Professional People Living In England) – come here in numbers and at times it's impossible to get near the bar. The usual beers are sold, as well as draught Harp lager and Smithwick's, usually very difficult if not impossible to find in England, and you can catch up on the Irish papers while you wait for someone. The music can be very good at times and food is available at lunchtimes and evenings in the bar or restaurant. It's an Irish menu, which means dishes with lots of seafood, and Irish stew like your grandmother never made is nevertheless delicious and fragrant with herbs. The weekdays are better times to come to Minogue's as the weekends can be horribly busy. There's music here most nights, and it varies from the so-so to a really good, authentic Irish traditional seisiún.

Patisserie Bliss
428 St John Street EC1
071-837 3720

Open: Mon–Fri
8 a.m.–8 p.m., Sat,
Sun 9 a.m.–6 p.m.
No credit cards
Average: £6

The Angel is an unlikely spot to find the best coffee and pastries in North London. A strong cup of coffee and an almond croissant here should set you up for the rest of the day. The problem with Patisserie Bliss is that it is so small and so popular that unless you get there early in the morning or during the mid-afternoon you are unlikely to find a seat: the customers seem to lack the usual English reserve and sit and talk loudly for hours. It's a great place to go for breakfast any day; if you like people-watching wait for a seat, but if not get a takeaway and walk up to Camden Passage or down to Regent's Canal just behind these buildings and enjoy an oasis of peace in one of London's busiest areas.

The Pipe of Port
325 Essex Road N1
071-226 4078

Open: Mon–Fri
11.30 a.m.–3 p.m.,
5.30–11 p.m., Sat
7–11 p.m.
Credit: A, Amex, DC, V
Average: £30

The idea at the Pipe of Port, it seems, is to combine a touch of early nineteenth-century English gloom with a drop of the stuff that never fails to make you happy one minute and broke the next – champagne. A wide range of vintage and non-vintage champagnes are enjoyed by a clientele that's a bit cocky for my taste but then what would you expect? The food is Olde English fare – grilled steak and steak, kidney and mushroom pies. It's better in the evening than in the afternoon, which can be calmer – but who wants to be calm if you've had a good day on the market and are spending all that money on a glass of the good stuff?

The Quality Chop House
94 Farringdon Road
EC1
071-837 5093

Open: Mon–Fri, lunch
midday–3 p.m., dinner
6.30 p.m.–midnight;
Sat, dinner
6.30–midnight, Sun,
lunch midday–4 p.m.,
dinner 7–11.30 p.m.
No credit cards
Average: £30

This Victorian dining room, dating back to the 1870s, was recently taken over by Charles Fontaine, formerly the chef of the Caprice in Piccadilly (see Westminster and St James's). He has remained true to the original idea of a dining room serving good basic fare including sausages and mash, steak, liver and lots and lots of chips which are accompanied by ketchup and pools of gravy. For vegetarians there are omelettes with mushrooms and there's also some fish dishes. The food is second to none and is not too expensive, and if you don't fancy wine you can always slurp at a big mug of tea. Because the approach is simple and rewarding, and because the Guardian newspaper's offices are across the road, it is very difficult to get a table in the afternoon. The restaurant's original booths makes it difficult to have an intimate conversation here, as it's likely you'll have to share, but that can be interesting as the journalists who have had one too many might let something slip.

The Slug and Lettuce
Islington Green N1
071-226 2864

Open: Mon–Sat
11.30 a.m.–11 p.m.,

Islington has embraced the consistent charm of the Slug and Lettuce, where vast quantities of local beer are drunk by local people, sitting at the scrubbed oak tables. Situated on the Green, this pub is the main meeting point for people heading out into the night. Bistro-style home-made food such as goujons of chicken with asparagus at £4.95 is available, and in

Sun midday–3 p.m.,
7–10.30 p.m.
Credit: A, V
Average: £20

**Upper Street Fish
Shop**
324 Upper Street N1
071-359 1401

Open: lunch, Tues–Fri
11.30 a.m.–2 p.m. Sat
11.30 a.m.–3 p.m.,
supper, Mon–Sat
5.30–10 p.m.
No credit cards
Average: £21

the evening there's a separate tapas-like menu serving dishes such as garlic mushrooms and devils on horseback. Puddings include orange slices with brandy cream sauce, and various crumbles.

If you want to know the real gossip of Islington you need go no further than the Upper Street Fish Shop, where the proprietor Olga knows everything worth the telling. She's a small, energetic woman who maintains the best fish and chip shop for miles – it's clean, fast and delicious. The most popular dish here appears to be cod, chips, mushy peas (£6.70) and a big mug of tea. Starters include a smoked-salmon pate, mussels deep-fried on a skewer and a milky fish soup with chunks of haddock and cod, and cost £2. Home-made treacle tart, Bakewell tart, bread-and-butter puddings and other traditional puddings are all gorgeous.

The Upper Street Fish Shop sits conveniently opposite the Screen on the Green cinema (see separate entry), which makes it a perfect end or beginning to an evening and also helps to keep the prices down. It's not licensed, but they don't mind you bringing your own, and there is a decent choice from the Oddbins across the road. Their takeaway service is even cheaper, and the food looks just as good wrapped in newspapers as it does on a plate.

SHOPPING

Aria Table Art
133 Upper Street N1
071-226 1021

Open: Mon–Sat
10 a.m.–7 p.m.
Credit: A, Amex, V

The eighties craze for beautiful and functional design led to an explosion of shops such as Aria, which sells polished, gleaming silver, thin and perfect enough to split a hair twice. Printed plates, abstract vases and pens or watches made from industrial materials (from £3.95 to £395) stand austerely beside metal candlesticks (from £15) and lampstands. Aria doesn't give much of a sense of warmth but it does encourage the modern, which in Islington has to be a good thing.

Beller's
193 Upper Street N1
071-226 2322

Open: Mon–Wed, Fri,

This old-style drapery and underwear shop, which caters for both men and women, has maintained a high standard. Discreet fittings allow you to get your smalls right after years of telling yourself that what looked good actually felt comfortable as well. From jockeys to boxers and winceyette pyjamas (£7.99), there's something to fit every man, and women can indulge in anything from the silkiest of silk to a functional Playtex bra (prices start at £1.95 for bras, with cotton briefs from £1.25). The shop also does a decent range of cut-price towels, pillowcases and delicious cotton sheets. The staff knows exactly what they are doing and make a point of making you feel comfortable before you have even started putting the bits and pieces on.

Broadhurst and Clarkson and Co.
63 Farringdon Road
EC1
071-405 2156

Open: Mon–Fri
8.30 a.m.–5 p.m., Sat
10 a.m.–4 p.m.
Credit: A, V

Hidden on a road developed into a financial citadel, this shop for the amateur and professional astronomer is a small but important blimp in the galaxy. It has everything from solar-powered radiometers to sixteen-inch illuminated globes. They specialise in telescopes (prices from £150 to £40,000) and have everything from a voyeur's people-watcher to something big enough to pick up the footprint of an astronaut in the lunar sand. On the less serious side there is the Galileo thermometer, a glass cylinder filled with liquid and weights which still manages to give you the temperature, and you can get a pair of binoculars for £50. You can also buy photos of London as seen from space.

Camden Passage
off Upper Street N1

Open: shops, Tues,
Thurs–Sat
10 a.m.–5 p.m.; market
Wed 7 a.m.–2 p.m.,
Sat 9 a.m.–3.30 p.m.
Credit: ask

This mixture of grand terraced houses and antique shops, with its combination of the rare and the silly, is probably the most stylish and classy open market in London, and was opened in the 1960s on two old bomb sites. With over 200 shops and on market days 150 stalls, Camden Passage is also the capital's largest antique centre. Compared to Portobello Road (see Notting Hill) or Camden Market (see Camden), Camden Passage is a very civilised set-up where everyone looks rich and nonchalant about whether they want to sell you something in the first place – a very good way of making you think you ought to spend some money. On Wednesday mornings or Saturday afternoons the market is busy but not uncomfortable, and the shops offer enough variety to make it worth your while wasting a few hours searching for anything from an African mask at Ian Auld's in the Gateway Arcade to an old uniform and breastplate at Military Antiques opposite.

GET STUFFED

Sat 9 a.m.–6 p.m.,
Thurs 9 a.m.–1 p.m.
No credit cards

North ISLINGTON

Canonbury Bookshop and Toyshop

268 Upper Street N1
071-226 4872

Open: Mon–Sat
9 a.m.–7.30 p.m.
Credit: A, V

The children's department in this store provides enough titles and distractions to keep children of all ages amused at least long enough for you to chase that book you've been looking for. The staff are helpful and if what you want is not in their extra-ordinary floor-to-ceiling collection they will find it for you, order it and have it delivered if you can't get back to collect it. I think that the nicest thing about this shop is that you don't get the feeling you're entering one of the high-street chains which look as if they have everything but really stock very little, especially of local interest.

Cover Girl Shoes

44 Cross Street N1
071-354 2883

Open: Mon–Wed, Fri
10 a.m.–5 p.m., Thurs
10 a.m.–7 p.m.
Credit: A, DC, V

Halfway up Cross Street an anonymous-looking shop-front covered with brown velvet curtains hides what is possibly the oddest shop in Islington. Cover Girl promises to transform you from 'man into woman' in 60 minutes. They can offer an attractive dress or a trendy skirt, a curly or tailored wig, a selection of patent-leather shoes with six-inch heels and, to top it all off, panties, briefs or bloomers. It's all available through the post at a decent price (your basic high-heel court shoe is £46) and gives a finished effect which is feminine and sophisticated. The staff are straightforward and helpful and treat each inquiry and if it's the most common in the world. If you want to read up on the subject before committing yourself, there are many books available here.

G. Gazzano and Son

167 Farringdon Road
EC1
071-837 1586

Open: Tues–Fri
8.30 a.m.–6 p.m., Sat
8.30 a.m.–5.30 p.m.,
Sun 10.30 a.m.–2 p.m.
No credit cards

Up the road from the Guardian newspaper building is this Italian deli, which looks like it might be a smutty bookshop or a peep parlour. Once inside though, the only vice to tempt you will be gluttony. There is a tremendous selection of olives – in orange peel, in olive oil or with hot spices and flu-killing garlic (£2.40 a pound), which won't do much for your social life but which taste amazing. As well as the normal range of Italian foods, Gazzano's also does wonderful Parma ham at £10 a pound. Parmesan is £4.25 a pound.

Get Stuffed

105 Essex Road N1
071-226 1364

Open: Mon–Sat

The shopfront of this taxidermist's is a stuffed menagerie of upright kangaroos, lions' heads, ducks, weasels, giant owls, ferrets making a kill, a fox, and the tired-looking skin of a monkey. These very dead creatures stare at you intensely, begging you to enter

10.30 a.m.–4.30 p.m.
No credit cards

**The Glorious
Clothing Company**
60 Upper Street N1
071-704 6312

Open: Mon–Sat
11 a.m.–6.30 p.m.
Credit: A, V

The House of Steel
400 Caledonian Road
N1
071-607 5889

Open: Mon–Fri
10 a.m.–5.30 p.m.,
Sat by appointment
No credit cards

Olga Stores
30 Penton Street N1
071-837 5467

Open: Mon–Sat
9 a.m.–8 p.m., Sun
9 a.m.–2 p.m.
No credit cards

Steve Hatt
88–90 Essex Road N1
071-226 3963

Open: Tues, Wed, Fri,
Sat 7.30 a.m.–5 p.m.,
Thurs 7.30 a.m.–1 p.m.
No credit cards

this macabre world. All the animals are for sale at prices ranging from £30 to £500, and a pheasant will set you back £125 plus VAT.

This shop stocks an amazing selection of women's second-hand and antique clothing from the twenties straight through to the seventies. The turnover is very fast and what you like today may be gone tomorrow, so you'll need to make quick decisions. Dresses from the twenties and thirties cost around £60, depending on the condition, and sixties trousers are between £15 and £24. There are also accessories such as bags, gloves and sunglasses available.

Packed from floor to ceiling with eighteenth- and nineteenth-century ornamental metalwork, this is an enormous warehouse containing every conceivable piece of metal furniture or accessory. Has metal had its day as a feature in every dream home? I fear not – a twist of Gothick here meets the modern in the designs of House of Steel owner Judith Cole, who seems to be adapting traditional designs very successfully. Bronze, brass or iron lamps and chairs start at between £50 and £150.

This Italian deli serves the local community with a fine selection of Italian cheeses, pastas and, most notably, sauces. These vary from the adventurous, such as squid sauce (£1), which goes well with spaghetti, to homemade pesto (£2.20 for five ounces), which is perfect with any pasta. All of the various ingredients needed for Italian cooking are sold in Olga Stores, as well as fresh olives with garlic or mushrooms, and a fine selection of olive oils. The deli can also put a fine sandwich together for a takeaway, and there is a selection of strong Italian coffees. Small and friendly, Olga Stores is definitely one of Islington's favourite shops.

This fishmonger's, which is one of the best in London and a favourite with the local community, offers a variety of fresh fish such as mullet and swordfish, as well as excellent seafood and the odd saddle of hare, freshly dressed pheasant or pigeon, and samphire grass when in season. Scottish smoked salmon is about £11 a pound, beluga caviar £27 for a 90g tin and pheasant about £7 a brace. They know their stuff here, but are not in any way patronising if you don't – they will spend as long as it takes explaining the best way to cook what you buy.

L. Terroni
138 Clerkenwell Road
EC1
071-837 1712

Open: Mon–Wed, Fri
9 a.m.–5.45 p.m.,
Thurs 2–5.45 p.m., Sun
10.30 a.m.–2 p.m.
No credit cards

This wonderful deli is open every day of the week but is most popular on Sundays, when people flood in after Mass in St Peter's Church next door. All of London's Italian community seems to be here buying olive bread, home-made pasta (60p for 500g), cheese and olives, all the while swapping stories about who is doing what to whom. The older people who use the deli speak in Italian but the younger customers boast or gossip in English, which can make a visit here very entertaining. Terroni's gives you an idea of what Clerkenwell must have been like in the days when it was London's 'Little Italy'.

Theorem
4 Cross Street N1
071-354 9713

Open: Mon–Sat
9 a.m.–6 p.m.
Credit: A, Amex, DC, V

For those of us who are a little bit more adventurous, Theorem offers green, yellow, orange, violet, pink and blue hair extensions from £35 for a quarter head and £120 for a full head, as well as all the usual hairdressing services. Their slogan challenges us all to 'climb aboard the mane train'. I accept that hair can be fantastically boring to put up with, but what do you do if once you've attached one of these extensions you don't like it?

**G.W. Walford
(Booksellers)**
182 Upper Street N1
071-226 5682

Open: Mon–Fri
9.30 a.m.–5 p.m.
Credit: A, Amex, V

If you're looking just to waste some time before meeting someone this antiquarian bookshop is the wrong place to do it, but if you're genuine about your interest in books, it's definitely the place for you. Illustrated topographical and natural-history books, all in perfect condition, are in abundance here, at prices ranging from £5 to £5,000. There was a time when books were still regarded as precious and worthy of care, and this establishment continues the tradition of selling and caring for books.

ENTERTAINMENT

**The Almeida
Theatre**
Almeida Street N1
071-359 4404

Open: bookings
Credit: A, Amex, DC, V

The building housing the Almeida Theatre was once a nineteenth-century scientific institute which, like most of the surrounding area, was left to crumble and become little more than a pit in which cockfighting, followed by the odd song-and-dance routine, was the principal entertainment. The building was taken over by the Salvation Army, and changed the tone of the street until 1956, when it was turned into a factory and showroom for carnival novelties by the extraordinary Mr Beck, a notorious transvestite who proudly strolled up and down Upper Street in his Sunday best until his son, finding him wearing his wife's clothes, murdered him.

In the 1980s the Almeida Theatre restored and modernised the space, leaving the original brickwork in view and doing much to enhance the modern and progressive work of touring companies such as Theatre de Complicité, Cheek by Jowl and the Abbey Theatre. Under the auspices of Pierre Audi, the Almeida was turned into a cosmopolitan and innovative theatre. New European plays and classic plays seldom performed in Britain found a home here under the artistic direction of actors Ian McDiarmid and Jonathan Kent, who somehow managed to attract writers of the stature of Harold Pinter to premiere new work and entice talents such as Glenda Jackson, Diana Rigg and Nick Hytner to work for Equity's minimum fee. The combination of the Almeida's intimate atmosphere and its epic theatre has seen the company do very well over the past couple of years, with good audiences coming to watch precise if sometimes over-the-top productions of anything from Euripides to Dryden.

Bernard Park
Barnsbury Road N1
071-278 9494

Open: Mon–Fri
9.30 a.m.–midday,
1–4 p.m.

The local council, if unpopular with tax-paying parents, is a big hit with the under-fives who appreciate this patch of land where they can run wild and free and which seems to belong to them and to them only. If you are about to juice your child in the liquidiser because of his or her intransigent screams, this is the place to change the mood and relieve yourself for five minutes at least.

The Duke of Wellington
119 Balls Pond
Road N1
071-249 3729

Open: Mon–Sat
6 p.m.–midnight, Sun
7–10.30 p.m.
No credit cards

Once a highly respected jazz venue, this pub is now an equally popular gay and lesbian bar which can get packed at weekends. It's a friendly, relaxed and welcoming local. The back room, where the music used to be, is now a women-only space with a pool table and bar, and is open from 8 p.m. to midnight every night except Sunday.

Bar food – pasta and pasties – is available at around £1.50–£2.

On Friday nights there's free live music.

293

The Hare and Hounds

181 Upper Street N1
071-226 2992

Open: Mon–Sat
11 a.m.–midnight
No credit cards

R&B, Country and Western and bad rock 'n' roll all feature in this North London bar, which seems to give anyone with facial hair or a poncho a chance to perform. It can be good but is often terrible, though very popular indeed with the locals.

It all starts at 9 p.m. on Friday and Saturday nights, and admission will cost you £2–£3 at the door. There's no food, though.

Highbury Fields

Highbury Terrace N5
071-226 2334;
football bookings
071-607 7331

No credit cards

During the Great Fire in 1666, 200,000 people from all parts of London society gathered in these fields with what little they had managed to salvage from the flames. The $27^1/2$ acres were bought by the district in 1885 and are now available for the use of the public. The facilities are decent and well used. Registration and booking is required up to three days in advance for one of the eleven all-weather courts or pitches offering football, tennis or athletics. The floodlit areas stay open from 8 a.m. to 9 p.m., but the others close at dusk. You always need to book the football pitches, and while you can use any free tennis court you can, for £7 a year, get a registration card that allows you to book a court ahead. There's also an indoor swimming pool here.

The King's Head

115 Upper Street N1
071-226 1916 (box
office), 071-226 0364
(pub)

Credit: A, V in theatre
only

This theatre pub is one of the London Fringe's most important, and manages to attract good performers and writers such as Steven Berkoff. Founded in 1970, during a period when there was an explosion of new writing and a dearth of venues other than conservative West End theatres, the King's Head now specialises in work from up-and-coming young writers as well as in musical revivals. For the past couple of years it has been under threat of closure due to a lack of funds – their annual council grant would barely cover the lighting bill.

The pub itself is crowded with theatre memorabilia and has a fake forties feel about it which is highlighted by the policy of asking for payment in pounds, shillings and pence.

The Lilian Bayliss Theatre

Sadlers Wells, Rosebery
Avenue EC1
071-837 4104;

Situated behind the main Sadlers Wells theatre and named after the woman who saved the Wells from demolition in the 1930s, this studio space was opened in 1988 and has yet to capture the public's imagination. It is, however a fantastic venue. So far

071-713 0093 (for
those with hearing
difficulties)

Credit: A, Amex, DC, V

**Little Angel
Marionette Theatre**
14 Dagmar Passage N1
071-226 1787

Credit: A, V

**Old Red Lion
Theatre Pub**
418 St John Street EC1
071-837 7816

Open: Mon–Fri
11 a.m.–3 p.m.,
5.30–11 p.m., Sat
7–11 p.m., Sun
7–10.30 p.m.
No credit cards

Paradise Club
1 Parkfield Street N1
071-354 9993

Open: Thurs–Sat
10 p.m.–6 a.m., Sun
3.30–11.30 p.m.
No credit cards
Admission: £7–£13

the theatre has put on a mixture of new, experimental work and classic European plays from the likes of Ibsen, but although the performances have had favourable press they have not yet hit the mark with London's theatre-goers. More recently the Lilian Bayliss has seen performances by music- and dance-based companies, and there is an increasing amount of community and education projects taking place here.

Supposedly the best puppet theatre in Europe, the Little Angel is tucked away deep in the heart of Islington's backstreets, but that never deters marauding bands of noisy children making their presence felt every weekend. For over 30 years the puppets have been brought to life on stage and in the workshops next door, where emergency repairs are made to favourite characters, and new heroes and villains such as Lancelot the Lion are created.

A building has been here in one form or another since the end of the eighteenth century. It is supposedly where Thomas Paine began what was to become *The Rights of Man*, the inspiration for the French Revolution and the basis of the US Constitution. The theatre has never seen writing of this importance since, but many young playwrights are given the chance to stage their work upstairs in the theatre club. The club is also a respected venue on the comedy circuit, which is not to say that everyone allowed on has any talent, and listening to someone painfully trying to be funny can be a horrific experience. But then again, some of the best writing and acting talent to emerge recently has come from this type of performance. Ring for times and details.

This nightclub is Islington's busiest gay haunt, offering enough space and choice of entertainment for anyone. It attracts a friendly and relaxed, if somewhat cruisy, crowd and is deservedly popular.

It has two dancefloors, a games room and three coffee bars, and the whole place is hot, busy and full of men looking for a nice way to end the evening. Its long opening hours make the Paradise Club an ideal place to spend some time.

Sadlers Wells
Rosebery Avenue EC1
071-278 8916

Credit: A, Amex, DC, V

Beneath a trapdoor at the back of the stalls is the well which gives its name to this theatre, built in 1931 to the design of Frank Matcham. The well supposedly holds miraculous healing powers and during the Middle Ages belonged to Clerkenwell Priory. During the Reformation it was forgotten about until 1683, when the entrepreneur Thomas Sadler reopened it. To make a day out of a visit to the well Sadler put on what he described as entertainments, which included staged plays and magic shows. He also sold food and drink so that a visit was a complete event for the rich merchants who journeyed with their families to sample the waters, and the patent medicines and ales Sadler made from them.

In 1765 the old wooden house built with Sadler's money was pulled down and replaced with a handsome new building. In 1806 and 1826 attempts were made to turn the Wells into a racetrack, but although the soft ground was perfect for horses, the idea never took off. During the middle of the eighteenth century a regular theatre played host to the genius of Edmund Kean and the the clown Grimaldi, who brought the *commedia dell'arte* alive in what was now one of the city's favourite attractions.

Industrial London brought brutal change to the area. Large tracts of land were taken over for factories and Islington's reputation dwindled, as did that of the theatre, until the robust and spirited Lilian Bayliss reopened Sadlers Wells in 1931, giving it the dubious title of the 'Old Vic of North London'. Having been everything from a pickle factory to a boxing arena the theatre is now a home for visiting dance companies, performing everything from avant-garde works to flamenco. The D'Oyly Carte company performs Gilbert and Sullivan regularly here and contemporary dance and ballet is performed by both national and visiting companies. The tradition of colour and drama which Grimaldi brought to the theatre is carried on by the likes of Lyndsay Kemp, who calls the theatre his second home.

The Scala Cinema
275–277 Pentonville
Road N1
071-278 0051

The Scala Cinema was originally based in Scala Street, just off Charlotte Street in the West End, when it was without a doubt the most popular independent cinema in London. The cinema's popularity made it

No credit cards

necessary to find the Scala a new and larger home, which they discovered in the middle of the Kings Cross and Islington area. Now the Scala is in a huge Victorian gothic building which was once a monkey house: the waiting area upstairs, where you can buy tea, coffee and snacks, is vast, high and covered with murals relating to cinema throughout the decades.

The Scala continues its repertory tradition and often shows controversial movies which mainstream cinemas decide to pass by – as these are often certificated you need to be a member of the cinema club, but membership costs only 50p a year. At weekends there are all-nighters based around particular themes: Metal Machine Men night featured *The Terminator*, *Terminator 2*, *Robocop*, *Robocop 2* and *Total Recall*. Whew. They have recently got into very hot water by allegedly showing Stanley Kubrick's *A Clockwork Orange*, that extraordinary film of youthful violence which the director banned from showing in the UK.

The Screen on the Green
83 Upper Street N1
071-226 3520

Credit: A, V

Commercial Hollywood and art-house films play back to back in this exotic little cinema. It has all the glamour of an early twenties picture-show house, and the building is constantly lit with bright neon, giving the feeling that something special might just be going on here. It remains a favourite haunt of Islington's gloomy artheads, even though they tend to look out of place in the queue to see the latest offering from Michael J. Fox. Cheap seats are available on Mondays and there are late shows on weekends.

Tower Theatre
Canonbury Tower,
Canonbury Place N1
071-226 3633

Credit: A, V

This building, the oldest in Islington and apparently haunted, was once part of the sixteenth-century Canonbury manor which was home to philosopher Sir Francis Bacon and, in the following century, playwright Oliver Goldsmith. Now it is the residence of the Tavistock Repertory Company, who perform a mixed bag of musicals and contemporary plays once a fortnight, though the theatre is closed from July to September.

East

The City

THE CITY

*t*he City of London is one square mile of uniformed wealth, the home of the Bank of England and the Stock Exchange. Until cheaper rents and new technology took most of it elsewhere, the City was also the home of the newspaper industry, based in Fleet Street, a name which has become synonymous with the British press. Bankers, brokers and bond dealers arrive in the district any time after 6 a.m. and suddenly what seemed to be a dead zone becomes the pumping heart of the capital. Nobody really lives here and at night the streets look as if the three-minute warning has been called. During the day most bars and restaurants are only open for lunch, and there is a distinct lack of mid-price café-style places where you can sit and have a good cup of coffee and a snack. The restaurants are expensive and aimed at the high-flying City folk, and are totally inappropriate for relaxing in. At the other extreme there's a multitude of sandwich bars ranging from the awful to the exceptional, but most of them have a takeaway service only – there are not a lot of outdoor seating arrangements in the City.

So why would anyone who is not a power-dressed trader want to come into the domain of the Masters of the Universe? Perhaps because, despite the lack of refreshments on offer, a walk around the Square Mile is a stimulating history lesson. This is where the Romans created the original Londinium fortress which became a centre for European traders. It was here that

the Great Fire of London began in a bakery in 1666 and destroyed the cramped small streets and houses as well as getting rid of the plague of diseased rats which had been threatening to kill off the population. The great architect Christopher Wren's plan to create long avenues leading from St Paul's to Westminster was thwarted by the petit bourgeoisie who would not allow him to get rid of the bricks and mortar which made up the slums and which were as dear to them as their families, if not more so. The attitude that what you own is an indication of your own self-worth still seems to be around today.

Wren's plans were given a second chance when the City was destroyed a second time during the heavy bombing of World War II. This time the redevelopers moved in on a major scale, creating some of the worst examples of modern architecture in Europe. High-rise glass and metal towers seemed to go up overnight as the City's space was strangled by corporate insensitivity. The office developments might have meant a boom period for the building trade but they were an architectural graveyard for new designers. When Lloyds the underwriters commissioned Richard Rogers to design their new headquarters, built in 1986, the reactionary elements in the City balked at the plans and laughed at the finished building. It is in fact a work of brilliance and it's worth a trip just to see it (see separate entry).

I have never much enjoyed the highly regulated and traditional air of the City and prefer the village life to be found in places like Islington, Camden and Notting Hill, where a mix of cultures and buildings create a base good enough to be called a home. The new people of the City are for the most part commuters who bring nothing to the place and leave as soon as they can. New technology is making many people's jobs obsolete, so maybe by the end of the century this quarter will have to be redefined. Canary Wharf, the so-called 'Second City' (see The Thames), is intended to attract many of the big city firms with its low rents and easy parking. But the financial problems of the developers have turned Canary Wharf into a major white elephant, and in any case the area does not have the rich history or the easy access which makes the City so attractive for some.

I tend to look for mystery in the City and never find it. The best time to go and walk around is either in the evening, when it is very quiet (most pubs and bars shut at nine), or the weekend, when nothing stirs.

HOW TO GET THERE

Tubes
- Aldgate
- Bank
- Barbican
- Blackfriars
- Cannon Street
- Chancery Lane
- Holborn
- Liverpool Street
- Monument
- Moorgate
- Old Street
- Temple
- Tower Hill
- St Paul's

Buses
- Aldersgate: 4, 172, 502
- Bishopsgate: 8, 67
- Chancery Lane: 8, 17, 22B, 25, 45, 46, 171A, 501, 521
- Cheapside: 8, 22B, 25, 501
- City Road: 43, 76, 214, 271, X43
- Clerkenwell Road: 55, 56, 153, 243, 505
- Goswell Road: 4, 56, 153
- Holborn Viaduct: 8, 17, 22B, 25, 45, 46, 171A, 243, 501
- Houndsditch Minories: 5, 15, 15X, 25, 42, 78, 100
- Moorgate: 21, 43, 76, 133, 214, X43
- Old Street: 55, 243, 505
- Shoreditch High Street: 5, 43, 55, 243, 505
- Threadneedle Street: 25

SIGHTS AND SITES

All Hallows by the Tower
Byward Street EC3
071-481 2928

Admission to
museum: £1

There has been a church on this site for the last 1,300 years – the Saxon arches here date back to AD 675 – and this building serves as the parish church for HM Customs and Excise and the London World Trade Centre. Though the outside walls are original, the middle of the church and the roof are new, rebuilt after they were destroyed during the Blitz. Diarist Samuel Pepys watched the Great Fire of London from the church tower here. Depending on where you stand, All Hallows by the Tower is the first or last church in the City and is the only church here to have records going back as far as 1500. These are on show in the Undercroft Museum, where you can also see the remains of a Roman pavement. Admission here is by application to the church, and costs £1.

There is a brass-rubbing centre here, open Monday to Saturday from 9 a.m. to 4 p.m. and on Sundays from 12.30 to 4 p.m.. The charges vary according to the brasses rubbed, and it's a great way to keep kids amused. The Tower of London is not strictly in the City, but you can get a good view of it from Tower Place, just by the church.

Bank of England Museum
Threadneedle Street
EC2 (entrance in
Bartholomew Lane)
071-601 5792/5545

No admission charge

At the very hub of London's financial centre is the Bank of England, once satirised by James Gillray as 'The Old Lady of Threadneedle Street'. Like the Lloyds Building, the bank has been forced by terrorist threats to close off the building to the public, but you are still free to walk around the museum and see the pikes and muskets used to defend the bank in earlier times. The museum's displays trace the history of the bank from its founding by Royal Charter in 1694 to today's high-tech world, and from ancient gold bars to various coins and banknotes. Other features include interactive videos, which can be found in the eighteenth-century banking hall designed by Sir John Soane and which give a fascinating insight into the workings of the bank today, normally quite incomprehensible to the uninitiated. You can also get information on gilt-edged stock and securities, and the foreign currency and money markets, at a dealing desk similar to those in everyday use at the bank itself.

The Barbican Centre
Silk Street, Barbican EC2
071-638 4141

A 'barbican' is part of the outer line of defence of a city or castle, and within the modern-day Barbican complex lies part of the old Roman and medieval city walls. During the last war the site where the Barbican now stands was devastated by German bombers, leaving a space big enough for architects Chamberlin, Powell and Bon to envisage a residential neighbourhood with open spaces and bustling with schools, shops and art centres. Despite their idealistic plans, the Barbican is regarded by many as a brutalist concrete nightmare – a maze of flats in tower blocks surrounding a huge arts centre which now houses the Royal Shakespeare Company, the London Symphony Orchestra and the Guildhall School of Music.

For all its ugliness the Barbican has attracted droves of people to its small, compact apartments. Easy access to the nearby business district makes it a perfect location for City folks, and the convenience and security attract celebrities and those lucky enough to be able to afford a metropolitan stopover as well as a country home. It is here that Shakespeare and Milton lived, and Oliver Cromwell was married in St Giles' Church. Nowadays it's the likes of Labour Party leader John Smith and various media personalities who use this fortress as a home. The quiet evenings, when the towers are lit and look dramatic and proud, must attract the high and mighty here, but in the afternoons, especially on rainy English days, the place is terribly bleak.

There's acres of entertainment to be found in the rather dark and foreboding Arts Centre. When it was opened by the Queen in 1982 it was trumpeted as the City's 'gift to the nation', and since then thousands of visitors come each year to hear the resident London Symphony Orchestra and watch performances by the Royal Shakespeare Company (see separate entry). The Barbican Hall sees over 300 concerts each year and recent visiting greats include the French modern composer and conductor Pierre Boulez and the jazz-bluesman Ray Charles. The Barbican Art Gallery has consistently shown good and innovative work. Though the centre has its critics, the quality of the work put on is second to none.

Charterhouse Square, EC1

This small secretive square is worth a mention, if only for its small school where the great writer Thackeray taught and where Baden-Powell, the founder of the Boy Scout movement, enjoyed his formative years. Charterhouse was formerly a medieval monastery which, like all the others, met with the wrath of Henry VIII's manic dissolution of all things Romish. Thomas Sutton, a philanthropist during the Stuart dynasty, had the buildings converted into a school for poor boys and a home for the aged.

Pensioners still use the peacefulness of the square as an escape from city life, and it is strange to think of this hushed place so close to the bloody and noisy Smithfield Market. The square has a character of its own. A mixture of Georgian, Regency and the inevitable modern buildings give the square a mixed-up look but the stunning 1920s purpose-built block Florin Court is worth a visit. Its curves and undulations are as sexy as architecture can get.

Charterhouse Square is the other London, so quiet at the weekend that it is rare to see anyone walking around. Sir John Betjeman lived nearby in Cloth Fair, and around the corner from his house is London's oldest church, St Bartholmew the Great, which is one of the finest remaining examples of Norman architecture. Built in 1123, it gives you an idea of how majestic monastic churches were before Henry VIII had his way. Although much has been done to change the area, streets such as Cloth Fair still keep a whiff of seventeenth-century life about them.

Exmouth Market, N1

Open: Mon–Sat
9 a.m.–4 p.m.

There has been a street market here since 1892. Serving the local businesses, Exmouth Market is busiest during the weekday lunch period, and the peak days are Tuesday, Thursday and Friday. At the end of the market there's a stall selling traditional English eels, cockles and mussels, which are definitely an acquired taste. Whether you think the taste worth acquiring is up to you. The most imposing building here is the Church of Our Most Holy Redeemer, the only church in London built in the Italian basilica style. The church occupies the site of the Pantheon, which was notorious for its bawdiness and badness. Unfortunately for the hedonists who patronised the place, it stayed open for only six years.

Between 1822 and 1829 the father of all clowns, Joey Grimaldi, lived at number 8, within walking distance of Sadlers Wells.

Finsbury Circus, EC2

Finsbury Circus was laid out in 1815 by William Montague to the design of George Dance. It occupies what was once open fields; the Bethlehem Royal Hospital stood here before it moved to Lambeth. The beautiful buildings which once ringed the green area have gradually been replaced by offices. The south-west quadrant was built in 1849 and the south-east in 1901. The most interesting area, though, is Lutyens House, designed by Sir Edwin Lutyens in 1924 and a great example of the famous architect's use of the functional and the futuristic. The circus garden is popular with office workers, who come here to eat lunch on a nice day, and there are often free concerts here, as well as the chance to have a game of bowls.

Finsbury Square, EC2

Finsbury Square was the first place in London to have gas lighting. One of the city's most famous bookshops was located here – known as the Temple of the Muses, it was owned by James Lockington. This enormous shop had a frontage that was 140 feet long, and when Lockington was in a flag was raised on the dome above the building.

Finsbury Square was badly bombed during World War II; reconstructed, it is now a home for insurance firms. Famous residents include the Austrian composer Anton Bruckner, who lived at number 39 in 1871, and the explorer David Livingston, who spent some time in the square in 1856, before one of his trips into the jungle.

John Wesley's House and Chapel
47 City Road EC1
071-253 2262

Open: Mon–Sat
10 a.m.–4 p.m.; Sun
after 11 a.m.
service–2 p.m.
No credit cards
Admission: adults £3,
concessions £1.50,

The chapel is the mother church of Methodism and the place where Wesleyan philosophy was born. On 21 April 1777, at the age of 74, John Wesley himself laid the foundation stone of this building, and he is buried at the back of the chapel; his mother Suzannah lies across the road in Bunhill Fields, along with John Buchan and Daniel Defoe. The soil needed to cover the reclaimed swampland on which it is built came from the excavations for the foundations of St Paul's. During the 1970s the building was restored and once again put to use. It is well worth a visit to see the chapel museum and the pious man's house, which is

family £8

now a museum and stands as it did when he lived here. The chapel's other claim to fame is that ex-Prime Minister Margaret Thatcher was married here. The museum has a shop selling gifts and books.

Lloyds
Lime Street EC3
071-327 6210 (shop)

Open: viewing gallery,
Mon–Fri 10 a.m.–2 p.m.

Lloyds is the world's most famous insurance society, having grown from a small seventeenth-century firm based in a coffee house to a huge business insuring everything from film stars' legs to space flights.

In 1986 the company moved to this new building. Designed by Richard Rogers, it has caused more of a fuss in business and art circles than any other new building this century. Some people love it and others can't stand it – and the people who work here are also in two minds about it. The market floor is the focal point of the building and has a glass-roofed atrium the same height as St Paul's. Walking in here is like entering another world. Escalators climb the building, staggering the imagination. The scenes which take place here are often just as staggering – I have never been able to understand the enormity of the risks and the sums involved. The building adds some fun to this madness and is as important to the twentieth century as St Paul's was to the seventeenth. The industrial construction materials are all on view and not hidden away, which adds to the impact of the building. It's not a very English construction, nor the type that insurance brokers usually like, but it's here and it's staying. You used to be able to enter the viewing gallery but recent security alerts and terrorist threats have stopped that and now no members of the public are allowed in.

Monument
The Monument Street
EC3
071-626 2717

Open: Mon–Fri,
March–September
9 a.m.–6 p.m.,
1 November–30 March
9 a.m.–4 p.m.,
Sat, Sun,
May–September
2–6 p.m.

This tower was designed by Sir Christopher Wren to commemorate the Great Fire of 1666, which decimated 436 acres of buildings and all but destroyed the City. It was built in the 1670s from Portland stone as a single Doric column. At 202 feet – the distance westwards from the bakehouse in Pudding Lane where the fire broke out – it is the tallest free-standing column in the world. A 311-step spiral staircase leads to the top where a flaming gilt bronze urn symbolises the Great Fire. The climb is steep and many people turn back, but it's worth it – the view from the top is magical and all London's strange juxtaposition of old and new buildings can be seen clearly stretching out

No credit cards
Admission: £1

before you from the City to the Embankment and beyond to south of the river. In the eighteenth century the Monument became a favourite place for people to come who wanted to end it all, though now they tend to chuck themselves under tube trains instead. On the west side of the Monument is an interesting bas-relief by Caius Gabriel Cibber, showing Charles II, in Roman dress, coming to the aid of London as the flames lap in the background.

If you walk down Fish Street from here to Wren's church of St Magnus the Martyr, you can see the ancient footpath which led to the first London Bridge.

Museum of London
London Wall EC2
071-600 3699

Open: Tues–Sat
10 a.m.–6 p.m.,
Sun midday–6 p.m.
Admission: £1.50–£3
Credit: A, V

If you are really interested in this city, then this terrific museum should be your first stop. The building was designed by Powell and Moya in 1975 and stands on the west gate of the old Roman fort. It holds artifacts which tell you everything you need to know about London. It's all very accessible here as everything is arranged chronologically, making it very entertaining to see how things changed so quickly from Roman times, through the Middle Ages and up to the present day. There is also a comprehensive collection of costumes which are in near-perfect condition and displayed to their best effect.

The museum has a small cafe and garden, open the same hours as the museum, which is good enough to spend a bit of time in. Don't expect to have a wonderful lunch, but the snacks and the tea are fine.

St Botolph without Aldgate
Aldgate High Street EC3
071-283 1950

For the last thousand years there has been a church standing on this site, which was originally outside the old gateway in the city wall (the Aldgate), and beside the bridge which crossed the city moat (the Hounds Ditch). It was a place for travellers entering or leaving the city to seek peace and quiet. The church is dedicated to St Botolph, a seventh-century Benedictine monk who was a sort of English St Christopher, the patron saint of travellers. The mercantile connections of the church are evident in the memorial just inside the door, erected in 1612 by the Right Worshipful Company of Merchant Tailors for a certain Robert Dow, who performed 'divers charitable deeds'. Opposite him is a bust of Sir John Cass, a former sheriff of the City, Master of the Carpenters Company and the man who founded the school near the church. Daniel Defoe, the author of *Robinson Crusoe*, was married here in 1683. Two pits were dug in the churchyard here during the Great Plague, and in four months 5,136 bodies had been flung into them.

The present church was built in 1741 to the design of George Dame the elder, who had designed the Mansion House two years earlier. Its neo-classical feel contrasts with Christopher Wren's multitude of churches in the City's square mile. The church's unusual ceiling was added later by J. F. Bentley (1839–1902), the architect responsible for Westminster Cathedral.

St Mary-le-Bow Church

Cheapside EC2
071-248 5139

Open: Mon–Thurs
7.30 a.m.–6 p.m., Fri
7.30 a.m.–4 p.m.

This church, designed by Christopher Wren, was built in 1680 on the site of an older Norman church, of which the crypt still survives. The tower and steeple are among Wren's finest and they house the famous Bow Bells, within whose sound all true Cockneys are born. Like that other Wren church, St James's in Piccadilly, St Mary-le-Bow has now thrown open its doors to market forces and has opened a restaurant in the crypt, called The Place Below (see separate entry). The crypt itself is known for its famous 'wall of arches' which are quite spectacular.

St Paul's Cathedral

St Paul's Churchyard
EC4
071-248 2705

Open: viewing,
Mon–Sat
9 a.m.–4.30 p.m.;
services, Mon–Sun
between
7.30 a.m.–6 p.m.
Admission:
£1.50–£2.50
Credit: A, Amex, DC, V
(shop only)

St Paul's is best approached from Fleet Street, where the absolute magnificence of Christopher Wren's achievement can be seen in all its glory. It was commissioned by Charles II after the Great Fire of London in 1666 and built between 1675 and 1709. The fact that Wren managed to complete the building in half a lifetime and without much political interference is an indication of the esteem in which the architect was held by the King. It is a masterpiece and the collection of memorials and sculptures inside are as interesting as, if not better than, those seen on the walls of London's galleries. The crypt is the largest in Europe and within it lie great painters and writers such as Reynolds and Walter de la Mare, and of course Wren himself.

To get a view of London as good as the one from the Monument (see separate entry), a climb to the top of the dome is recommended. The first stage is the Whispering Gallery, where the bizarre acoustics will send the slightest sound echoing around the walls. After this a steeper and more difficult climb will bring you to the Stone Gallery. From here a wonder-ful view of the river and the City spreads out before you. If you are fit and keen you should head up further still, to the Golden Gallery, and take in an inner view of St Paul's which will show you how beautiful this place of worship is. There are guided tours at 11 a.m., 11.30 a.m., 2 p.m. and 2.30 p.m.; costing from £3-£5, they can be very worthwhile.

Temple of Mithras

Temple Court, Queen Victoria Street EC4

This was discovered in 1954 and has since been carefully restored. You can now see the remains on a paved area near Bank Station. The Mithras cult was an odd one and we know little about it other than that Mithras was a Persian god of light who sym-bolised a type of honesty and courage which ap-pealed to the Roman soldiers who prayed here. They had to do this secretly, as the Christians did not allow any pagan gods to be worshipped. Other deities found here can be seen in the Museum of London. I particularly like the stone god that hides itself from the gaze of others.

Smithfield Market, EC1

071-236 8734

Open: Mon–Fri 5–10.30 a.m. Admission free to public

Originally the site from which horses were traded in the twelfth century, Smithfield became a cattle market and later a slaughterhouse – the blood was said to flow into St John Street. When the authorities decided that noisy drunken herdsmen were causing enough chaos, they decided to clean up the area, and in 1855 Smith- field was redesigned by Horace Jones. It became known as 'Dead Meat Market' as carcasses were thrown from hook to hook by the bummarees, who are a strange breed of butcher-porter. They are regarded as being very important and the custom of each retiring bummaree handing down his position to a member of the family keeps Smithfield locked into tradition.

The market is under serious threat of closure as it did not meet EEC standards of hygiene, and regard-less of its romantic past has been forced to move into a world of technology and restrictions. The beautiful iron stations will undoubtedly be taken over by developers keen to attract the cashmere and trinkets brigade from the Piccadilly arcades.

The market serves the meat trade and is not really the place to come for a pound of sausages.

The sight of bloodied aprons and carcasses is not

one for the fainthearted, but a drink at 6.30 a.m. in the Fox and Anchor (see separate entry) will steady the nerves and open the eyes to the bizarre attractions of London nightlife. It is quite normal to find clubbers, still shaking after a night on the town, standing shoulder to shoulder with the blood-covered porters, and neither tribe seems to pay any attention to the other's bizarre attire. It's just another night.

The Tower of London

Tower Hill EC3
071-709 0765

Open: Mon–Sat
9.30 a.m.–5 p.m.
Credit: A, V
Admission: adults
£6.40, under 15s
£3.90, concessions
£4.80, family ticket
£17.50

The history of London can be read in the stones of the Tower of London. It stands on a site originally occupied by a Roman fortress used as a seat of power by successive invaders. William I began to construct the tower here and it was Edward I who completed what was to become a palace, a prison, a place of execution and a menagerie – today it is best known as a museum and the place where the Crown Jewels are kept. The first prisoner to be kept here was the Bishop of Durham, who was imprisoned in 1101 for selling benefices. During the reign of King John the Tower was seized by his barons in a successful attempt to make him sign the Magna Carta.

During the reign of Henry III in the thirteenth century the menagerie at the Tower grew to include leopards, lions, snakes and bears. It was again used as a place of imprisonment when the young Edward III was incarcerated here. Richard, the Duke of Gloucester, is said to have become king by having the two young princes executed, but recent examinations of the genuine records seem to prove him innocent – perhaps the most slandered man of all time.

Henry VIII enjoyed sentencing people to the Tower, and two of his wives, Anne Boleyn and Catherine Howard, met their end here. At this time it was a place much feared by the people of London. Bloodstained as it was, it was a strange choice for a palace, which is perhaps why James I, who came to the throne after the death of Elizabeth I, was the last monarch to live here. He had a macabre interest in the Royal Menagerie and would frequently order bear-baiting and dog fights to take place.

There have been regular attempts to steal the Crown Jewels, which date from the seventeenth century, although a few pieces date back to the Middle Ages.

The crown was made for the coronation of Queen Victoria. Every night the ancient Ceremony of the Kings takes place here when the Chief Yeoman Warder ensures the safety of the Tower and the jewels.

At night the view of the Tower and Tower Bridge is one of the very best London has to offer. Tours and talks concerning the Tower and its bloody history take place regularly here, but it is at night that the grim past of this fortress becomes all to easy to remember.

Whitbread Brewery
Chiswell Street EC1
071-606 4455

Whitbread's is one of the last surviving eighteenth-century breweries, and its six-acre site is an architectural jigsaw of eighteenth-, nineteenth- and twentieth-century buildings, now converted into offices. Partners' House, which fronts on to Chigwell Street, dates back to 1697 and earned its name in the nineteenth century as a place for the partners to meet. The Portolundrum, completed in 1784, with its fine timber roof, is now a conference and banqueting hall, and the old delivery yard, which dates from 1860, has recently been restored and now looks like the working yard it once was. The Speaker's Coach is kept here, though it has been seen on the streets of London only about five times since 1911. The stables and yards used to be open to the public, but the brewery's famous shire horses have now been moved to Kent. Perhaps it is as well that you can now see only the beautifully restored facade and forget about the modern offices behind it.

EATING AND DRINKING

Ashley's Bar and Grill
10 Copthall Avenue
EC2
071-256 8162

Open: Mon–Fri, bar
11 a.m.–11 p.m., grill
7.45 a.m.–3 p.m.,
restaurant
11.30 a.m.–2.30 p.m.
Credit: A, Amex, V

It is difficult to describe the food here, which usually consists of a mix of all things good in European cooking.

The grill, which opens early for an English breakfast, serves up grilled meat or fish in quite a simple way, with each dish garnished as much as required and no more.

The restaurant, however, is altogether different. The menu is rich and imaginative, dealing with lamb and salmon in an almost Japanese manner, marinated in rich sauces, including soy.

On Thursdays in the bar there's usually live music,

Average: grill room
£30, restaurant £50

Birley's
12/13 Royal Exchange
EC3
071-929 0822

Open: Mon–Fri
6.30 a.m.–3 p.m.
Credit: A, Amex, V
(delivery service only)

Corney and Barrow
118 Moorgate EC2
071-628 2898

Open: Mon–Fri, lunch
midday–3 p.m., snacks
midday–9 p.m.
Credit: A, Amex, DC, V
Average: £50

Cozys
11 Sun Street EC2
071-247 9445

Open: Mon–Fri
7 a.m.–11 p.m.
Credit: A, Amex, DC, V
Average: bar £20,
restaurant £42

which filters down into the rest of Ashley's and makes for a sensual evening if you feel that's what's required.

With its sparkling, airy interior, wooden floor, marble counters and brass light fittings, Birley's is the best of this area's many sandwich bars. It's clean, friendly and efficient and you can get an excellent coffee (from 50p) or freshly-squeezed juice (£1) or a mineral to drink along with your made-to-order sandwiches to take away. Turkey and bacon salad sandwiches are £2.95, and bacon and avocado £2.70. It's possible to get a full meal to take away here, as they sell soups and puddings, including a wicked chocolate brownie and tiramisu. They will deliver anywhere within EC1, EC2, EC3 and EC4 between 10.15 a.m. and 3 p.m.

There is a chain of Corney and Barrow wine bars in London – including one under the Lloyds Building (see separate entry) – but this is definitely the best. The design of the restaurant, which looks like an ocean liner run aground, is more impressive than the food. The menu is short, changes regularly and offers decent French food, but it's not particularly memorable considering the steep prices. You can get a set two-course lunch for £21.95 or three courses for £26.95, and if you leave your table before 1 p.m. the prices go down to £14.95 and £17.95 respectively. As the restaurant is in a basement below the C&B wine merchants, with their long and impressive list, the selection of wines here is excellent. The service here is second to none and there is a button on each table so you can summon the waiters should you need them – they actually turn up quite promptly. It's worth coming here to sample a bottle of nice wine but I don't suggest you stay for much else.

Cozys, which looks more like a country pub than a City wine bar, though the wine vaults are said to take up much of the space beneath Sun Street and to have passages leading in all kinds of directions. The underground passages I could live without, but Cozys is a little bit special, especially in the early hours when it opens up for breakfast to feed the hungry bankers. They also do bargain deals on end-of-bin lines, which are usually very good, and they have a remarkable choice of over 200 wines on their list – I can think of no other place with such a wide and varied selection.

A full English breakfast here costs about £11, and in the bar you get a choice of about a dozen dishes, including smoked-salmon sandwiches, scampi and chips and vegetarian dishes. The restaurant section does more serious food but is considerably more expensive.

East West
188 Old Street EC1
071-608 0300

Open: Mon–Fri
11 a.m.–9.30 p.m.,
Sat, Sun
11 a.m.–3 p.m.
Credit: A, V
Average: £8

This vegan food bar and cafe is one of the few places to eat in the Old Street area, though it's more of a New Age complex than a restaurant. If you're interested in vegan food and ideology this is the natural place to come to learn more. The food is served at the counter by pale-skinned cooks who know a real vegan when they see one. The main dishes change each day but you can rely on them being balanced and simple, and they vary in price from about £4 to £6. There's also a wide range of salads, and soups at £1.60. I quite like the puddings which are all made without sugar, dairy products or animal fat, but I'd rather have something with heavy cholesterol. The restaurant is packed at lunchtimes and in the early evening, when you're likely to bump into pop-star converts, such as Boy George, nibbling on a macrobiotic delight.

El Vino
1 Hare Place, 47 Fleet
Street EC4
071-353 5384

Open: Mon–Fri
11.30 a.m.–3 p.m.,
4.30–8 p.m.; restaurant
12.15-3 p.m.
Credit: A, Amex, V
Average: £28

As they proudly announce everywhere they can, this wine bar has been pouring good wines and sherries down the throats of London's journalists and traders for over a hundred years. It was here that Fleet Street hacks spent their inflated salaries drinking the day and night away and swapping stories and jobs. Once it was famed for allowing only men to be served at the bar, but in the eighties this was declared illegal and the owners were forced to accept women. Drink is the thing here but the food, which comes in the shape of cold meats or ploughmans' lunches, is good enough and unpretentious – unlike the stuff served by many of El Vino's rivals. They do have a dress code – men must wear ties and jackets, and women skirts or dresses – and it's very strictly adhered to.

The Fox and Anchor
115 Charterhouse Street
EC1

The doors to this pub open at 6 a.m. and from 7 a.m. until 10.30, when breakfast ends, it's chaos as the bummarees from the nearby Smithfield Market order

071-253 4838

Open: Mon–Fri
6 a.m.–11 p.m., Sat
8 a.m.–1 p.m.
Credit: A, V
Average: £25

The Green Man
7 Bucklersbury EC4
071-248 1363/3053

Open: Mon–Fri
11 a.m.–9.30 p.m.
Credit: A, V
Average: £15

The Lamb Tavern
10 Leadenhall Market
EC3
071-626 2454

Open: Mon–Sat
11 a.m.–9.30 p.m.
Credit: A, Amex, V

The Place Below
St Mary-le-Bow Church,
Cheapside EC2
071-329 0789
Open: Mon–Wed
7.30 a.m.–3 p.m,
Thurs, Fri
7.30 a.m.–3 p.m.,

up platefuls of bacon, sausage, egg, black pudding, mushrooms, beans, fried bread, liver and kidneys (£6.50), with a pint of beer to wash it all down. It's not only porters who flock to the Fox and Anchor but also medics coming off night shift at the nearby Bart's hospital: at times it's difficult to tell the difference between the butchers and the surgeons ploughing through their food with what appears to be an unhealthy appetite. Breakfast in the Fox and Anchor is an experience not to be missed, and if you have been dancing all night you'll find plenty here to recharge your batteries. Between midday and 2.30 p.m. steaks and grills are available (£10 for steak served with chips and vegetables).

For such a tiny street Bucklersbury has two great pubs, the Shades (see separate entry) and this one, which also has a restaurant downstairs. The Green Man has been under threat of demolition for fourteen years – but looking round at the beautiful wood panelling and the tartan-clad walls, I can see that the place is worth preserving. They serve a selection of Youngers ales here, as well as snacks such as shepherd's pie, cottage pie, steak and kidney pie and sausages.

Pubs in the City can often be a waste of time, but though this one is as busy as the rest in the district, at least women can spend time here without being troubled by loutish males. A pint of Beamish stout to chase away incoming colds is £1.85, and it's worth every drop. Good pub food, such as roast beef on French bread (£3.70) and toasted sandwiches, is available if you're peckish. On the first floor there's also a non-smoking bar which should come as a great relief to those who find that the smoky atmosphere of some pubs a real turn-off.

Winner of the *Time Out* Vegetarian Restaurant of the Year award in 1992, The Place Below serves up imaginative and beautifully presented food and is perfect for breakfast and lunch. You can also hire the room – a beautiful Norman crypt with spectacular arches – for parties, weddings and so on. Minestrone soup, pasta with fennel, mushrooms and cheese and a chicory, walnut and Stilton quiche are all delicious.

6–9.30 p.m.
No credit cards
Average: breakfast £8,
lunch £20, dinner £30

Rouxl Brittania
Triton Court, 14 Finsbury
Square EC2
071-256 6997

Open: Mon–Fri – cafe
7.30 a.m.–4 p.m.;
restaurant
midday–2.30 p.m.
Credit: A, Amex, DC, V
Average: cafe £30,
restaurant £40

The Shades
5–6 Bucklersbury EC4
071-248 0523/6218

Open: Mon–Fri
11.30 a.m.–9 p.m.
Credit: A, Amex, V
Average: £10

**Stephen Bull's
Bistro and Bar**
71 St John Street EC1
071-490 1750

For puddings try fresh fruit salad or bread pudding.
You can get a good breakfast here or just come in
for a snack – the place isn't licensed (being a church
and all that) but you can bring your own and they
don't charge any corkage. A great place and well
worth knowing about.

This cafe-and-restaurant complex, set in the marble
atrium of an office block, is the new baby of the
famous French chefs the Roux brothers.

Pre-packaged food of the highest quality is on offer
in the cafe – omelettes and fish-based pasta dishes
average around £5. The restaurant offers a set menu
each day. This averages £20 per person and the three
courses included are not incomparable to the class
and invention of the brothers' other establishments
such as the Waterside Inn in Bray (near Marlow on
the Thames) and the Gavroche (see Mayfair). My
favourite dish is the Toulouse sausage in a thick
onion-based sauce, accompanied by a large plate of
fries, and the restaurant does a set three-course lunch
at £18.95 a head.

Bucklersbury is one of London's most ancient Roman
streets and is more than 900 years old. In the
thirteenth century it was a home for prosperous
merchants, but now, unfortunately, the whole area is
under threat of redevelopment – try to see it as soon
as you can and get an idea of what the City of London
used to be like. The Shades pub was first built in 1795
and rebuilt in 1874. It features a huge bar that
stretches along one wall, old wooden panelling and
early prints and photographs. There's a low-key,
traditional feel to the place that is very welcoming,
and which is a welcome contrast to the brash, loud
wine bars that infest the City. Between 11.30 a.m. and
2.30 p.m. they serve hot food such as shepherd's pie
or sausages, as well as salads, sandwiches and snacks.
There's no puddings, unfortunately, but the Shade is
still a haven in the City. Well worth a visit.

This restaurant and bar is the place to come for head
chef Stephen Bull's intelligently planned modern
food, served in understated surroundings. Bull also
has a highly regarded restaurant off Marylebone High
Street, but the prices in this bistro are much cheaper

Open: bar
11.30 a.m.–3.30 p.m.,
5.30–11 p.m.;
restaurant, lunch
midday–11 p.m., dinner
6–11 p.m.
Credit: A, V
Average: £40

than you'd expect. Starters when I was last at Stephen Bull's included a terrine of leeks and langoustines or cauliflower soup with Cashel Blue cheese and lovage cream; tempting main courses include a saddle of lamb with salpicon of liver and kidneys and grey mullet with red wine sauce and black trumpet mushrooms. For puddings try the delicious lemon and lime curd pots with crumbled biscuits or the Viennese blackberry tart. One of the best places to eat in the City, without doubt.

Sweetings

39 Queen Victoria
Street EC4
071-248 3062

Open: Mon–Fri
11.30–3 p.m.
No credit cards
Average: £38

You must try this fish restaurant if you have any intention of coming into the City. It's an institution in the Square Mile and therefore it's very difficult to get a seat here at one of the series of bars – just snatch a place as soon as you see one. This is British food and service at its best. The atmosphere is electric and very loud as waiters shout orders to assistants who quickly appear carrying plates of whitebait, oysters or prawns, all fresh. It's not a bad place to watch depressed bond dealers drowning their sorrows or resuscitating their flagging spirits with a plate of Mediterranean prawns and a bottle of Chablis, and for what it is, it's not that expensive. The wine list is trad French with a mixture of averagely priced good wines and expensive once-in-a-lifetime bottles. It's open only for weekday lunch, so don't make the mistake of heading down into this graveyard of an area in the evening or at weekends.

Tatsuso

32 Broadgate Circus
EC2
071-638 5863

Open: Mon–Fri, lunch
11.30 a.m.–2.30 p.m.,
dinner 6–9.30 p.m.
Credit: A, Amex, DC, V
Average: £80

One of the few restaurants in the City which opens again in the evening, this is a high-class Japanese restaurant overlooking the ice-hockey pitch in the middle of the Broadgate development. In the afternoon the set lunches (from £13.80) served in the sushi bar are popular with local businessmen, but it is in the evening that the place starts to become interesting when it suddenly becomes very Japanese as homesick men on London trips come here in droves. There is no karaoke machine and none of the smiling subservience which can be so annoying in Japanese restaurants. This place offers just good Japanese food, cooked and cut before your eyes. Because it gets very busy you'll need to book the restaurant, and there is a minimum charge of £40 per person. You can also eat in the tatami room which seats six shoeless diners in the quiet of a closed and sedate place. It is, however, fantastically expensive.

SHOPPING

Freshlands Wholefoods
196 Old Street EC1
071-250 1708

Open: Mon–Fri
8.30 a.m.–7 p.m., Sat
8.45 a.m.–5.30 p.m.
Credit: A, V

Founded in 1976, Freshlands is one of London's pioneering wholefood shops and it has built up one of the widest ranges of organic foods available. The shop is divided into two floors: upstairs is the organic vegetables and dairy products, staple grains, nuts, dried fruits, oils, tofu and other foods, and downstairs you will find vitamin supplements, cosmetics, water filters and so on, including a selection of Japanese seaweeds which seem to be a universal panacea. There's lots of non-wheat products here for anyone with allergies, and you can buy delicious home-made food, cooked on the premises and mostly vegan, to take away. It's an extremely well run and well stocked shop, and the staff are friendly and approachable and will gladly help you out with information as well as leaflets. Freshlands is also perfectly situated next to the East-West centre (see separate entry).

Leadenhall Market
Leadenhall Market EC3
071-260 1530

In the fourteenth century a meat and fish market occupied a series of courts behind the grand lead-roofed City Mansion, the Leaden Hall, on Leadenhall Street. The site was leased in 1408 by Dick Whittington, who bought the freehold in 1411 and presented it as a gift to the City in his third term of office as mayor. The present wrought-iron and glass-roofed building was designed by Horace Jones in 1881, and the market was recently restored and redecorated in consultation with English Heritage who have done their very best to recreate the character of the Victorian market. It has an amazing roof with a blue dome and gold stars, covering the cobblestones and old-fashioned delivery bikes propped against traditional shopfronts. Red-and-black-uniformed bootboys will shine your shoes for £1.50 – it's an extraordinary place to come across among the ultra-modern buildings of this modern financial centre, only minutes from Lloyds. At lunchtme yuppie wage slaves pour in here to snack at one of the eateries or buy their groceries. There's 37 retail units on the ground floor with ten more upstairs, and it definitely provides the best shopping, eating and browsing in the area.

The market keeps City hours; most shops close at about 3 p.m., though restaurants tend to stay open until about 8 p.m. – it's best to check.

Royal Exchange
Threadneedle Street EC3

Sandwiched between Threadneedle Street and Cornhill Street is the Royal Exchange. It used to house the London International Financial Futures and Options Market, but the futures exchange has recently moved to Cannon Bridge. Opposite the old entrance to the building and linking Cornhill Street and Threadneedle Street is a paved area planted with trees and dominated by the imposing figure of Paul Julius Reuter – the world news organisation that he founded in 1851 and that bears his name is housed in number 1, Royal Exchange. Today, though, the area bustles with traffic, and there's a good supply of shops to serve the passing trade. On the Cornhill side there's a jeweller's at number 1 and designer goods from Hermes at number 2. Next door you can pick up embossed luggage, briefcases and wallets from the famed but terribly expensive Louis Vuitton, and at number 7 is Penhaligon's, which sells its traditional bottles of cologne and flower scents at a price. At number 9 is Geoffrey's, a real old gentleman's barber's and manicurist's where you can get a shave with hot towels for £13 and a haircut for about £15 while seated in a huge old-fashioned swivel chair and staring at the various coats of armour on the walls.

There's something to suit just about everyone here – further along you could stop off at the Greenhouse Champagne and Oyster Bar or indulge in some of the finest chocolates in the world at Bendicks. Feed the mind at Ash Rare Books at number 25, stockists of antiquarian books and prints – you could get a first edition of *Under Milk Wood* here for £100, and £250 will buy you the first edition of *David Copperfield* in book form, bound up from the parts published monthly. And Carter at number 30 is the perfect shop for the English weather, stocking hundreds of brollies squeezed into every available nook and cranny.

Thorntons
43 Cheapside EC2
071-248 6776

This traditional old English chocolate shop offers as good a selection of dark chocolate and toffee cream-based delights as you will see anywhere, including Switzerland and Belgium. This is one of many Thorn-

Open: Mon
10 a.m.–6 p.m.,
Tues–Fri 9 a.m.–6 p.m.
Credit: A, V

tons branches across London but seems a little less flashy than the others and concentrates more on the goodies. If you're thinking about your teeth you'd be wise not to come in, but if you want some tough toffee to get your jaw moving as it never has before, come here as quickly as possible. The chocolates they sell here are hand made and so cost a little more than the normal manufactured stuff – a small 8oz bag averages out at around £3.90 – but they're worth it.

ENTERTAINMENT

**Community Health
Foundation**
188 Old Street EC1
071-251 4076

Credit: A, V

Sharing a building with the East West restaurant (see separate entry), the Community Health Foundation has been in existence since 1976. Many of the courses it offers have evolved from Eastern preventative approaches to health care, and they include massage, acupuncture and shiatsu, all of which are powerful antidotes to stress and the strain caused by city life. Local office workers seeking an alternative to the liquid lunch can come here during the week for a shiatsu massage. You can also have a Pilates session here – it's a brilliant form of exercise which improves posture and strength without putting too much strain on any part of the body.

Ironmonger Baths
1–11 Ironmonger Row
EC1
071-253 4011

Open: Sat, all facilities
9 a.m.–5 p.m.,
Mon–Fri, pool
7.30 a.m.–8 p.m.,
Turkish baths, gym,
sauna, sunbeds
9 a.m.–9 p.m., Sun,
Turkish baths, sauna,
sunbeds 9 a.m.–midday
No credit cards

These beautiful, traditional baths have been here since the 1930s, and are a treasure to find in the City. A Turkish bath and a body scrub will make you feel as relaxed as a newborn babe and costs £8.50. All tension will drain from you as you move from steam rooms to dry heat rooms and plunge in the pool. If you're in a hurry you can settle for a swim, which costs £1.85 during peak hours or £1.55 off peak. The Turkish baths and sunbed are open exclusively to women on Mondays, Wednesdays, Fridays and alternate Sundays; women's days in the sauna are Tuesday, Thursday and Saturday. The other days are for men only. It's a wonderful experience – if everyone had a Turkish bath and a massage a week, there'd be no more war . . . Times of courses vary – ring first to check.

The Pit
The Barbican Centre,
Silk Street EC2

This theatre, smaller than the Barbican's main theatre, is where the RSC puts on its more experimental work which is often more rewarding than what is on in the

071-638 8891

Credit: A, Amex, V

main house. It seems as if the actors and directors are under less pressure here and can try out new ideas without worrying about the commercial implications. New plays are performed here and they also approach the Greek classics with an uncompromising attitude.

If critical acclaim and box-office success are met with here, the work will often be moved up to the bigger theatre. The Pit is a small intimate space where you sit hanging over the actors, which means that you can see every movement, from lips to hips, giving you an idea of how good these actors really are. Recent productions include *The Last Days of Don Juan*, *Edward II*, with Simon Russell Beale, *Troilus and Cressida*, directed by Sam Mendes, and the sell-out *'Tis Pity She's a Whore*. It's one of my favourite theatre spaces in London and I've seen some truly great acting here.

The Royal Shakespeare Company
The Barbican Theatre, Barbican Centre, Silk Street EC2
071-638 8891

Credit: A, Amex, V

The Barbican theatre can seat 1,166 people, which gives an indication of the pressures on the theatre company to provide a commercial selection of the Bard's work. A solid core of associate artists, actors, directors and designers have tried to maintain a policy of innovation and accessibility without ever compromising the beauty and vigour of Shakespeare's words and, although the theatre has been criticised by actors as being an uninspiring bunker, the productions, which are previewed in Stratford, always seem to travel well and play to big audiences. As well as Shakespeare, they also put on productions of world classics. Bunker or not, the theatre is probably the most comfortable in Britain, giving the public a chance to sit back and actually relax and enjoy the legroom if the show is not so good. There are no aisles in the stalls and each row leads to an automatically controlled door which suggests that once you are in you are in for the duration.

Recent productions include *King Lear*, with John Wood, and Terry Hand's production of Chekov's *The Seagull*. The pressure of looking after this institution has been handed down from Sir Peter Hall to Trevor Nunn, and now lies with Adrian Noble, who is certain to put his own stamp on the concrete blocks.

The Slaughterhouse Gallery

63 Charterhouse Street
EC1
071-490 0847

Open: Mon–Sat
11 a.m.–6 p.m.
No credit cards

Walking along Charterhouse Street, admiring the cast-iron avenues of the meat market, it is very easy to miss the Slaughterhouse Gallery. This was originally a Victorian abattoir serving the market next door, and very few of the original features have been changed. The air is tight and dense enough to make you think the gallery can't possibly be what it says it is, but hanging on the wall is art of some description, normally preliminary sketches for what lies in the real basement, further down some rickety old steps. The walls drip water and there are channels in the floor which were presumably designed for the blood to flow down. Theatrical to the end, the owners have positioned large, memorable pieces of contemporary sculpture under direct spotlighting. The effect is eerie and disturbing. There is no other gallery in London which has managed to create such a complete atmosphere. Its ambiance is not exactly inviting, but somehow it seems to draw you in.

The artists are often unknown and uncompromising in their choice of imagery, which to the naked and innocent eye seems to be verging on the macabre, but this is very appropriate to the space. Prints and sculpture can be had for £150–£4,000 – prices vary but are reasonable by West End standards.

Tower Hill Pageant

Tower Hill Terrace,
Tower Hill EC3
071-709 0081

Open: April–October
9.30 a.m.–5.30 p.m.,
November–March
9.30 a.m.–4.30 p.m.
Credit: A, Amex, V
Admission: adults
£4.50, children and
OAPs £2.50

Billed as London's first dark ride museum, this is the place to come to run through 2,000 years of London's history in fifteen minutes flat – and all from the comfort of an automated car. Situated in old Victorian wine vaults and inspired by the Museum of London's (see separate entry) archaeological digs along the City waterfront, the pageant features historically accurate reproductions of London scenes from early Roman settlements, through seventeenth-century coffee houses to the Blitz and on to today. With its moving figures and authentic smells of marshland and docks, it keeps kids enthralled.

In the Tower Hill terrace is Virtual Quest. Opened in January 1993, this is a virtual-reality games quest, featuring various different virtual-reality machines. You can choose to become an elf or a dwarf, or to remain human, and battle mythical creatures in a three-dimensional world loosely based on Dungeons and Dragons. It's a fun one-off experience and costs

£2 – for £5 you can join a gaming club which entitles you to buy time so that you can pick up your last game exactly where you left off. For die-hard enthusiasts.

Turnmills
63b Clerkenwell Road
EC1
071-250 3409

Open: Mon–Thurs
6 a.m.–2 a.m., Fri
6 a.m.–9 a.m., Sat
8 p.m.–midday, Sun
10 p.m.–6 a.m.
Credit: A, Amex, V
Admission: Mon–Thurs
free, Fri–Sun £6–£10

At the weekend the small, quiet, well-kept streets in this area hide one of the greatest secrets of London. A pounding bass beat seems to be coming from underground. It is. Across Clerkenwell Road, a minute from the Green, is Turnmills, a virtually 24-hour nightclub (soft drinks are served outside club opening hours) whose only giveaway is a baseball-capped doorman who can tell in a second if you are the right type of person to go in. The Sunday afternoon event is aptly titled Sunday Roast, and when I went the violent red lights seemed to indicate a descent into an inhospitable zone where only something bad could face an innocent like myself. At 1 p.m. the long corridor which serves as a bar and as access to the dancefloor was crammed full of bedraggled but very much alive and gyrating bodies.

The doorman told me that until 10 a.m. the high-octane electro sound of Trade, a gay club, had played to a full house. The club was then cleaned, restocked and rearmed with records for a different crowd. He has few memories of ever having had trouble here – the only time there's ever problems is when they have to tell people to leave.

SWEETINGS

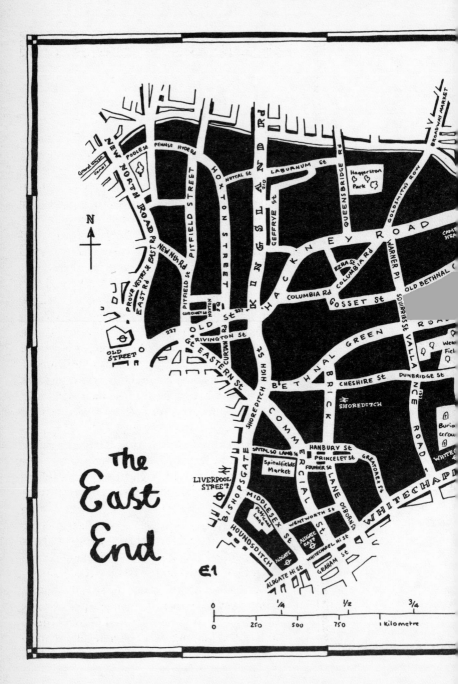

The East End

E1

*t*he core of the East End is probably White-chapel. Named after the whitewashed St Mary's Church, the area has for centuries been the first stopping-off point for immigrants, from Huguenot weavers to Bangladeshi refugees. By the nineteenth century this intensely poor area was home to a mix of Irish, Germans and Sephardic Jews who saw its sweatshops, soup kitchens and low-life lodging houses as a better prospect than the life they had left behind.

From watermen to coal whippers to tailors, Whitechapel became, in the words of William Booth, the founder of the Salvation Army, 'the Eldorado of the east, a gathering together of poor fortune seekers'. It was also the haunt of Fagin's young criminals in *Oliver Twist*, and was the place where they learned their tricks and disguised themselves as 'swells' before picking the pockets of West End gentlefolk.

The steady influx of Jewish refugees from the pogroms in Eastern Europe at the turn of the century gave the area a ghetto-like atmosphere and English was seldom heard as this once quiet quarter of the City of London became the setting for synagogues and delis, and the training ground for the likes of Alfred Marks (of Marks and Spencer) to catch the bug of selling people what they wanted at a price they could afford.

Throughout the twentieth century, the Jewish community has moved to more prosperous parts of London such as Finchley and Golders Green in East London, but their children still return to sample the food from the restaurants and delis

that remain. The Jewish immigrants have now been replaced by Bengali, Bangladeshi and Somali refugees fleeing political turmoil and famine in their own countries. Now the streets of Whitechapel have taken on a new character, with a proliferation of clothing stores and cheap Indian cafes selling what is probably the best food of its kind in London.

The area we now know as Spitalfields was built on the muddy fields east of the old medieval priory which once stood in this area. The hospital of St Mary Spital was founded in 1197, but had a history of bad debt and bankruptcy and by the sixteenth century had two people in each of its 180 beds. As London swelled in size at the end of the seventeenth century, Spitalfields served the overspill from Aldgate, and the unruly locals of the area were joined by French Huguenots who had fled their own country after the edict of Nantes in 1685. Their silk-weaving skills soon made them prosperous and the fine houses they built still stand in aptly named streets such as Fournier and Princelet. When the weaving trade declined in the nineteenth century the gracious Georgian streets degenerated into slums, and Jews arriving at the docks after fleeing the pogroms after Tsar Alexander's death filled the cheap accommodation. Despite the bad conditions of the area the new inhabitants carried on Spitalfields tradition as a textile area, though working in fur and tailoring rather than silk.

During this period the area gained its most legendary visitor. Jack the Ripper's identity has never been uncovered, but over a period of three months he left his mark on six victims, each of whom was killed inside a square mile in the Spitalfields area. On organised walks through the backstreets (071-624 3978) it is still possible to imagine the movements of the Ripper as he stalked the unfortunate women who fell victim to his savagery.

As in Whitechapel, Jewish settlers have now been replaced by Bengali and Bangladeshi families. The rag and leather trades still flourish in the area, although the goods produced tend not to be of the highest quality. Apart from manufacturing, the locals find work in the nearby Brick Lane and Petticoat Lane markets and the Truman's brewery, but not enough has been done in the area to lift the gloom of centuries of underdevelopment and poverty. The Huguenot houses have been reclaimed by architects and artists (there is a higher concentration of artists in the Spitalfields and Bethnal Green areas than anywhere else in the world) who have shown great sensivity towards the original design of the interiors. The controversial artists Gilbert and George have made their home on Fournier Street into a work of art, as has the tailor Timothy Everest, who is based on Princelet Street. Such houses stand in stark contrast to the poverty which surrounds them.

HOW TO GET THERE

Tubes
- Aldgate
- Aldgate East
- Bethnal Green
- Liverpool Street
- Old Street
- Shoreditch
- Whitechapel

Buses
- Bethnal Green Road: 8
- Bishopsgate: 8, 22B, 26, 35, 47, 48, 149, 505
- Hackney Road: 26, 48, 55
- Great Eastern Street: 5, 43, 55, 243, 505
- Middlesex Street: 5, 78, 100
- Shoreditch High Street: 5, 6, 8, 22A, 22B, 35, 43, 47, 48, 55, 67, 78, 145, 243, 243A, 505

THE BASS CLEF

SIGHTS AND SITES

**Bethnal Green
Museum of
Childhood**
Cambridge Heath Road
E2
081-980 2415

Open: Mon–Thurs, Sat
10 a.m.–5.30 p.m.,
Sun 2.30–6 p.m.
No admission charge

One of the best museums around and a branch of
the Victoria and Albert Museum, this is a place to
revel in toys and games past from early toy theatres
to Action Man. It's great for keeping kids quiet, and
there are lots of organised events.

Occasionally special exhibitions are mounted here:
recently 'Trash or Treasure' examined 400 years of
children's literature through a display of the extensive
Renier Collection.

There is also a shop here, selling gifts, cards and
toys.

Brick Lane, E1
Open: market Sat, Sun
8 a.m.–1 p.m.

This street got its name in the sixteenth century from
a nearby brick factory and was once home to Huguenot silk-weavers. The area still has a ghetto-like feel
to it and at night has a mysterious, magical atmosphere, the like of which I have felt only in a Moroccan
casbah. The market is eye-openingly poor and offers
a selection of tat and bric-a-brac at very low prices,
though if you have a good rummage through you
could find a genuine bargain. Brick Lane is lined with
restaurants, many of them unlicensed, where the
cheapest and best Indian and Bangladeshi food can
be found. Most of the restaurants look and feel the
same and it is difficult to get a raw deal here.

Christ Church
Commercial Street E1
071-377 0287

Open: Mon–Fri
12.30–2.30 p.m., Sun,
Matins
10.30 a.m.–12.30 p.m.,
Evensong
6.30–7.30 p.m.

This church, designed by Nicholas Hawksmoor and
built between 1714 and 1729, remains a proud
monument to the great architect. Its most outstanding features are the portico of four Tuscan columns,
and the barrel-vaulted arch in the middle, which
meets the rest of the building through the octagonal
spire. Intended to bring a modicum of religious
sensibility to this anarchic district, the money to build
it was raised through a new coal tax. Between 1729
and 1858, about 67,000 people were buried in the
churchyard, and another thousand in the crypt.

Today, the flat coffered ceiling looks down on an
empty church which has fallen on very hard times,
though the Friends of Christ Church are ensuring that
it is restored, albeit very slowly indeed. The crypt is
used by homeless people to shelter from the bad
weather and also functions as a clinic for alcoholics.
In June each year there is a live music festival

featuring baroque and modern music; John Taverner and Gavin Bryars have both premiered their work here.

Geffrye Museum
Kingsland Road E2
071-739 9893

Open: Tues–Sat
10 a.m.–5 p.m., Sun
2-5 p.m.
No admission charge
Credit: A, V

The buildings housing this museum were originally eighteenth-century almshouses, constructed in 1715 at the bequest of Sir Robert Geffrye to serve as a home for ironmongers' widows. Converted in 1914, it's bang in the centre of London's furniture and cabinet-making district and holds a permanent collection of furniture and complete rooms which chronicle the development of furniture-making from Tudor times to the 1960s. The authenticity of the rooms make a trip here an interesting walk through time, and give you the impression that our ancestors paid scant attention to their comfort. I like this place a lot as it's never too busy and the setting is one of the most unusual in London; try to visit the traditional walled herb garden which is open from April to September. In the centre of the museum, tucked behind the chapel, there's a coffee bar selling tea, coffee and soft drinks for 40p, as well as delicious big cakes (£1), crisps and biscuits, though you may prefer to take a ten-minute walk to Brick Lane where you can get a decent meal for under a fiver. The shop sells books on herbs, gardening and furniture design, as well as souvenirs and gifts. There is also a library where you can read in peace and quiet.

Whitechapel Art Gallery
80–82 Whitechapel
High Street E1
071-377 0107

Open: Tues, Thurs-Sun
11 a.m.–5 p.m., Wed
11 a.m.–8 p.m.
No admission charge

The Whitechapel area owes a great debt to the pioneering Canon Augustus Samuel Barnett, who decided that something had to be done to save the souls of the people from the continuing poverty, and his Whitechapel Art Gallery, designed by C. H. Townsend at a cost of £8,427, was started in 1897 and opened in 1901.

There is no permanent exhibition here; instead, the curators put on several shows a year of excellent work by new and established artists. In general the work moves between the modern and the conceptual and artists who have shown here recently include painters Juan Gris, Ian McKeever and Sean Kelly and sculptor Jacob Epstein. Some sculptures are also exhibited in the nearby Spitalfields Market (see separate entry). Shows tend to run for six to eight weeks and the gallery is closed for about ten days between

exhibitions – therefore it's best to ring first to check what's on. The annual Whitechapel Open gave many local East End artists the chance to show their work in this magnificent gallery, but now, sadly, it looks as if 1992 was the last year this great and important show took place.

There is a cafe upstairs which sells good wholefood such as mushroom quiche with green salad and cauliflower soup. The food is all made on the premises and is consistently priced at about £1.50 for soup and £3-£4 for a main-course dish. There is also a selection of well-laid-out salads at about £2.80 a plate. The bookshop offers a good range of catalogues and cards, not all necessarily related to the current exhibition. There is full wheelchair access to all parts of the building.

EATING AND DRINKING

Bloom's
90 Whitechapel High
Street E1
071-247 6001

Open: Mon–Thurs
11 a.m.–9 p.m., Sun
11 a.m.–2 p.m.
Credit: A, Amex, DC, V
Average: £25

This restaurant is a serious nostalgia trip – everything is as it was 50 years ago, when places like this served kosher food to Whitechapel's large Jewish community. Today the busy chattering classes of North and East London eat, talk and enjoy the meaty dishes, all served with generous helpings of rye bread. It can be unexpectedly expensive, but if you keep with the Bloomburger and onions (£5.90) or the frankfurters with sweet and sour cabbage (£5.40), and don't go overboard with wine from the adequate list, you should be able to keep the final bill at a very reasonable level. The service can sometimes be very abrupt if you don't know what you want, but the food and the atmosphere definitely make it worth a visit.

Cafe Ezra Street
Ezra Street E2

No credit cards

There's a hippy feel to this red-tiled and white-walled place, which every Sunday morning will serve up a half-pint mug of real coffee for just 60p. Its popularity is obvious from the queues that form here on market day,·when it's well-nigh impossible to get a perch on one of the high stools inside. However, you can sit outside on wooden let-down benches and watch the troops of green-fingered gardeners clutching huge armloads of flowers and bedding-out plants. There's usually some rather good Irish traditional buskers playing outside as well, which should put a jig in your step. The grub is great – sugary Chelsea buns are 40p, delicious home-made cheesecake £1.20, soup and bread £2, and there's also a good selection of bagels and platzels. In hot weather the home-made lemonade is fantastic.

The Clifton
126 Brick Lane E1
071-377 9402

Open: midday–midnight
Credit: A, Amex, DC, V
Average: £25

With its huge Pakistani portrait murals and modern, light decor, this is not your average Asian eatery and it easily beats off most of the competition in the quality stakes. All the usual favourites are here – especially good are the onion bhaji, the fish curry and the fried bhindi (okra) with onions and chilli. Most main-course dishes cost around the £4.50 mark, though the seafood comes out a little more expensive, at about £7.50. The chef, who comes from southern India, has been at the Clifton since 1969, which is a guarantee of consistency in the quality of the food. Definitely one of the best places, if not the cheapest, on Brick Lane.

F. Cooke
150 Hoxton Street N1
071-729 7718

Open: Mon–Thurs
10 a.m.–7 p.m.,
Fri, Sat
9.30 a.m.–8.30 p.m.
No credit cards
Average: £4

The Cooke family is one of three London clans who control the pie-and-mash business, each of which jealously guards its own recipe. Exactly why is beyond me, as I have never been able to understand the charm of squashed-up eels and the poisonously coloured green 'liquor', which is made from parsley and which I find quite disgusting. However, it's incredibly popular with a lot of people and the shops themselves are often worth a look. This one is extraordinary, with its wall-to-wall tiles and shining mirrors. It's all a part of the working-class London which has yet to be taken over by the middle classes.

**The Dove Free
House**
25–27 Broadway
Market E8
071-275 7617

Open: Mon–Sat
11 a.m.–11 p.m., Sun
11.30 a.m.–3 p.m.,
7.30–10 p.m.
No credit cards
Average: £15

Like the Hackney Empire (see separate entry), the Dove free house is a little off the map of this book, but merits an entry by being perhaps one of the very best pubs in the East End, if not the whole of London. Located on Broadway Market, a very bleak and miserable little street, this haven acts like a magnet for a friendly, mixed crowd of locals, young trendies and students: when it first opened in 1991, owners Lee and Al consciously set out to make the Dove a place where everybody, but women in particular, can feel comfortable on their own. And they have succeeded magnificently: the pub is a great place to come for a read of the papers, a game of chess or

indeed any of the 30 games they have here, or to listen to excellent music varying from swing and jazz to Irish traditional, classical, blues and cajun. On Saturdays football fans can come to watch the game – everybody gets a free hotdog, which is a nice touch.

The food at the Dove is excellent, too – there's always two vegetarian dishes as well as something delicious for the carnivores, and a terrific vegetable soup that's really closer to a stew. Worth a special mention is the salad platter: a vast wooden bowl piled high with lettuce and five imaginative and delicious salads such as red bean, melon and leek. At £2.50, this is the bargain of the year. Also try to check out the cherry, ginger and (especially lethal, this) garlic-flavoured Absolut vodkas, the Lovey Dovey cocktails (£2.50) and, in season, the Galway Bay oysters, washed down with a pint of properly poured Guinness. Warm, friendly and welcoming, the Dove is a real oasis in an area which badly needs one.

The Kosher Luncheon Club
Morris Kasler Hall, 13
Greatorex Street E1
071-247 0039

Open: Sun–Fri
midday–3 p.m.
No credit cards
Average: £14

One of the last examples of a tradition of East London kosher luncheon clubs, this is a huge room which at one time was a soup kitchen and which has walls adorned with notes of appreciation from all over the world. The food is served in the cleanest kitchen I have ever seen and is served by the friendliest people I have ever met on all my trips into the East End. There's a big emphasis on fish, either traditionally fried in matzo meal and served with chips or the more exotic East European spiced herring and bean and barley soup at about £1.80. There is also a selection of desserts at £1.50. When a busload of people rolls in from anywhere from Golders Green to New York, there is a terrific atmosphere here. It's a favourite with actor Steven Berkoff, who comes here to recharge his batteries with the club's lox or latkes. It costs 10p to join the club, which is not particularly expensive or exclusively Jewish, and it's an incredibly welcoming place, especially on a cold, wet London day.

The Market Cafe
5 Fournier Street E1
071-247 9470

Open: Mon–Fri
12.30 p.m.–1 a.m.

When I wandered past this cafe, situated in a street of old, wooden-shuttered narrow Huguenot houses, it was getting a lick of paint to its bright tongue-and-groove interior. The Market Cafe is a good stopping-off place if you need to escape the bustle of Brick Lane nearby or Spitalfields opposite. The food is

No credit cards
Average: £10

good, typical caff fare and is great first thing in the morning, and the cafe itself is a great favourite with local market stallholders and artists – there is a higher concentration of artists in the East End than anywhere else in the world.

Nazrul
130 Brick Lane E1
071-247 2505

Open: Mon–Sat, lunch
midday–3 p.m., dinner
5.30–midnight; Sun
midday–midnight
No credit cards
Average: £15

This restaurant has the simplest decor on Brick Lane (and that's saying something), and the formica tables tell you that the owners don't really go overboard on presentation. The food, though, could feed a boatload of Huguenots for a week – kebabs, curries and simple vegetable dishes are all good. Everything is fresh and perfectly cooked. Curries cost from £3 to £5 and starters, which include delicious onion bhajis, come in at around 60p to £1.50. The place attracts a lot of local artists and if you get talking it's not at all a bad place to find out what is happening in the art world.

The Royal Oak
73 Columbia Road E2
071-739 8204

Open: Mon–Sat
11 a.m.–11 p.m., Sun
8 a.m.–3 p.m.
No credit cards

The Royal Oak is a typical East End pub, complete with darts, pool table, slot machines and constantly blaring TV – and the best thing about it is that it opens very early on Sunday mornings for the Columbia Road flower market (see separate entry). From 8 a.m. on, lots of trader stop off here for a swift half and a bite to eat – there's bagels, pies and bacon rolls available, as well as coffee and tea. Good if you've been virtuous and got to the market early.

Salique's
32 Hanbury Street E1
071-377 5232/2137

Open: Mon–Fri, lunch
midday–3 p.m., dinner
6 p.m.–midnight; Sat,
dinner 6 p.m.–midnight
Credit: Amex, DC
Average: £25

This restaurant has more a West End than an East End feel about it, with its smart blue and white napery and light interior. It comes well recommended as serving some of the best food in the area and is much more than just a place to come to for a post-pub curry. Prices are reasonable, with a vegetarian thali (vegetable curry, aloo gobi, tarka dall, yoghurt chana, nan and pilau rice) costing £6.95, lamb pasanda (marinated lamb with spices and fresh cream) at £5.25 and tandoori chicken at £5. Definitely on the trendy side for Brick Lane.

The Ten Bells
84 Commercial Road E1
071-377 2145

Open: Mon–Sat
11 a.m.–11 p.m.,
Sun midday–3 p.m.,

There has been a pub on this site, directly opposite Spitalfields Market, on the corner of Fournier Street, since 1753. The Ten Bells achieved notoriety as the 'Jack the Ripper' pub as it was in here his six victims drank. Now the Ten Bells is a regular stopping-off place on the the Original London Walks (071-624 3978) and Historical Walks (071-668 4019) tours of

7–10.30 p.m.
No credit cards

London. It boasts a wall of old photographs of the pub and the market in the surrounding streets, and there are some new snaps of celebs like Anthony Perkins sitting down and enjoying a drink here. If he has time the landlord is quite happy to spend some of it telling stories about the pub's history, and in general the Ten Bells is a friendly place for a pint. Pub food such as pies and snacks are available at about £1, and on Sunday mornings there's live music here.

SHOPPING

Ambala Sweet Centre

55 Brick Lane E1
071-247 8569

Open: Mon–Sat
10 a.m–8 p.m., Sun
9.30 a.m.–7.30 p.m.
No credit cards

You have to have a very sweet tooth indeed to fully appreciate the trays of home-made Indian delicacies on sale here. Pista halva (pistachio halva) costs £2.60 a pound and habshi halva (pistachio and cashew nuts with milk and almonds) is £3.60 a pound. They also have delicious gulab jamun, which should be familiar to anyone who frequents Indian restaurants and which will set you back £1.80 a pound. Don't be put off by the garish colours, for the green chunks of pista burfi are delicious, and if you're not sure what you want they might let you have a taste first.

Atlantis European Ltd

146 Brick Lane E1
071-377 8855

Open: Mon–Sat
9.30 a.m.–6 p.m., Sun
10 a.m.–4 p.m.
Credit: A, V

This building was once part of the old Truman's brewery, founded on this site in 1666, the year of the Great Fire of London. The brewery is now owned by Grand Met and used mainly as offices, though its canteen now houses the Brick Lane Music Hall (see separate entry), and the building housing Atlantis was originally the place used to steam-clean the barrels, which were then refilled in another part of the establishment – you can see the pipes in the ceiling and the dips and bumps in the floor for drainage. The four floors of the building house studio spaces and a gallery, but Atlantis is chiefly known as one of the best art-materials suppliers in London, and is used a great deal by local artists. You can buy everything from wood for stretchers to canvases and paper; the range and value is second to none. It's especially good for Spectrum oil and acrylic paints and screen-printing materials. Atlantis also has a mail-order service on art materials.

Beigel Bake

159 Brick Lane E1

At the weekend, deep into the small hours, carloads of sweating ravers who have danced the night away

071-729 0616

Open: 24 hours
No credit cards

converge on this place to refuel their batteries. The bagels – or beigels – are ring-shaped rolls of heavy, sweet bread which taste best filled with smoked salmon and cream cheese, though there is a range of other fillings. This round-the-clock bakery is a great place to find out what's going on and is an eye-opener if you ever thought London nightlife had died a death. The last time I was here the queue was a mix of dancers, Jewish cab drivers, gamblers, prowlers and growlers, all starving. It's also very popular on Brick Lane market days with stallholders popping in for hot coffee.

**Columbia Road
Market**
Columbia Road E2

Open: Sun
8 a.m.–1 p.m.

During the week Columbia Road is more or less deserted, but on Sunday mornings it sees a famous market for flowers and plants at prices which are said to be the cheapest in London. Everything from chrysanthemums to Dutch sunflowers are available here, as well as a huge selection of bulbs, shrubs and bedding-out plants, and all are worth haggling over. There are some great bargains to be had – five weeping figs grafted to make a five-foot, beautifully shaped little tree, which must have taken twelve years to grow, can be had for about £30 and will brighten up any room. Smart shoppers arrive either early in the morning, to get the best-quality plants and avoid the crowds, or later – the closing time of 1 p.m. is strictly enforced and you could snap up a bargain from a trader anxious to pack up and go home.

The popularity of the market means that a number of trendy small gift shops, as well as garden shops, have opened along the street, and there's also a good selection of cafes to choose from. The atmosphere along the market, which is always jammed with people clutching fragrant, colourful sheafs of blooms, is great, particularly in summer.

Elvisly Yours
107 Shoreditch High
Street E1
071-739 2001

Open: Mon–Fri
10 a.m.–6 p.m.
Credit: A, Amex, V

This amazing shop, which has been here since 1982, sells just about everything to do with the King, and also runs the small Elvisly Yours fan club for its customers. It's the only shop in Britain dedicated entirely to Presley and is the first stopping-off point for foreign fans visiting England. Die-hard Elvis fans can buy soap with an everlasting image of the man himself for £1, mugs at about £3 each, ties at about £2 and commemorative plates for about £13. About the only things they don't sell are costumes – would-be Elvis impersonators are advised to go to a theatrical costumer instead.

S & B Evans and Sons Ltd

7a Ezra Street E2

071-729 6635

Open: Fri
9 a.m.–5 p.m., Sun
9 a.m.–1.30 p.m.
Credit: A, V

This shop has been a feature of Columbia Road market since 1982, and has been in its current premises since 1986. Because of its location – by the plant market – the main demand here is for plant pots and wall pots (from 30p), but they also sell terracotta plaques and decorations, as well as glazed mugs which cost £4.30. They are beginning to stock more water-oriented items now – these include fountain pieces for ponds as well as free-standing fountains, costing from £80. All their terracotta and glazed pots carry a ten-year guarantee against frost damage.

The Flower Room

96 Columbia Road E2

071-739 7555

Open: Sun
9 a.m.–2 p.m., and by
appointment
Credit: A, V

Angela Flanders, the owner of this tiny shop on the end of Columbia Road, is an interior designer, and it shows – the Flowers Room is absolutely exquisite, with its tongue-and-groove interior and hand-stencilled borders, all in pale green and mustard-cream. The Flower Room smells as delicious as it looks – pot-pourri is made here, and they also stock a range of aromatic and burning oils, as well as various burners. One wall is stacked with candles, ranging from thick church candles – a box of 25 nine-inch candles is about £17 – to beeswax and handcrafted alternatives. There are clusters of wall sconces at £30 a pair, and candle fittings of all sorts – hand-marbled paper candlelamp shades range from £5.50 to £7.95. It's a specialist shop but well worth a visit.

Fred Bare Hats

118 Columbia Road E2

071-729 6962

Open: Sun
9 a.m.–2 p.m., and by
appointment
Credit: A, V

An old marketing slogan says 'If you want to get ahead, get a hat', and Fred Bare's is definitely the shop to pick up something great to put on your bonce. Hanging and perching in every available corner, there's a fantastic array of all sorts of big hats, little hats, caps, berets and bowlers, ranging in price from £8 upwards. The designs are all exclusive to the shop, and at any one time there's a selection of about 80 to choose from. Summer hats with a driftwood trim cost £80, as do neat winter Homburgs and bowlers decorated with found objects from the Thames beach. The famous Fred Bare brimmer, in linen, velvet or suede, costs from £20 to £60, and tartan berets are £8.

Freedom Book Shop
Angel Alley, 84b
Whitechapel High Street
E1
071-247 9249

Open: Mon–Fri
10 a.m.–6 p.m., Sat
10 a.m.–4 p.m.
No credit cards

Anything considered subversive literature is proudly displayed in this bookshop, next door to the Whitechapel Art Gallery (see separate entry). They specialise here in anarchist writings which promote the idea of a radically different society, selling anything from pamphlets to books on anarchist theory and philosophy – Freedom Press is also based in the building.

It may sound intimidating but the shop is actually very friendly and welcoming, and a fascinating place to browse.

The Garden Studio
146 Columbia Road E2
071-613 2424

Open: Tues–Sat
10 a.m.–6 p.m., Sun
9 a.m.–2 p.m.
Credit: A, V

This shop recently helped the Windsor Castle nurseries clear out their old potting sheds, collecting thousands of old-fashioned Long Toms – hand-thrown terracotta flowerpots. Inspired by these, the Garden Studio has commissioned similar pots for sale in the shop, and you can buy them here at prices ranging from about £3 to £18. But the Garden Studio goes far beyond the pot – in fact, this three-roomed shop, with its rough brick interior and wooden floors, is a gardener's dream and is the pick of all the garden shops on Columbia Road. Everything for the garden, from sundials and statues to wooden-handled steel spades (£80) and forks is available here. Citrus pot-pourri is £2.50, bride's lavender £3.50 and gardening gloves cost between about £4 and £10. Just a browse here will give you some wonderful ideas, whether you've a city balcony to grow herbs on or a country garden complete with English lawn.

Idonia van der Bijl
122 Columbia Road E2
071-729 7976

Open: Sun
8 a.m.–2 p.m.
Credit: A, V

This shop has been here for five years and is so successful that Idonia van der Bijl has recently opened a second, in Bloomsbury's Museum Street. She designs her own range of decorated teapots, mugs, bowls and so on, with motifs of bright irises against rich blue-green backgrounds. They also stock wirecraft, imported directly from Zimbabwe, Botswana and South Africa so that the money paid goes straight to the local craftsmen who make the goods. Also on sale is beaded ware, bought from Operation Hunger, a charity which has set up cooperatives for the unemployed in South Africa. A beautiful beaded mug would cost you about £12.50.

S. Jones Dairy
23 Ezra Street E2

Open: Fri, Sat
8 a.m.–1 p.m.,
3-5 p.m., Sun
9 a.m.–1 p.m.
No credit cards

I always feel as if I'm stepping back in time when I enter this traditional establishment with its dark wooden shelves, long marble-topped counter and selection of huge cheeses and provisions. Jams, marmalades, fruit juices, and fresh bread are all available here; fresh eggs cost £1.90 a dozen, Colombian coffee about £1.65 a half-pound, and Earl Grey tea just over £1 a pound. Best of all, though, are the cheeses – among the many on display are huge slabs of Cheddars and delicate, crumbly Caerphilly at £3 a pound.

Paris and Rio's
93 Columbia Road E2
071-729 1147

Open: Mon–Wed, Fri,
Sat 9 a.m.–7 p.m.,
Thurs, Sun
9 a.m.–2 p.m.
No credit cards

This fab family-run delicatessen, the best and most popular in the area, has a huge array of tempting foods, with lots of homemade Spanish and Italian dishes such as various types of tortilla, at £1.50 a portion, to take away. It's definitely the place to come if you've friends coming round and have run out of time. Spanish hams, dried fish, sun-dried tomatoes, marinated olives and various cheeses are all enough to make you salivate on the spot. Italian seafood salad costs £1.75 for a quarter of a pound, stuffed peppers £2.80 a pound, chicken kebabs £1.50 each and home-made pasta such as ravioli is about £3.50 a pound. Paris and Rio's really deserves its popularity with locals and Columbia Road market-goers.

Petticoat Lane Market, E1

Open: Wentworth
Street, Mon–Fri
7 a.m.–2 p.m., whole
market, Sun
7 a.m.–2 p.m.

The original Petticoat Lane market, which dealt in clothing, was formed around the short paths uniting the French, Spanish, Portuguese and Italian communities. The influx of Jewish immigrants to the area caused the market to expand greatly and, much to the horror of the local Christians, Sunday trading began to take place. Today there is still a strong Jewish feel to the market but the high concentration of Asians in the neighbourhood has brought new wares to a market where anything from a stuffed animal to a donkey can be bought at a reasonable price. There are moves afoot to take Petticoat Lane upmarket, and already there are stalls selling herbal remedies and Levis 501s, but for the most part the goods on sale here are very tacky and most of the clothes are unwearable. Come here for the atmosphere but go to nearby Spitalfields market for shopping.

SCP

135–139 Curtain Road
EC2
071-739 1869

Open: Mon–Fri
9.30 a.m.–6 p.m., Sat
10 a.m.–5 p.m.
Credit: A, V

This old warehouse, at one time a furniture factory, is situated in the middle of an area once famous for its craftsmen. SCP continue this tradition by selling the work of new designers such as Jasper Morrison and Matthew Hilton, as well as twentieth-century classics from the likes of Le Corbusier, Mies van der Rohe and Rietveld. Considering the quality of the work on show, the prices are not at all bad in comparison to the big central stores selling similar furniture – a Morrison sofa will cost from £1719 plus VAT and one of his beautiful small ottoman stools around £338, but they are very rare and you will never see anything like them again. The people here will do their best to help you through tough decisions, and you can spend as much time as you want just sitting and looking.

Shhh

22 Coronet Street N1
071-613 5458

Open: Mon, Wed–Sat
11.30 a.m.–6.30 p.m.
No credit cards as yet

This sex shop created quite a stir when it was first opened in 1992. Shhh caters for women only, and men are allowed in only if accompanied by a woman; as a result the shop has a very relaxed atmosphere where you can feel at ease as you browse. There's an extensive range of vibrators, starting at £6 – the most popular is the Jessica Rabbit, which retails at £25.50. Other sex toys include clitoral stimulators, Thai beads, Chinese love balls and dildos, including special lesbian models designed by women for women. All the toys are market researched and conform to the relevant British Standard.

Shhh also has a large range of underwear and rubberwear and a made-to-order leather service where you can have your fantasy outfit created exactly as you want it. The shop is also one of the best places to get leather jeans made to measure: the competitive price of £150 includes a refit after six months to take care of any baggy trouser knees or bums. The staff are all very friendly and helpful, especially if you have never been in this kind of shop before and aren't sure what exactly it is you want.

Spitalfields Market

65 Brushfield E1
071-247 6590

Open: Craft and food

There has been a vegetable market here since 1682. In 1856 the sight was bought by ex-market porter Robert Horner, who invested the enormous sum of £80,000 on transforming the place with new buildings which included heated cellars for the ripening of fruit.

East

market, Mon–Fri
11 a.m.–3 p.m., Sun
9 a.m.–3 p.m.; shops,
Mon–Fri 9 a.m.–6 p.m.
Credit: ask

In 1920 the Corporation of London restored the building at a cost of £2,000,000, and the new market was opened in 1928. However, the fruit-and-veg market has now moved east to Leyton and now this three-acre site is devoted to a mad, eccentric mix of stalls, selling everything from organic food to clothes and records, sports facilities, including skateboarding ramps and rollerblading circuit, and sculpture and art displays. You can also play football or tennis here. The goods on sale are similar to those you'll get in places like Camden Lock (see Camden), but Spitalfields is a more manageable size and less tiring and crowded. There's a big selection of food stalls where you can eat Singapore noodles, Belgian crepes, Spanish paella or good, old-fashioned English caff food.

Timothy Everest
4 Princelet Street E1
071-377 5770

Open: Mon–Fri
9.30 a.m.–6 p.m., Sat
10 a.m.–4 p.m.
Credit: A, V

Timothy was trained in the home of tailoring, Savile Row (see Mayfair), but always knew that he wanted to start his own business. Realising that there was a market for bespoke suits amongst those who normally spent inordinate amounts of money on off-the-peg designer wear, he offered tailoring at an irresistible price. Instead of the £1,500 price tag which was the norm for a Savile Row suit, he charged around £500 for something completely individual. Since then he has left the charmless West End and set up here in an old Huguenot house, which has previously served as a bordello and a synagogue. Through word of mouth and some very favourable press, Timothy Everest has built up a clientele which includes corporate raiders and politicians as well as those quieter types who just love quality cloth and good taste.

Wellard 'n' Wikid
116 Columbia Road E2
071-739 1793

Open: Sun
9.30 a.m.–2 p.m.
No credit cards

Run by four local jewellery designers who have a workshop around the corner, this shop makes for a welcome change from the garden shops lining Columbia Road. It's been going since 1988 and in addition to the jewellery (prices from £5 to £40) they also have a range of T-shirts and socks designed by a Japanese woman who lives locally. The earrings and brooches are all fun, colourful and much cheaper than they would be in the West End where high overheads push up prices. There's a great selection of little animal brooches which would make unusual and stylish presents.

ENTERTAINMENT

The Bass Clef
35 Coronet Street N1
071-729 2476

Open: Sun–Thurs
10 p.m.–2 a.m., Fri,
Sat 8 p.m.–2 a.m.
Credit: A, Amex, DC, V
Average: £20
Admission: £3.50–£6

Hidden deep in the backstreets of Hoxton, the Bass Clef pumps out Latin, funk, African and jazz seven nights a week. It's small, dingy, dark and really quite disgusting, but you haven't lived until you've be-bopped a night away in this remarkable venue. It has recently begun experimenting with evenings of House and rare groove, but it's still best for jazz and, on Saturday nights, live African music – phone first to check the week's events. There's a restaurant in the club where you can get a meal or a snack – the food is reasonable and there's always a vegetarian selection. On Friday and Saturday nights admission to the Tenor Clef next door is included in your entry fee – this quieter place is more of a listening venue with more laid-back jazz. Highly recommended.

Brick Lane Music Hall
152 Brick Lane E1
071-377 8787

Open: Wed–Sat from
9 p.m.
Credit: A, V
Admission: dinner and
show £20 per person

Located in the canteen of an old brewery, the Brick Lane Music Hall is a step back in time. As soon as you come in, you're greeted by Paul, a real pro who is especially charming with older ladies, and who will take you to your table, where you have a three-course meal before the show. The food is very traditional East End kosher nosh – huge portions of boiled beef or trout, served with lots of vegetables and potato latkes, followed by gigantic steamed puddings. The show itself begins with the incredibly jovial MC, Vincent Hayes, getting things going with a bit of audience participation, and from then on you're definitely in the land of sing-along, painfully bad but very funny jokes and double entendres, and terribly schmaltzy Victorian tunes. If you're in the right mood and are ready to leave your credibility at the door it can be great fun, and it is a terrific place to take older relatives, who always seem to have a ball here.

Considering that it's a kind of Victorian theme park in miniature the music hall is surprisingly free of tourists – most of the crowd seem to be Eastenders who know all the songs and join in lustily. At £20 a head for dinner and the show, it's great value.

Hackney City Farm
1a Goldsmiths Row E2
071-729 6381

Hackney City Farm, founded in 1984 by the Greater London Council, is a little treasure. Here city kids and relocated adults can wander happily gazing at

Open: Tues–Sun
10 a.m.–4.30 p.m.

chickens, ducks, geese, sheep, goats, lamb, pigs and rabbits. In early 1993 the farm completed some new buildings to house indigenous wild animals such as field mice, foxes and hedgehogs, lent to the farm by animal sanctuaries and London Zoo (see Camden). There's also a butterfly tunnel, where butterflies are bred and reared, and a large herb and vegetable garden, as well as an orchard. The whole farm is wheelchair-accessible and there is an induction loop for the hard of hearing. Other facilities here include a pottery, a cafe serving cakes, sandwiches and soups, and even juggling classes – ring for details if you feel like trying this addictive activity. You can buy honey and guaranteed samonella-free eggs here as well. It's a wonderful place that's very popular with inner-city children, and is a great place to come after a tour around the flower market – just a pity, really, that its ever-reducing grant ensures that the farm is always struggling to survive.

Hackney Empire
291 Mare Street E8
081-985
2424/081-986 9666

Credit: A, V

Designed by the great architect Frank Matcham and built in 1901, in its time the Hackney Empire saw the greats of variety and music hall, including Marie Lloyd and Charlie Chaplin, and in its heyday a single bill might combine Verdi arias with juggling, tap dancers with flamenco, and fire eaters with scenes from Shakespeare. Louis Armstrong, Liberace and Tony Hancock all played the Empire in their day but the theatre went into a decline and spent 25 years as a bingo hall before its gala reopening in 1986.

Now the Hackney Empire is famous for what it terms New Variety – performers such as Harry Enfield, Julian Clary and Lenny Henry have all appeared here. But the Empire does not limit itself to comedy: recently it has staged an English-language production of Mozart's Don Giovanni, and has become a popular venue for performances of Irish and Caribbean music, as well as hosting gay and lesbian evenings, dance and mime events, and shows for children and the elderly. The black talent show – the 291 Club – draws audiences from all over the country.

The Hackney Empire Preservation Trust was established to oversee the creation of a new, state-of-the-art theatre within Matcham's original design, at a cost of at least £5,000,000. It's a worthy project: the Hackney Empire is an oasis in North-East London and would be sadly missed by locals and visitors alike.

South

Battersea

SW11

RIVER THAMES

BATTERSEA PARK

Prince of Wales Drive

BATTERSEA PARK ROAD

Queenstown Rd

BATTERSEA POWER STATION

BATTERSEA PARK

SW8

QUEENSTOWN ROAD

NINE ELMS

NEW COVENT GARDEN MARKET

Albert Bridge Road

Battersea Bridge Rd

Battersea Church Rd

Westbridge Rd

Battersea High St

Vicarage Cr

Lombard Rd

York Rd

York Gdns

Plough Road

Grant Road

Falcon Road

Latchmere Road

Eversleigh Road

Broughton Road

Silverthorne Rd

Queenstown Road

WANDSWORTH ROAD

Wandsworth Road

Heathbrook Park

CLAPHAM JUNCTION

St John's Hill

St John's Hill 2

LAVENDER HILL

160

835

Elspeth Rd

Stormont Rd

Cedars Road

North St

Old Town

North Side

The Pavement

St Alban's

Clapham High St

Clapham Park Rd

CLAPHAM PARK

Battersea Rise

100

C. Comm Nth Side

CLAPHAM COMMON LONG RD

CLAPHAM COMMON

St John W. Side

Northcote Road

Broomwood Road

Ballingbrook Grove

THE AVENUE

CLAPHAM COMMON WEST SIDE

Clapham Common West Side

Windmill Dr.

CLAPHAM COMMON SOUTH SIDE

Windmill

Cavendish Rd

Abbeville Road

Crescent La

THURLEIGH ROAD

Bellevue Rd

NIGHTINGALE LANE

THE AVENUE

CLAPHAM SOUTH

SW4

Cl

N

*a*lthough Battersea is only over the bridge from the lively village of Chelsea it's not as interesting a place as you might think. In many ways Battersea is like Fulham – it's a place where people live rather than play; when they want to go out they use the many services Chelsea or the nearby West End has to offer.

South of Battersea and divided from it by the long road of Lavender Hill, is Clapham, home of the Soane ('s only fifteen minutes from Sloane Square), a variant on the Sloane Ranger. The industrial boom of the nineteenth century brought many migrant workers to London, and the rows of terraced houses which line the streets of Clapham date from that period. In the eighties these houses were bought by young professionals convinced by estate agents that this was an area where property values would go up and up – which they have, to a certain extent. The influx of young people did encourage a few brave entrepreneurs to try to do something here – some of the resulting enterprises have closed, some have stayed.

There is a scattering of restaurants and theatres in Battersea and Clapham, but there's no doubt that most places worth a visit are across the water, and Battersea's chief interest is as a small residential area with a fantastic park (see separate entry) overlooking the river. Clapham also has a large tract of land, known as Clapham Common (see separate entry); over 200 square acres, the Common is now surrounded by big

merchant houses, built in the nineteenth century and owned by London's monied classes.

HOW TO GET THERE

Tubes
- Clapham Common
- Clapham Junction
- Clapham North
- Clapham South
- Stockwell
- Vauxhall
- Wandsworth Common
- Wandsworth Road

Buses
- Battersea Bridge Road: 44, 45A, 49, 219, 249, 349, N19
- Battersea Park Road: 44, 45A, 49, 219, 344, N19, N88
- Battersea Rise: 77, 219
- Bolingbroke Grove: 249, 349, G1
- Clapham Common South Side: 60, 155, 189, 355, N87
- Clapham High Street: 45A, 88, 155, 355
- Landsowne Way: 2
- Lavender Hill: 45A, 77, 77A, N68
- Nine Elms Lane: 44, 344
- Northcote Road: 249, 349, G1
- South Lambeth Road: 2, 2A, 2B, 88, 155
- Wandsworth Road: 77, 77A

ARDING AND HOBBS

SIGHTS AND SITES

During the sixteenth century the land which is now Battersea Park would be overwhelmed each year by gypsies, thieves and London's riff-raff, who turned the district into a gambling den where fortunes were made, lost and told. The regular Sunday fairs here caused so much trouble that the government was forced to intervene. Three hundred years later, however, the quiet park is a popular weekend venue for Londoners of all sorts. The rich middle classes seem to have adopted it as their own – they all seem to have dogs with ridiculous names and show no embarrassment when shouting these names out loud.

The park is equally popular with young families, as on the North Carriage Drive there is a children's zoo which gives city kids an idea of what life on a farm is like. For grown-ups there are tennis courts and floodlit football pitches, and for art lovers there are two pieces of sculpture worth looking at – Henry Moore's 'Three Standing Figures' and Barbara Hepworth's 'Single Form'. At Easter time there is a fair, which brings a carnival spirit to the area, and a famous, charity-organised Easter parade. Every now and again circuses come to the park, most recently and memorably the wonderful Archaos.

The Lakeside Cafe (071-498 2577) serves up decent hot and cold meals all year round and is a very welcome stopping point.

This magnificent building was built to the design of Sir Leonard Pearce, engineer-in-chief of London's Central Electricity authority; the exterior brickwork elevation was the work of the great architect Sir Giles Gilbert Scott, the man responsible for Liverpool's overwhelming Anglican cathedral and who embraced the task of building a power house of another kind. It's actually two stations: A Station was constructed between 1929 and 1935, and B Station was commissioned in 1944 and completed in 1955.

Battersea Power Station is probably familiar to a lot of people from the cover of the Pink Floyd album *Animals*, which features a pig floating above the building. It is now obsolete as a working station, but the word is that it will be redeveloped into a theme

park of technological advancement, though the project is on hold at the moment. I am delighted that the shell of the building at least will survive, but many Londoners see it as yet another blight on the horizon.

Clapham Common, SW4

In the eighteenth century Clapham Common was nothing more than a wild tract of land infested with vermin, and in 1722 a concentrated series of raids was organised in an attempt to destroy the common's huge population of rats, hedgehogs and polecats. Throughout the eighteenth century wealthy merchants and literary or political men such as Wilberforce and Lord Macaulay had large houses built in Clapham, and in 1745 the Duke of Cumberland, the butcher of the Scottish uprisings, camped his men on the Common. In 1781, in an attempt to give the area some respectability, the weekly fair, which had featured anything from bare-knuckle boxing to ferret-racing, was abolished. After a tree was planted on the common by the son of the adventurer Captain Cook, the spot became known as a place to air your political or religious views.

Worth noting is the sculpture on the north side by Charles Barry, called 'The Woman of Samaria' and erected here in 1894. Today the common is used mainly by people walking dogs, or children. There's also a pond near Southside where you can sail your model boat, if that's your sort of thing, and there are a few places where you can get refreshments.

EATING AND DRINKING

Battersea Village Rickshaw
15–16 Battersea Square, Battersea High Street SW11
071-924 2450

Open: lunch, midday–2.30 p.m., dinner 6–11.15 p.m.
Credit: A, Amex, V
Average: £25

Inside this fine Indian restaurant is all potted fronds, pale walls and traditional framed prints – a tasteful and understated setting, unusual for an Indian restaurant but perfect for the food which comes highly recommended. The dishes are a mixture of food from all over the subcontinent and the menu, called the Spice Trail, is unusually informative and tells you about each region and the cooking methods used. The Battersea Garden Rickshaw is more relaxing than many restaurants, but no more expensive. The restaurant serves Kingfisher, Tiger and a good selection of bottled beers for about £2.30. There's also a branch in Covent Garden.

Blues Brothers

50 Clapham High
Street SW4
071-622 0070

Open: midday–midnight
Credit: A, Amex, V
Average: £25

This bar-restaurant is where Clapham's trendy few come to eat and pour scorn on each other. The dishes are in the Modern British mode and tend to be a bit overambitious, mixing French with Chinese and whatever else seems to take the chef's fancy. On weekdays from midday to 6 p.m. there's a light bites menu offering dishes such as nachos, barbeque ribs and pasta for around £4. If you're not hungry you can sit and nurse a drink for a while – there's a happy hour from 1 to 4 p.m. and from 6 to 8.30 p.m., when cocktails are half price. If you're in the neighbourhood pop in to see what the locals are up to.

Buchan's

64 Battersea Bridge
Road SW11
071-228 0888

Open: lunch, Mon–Sat
12.1–2.45 p.m.,
dinner, Mon–Sat
5.30–11 p.m., Sun
7–10.30 p.m.
Credit: A, Amex, DC, V
Average: £30

Named after the Scottish author John Buchan, this restaurant serves food with a tenuous Scottish link – Scots game and fish is mixed with food from the auld alliance of France. The result is not bad at all – a Scot away from his homeland can find it's enough to stir the emotions as the Drambuie is poured and the haggis (£3.50 as a starter) is served with a whisky sauce. It's all a bit kitsch but it's as good as any other place in the Battersea region. Rack of lamb with Provencal herbs and a casserole of pheasant with chestnuts and whisky are both about £10. On Sundays there's a set lunch menu at £10.50 for three courses.

Flumb's

67-69 Abbeville Road
SW4
081-675 2201

Open: restaurant
10 a.m.–3 p.m.,
6.30 p.m.–12.30 a.m.;
bar 10 a.m.–11 p.m.
Credit: A, Amex, V
Average: £35

Named after the owner's fabulous mum, whose oil paintings adorn the walls, Flumb's is a friendly eaterie ideal for a quick snack or a more substantial meal. It consists of several rooms on different levels, and has a friendly, cosy feel about it. Friends of the owners have painted murals to decorate the place, including a striking jungle scene, complete with parrots who watch over you as you tuck into the good and varied grub. Vegetarians are well catered for, with specials including warm potato salad with grilled polenta and red onions, served with a mustard vinaigrette. Meateaters can enjoy a seared beef salad with wine dressing or a cumin-and-coriander-crusted poussin with roast vegetables.

Fungus Mungus

264 Battersea Park
Road SW11
071-924 5578

There's no need to go inside Fungus Mungus to realise that you're in for a different sort of experience – the frontage is painted with swirling psychedelic patterns and the door handle is a giant green ear. Inside, it's not the junk shop you could easily mistake

South

Open: midday–midnight
No credit cards
Average: £15

it for but a dark and cosy cafe and bar with huge dripping candles and a motley collection of wooden tables and chairs. Call in here for a drink, a snack or just to mellow out and enjoy the good vegetarian and vegan food. Bar snacks such as potato skins with garlic mayonnaise or hummus and bread are £1.50, a leek and broccoli stroganoff is £6.95, and stuffed Mediterranean vegetables will set you back £6.50. There's lots of unusual beers for sale and the place has a very early seventies feel that is strangely seductive . . .

Harvey's

2 Bellevue Road SW17
081-672 0114

Open: Tues–Sat, lunch
12.30–2 p.m., dinner
7.30–11.15 p.m.
Credit: A, V
Average: £100

This is the home of the much-loved and much-hated young chef Marco Pierre White. Though he can act like a rude schoolboy when criticised, which seldom happens, White is undoubtedly a talented young man and has come up with several dishes which are worthy of his background as a trainee with the Roux brothers. However, I have gone to this restaurant several times and the food has never been consistent.

There is no à la carte – dinners cost £48 for a choice of ten starters and twenty-five main courses, as well as puddings, and lunch is £24 for three courses. The food can be truly wonderful but it is incredibly expensive. The wine list can be daunting and there is little on offer for under £20. It's a good place to bring someone for a romantic evening, but remember that things might not go quite according to plan. White has recently opened Harvey's Canteen in Chelsea Harbour, which is cheaper – we wait to see how it develops.

Jack's Place

12 York Road SW11
071-228 8519/1442

Open: Tues–Fri, lunch
midday–3 p.m., dinner
6–11 p.m., Sat dinner
6–11 p.m.
No credit cards
Average: £24

You could be forgiven for walking past this restaurant, but don't. Jack's Place is definitely worth a detour as it has won several Les Routiers casserole awards in recognition of its outstanding quality and value for money. Jack used to be a lorry driver – he's now a Freeman of the City of London and his wonderful personality can be felt all over the dining room.

The blue and white checked tablecloths give Jack's Place a French feel borne out by the owner's attention to the food. Try the Sunday roast lunch – there's a choice of ten starters, roast chicken, lamb or beef, or trout, for the main course, plus puddings and coffee – all for £12. Not surprisingly, reservations are advisable.

Love Shack

162 Clapham High
Street SW4
071-622 4821

Open: Tues–Fri, lunch
11.30–3 p.m., dinner
6.30–11 p.m., Sat,
lunch
11.30 a.m.–3.30 p.m.,
dinner
6.30–11.30 p.m., Sun
midday–9 p.m.
No credit cards
Average: £15

C. Notarianni and Sons

142 Battersea High
Street SW11
071-228 7133

Open: Mon–Fri
midday–3.30 p.m.,
6–11.30 p.m., Sat
6–11.30 p.m., Sun
midday–3.30 p.m.
Credit: A, V
Average: £15

Il Rincon Latino

148 Clapham Manor
Street SW4
071-622 0599

Open: Mon–Sat
11 a.m.–midnight
Credit: A, Amex, V
Average: restaurant
£28, tapas £33

Tea Rooms Des Artistes

697 Wandsworth Road
SW8

A recently opened and definitely groovy addition to Clapham's food scene, this vegetarian restaurant boasts wacky love murals, hearts on the windows, massive paper flowers and slogans such as 'far-out' and 'groovy' painted in gold on the walls.

Catch the Love Shack in the right mood and you'll have a great meal here. The food is all freshly prepared – try the delicious deep-fried parsnip chips with sweet chilli dip (£1.75), followed by a savoury crepe with wild mushrooms, cream and broccoli. Finish off with a sweet crepe made with Grand Marnier or with citron and lean back and relax with a cappuccino or herb tea.

There's a slogan on the wall stating 'No Sloanes'. Yeah man.

The Notarianni family have been in and around this area since 1937, making ice cream and pasta. The shop got itself a drinks licence in 1988 and is now a high-street pizza parlour mingling 1930s ice-cream recipes and modern tastes in the form of pizza. You can still come in just for an ice cream, though, which is good news for addicts. Their latest venture at this venue features a very fifties nostalgia – with its jukebox and decor – but the food is tried and tested from another era. The pizzas are as good as I have had anywhere else in London, and the coffee is perfect. Pizzas range in price from about £4 to £5 and gnocchi are £5.20; to round it all off try a sinful knickerbocker glory or sundae at £3.50.

Run by two half-Spanish, half-Colombian sisters, Gloria Ricot and Clara Gomez, this cool-looking modern restaurant has a friendly atmosphere which is much appreciated by the locals who flock here for tapas such as Galician-style octopus at £3 or mushrooms in garlic at £2.50, or for something more substantial such as monkfish in tomato sauce with prawns, cockles and potatoes (£9).

A great place, Il Rincon Latino is highly recommended.

A rambling haven for bohemians, poets and those of us who like looking at other people, this is my favourite spot in South London. It's called a tea room but it is actually more of a bar, with food, wine and

071-720 4028

Open: Tues–Thurs
6 p.m.–midnight, Fri
4.30 p.m.–1 a.m., Sat
midday–1 a.m., Sun
midday–midnight
No credit cards
Average: £25

Teatime
21 The Pavement SW4
071-622 4944

Open: 10 a.m.–6 p.m.
No credit cards
Average: £10

Arding and Hobbs
315 Lavender Hill
SW11
071-228 8877

Open: Mon, Wed
9 a.m.–5.30 p.m., Tues
9.30 a.m.–5.30 p.m.,
Thurs 9 a.m.–8 p.m.,
Fri, Sat 9 a.m.–6 p.m.
Credit: A, Amex, DC, V

Artvend
24a Abbeville Road
081-673 6661

Open: Mon, Tues,
Thurs–Sat
10 a.m.–6 p.m.
Credit: A, Amex, V

beer (but not spirits) available. The food available (the menu is chalked up on the board) consists mainly of vegetarian and fish dishes such as lasagne or prawn curry. The people who come here are young, but the music is kept quite low, which means it is possible to have a conversation here. On Tuesday and Sunday evenings there's live jazz, which suits the mellow, laid-back atmosphere of the place. Tea Rooms des Artistes has one of the best and least pretentious atmospheres in London and sometimes makes you feel as if you're in a totally different kind of city.

These pale green tea rooms on two floors have been attracting Clapham's well-heeled residents for years. There's a few too many dried flowers on the wall for my liking, but no one can complain about the food: delicious cake, crumpets and muffins, scrambled eggs with cream on toast and kedgeree. There's also cucumber sandwiches. Afternoon tea – sandwiches, tea and cake – costs about £7. Teatime is the relaxing sort of place where you can unwind with the papers untroubled.

SHOPPING

This is the Harrods of South London – it's part of the Allders chain but offers enough variety to make it worth a visit. The locals swear by it and, in keeping with the traditional North-South rivalry, swear that there's nothing in Harrods that you can't get in Arding and Hobbs.

The store's five floors hold everything you would expect to find in a good department store – clothes, furniture, cosmetics, kitchen equipment, stationery – and on the third floor there's a restaurant which stays open until half an hour before the store closes. Your best bet if you want to avoid Central London crowds.

One of those gift/interiors shops that seems to sell everything, Artvend is the place to come to pick up a present that is sure to be welcomed. Square glass vases, candlesticks, stationery, frames, jewellery and cards galore are all available here. The shop also stocks the Neals Yard range of creams, aroma oils and body products in the familiar blue glass jars and pots. It's also a good place to go for Kaz Lever's mermaid-pattern ceramics – a large bowl is £54 and a mug £22.

The Dogs' Home
4 Battersea Park Road
SW8
071-622 3626

Open: Mon–Fri
10.30 a.m.–4 p.m.,
Sat, Sun
10.30 a.m.–3 p.m.
No credit cards

If you've been thinking about spending a lot of money on a dog, think again. Battersea Dogs' Home looks after a collection of strays and unwanted animals which have been taken in and given a temporary home. Most of them are well-behaved, good animals who deserve a good home. Some of them have been treated badly, and others are Christmas presents which kids don't want any more.

The people who look after the animals are professionals and can get fed up very quickly with people who waste their time. The dogs cost between £45 and £60; they have all been deloused and they are all in need of a permanent home.

Jacques
151 Northcote Road
SW11
071-738 2252

Open: Mon–Sat
10 a.m.–6 p.m., Sun
midday–5 p.m.
Credit: A, V

The people who run Jacques have had a successful stall in Northcote Road Antiques Market (see separate entry) since 1988, and this shop has been open since 1990. They stock mostly Victorian and early twentieth-century pieces, as well as some Georgian antiques. Among the jewellery on display is a case of gentlemen's fob watches. Jacques is the kind of place that should appeal to the old and young fogeys who moved to the Battersea area when it was gentrified in the eighties, but some of the goods on sale are very beautiful.

New Covent Garden Market
Nine Elms Lane SW8
Open: Mon–Fri
4 a.m.–11 a.m.

No credit cards

This huge commercial market is where most of the flower stalls in London get their goods from. It is also a fruit and veg market which supplies most of the restaurants and stalls in London. Everything is sold in bulk, which means that you must buy at least five boxes of each thing – it's not the place to go if you're looking for a couple of pounds of cheap carrots. Also, strictly speaking it's a wholesale market only, but it's up to individual traders whether or not they'll sell to you. The flower market is slightly less intolerant of people who just want to have a look at what goes on in the early hours. The strange exotic plants can be bought in ones and twos – they start at £50, but remember that they can go for £100 in the shops. During the winter months the flower market is also open on Saturday mornings, from 4 until 9.

There are a couple of cafes, both of which are

traditional greasy spoons. One of them opens at 10 p.m. and stays open until the morning, and the other opens when the market does, at 3.30 a.m.

The entrances can be difficult to find – the main entrance for motorised traffic is signposted on Nine Elms Lane, and pedestrians can gain access through the gate on Wandsworth Road, near the junction with Nine Elms Lane.

Nine Elms Sunday Market

Nine Elms Lane SW8
0895 639 912

Open: Sun
9 a.m.–2 p.m.
No credit cards

London has so many markets that you might think there isn't room for another but there is – and this one, next door to the flower market, specialises in household bits and pieces. Everything from underwear to new brooms is here, but would you really want it? This market is absolutely crazy on Sundays, when busloads of people get off at the front doors and squeeze in looking for a bargain. It is near Battersea Park (see separate entry), though, so you might want to come here first before enjoying a river view and a bit of green grass.

Northcote Road Antiques Market

155a Northcote Road
SW11
071-228 6850

Open: Mon–Sat
10 a.m.–6 p.m., Sun
midday–5 p.m.
No credit cards

This indoor antiques market has about 30 stalls, as well as a small cafe where you can ponder over your purchases. Some stalls are very specialist – there's a fine collection of old shop signs, glass-stoppered pharmacists' bottles and old tobacco and cigarette tins, piled in Edwardian display cases. Mostly, though, the stalls sell pretty general goods; it's the place to come to pick up old linen, china, small pieces of furniture, big old baskets, and lighting and glassware – a beautiful 1930s green glass rosebowl cost £120 when last I visited. If you're genuinely interested in antiques it's probably a good idea to pop next door to Kerry Wood's antique shop at number 156.

Whittard and Co.

73 Northcote Road
SW11
071-924 1888

Open: Mon–Sat
8.30 a.m.–5.30 p.m.
Credit: A, V

Tea and coffee specialists Whittard and Co. opened this shop in 1987, and since then the place has become ever more popular with the locals, who come here to buy the distinctively packaged Earl Grey or Lapsang Souchong tea at £4.80 a pound, or ground Colombian coffee at £4.60 a pound. You can buy a gift set of different teas for £4.95, and they are currently in the process of expanding the range of those available. As well as tea and coffee you can pick up some gifts here – big stripy breakfast cups and saucers cost from £3.95, and they also have a range of hand-painted mugs from Italy. It's a deliciously fragrant place, and well worth a visit if you live or travel to the area.

ENTERTAINMENT

BAC
Lavender Hill SW1
071-223 6557

Open: Tues–Sat
10 a.m.–10 p.m., Sun
11 a.m.–6 p.m.
Credit: A, V

It's looking a bit run down but the Battersea Arts Centre is in many ways quite a radical arts house with theatre productions of a very high standard. The exhibition space is well used and is not a home for twee pictures by the local art club – the centre has tried, successfully in my opinion, to put on new shows dealing with contemporary issues. Recent shows have included 'The Sea of Sun', a site-specific installation by Andrew Sabin which was shortlisted for acquisition by the Tate. Recent productions in the main theatre include the controversial *120 Days of Sodom* and Roy Smiles's S*chumks*. On Tuesday evenings the centre features 'pay what you can' theatre, and each Friday there's cabaret in the studio. In recent years young dance companies have been encouraged to come here and use the available space, which they have done to great critical acclaim.

There is a cafe in the building, which is open for the same hours as the main arts centre.

The Clapham Picture House
Venn Street SW4
071-498 3323 (box office); 071-498 2242 (programme details)

Credit: A,V

The Clapham Picture House opened in December 1992 and is a welcome addition to a part of town previously ill served for entertainment. The cinema shows commercial films in rep and has a well-designed modern interior with a nice bar where you can get snacks as well as a selection of bottled beers, wines and spirits. The walls are hung with paintings, all of which are for sale at reasonable prices. The whole place feels clean and fresh – perhaps it just hasn't had time to get the thrashed feeling we associate with cinemas.

The Grand
Clapham Junction SW11
071-738 9000,
091-963 0940 (credit card bookings)

Credit: A, V

Across the road from Clapham Junction station (the busiest in Britain) is the Grand. Part of the Mean Fiddler group which also runs Subterrania (see Notting Hill and Bayswater), this venue has succeeded in winning itself a large and loyal following since it opened in December 1991. It's housed in an old theatre which has recently been done up and looks very stylish, with a good bar at the back. Downstairs

is the standing area and they have recently opened the balcony as a place where you can sit and watch the music in quiet – the venue can now hold 1,600 people. The sound is always very good, and acts as varied as Abba impersonators Bjorn Again, Green on Red, Mary Coughlan and Jools Holland have all played here recently, and the atmosphere here can be great on a good night. The Grand is a sorely needed and valuable addition to nightlife south of the river, and at only four minutes from Waterloo, is easily accessible from central London.

**The Grace Theatre
at the Latchmere**

503 Battersea Park
Road SW11
071-228 2620 (box
office)

Credit: A, V

Located above a big old pub with brown tiles and hanging baskets which is establishing a good local reputation for its food, the Grace Theatre has recently been done up. It now has a modern feel to it with its mirrored bar, blue carpets and white walls. The theatre space seats 85 and concentrates on showing new and experimental pieces. Between April and June 1993 their German Festival features performances of Brockner's *Painted Youth* and a new translation of *The Robbers*, by Schiller. Worth supporting, if only because the area has little in the way of live theatre.

TEATIME

Brixton

SW9

SW2

SE24

Cam

*f*or much of its history Brixton was largely wasteland, but its proximity to the centre of London ensured that it was developed in the nineteenth century as a suburban residential area for London businessmen. Their large, well-appointed houses, set well back from the road, were later joined by humbler dwellings, intended for the clerks and skilled workmen who had taken advantage of the area's cheap accommodation and quick access to the City. In 1860 the railway system arrived in Brixton, bringing even more people to this quiet leafy suburb. Towards the end of the century, however, the character of Brixton had completely changed and the big houses had been converted into lodgings used by labourers and actors who favoured the area because of its proximity to the West End.

In the early 1950s this same availability of central and cheap lodgings made Brixton popular with West Indian immigrants, who initially settled in the Somerleyton Road and Railton Road areas. Over the next twenty years or so the area became known for its poverty and decrepitude, but plans for wide-scale redevelopment of the area were dropped in the mid–1970s, and Brixton was left to waste away as an area of high unemployment and social deprivation.

In 1981 there were serious riots here; night after night local youths fought hand to hand with the police and much of the area was seriously damaged by fire and vandalism. The unrest did at least lead to the government realising that the area needed some serious

financial input and that community relations between the police and the local community were at an all-time low. Since 1988 Brixton has received about £3 million in EEC aid, most of which has been used for projects relating to the long-term unemployed, women, ethnic minorities and the disabled. Since 1987 the area has also received over £73 million from the government and in 1991 Brixton won the City Challenge Bid, run by the Department of the Environment and worth £37 million over five years, to be spent on inner-city regeneration. It remains to be seen what these funds will do to the place.

Brixton's unfortunate reputation as a dangerous and troubled place often stops people from coming here. I've never encountered any danger here – and in summer, when there are concerts in Brockwell Park (see separate entry) and loud music on all the streets, Brixton is one of the best and most lively areas of London to spend some time. The centre of the area is Brixton Market (see separate entry), which takes place every day and on weekends becomes a sprawling mass of stalls where you can buy anything from antique Levis to quite good art. It's a young place by nature and seems to attract flamboyant people who see the streets as a stage on which they can perform.

At one time a village, Camberwell was famous for its flowers and fruit trees, and gets its name from the well here which was thought in medieval times to have medicinal properties, especially for those with crippling diseases – the name Cam comes from the old Celtic and means crooked. Camberwell Green was the site of an ancient annual fair and on the south side there once stood a country mansion reputed to be the home of Sir Christopher Wren. The local parish church of St Giles, on Camberwell Church Street, was designed in the gothic style by George Gilbert Scott in 1844, and in the churchyard lies the body of Mary Wesley, wife of the pious John Wesley and regarded as something of a shrew.

As South London grew during the Industrial Revolution it became highly developed. Row upon row of cheap housing was built along the Georgian splendour of Camberwell Grove (see separate entry). Today the inhabitants of Camberwell range from students to stockbrokers who all seem to enjoy the proximity of the area to the centre of London. In recent years, however, there has been a concerted effort to give the area an identity of its own, with new restaurants and bars opening up overnight. Few of these places ever stand the test of time but those which have prevailed are worth a visit if you are ever in the neighbourhood.

HOW TO GET THERE

Tubes
- Brixton
- Clapham North
- Elephant and Castle
- Kennington
- Oval
- Queens Road
- Stockwell

Buses
- Acre Lane: 35, 37, 189
- Brixton Road: 3, 59, 109, 133, 159, 196
- Camberwell Church Street: 12, 36, 36B, 171
- Camberwell New Road: 36, 36B, 185
- Camberwell Road: 12, 35, 40, 45, 45A, 48, 171, 176, 184, P5
- Clapham Road: 45A, 88, 155, 355
- Coldharbour Lane: 35, 45, 45A, P4, P5
- Denmark Hill: 40, 68
- Dulwich Road: 3, 37, 196, N3
- Grove Lane: 176, 184, 185, N79
- Herne Hill: 40, 68
- Kennington Park Road: 3, 109, 159, 196
- Railton Road: 2, 3, 37, 196, N3
- Stockwell Road: 2, 2A, 2B, 45A
- Tulse Hill: 2A, 2B, N2
- Walworth Road: 12, 35, 40, 45, 45A, 68, 171, 176, 184, P5

CAMBERWELL GROVE

SIGHTS AND SITES

Black Cultural Archives

378 Coldharbour Lane
SW9
071-738 4591

Open: Mon–Sat
10 a.m.–6 p.m.;
archive, Mon–Fri
10 a.m.–4 p.m., by
appointment
No credit cards
No admission charge

Opened in 1990, the Black Cultural Archives Museum looks at the heritage of black people in Britain and redresses the lack of acknowledgement given to the contribution made to British life by Afro-Caribbean people. The museum also celebrates the achievements of black people around the world and holds regular exhibitions and lectures on the subject. The museum, with its displays of African artefacts, has become a popular Brixton meeting place and the shop has put together a good selection of books, crafts and clothes which all reflect Afro-Caribbean culture. On a recent visit the gallery section had an exhibition of work by local artists, who had caught the mood of the market perfectly, as well as work on the theme of mothers and fathers. All the exhibits were impressive, and very reasonably priced, and the place was busy with local young people looking and asking questions.

Brockwell Park

Herne Hill SE24
071-926 6900

Open: summer
6.30 a.m.–10 p.m.,
winter
7.30 a.m.–4.30 p.m.

This park, which stretches over 207 acres in all, is the location for Lambeth's major event of the year – the Lambeth Country Show, held each July and featuring fairs, animals, stalls, music, a city farm and much more. Free concerts are held here in the summer, often with reggae bands, and on Guy Fawkes Night the council puts on fireworks for the locals. There's many sports facilities here – tennis and bowls (071-926 1078), football (071-926 6900) and an area for skateboarding and BMXing. If you just want to get away from the hustle and bustle of Brixton, there's a traditional walled English garden, and with its duck pond, aviary, play area and one o'clock club, the park is a great place to take city kids.

Camberwell Green, SE5

This acre of land is surrounded by all of the worst elements of London life – very dull house conversions and rows of cars, and all signs of nature appear to have been eliminated. It was originally the site of an ancient fair, held every year until the late nineteenth century and was so good that it apparently rivalled Greenwich Market. The most famous visitor to the Green was Mendelssohn, whose 'Spring Song' was originally 'Camberwell Green'. That great poet and lover of nature, Robert Browning, was born in a house overlooking the Green, and I'm sure that if he could see what has happened to the place he would turn in his grave.

The most famous resident was supposedly Sir Christopher Wren, who had a large house on the south side. In the eighteenth century a new butterfly was discovered on the Green – called the Camberwell Beauty, it is now, unfortunately, extinct.

Camberwell Grove, SE5

This beautiful, tree-lined road has some of the best examples of Georgian houses in London. They were originally the homes of the well-off business families of the area, among the best-known being the Chamberlains – Joseph Chamberlain was born in 1936 at number 188. The physician John Coakley Lettsom had a huge country estate here, and was often visited by his friend James Boswell. The houses are now occupied by people who seem to take a great pride in restoring them to their former beauty.

Camberwell Old Cemetery
Forest Hill Road SE22

Another of London's Victorian graveyards which are no longer in use, Camberwell Old Cemetery is a great reminder of how seriously the Victorians took death. The Anglican chapel and the small Roman Catholic chapel were both destroyed during World War II, but the small, odd-looking building near the gate is authentic and was originally built as a gatekeeper's house. It's open seven days a week, but it's very creepy here and not a place where you would want to stay long in the evening. F. J. Horniman, the local tea merchant responsible for the Horniman Museum, lies buried here.

Camberwell College of Art
Peckham Road SE5
071-703 0987

This art school was opened in 1898; connected with the South London Art Gallery, it took over part of that building and was originally a technical school intended to assist young craftsmen with new ideas about design. It did not last very long in this form and around 1908 there was a shift in emphasis towards fine art and design which continues to this day. Camberwell's reputation has fallen by the wayside in recent years and the art school itself looks as if it could do with a serious injection of cash. I went to a recent degree show and was disappointed by most of what I saw, which is not usually the case with London art schools.

Cuming Museum

155–157 Walworth
Road SE17
071-701 1342

No admission charge

This museum, opened in 1906, recently won an award as one of London's best small museums, and specialises in the archaeological history of the Southwark area, from prehistoric times to the industrial age. It's based on the collections of the Cuming family, begun in 1782 and bequeathed to the nation in 1902. The displays include things as diverse as Roman sculpture and the personal effects of Michael Faraday, the man responsible for the use of electricity. There is also a collection of sculptures by George Tinworth, one of the major Doulton designers. There's a museum shop which sells books on local and general history, and gifts aimed at kids. The Cuming Museum is not a very well-known place but it's worth a visit and is a good place to capture a sense of London's development.

Horniman Museum

100 London Road,
Forest Hill SE23
081-699 2339

Open: Mon–Sat
10.30 a.m.–5.30 p.m.,
Sun 2-5.30 p.m.
No admission

Tea merchant F. J. Horniman was one of Camberwell's most famous and generous residents. A great traveller, he would bring back from his journeys any interesting artifact or musical instrument he could find, and in 1890 he opened his house three days a week so that the public could come and marvel at his treasures. The house was later demolished and replaced with the Art Nouveau building, designed by C. Harrison Townsend, which now stands. Above the entrance there is a beautiful mosaic panel which depicts in allegorical style the course of human life. In 1901, when the gallery was finally completed, Horniman presented it as a gift to the people of London.

The Horniman Museum contains over 6,000 musical instruments, 100 of which can be heard on the cassette guide, and is well worth a visit. There's an extensive reference library which is open during museum hours, but closed on Mondays and Sundays. In the grounds there's a nature trail, a live animal area and a bandstand where concerts are held in summer. The sixteen acres of gardens are open from 8 a.m. until dusk every day.

The Maudsley Hospital

Denmark Hill SE5

This purpose-built mental hospital, modelled on Continental mental clinics, is named after the eminent nineteenth-century psychiatrist Dr Henry Maudsley, who put up £30,000 for the building. It was established in direct opposition to the nineteenth-century asylum system of putting mental patients into huge barracks-like buildings. In 1898 a movement began to build a small hospital for acute and chronic patients, where research and teaching could also be carried out. The building was begun in 1913, and during World War I was used as a military, neurological teaching hospital (treating shell-shock cases), quickly gaining an international reputation for research. The hospital has been incredibly influential in psychiatry – the present-day Institute of Psychiatry originated here.

Since 1948 and the advent of the NHS, the Maudsley has been linked to Lambeth's Bethlehem Hospital, which was founded in Liverpool Street in 1676 and known as Bedlam.

Ruskin Park
Denmark Hill SE5
071-926 1045

Open: 7.30 a.m.–dusk

This 36-acre park is named after John Ruskin, the writer and critic who spent most of his life in this area, and up until the nineteenth century it bordered on open country. There is a fountain here, created by an unknown sculptor and dedicated to Felix Mendelssohn. You can also make use of various sporting facilities such as a bowling green, tennis courts and a football pitch – ring for details or to book.

The William Booth Training College
Denmark Hill SE5

Designed by Sir George Gilbert Scott and built in 1929 as a training college for the Salvation Army, this forbidding-looking brick building is a local landmark. The Salvation Army as we know it was founded in 1878 but had its roots in a series of missions set up in 1865 by the Booth family. Originally linked to the Methodist Church, the Sally Army is now a wholly independent institution. Today only about 130 students attend each course here, considerably less than the 500 who would once come here.

EATING AND DRINKING

The Brixtonian
11 Dorrell Place SW9
071-978 8870

Open: Mon, Wed
5 p.m.–midnight, Tues
midday–midnight,

This Afro-Caribbean restaurant-bar is well known in South London, not only for its authentic food but also for the linen drapes and moody lighting which seem to be a great attraction. Food is served in the bar – there's à la carte available here at lunchtimes – and in the upstairs restaurant, which serves a set dinner menu between 7 and 11 p.m., at about £19 for three

South

BRIXTON AND CAMBERWELL

Thurs–Sat
midday–1 a.m., Sun
5–11 p.m.
Credit: A, Amex, V
Average: £38

Cafe on the Hill
91 Brixton Hill SW2
081-671 6012

Open: Mon–Fri
7 a.m.–4 p.m., Sat
7 a.m.–1 p.m.
No credit cards
Average: £10

Cafe Pushkar
16c Market Row,
Coldharbour Lane SW9
071-738 6161

Open: Mon, Tues,
Thurs–Sat 9 a.m.–5 p.m.
No credit cards
Average: £12

**The Jacaranda
Garden**
11 Brixton Station Road
SW9
071-274 8383

Open: Mon–Sat
9 a.m.–11 p.m., Sun
11 a.m.–5 p.m.
No credit cards
Average: £15

courses. Traditional dishes from the West Indies are changed each week as the chef moves for inspiration from island to island. It might be worth checking what's on the menu before you go. Some of the locals think the Brixtonian has gone too far upmarket in order to attract monied South Londoners, but the bar as well as the restaurant has attempted to give the area a touch of class. There's a huge selection of rums available and throughout the evening there's good moody jazz belting out from the bar.

The Cafe on the Hill mixes traditional British caff food such as egg, bacon and sausages with Thai-based dishes such as vegetable curry and rice. Spicy chicken noodles or yummy ribs and fried rice cost £2.95, and soup and bread is 80p. The breakfast special – egg, bacon, sausage, beans and chips – is £2.25. Everything is homemade and delicious. Though it looks just like a normal caff – albeit a very clean one – the Cafe on the Hill is really much more interesting and is worth investigating.

This small vegetarian cafe, in the middle of the lively Brixton market, is very popular with travellers – of which there are many in the area – as well as with alternative types and arty-looking young people. It's named after Pushkar in India, which is a key place on the travellers' route. They serve good vegetarian food here – moussaka with salad is £3.10 and Caribbean fruit curry is £2.70. For dessert try a delicious pineapple upside-down cake at £1.60 or a fruit smoothie drink at £1.50.

This cafe is very popular with Brixton's large population of young people, and though it sounds exotic, the interior has definitely seen better times. It's a good place to go for a tea and piece of gooey chocolate cake after trawling around the market looking for a bargain. Rolls, sandwiches, salads and main course dishes are also available, at reasonable prices – the food is very Afro-Caribbean influenced.

The popularity of the place is a constant surprise to me but if you want to know what's happening in the area it could be a very good place to find out – they've got a notice board covered with posters and flyers relating to local happenings and events.

The Phoenix and Firkin

5 Windsor Walk SE5
071-701 8282

Open: Mon–Sat
11.30 a.m.–11 p.m.,
Sun 11 a.m.–5 p.m.
No credit cards
Average: £12

Pizzeria Castello

20 Walworth Road SE1
071-703 2556

Open: Mon–Fri
midday–11 p.m., Sat
5–11 p.m.
Credit: A, Amex, DC, V
Average: £16

Pizzeria Franco

4 Market Row, Brixton
Market SW9
071-738 3021

Open: Mon, Tues,
Thurs–Sat – coffee
8.30–11 a.m., pizza
11.30 a.m.–5 p.m.
No credit cards
Average: £16

Silva's Nest Restaurant

386 Coldharbour Lane
SW9

There has been a rash of Firkin pubs opening around London, all selling their own beers. This particular branch sells Rail Ale, Dogbolter and Phoenix, big malty beers which go down smoothly but have a horse's kick to them. The bare brick walls and the high, large space give you the impression that people come here for the beer rather than the atmosphere. It's very popular with people, mostly students, from the Hill. There is always food available, and it ranges from jacket potatoes to chicken Kiev. It's a quality place and the only pub in the area which actually makes an effort.

When I was trying to be a singer in a band I spent half my life rehearsing a few doors down from this pizzeria. The band would never communicate while we were practising, which was quite odd given that's what music is about, but as soon as we entered this place things would change. It's located near the Elephant and Castle, and is really the only reason for coming near this huge, unprepossessing concrete monstrosity, populated by a large number of homeless people. Here you can get a great pizza castellana, with artichokes, ham, olives, mushrooms and tomato, for about £5. The waiters here are very silly and quite funny but it is the pizzas which are the best thing about the place.

Franco's, in the heart of the covered market, is thought by many to be the best small restaurant in the district. The problem is that it's open only during market hours and on weekends gets so crowded that you may have to queue a long time for a table. There is a terrific range of traditional pizzas, all of them fragrant with herbs and garlic (if you want it), and you can also have calzone (about £5 and highly recommended), pizza-bread sandwiches (huge, served warm and absolutely delicious, good value at £4.10) and pasta. They also have starters and baked dishes. The cappuccino is good and the tiramisu yummy – in fact, Franco's is well worth queueing for.

This Portuguese-run greasy spoon is reputed to be one of the best in Brixton. During the week it is populated by local stallholders from the nearby market, but at the weekend it is swimming with

South

BRIXTON AND CAMBERWELL

071-274 4374

Open: Mon–Sat, lunch
11.30 a.m.–3 p.m.,
dinner 7–11 p.m.
No credit cards
Average: £20

Willow's Wine Bar
81 Denmark Hill SE5
071-701 0188

Open: lunch, Mon–Fri
midday–3 p.m.; dinner,
Mon–Sat
5.30–midnight; Sun
midday–11 p.m.
Credit: A, V
Average: £30

Acme Comics
391 Coldharbour Lane
SW9
071-274 7025

Open: 274 7025
No credit cards

The Bon Marché
442–444 Brixton Road
SW9

Open: Mon–Thurs, Sat
9 a.m.–6 p.m., Fri
9 a.m.–7 p.m.
Credit: A, V

bargain hunters who actually queue to get in, so it must definitely have something going for it. The Portuguese connection is not really reflected in the food but the Mediterranean temperament is definitely in evidence. I recommend the sticky jam pudding and the lump-free custard. Silva's is not the prettiest place in the world but it's cheap and a caff with a laugh.

The punter is the main man in this wine bar, unlike in many others which seem to treat customers so badly. The interior consists of bare stripped pine tables and the walls have no cliched images of France on them but instead some maps of the wine regions. The wines, which are quite reasonably priced, include Sancerres, St Emilions and Rhone Valleys and you don't have to eat here if you don't want to. You can have either a full meal or a snack – beef hotpot, salmon fishcakes and vegetable chilli are all £5. Desserts include a wicked marshmallow sundae at £2.55 and on Sundays kids under three eat free. All the food is fine, but the emphasis here is definitely on the plonk.

SHOPPING

A large inflated Spiderman adorns the window of this little shop, obviously casting a web to lure people in. On my last visit the place was packed with adult men and women scanning through American imports of the *Silver Surfer, Captain America* and brilliant early editions of *The Hulk*. The prices vary according to condition and age, and while new comics cost between 95p and £5, some of the rare comics can fetch as much as £100. They also sell T-shirts and tie-in material such as models and so on. In the basement there used to be a cartoon gallery, but unfortunately it's now closed due to flooding.

This shop, which holds only concessions, was originally the first purpose-built department store in England, developed by James Smith, a printer from Tooting who was partial to a flutter at Newmarket. His profits on the horses helped to pay for the store, named after the famous Bon Marché in Paris, but his luck ran out early in his brief reign as shopkeeper. After the 1940s the store fell into a sad period of decline and has never really recovered. At the moment it contains concessions – Top Shop, Dorothy Perkins, an optician's, Barratts Shoes – but the most popular and eye-catching stock is the Champion sportswear sold in the basement of the store (071-737 4654).

Brixton Market
Atlantic Road, Brixton
Station Road, Electric
Avenue, Popes Road
SW9

Open: Mon, Tues,
Thurs–Sat
9 a.m.–5.30 p.m.,
Wed 9 a.m.–1 p.m.
Credit: ask

This market first began in the 1880s in and around Electric Avenue, so called because the stalls would be floodlit with electric lighting. It was well known at this time for its fairground atmosphere and the collection of characters it attracted. In 1952 the authorities attempted to close the market but a public outcry saved it and it has continued to be the area's main attraction. During the week there are a number of stalls selling household items and cheap packets of food, but it is at the weekend that it comes alive, with young marketeers selling everything from second-hand clothes to herbal remedies and very good second-hand records. The market has a strong West Indian flavour and there are quite a few stalls selling genuine West Indian food and crafts.

Index Book Centre
10–12 Atlantic Road
SW9
071-274 8342

Open: Mon–Sat
10 a.m.–6 p.m.
Credit: A, V

This highly respected bookshop specialises in Afro-Caribbean politics and black activism in Britain and America, and is a good source of news about readings, lectures and events. They also have a children's section, tucked between Politics and History.The shop works on many levels, not only as a bookstore but as a place where people come to find out what is going on in the neighbourhood, and is always busy. The people who work here are informed and very helpful and if they don't have what you're looking for in stock they will get it for you. They have a fast order service which is useful.

Music Kiosk
104–106 Granville
Arcade SW9
071-274 4212

Open: Mon, Tues,
Thurs–Sat
9 a.m.–5.30 p.m.,
Wed 9 a.m.–1 p.m.
No credit cards

If you blink you could miss this small reggae, dub and soca booth in the heart of Brixton market, but you could never escape the throbbing sound of the bass which fills the air around. New sounds and old classics are all available here, and prices are negotiable. It can be difficult to get served, though, as there is always a crowd of people in front of the booth listening to the music.

It's very, very loud, so be prepared to have your eardrums burst.

Nasseri Fabrics
38 Atlantic Road SW9
071-274 5627

Open: Mon–Sat
9.30 a.m.–5.30 p.m.
No credit cards

If you're looking for a beautiful swathe of cloth to adorn your home or indeed yourself, this shop is definitely the place to come. They sell lengths of printed African fabric which would look great as clothes or as curtains – the staff are very helpful and will tell you which materials would look best on your sofa or your back. There is a very large selection of material and designs, and the prices are all very reasonable. It's a very little-known place and is definitely worth seeking out.

ENTERTAINMENT

The Brixton Academy
211 Stockwell Road
SW9
071-326 1022

Credit: A, V

This old art-deco cinema was ready for demolition until it was reinvented in the eighties as a live music venue. With acts from Lou Reed to Run DMC and Shabba Ranks, the Academy is to South London what the Town and Country Club is to the North. In recent years the club has been beset with problems, includings conflicts between local gangs, but these all now seem to have been resolved. Most dance and rock acts love playing here because of the good acoustics and the size of the auditorium, which can hold up to 2,000 people. If the band of the night gets things right the place can turn into a sweat pit. Check out what's on and get on down there.

Brixton Recreation Centre
27 Brixton Station Road
SW9
071-274 7774

Open: Mon–Fri
midday–10 p.m. Sat,
Sun 9 a.m.–8 p.m.
No credit cards

This large complex offers a brilliant variety of different indoor activities, including squash, badminton, basketball, martial arts, weight training, aerobics and, best of all, indoor wall climbing. Here you clamber up a wall set at 90 degrees to the floor, making your way as best you can by means of grips and handholds. You're protected by a large air cushion which makes falling half the fun. It costs £1.90 an hour. You don't need to be a member to to use the Brixton Rec, as it's known, and the heated 25-metre pool is great. The centre is a great addition to the community and deserves patronage.

The Fridge
Town Hall Parade,
Brixton Hill SW2
071-326 5100

Open: Tues, Fri, Sat

The Fridge is the brainchild of Andy Czezowski, the man responsible for the Roxy, London's first and best punk club, which has since disappeared. When the Fridge was first opened it was felt to be too cold in atmosphere for most people and the alternative bands who played live were always unhappy with the

10 p.m.–3/5 a.m.
No credit cards
Admission: £5–£8

acoustics. During the late eighties it was taken over by the new dance craze sweeping London and became incredibly popular. Jazzie B., the man behind Soul II Soul, did a regular stint here as DJ, which helped to make it even more successful. The Fridge remains one of London's most consistent clubs, with the weekend being most crowded. It attracts a very relaxed, friendly mixed/gay crowd.

The River

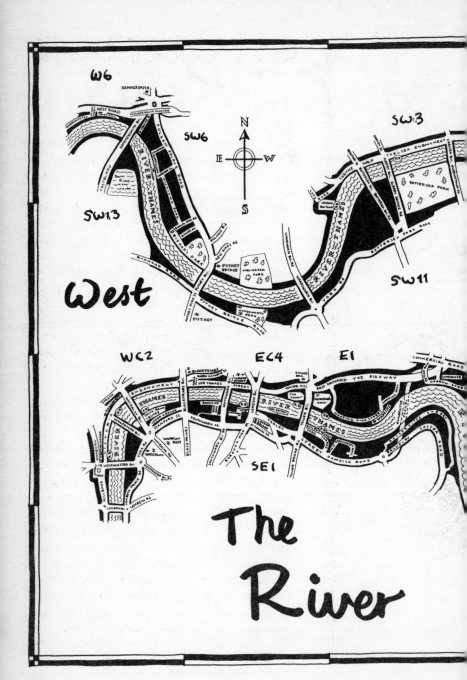

West

The River

*t*he serpentine trail of the Thames swings and sweeps through the once-uninhabited marshlands of the Thames valley from its source in Gloucestershire to its esturary in the North Sea in Essex. Around AD 48 the conquering Roman emperor Claudius established a fort and what was eventually to become a trading port here; the ancient pagan name Llyndum was changed to Londinium and the development of the city on the river began. But if a city brings easy access for traders it can also bring pillage and destruction and since its founding London has been burned, rebuilt, flattened, reborn, defeated and reclaimed. Pagans, Romans, Saxons, Danes and Normans have all proclaimed London as their own without understanding the fact that the city belongs to no one and that any power over it is exercised naturally by the river.

The Thames divides London into two cities which have definite cultural and economic differences – the South has always been the poor relation. From Roman times to the savage Norse attacks in the ninth century and the invasion of William the Conqueror, the area south of the river has been regarded as being outwith the city, and was always the first part of the city to be attacked. The Roman port of Southwark ('wark' meaning fort) was once a strong defence against threats and attacks from the river, but it was reduced to supplying the walled city with services that could not be found within. Blood sports, gambling, fornication and, later, play-

going, were all found on this side of the river. The first hospitals were also built here but these were used more for shelter than for medical care. It seems as though nothing much has changed in this respect as now the homeless and the mentally ill roam the streets of Waterloo and the South Bank in search of a place to put down a cardboard box to sleep in. During the reign of William the Conqueror the river was also used to set apart Westminster and the City of London, separating the trading centre from the pious seat of church and monarchy. By the thirteenth century Westminster was the principle law court of London; offenders would be sentenced here before being taken downriver to the Tower and their end.

Medieval noblemen would build their houses by the river for the convenience it offered – the roads were as bad then as they are now. During the heady Tudor period the river was the hub of London life, and was plied by ships importing everything from oil, grain and spices from the East Indies and Egypt to weapons, jewels and clocks. Very little other than cloth was ever exported in bulk, which indicates that our trade deficit has always been a problem. Corruption was rife in the wharves where London Bridge now stands as customs officials favoured English vessels over foreign ships and lightermen held the monopoly on what could be discharged on to the quayside, and parted with their knowledge of the changing tides only for a price. Sea criminals would be suspended on gallows in the middle of the Thames as a warning to others about the consequences of their corrupt practices. This sight was only one of many disadvantages of living on a river which also received refuse from the houses and wharves, and blood and offal from the butchers (who were supposed to dispose of this at high tide only), as well as excreta from the little huts parked over the water at some of the wharves and lane ends. The noise of livestock being moved on and off the ships could only have added to the atrocious conditions. There were some good points to life along the river banks – the Bakeries Company, which regulated bread-making in the capital was based in Thames Street by London Bridge, and the 2.5 million gallons of wine imported and controlled by the Vintners' Company at some time all lay around in warehouses along the river's edge. Prisoners in the Clink gaol, which overlooked the river, must have squirmed in frustration whenever they heard a new ship arriving with a fresh supply of booze.

At this point the Thames was the safest and fastest way of travelling through London, which was becoming vastly overcrowded, making the river the most suitable site for the pomp and ceremony so loved by the

English – Henry VIII especially enjoyed moving along the river from Hampton Court Palace to Westminster Palace, followed by a stately entourage. Until Victorian times the Thames continued to be the centre of London life and activity, though in later years it was often only the very poor who lived along its banks. It's a picture difficult to imagine now, with most of the docks closed due to their inability to cope with large container ships and the competition from other forms of transport.

The views from London's bridges give a sense of what a remarkable place this city is, but they also tell the tale of a wide but quiet river. Why are there not vast amounts of small passenger boats hurtling up and down? Why are there so few walkways and river parks from which to enjoy the spectacle of the water? And why is the traffic at a halt all the way along the Embankment when there's such a potential waterway over the wall? For a river once so full of life there is now an almost complete absence of river-based industry and leisure. It seems as if London has turned away from the Thames, forgetting that it should be enjoyed not only by the tourist but also by the citizen. There have been some signs of development, such as Docklands, the Canary Wharf business site – which some think is now a massive white elephant – and the high-rise, high-cost apartments and offices of Chelsea Harbour, whose facilities are all closed to the public, creating a fortress against the realities of London life. There are a few shops and restaurants here but not really enough to tempt you into the area, though there have been a few attempts to reclaim parts for people to enjoy, such as the walks around London Bridge, Borough High Street and along Butlers Wharf. But overall there seems to be no coherent plan to resurrect the fortunes of the river.

A journey down the river shows the diversity of London's past and the travesty of its cheap and ugly redevelopment, which has done nothing to rejuvenate it. It takes time and patience to seek out a sense of what the Thames and its banks must once has been like, but it is a magnificent stretch of water and deserves to have some public money put into it.

In this section I have concentrated on 'inner London' places. If you go further out to Kew and Richmond to the west, and Greenwich to the east, you will experience a much more gentle and docile river. For further information on riverside activities, see separate entries under Chelsea, Battersea and Clapham, Westminster and St James's, Covent Garden and the City.

HOW TO GET THERE

Hammersmith
Tubes
- Hammersmith
- Ravenscourt Park

Buses
- Fulham Palace Road: 74, 220, C4
- Great West Road: 190, 290
- Hammersmith Broadway: 9, 10, 11, 27, 33, 72, 190, 220, 266, 267, 283, 290, 295, 391, H91, R69, N11, N67, N93, N97, 415, 741

Fulham
Tubes
- Fulham Broadway
- Parson's Green
- Putney Bridge

Buses
- Fulham Palace Road: 74, 220, C4
- New King's Road: 22, C4

Lambeth
Tubes
- Elephant and Castle
- Lambeth North
- Waterloo

Buses
- Lambeth Palace Road: 77, 507
- Lambeth Road: 76, 77, 171A, 507, 511, P11
- York Road: 76, 77, 171A, 507, 511, P11

Waterloo and South Bank
Tubes
- Charing Cross
- Embankment
- Lambeth North
- Temple
- Waterloo

Buses
- Stamford Street: 149, P11
- Waterloo Road: 1, 68, 171, 176, 188
- York Road: 76, 77, 171A, 507, 511, D1, P11

River Buses
- Charing Cross Pier
- Festival Pier

Southwark and Borough
Tubes
- Burough
- London Bridge

Buses
- Southwark Bridge Road: 344
- Southwark Street: 17, 149, P11

River Buses
- Swan Lane Pier

Wapping
Tubes
- Wapping
- Shadwell

Docklands Light Railway
- Shadwell
- Tower Gateway

Buses
- Wapping High Street: 100
- The Highway: 100, D1, D11

River Buses
- St Katherine

Rotherhithe
Tubes
- Rotherhithe

Buses
- Brunel Road: 1, 225, N70, P11, 225, P14
- Lower Road: 47, 188, P13, P14, N47, N70
- Redriff Road: 1, 225, N70, P11, P14

Limehouse
Docklands Light
Railway
- Limehouse
- Westferry

Trains
- Limehouase

Isle of Dogs/Canary Wharf
Docklands Light
Railway
- Canary Wharf

Buses
- The Highway: 100, D1, D11
- Limehouse Road: 5, 15, 15B, 40, D1, D11, P14, N95
- Westferry Road: 277, D1, D5, D7, P14

Buses
- Westferry Road: 277, D1, D5, D7, P14, N8
- Marsh Wall: 277, D7, D8, D9, N8
- Canary Wharf: D8, D9, D11
- Preston's Road: 277, D6, D7, D8, N8
- Manchester Road: 277, D7, D8, D9, P14

River Buses
- Canary Wharf

THE PROSPECT OF WHITBY

SIGHTS AND SITES

**Battersea Bridge,
SW3 and SW11**

In the eighteenth century Henry Holland designed the first wooden bridge to cross the Thames here, at last joining Battersea Village with Chelsea. It was a huge success and it is thought that it was responsible for turning the village of Chelsea into a small town. The present bridge was designed by Joseph Bazalgette in 1890, and the area around it is most famous for the paintings of James Abbott McNeill Whistler, whose impressionistic view of the Thames at night he called Nocturnes.

Known as the Unlucky Bridge, Battersea Bridge keeps closing down. Its design made its arches lower than they should have been and since 1890 innumerable boats have crashed into it, weakening the structure. This, plus the strong north-to-south current caused by the bend in the river, makes steering through the five elegant spans rather tricky. Sometimes it seems easier to cross the Channel than the Thames – the 920,000 vehicles using London's 23 bridges every day are also beginning to take their toll.

Canary Wharf, E14
071-418 2345

Open: Canary Wharf
Tower, Sat, Sun
10 a.m.–5 p.m.
No credit cards
Admission: adults £3,
children and OAPs
£1.50, discounts for
groups of ten or more

Canary Wharf is supposedly an example of the new London. Dominated by the striking 50-storey Canary Wharf Tower (the highest building in London, designed by the architect Cesar Pelli), it has attracted tenants from the financial sector as well as the *Daily Telegraph* newspaper. The development, with its 10,000,000 square feet of office space, 500,000 square feet of shops, restaurants and other facilities, has now become something of a white elephant. The recession which has gripped the British economy since the late 1980s meant that there is an abundance of cheap office space available in the City of London, and it now looks as if the dream of a new city centre on the Thames will now come to naught.

Canary Wharf itself looks like a cross between Batman's Gotham City and downtown Manhattan, but it feels like a ghost town: there is no real heart to the place and shops selling Filofax inserts and Belgian chocolates do not really give any sense of community to a place. Its biggest problem is transport – the road system is a gridlocked nightmare and the Docklands Light Railway goes only as far as Bank tube station.

For a number of years now there have been plans to build an extension to the Jubilee Line, extending the Underground to Docklands, but the financial problems of the developers and the reluctance of the government to plough too much public money into the development has meant that the plans are continually in doubt.

The 12,000 council tenants who lived in the area, all of whom were ex-dock workers or the sons and daughters of dockers, have had to contend with a new type of person and a new image for Docklands, very little of which has any connection whatever with reality in their view.

The Design Museum
Tower Bridge SE1
071-403 6933

Open:
10.30 a.m.–5.30 p.m.
Credit: A, Amex, V
Admission: £3.50,
concessions £2.50

This long-awaited addition to London's cultural life came about through the passionate work of Terence Conran, the man behind Habitat and the Conran Shop. Upstairs there is a permanent exhibition which treats all design, from fridges to fountain pens, with the same respect. Recent exhibitions have featured Scandinavian design, home interiors and the work of the influential designer Phillipp Starck. The shop sells a wide range of designer items similar to those stocked by the Conran Shop – Alessi kettles, Starck lemon-squeezers and so on. There's also a wide range of books, cards and posters available.

So far the Design Museum has proved to be a bit far out of the way for people to visit it in great numbers, but there is a water service which drops you off very close, and the view along the river is worth the journey. There is a small cafe in the museum which does good coffee and pastries, but if you really want to splash out go to the Blueprint Cafe (see separate entry).

Fulham Palace
Bishop's Park, Fulham
Palace Road SW6
071-736 5821;
museum 071-736 3233

Open: Wed–Sun
1–4 p.m.,
March–October
2–5 p.m.
Admission: adults 50p,

Until 1973 this was the residence of the Bishop of London. The current building, with an ever-repeating pattern of dark purple bricks, dates back to the sixteenth century, although the various bishops have lived here since the eleventh century. Recent investigations into the origins of the palace have revealed that at one time there was a Roman settlement here. Until the 1920s the building was surrounded by a moat, which at a mile long was the longest in England. The palace is very impressive-looking and has a few interesting details which are well worth a look, such

accompanied children free, concessions 25p

as the Fitzjames Quadrangle, which you enter through an archway. There's also a battlemented tower with a bell turret.

There is a herb garden and a water garden open during daylight hours and there is a free guided tour on every second Sunday of the month. The museum is based in two rooms and features archaeology, paintings (including two paintings by the American Benjamin West) and stained glass, and also an exhibition on the history of the palace.

The Globe Museum
1 Bear Gardens,
Bankside SE1
071-928 6342

Open: Mon–Sat
10 a.m.–5 p.m., Sun
2-5.30 p.m.
Credit: A, V
Admission: adults £3,
concessions £2,
discounts for groups of
10 or more

This was the site of the famous Globe Theatre which was built in 1598 by Richard Burbage, the famous actor-manager. Shakespeare was a shareholder and a player here and had everything from *Romeo and Juliet* to *King Lear* and *Macbeth* performed on the stage of the Globe, which was an open-air theatre and so used only during the summer. In 1613 two cannons, fired during a performance of *Henry VIII*, set the thatch alight and the theatre was destroyed. It was rebuilt, but was later destroyed by the Puritans in 1642. This small specialist museum has been open for fifteen years, and celebrates not only the life of Shakespeare but also the Elizabethan theatre in general. The bookshop sells works on the great playwright and on that mad period when the City of London closed down its inns at night, forcing the residents to cross the river here to Bankside for their entertainment.

There is a shop selling gifts and souvenirs such as badges, key-rings and T-shirts.

Hammersmith Bridge, SW13 and W6

This was London's first suspension bridge, designed by William Tierney Clarke in 1824 and replaced in 1887 by Bazalgette's decorative suspension bridge, which still stands. It is possible to look downriver towards the east and Chelsea and upriver westwards towards Richmond, and the bridge is a good place from which to watch the annual Boat Race between Oxford and Cambridge each Easter.

Hammersmith Terrace, W6

This terrace of houses running along the side of the river bank was built around 1755. The houses face the river and have rather quaint gardens running down the front. The backs of the houses, which cannot be seen from the road, have stuccoed Doric porches. The houses were very popular with artists and writers, including the painter and faith healer Philip de Loutherbourg, the engraver Sir Emery Walker and Arthur Murphy, the actor and playwright.

The Hayward Gallery
South Bank Centre
071-921 0600

Credit: A, Amex, DC, V

Designed by Hubert Bennett for the Greater London Council, this building was opened in 1968. There are four exhibition galleries and the original intention was for it to provide a much-needed new arts centre for London, concentrating on contemporary work. I'm in two minds about the place. I hate going there but the exhibitions are so impressive that no art lover can stay away. The space lends itself to everything from installations to paintings and the rooms are connected by an intricate series of stairs and ramps.

On the top floor there is a small cafe which I think is one of the worst in London, though its setting gives it the potential to be one of the best – a problem that seems to run through the whole of the South Bank.

HMS *Belfast*
Morgans Lane, Tooley
Street SE1
071-407 6434

Open: 20 Mar–31 Oct
10 a.m.–6 p.m.,
1 Nov–19 Mar
10 a.m.–4.30 p.m.
Credit: A, V
Admission: adults £4,
children £1.75, OAP
£2 (reductions for
groups)

This 1938 cruiser battleship now sits moored just opposite the Tower of London throughout the year, giving enthusiasts a chance to see what life on a nearly modern ship is like. The biggest attraction, especially for men and boys, is always the six-inch guns, which would explain many of the world's problems. A walk through the multitude of gangways on board takes you past boiler rooms, cabins, gun turrets and the sick bay. The ship is in immaculate condition and gives even those with no love of war a chance to see how incredibly closely together sailors lived, and how difficult life on board must have been.

There is a permanent exhibition detailing the D-Day landings in which HMS *Belfast* took part, and also a gift shop.

Hungerford Bridge, WC2 and SE1

This pedestrian bridge runs parallel with the railway bridge taking commuters into Charing Cross, and links the station to the South Bank complex. It gets its name from the old meat market which once stood on the site of the station. The new Charing Cross complex, designed by Terry Farrell, overlooks the river and the South Bank, and there is the definite impression that it is the rich cousin looking at an impoverished relation. The bridge is a sad metaphor

for the things going on in the big city. Homeless kids beg and plead for money as the professional classes rush past them, staring fixedly at the ground. A walk across the bridge can be intimidating as trains hurtle past above your head.

Kelmscott House
26 Upper Mall W6
081-741 3735

Open: Thurs, Sat
2–5 p.m.
No admission charge

Kelmscott House was the home of Sir Francis Ronalds, who invented the electric telegraph in 1816. The poet and novelist George MacDonald lived here from 1868 to 1877, and then rented it to William Morris for the annual rent of £85. Kelmscott House gets its name from Morris's Oxfordshire manor; when Morris moved here the place was in a sad state of disrepair but he set out to make it into a beautiful home and thought that it 'might be made very beautiful'. The house still contains the fireplace designed by Philip Webb as a wedding gift for Morris, as well as Morris wallpaper designs. The main house is private, but in the basement the William Morris Society has mounted an exhibition of original designs, printing and presses. The coach house, which used to be the meeting place of the Hammersmith Socialist Society, is also open to visitors.

Lambeth Palace
Lambeth Palace Road
SE1
071-928 8282

Screened by high walls, this is the London residence of the Archbishop of Canterbury and is one of the few remaining medieval domestic buildings in London. The gatehouse was built by Henry VIII's right-hand man John Morton, a man famed for the way in which he devised new taxes. There are two entrances through the massive twin towers, one for carriages and one for pedestrians. The basic thirteenth-century fabric of the place has survived the Civil War and the Second World War, and through its many imposing halls you can sense centuries of conspiracy, collusion and heretical reform. The library, holding up to 1,250 books, is the oldest public library in the country. The palace itself is open to the public but the gardens behind are open on half a dozen occasions throughout the year – ring for details.

Limehouse, E14

Limehouse gets its name from the lime kilns which were once here in abundance, and throughout the Tudor period the area was renowned for its pure air. In the eighteenth century Limehouse was best known as a ship-building centre until a sudden influx of

Chinese sailors changed the place into a thriving Chinatown, the first in London. The area became notorious as a den of vice, and the now legendary opium and gambling dens attracted the poor and the wealthy into their dim and hazy quarters. Sax Rohman's fictional character Fu Manchu was based here. In the 1950s, however, the Chinese community either moved back to the Far East and Hong Kong or went up west to settle in and around Gerrard Street, now known as Chinatown (see Soho).

Today Limehouse is a comfortable living area for City bankers and scornful thespians who like the idea that their converted lofts were once the den of notorious outcasts. The appeal of a large apartment overlooking the river is obvious, but the ones around Narrow Street are very special.

London Bridge, SE1 and EC4

The original wooden London bridge was built around AD 100, and was used as a major river-crossing point by the Romans until about AD 400. Norse invasions which started from the Thames eventually destroyed the bridge, giving rise to the song 'London Bridge is Falling Down'. In 1305 the Scottish patriot William Wallace was beheaded and his head placed in the portico of the bridge's gatehouse – the beginning of a gruesome custom. To preserve the heads the executioner would par-boil them, place them in tar and then stick them on the portico, and the resulting horrific display was meant to stop further revolt in other parts of the country as well as in London. The Peasant Revolt of 1381 saw the bridge taken over by Wat Tyler's rebels. The great Thomas More's head was placed here in 1535.

By the eighteenth century the houses which had lined the bridge had been removed and replaced by a central arch, and in 1831 a new bridge of five stone arches was built by Sir John Rennie. Amazingly, this bridge was sold and re-created at Lake Havasu City, Arizona. The present, rather unspecial, structure was built by Mott, Hay and Anderson.

St George the Martyr
Borough High Street SE1
071-407 2796

In the twelfth century the church of St George the Martyr was part of Bermondsey Abbey, and was rebuilt in the fourteenth century; Henry VIII's lute player, Peter Carmelianus, was rector here. During the Puritan period the clergy and gentry finally got

Open: Wed
12.30–1.30, Sat
2–4 p.m.

around to repairing and beautifying the church, a process that took several centuries. The plaster ceiling depicting cherubs descending from clouds was the work of Basil Champneys in 1897. The new east window includes the kneeling figure of Little Dorrit, who in Dickens's novel was baptised and married here. The church is occasionally used for concerts and there are poetry readings here once a month.

St Katharine's Dock, E1

St Katherine's was the most westerly dock on the Thames, just below Tower Bridge on the north bank. The eighteenth-century warehouses and the nineteenth-century dock buildings which had seen so much of London's industrial and trading power grow over the years were finally closed down in 1968. A year later plans to redevelop the area into a complex of offices, restaurants, shops, a hotel and a marina got underway, and due to its location – only a short walk away from Tower Bridge and the Tower of London, it could hardly fail to attract Londoners and tourists alike. Today the complex employs 5,000 people and is visited by an average of two million people each year.

In 1978, Rupert Murdoch's British newspaper empire moved away from Fleet Street into a high-tech office site just east of St Katherine's, in Wapping. After a riotous beginning, when pitched battles were fought for a year between print workers and police over Murdoch's intransigent staffing arrangements, Wapping has now settled down and has become a successfully reclaimed part of London where nostalgia meets the modern world.

St Mary's Church
St Marychurch Street
SE16

St Mary's Church in Rotherhithe has a history of irreparable damage caused by the church's proximity to the river, and throughout the fifteenth century the locals found that the Church establishment left it up to them to find the money to rebuild the church. St Mary's was used by seamen and watermen and was eventually restored in 1715. The pillars here are made from ships' masts, thickly covered in plaster. The chairs and the altar were built with timber from the ship *Fighting Temaraire*.

The captain and three sailors of the *Mayflower*, which sailed to America in 1620 with a full complement of Rotherhithe men, are buried here in the churchyard. A wall plaque in the church tells of Prince Lee Boo, the son of a cannibal king, who rescued some members of a shipwreck and then came back with them to live and die in Rotherhithe.

Southwark Cathedral

Montague Close SE1
071-407 3708

Open: 9 a.m.–5 p.m.;
choral eucharist Sun
11 a.m., 3 p.m., Tues,
Fri 5.30 p.m.

Southwark Cathedral was famous in the early seventeenth century for its chaplain Sutton, who preached passionately against the vice that ran rampant in the area surrounding his church and all along the southern bank of the Thames. The large tower was completed in 1689, but the church itself dates back to the fourth century and has been rebuilt on many occasions. Towards the end of the nineteenth century it was decided that the church should become a cathedral catering for the growing population of south London. Some of the furnishings here are exquisite: the modern bronze sculpture by Kenneth Huges and the brass candelabra hanging under the central tower deserve special mention. There is also an oak effigy of a knight from about 1275, and a memorial to Shakespeare, carved in 1912 by Henry McCarthy. Every year a service in Shakespeare's honour is held for his birthday on 23 April – it would make Sutton turn in his grave. The cathedral is well worth a visit, and guided tours can be arranged – ring for details.

The cathedral is often used for musical performances, and there are lunchtime concerts each week.

Tower Bridge, SE1 and E1

071-407 5247

Open: 30 April–31
October
10 a.m.–6.30 p.m., 1
November–1 March
10 a.m.–5.15 p.m..
Credit: A, V
Admission: adults
£3.50, under 15s and
OAPs £2.50, under 5s
free, family ticket £10

The first stone of Tower Bridge was laid by the Prince of Wales in 1881 to the design of Sir Horace Jones to a brief requiring that the bridge had to have an opening span of 200 feet spare width and headroom of 135 feet. It's one of London's most popular bridges, and at night it is beautifully lit up and looks very dramatic. There are lifts which can convey passengers up to the high-level footbridge which is unfortunately no longer in use as it is considered highly dangerous. You can get an excellent view of the bridge from either side of the river, and when it is lit up at night it is a particularly romantic sight.

At the time of writing the bridge is closed for refurbishment, but it's planned to reopen in July or August 1993.

**Vauxhall Bridge,
SE1 and SW1**

This bridge is only one of the 32 which cross the length of the Thames but it is more interesting than many of the others, if only for what used to be situated around it. It was the first iron bridge to cross the Thames, linking Pimlico and the notorious Vauxhall Gardens which were famous in the eighteenth century for the parties held there. Those times are gone and Vauxhall now has the air of a place where nothing really happens, and can in fact be quite creepy, especially at night.

The Pimlico wharves opposite were developed by the great architect Thomas Cubitt in the 1840s. It's worth taking a good look at the bridge to see Alfred Drury and F. W. Pomeroy's eight statues of the arts and sciences, including one of Architecture holding a replica of St Paul's.

EATING AND DRINKING

**The Anchor
Bankside**
35 Park Street SE1
071-407 1577

Open: bar, Mon–Sat
11.30 a.m.–11 p.m.,
Sun midday–3 p.m.,
7–10.30 p.m.;
restaurant, lunch
12.30–2.30, dinner
Mon–Sat 6–10 p.m.,
Sun 7–9 p.m.
Credit: A, Amex, DC,
Forte Gold Card, V
Average: bar £10,
restaurant £40

This pub stands next to the site of the notorious Clink prison, destroyed by the Great Fire in 1666. You could easily get lost in this maze of small bars where once gathered the motliest crew of vagabonds and villains London has ever seen. There was a time when Shakespeare roamed the low-ceilinged dark rooms looking for inspiration in the bottom of a bottle, as did Dr Johnson and his Scottish groupie James Boswell. There is a wide range of beers available in this Courage pub, including its own Anchor ale, and a good selection of wines at reasonable prices – something rare in a London pub. Bar food is served at lunchtimes and in the evening beef and ale pie or roast chicken, served with potatoes and vegetables, will set you back between £3.50 and £4.50.

Upstairs there is a restaurant serving traditional English food, with an emphasis on fish. For parties of ten or more there is a special set menu at £12 for three courses – call first to book. House wine is a reasonable £7.95.

The Angel
101 Bermondsey Wall
SE16
071-237 3608

This Courage pub was built in the fifteenth century and has a brilliant view of Tower Bridge on one side of its pillared balcony, with the City and the rest of London on the other. The river pub is very much the theme here, with wrought-iron lamps, a ship's wheel and various knickknacks and old maps adorning the walls.

You can eat pub food such as sausages and mash or shepherd's pie here, though there is a small, reasonably priced restaurant which is very popular in summer. It serves mostly fish dishes and the renowned Greenwich fish pie, which is a bargain at £4.

Open: bar, Mon–Sat
11 a.m.–3 p.m.,
5.30–11 p.m., Sun
midday–3 p.m.,
7–10.30 p.m.
Credit: A, Amex, DC, V
Average: £34

Black Lion

2 South Black Lion Lane
W6
081-748 7056

Open: Mon–Sat
11 a.m.–11 p.m., Sun
7–10.30 p.m.
Credit: A, Amex, DC, V
Average: £10

This Watney's pub dates back 400 years and is featured as the Black Swan in A. P. Herbert's *The Water Gypsies*. The people who run it are quite keen on quiet games such as cribbage, chess and backgammon, which you can play in the single bar, but the main attraction of the place, apart from its good view of the river, is the prize-winning garden which looks incredible in the summer. There are three special dishes available each day about £4, as well as steak and kidney pie and the usual crisps, sandwiches and so on. The beers range from real ale to Australian lagers and are very welcome after a walk.

The Blueprint Cafe

Design Museum, Butlers
Wharf SE1
071-378 7031

Open: lunch
midday–3 p.m., dinner
7–11 p.m.
Credit: A, V
Average: £40

Named after the seminal architectural magazine *Blueprint* and situated above the Design Museum, this place has a glass frontage which overlooks the river and in the evening captures the spectacular lighting of Tower Bridge. In the summer the balcony is the place to sit – although it can be chilly, it is a brilliant position from which to enjoy the view. The food falls into the Modern British category but is really a mixture of Italian and French with a dash of British initiative. There's a decent selection of house wines and the prices are reasonable considering the position and reputation of this elegant Bauhaus-style building, which attracts London's fashion and photography crowd and the new locals who have moved into the converted warehouses next door.

The Dove

19 Upper Mall W6
081-748 5405

Open: Mon–Sat
11 a.m.–11 p.m., Sun
midday–3 p.m.,
7–10.30 p.m.
No credit cards

This very pretty eighteenth-century pub lies on the best stretch of the river in London at Hammersmith. There is an upstairs terrace covered in grapevine from which you can get a perfect view of the Thames. The dark oak beams give the bar a very traditional Olde England feel which is given even more credibility when you know that Charles II's mistress Nell Gwynne drank here, as did the authors Graham Greene and Ernest Hemingway. The other good

Average: £12

snippets of information about the Dove is that it is in the *Guinness Book of Records* for having the smallest bar room – four feet two inches by seven feet ten – and that James Thomson wrote 'Rule Britannia' here.

Basic pub food such as shepherd's pie, chilli con carne and Sunday roasts are available, at around £4.50 for a main-course dish. It's served from midday to 3 p.m., and in summer you can also eat here between 5 and 9 in the evening.

Downtown Suleman's
1 Cathedral Street SE1
071-407 0337

Open: Mon–Fri, lunch
midday–2.30 p.m.,
dinner 7–11.30 p.m.
Credit: A, Amex, V
Average: £20

The idea here seems to be that no cuisine in the world should be ignored, and this 1950s-look restaurant has embraced Chinese, American and European food without ever worrying about upsetting the purists. The menu changes every six weeks, which makes it difficult for me to recommend any particular dishes. The best thing to do is to try your luck with a number of different dishes, especially the Chinese and Thai-influenced ones. A set meal costs £10 a head between 5 and 7.30 p.m., and changes weekly. There is also a cocktail happy hour here between 5.30 and 7.30, and you don't have to eat if you don't want to. Downtown Suleman's is a perfect place to eat before going to the theatre or catching a movie on the South Bank.

East of the Sun/West of the Moon
Gabriel's Wharf, Upper
Ground SE1
071-620 0596

Open: Mon–Fri, Sun
11 a.m.–12.30 a.m.,
Sat 11 a.m.–1 a.m.
Credit: A, Amex, DC, V
Average: £28

This restaurant, which is on two floors, can be quite a confusing place, as the chef is perfectly happy to serve up any dish from any part of the world. The menu is long and very varied, which can often be a bad sign, but surprisingly, everything seems to work here. Moldavian fish stew, dim sum or latkes are well prepared and very edible indeed, and upstairs the main courses average at about £9, compared to £6 downstairs. There's no set menu but there are daily specials which cost about £5-£6. East of the Sun/West of the Moon is a bright, airy venue with good views of the river, and has become very popular with people from London Weekend Television, which is based next door. The technicians tend to prefer the cheaper cafe next to the restaurant, which has less choice and less ambiance.

The Founder's Arms
Bankside SE1
071-928 1899

The newest pub on the river is called after the foundry which once stood here; the bells of St Paul's Cathedral were forged there. It has a splendid view

Open: Mon–Sat
11 a.m.–11 p.m., Sun
midday–3.30 p.m.,
7–10.30 p.m.
Credit: A, Amex, V
Average: £30

of the City and St Paul's across the river, and is worth dropping in for that alone. However, most people come for the good Young's beer, which is brewed further up the river, and the people standing at the J-shaped bar tend to be either journalists or bank folk in for a quick one at lunchtime or on their way home.

The restaurant offers an à la carte menu only, and concentrates on fresh fish and steaks. Starters are about £3, main courses £9 and desserts £2.50.

The Grapes
76 Narrow Street E14
071-987 4396

Open: Mon–Fri
midday–3 p.m.,
5.30–11.30 p.m., Sat
7–11 p.m., Sun
midday–3 p.m.,
7–10.30 p.m.
Credit: A, Amex, DC, V
Average: £40

This Taylor-Walker pub is supposedly the place where Dickens based the Six Jolly Fellowship Porters in *Our Mutual Friend*. The people who run the Grapes have made sure that a brisk clean-up of the interior has brought it into the world of yuppies and ruppies (river-based yuppies). From the verandah of the bar there are good views of the lofts along the river and the major development of Canary Wharf.

The bar itself sells real ale, bar snacks and fish dishes, but is principally famous for having very good oysters in season – depending on the season, half a dozen will set you back from £7.

The Mayflower
117 Rotherhithe Street
SE16
071-237 4088

Open: Mon–Fri
midday–3 p.m.,
6–11 p.m., Sat
midday–3 p.m.,
6.30–11 p.m., Sun
7–10.30 p.m.
Credit: A, V
Average: £12

The Mayflower is a reminder that it was from this spot that the pilgrims' ship crossed the ocean with a crew made up of local Rotherhithe men. There is a jetty leading on to the river here, and in summer it is used by the residents even though there is a sign warning that it is dangerous. Inside the pub is dark with authentic beams creating an olde-worlde atmosphere which works well.

The Mayflower is a Charrington pub which has made an effort to sell good pub food, including a mixture of the traditional, such as ploughman's, and a variety of spiced sausages, including Cajun. The pub is very popular, not only with ex-seamen but also with the new inhabitants of Wapping and the Isle of Dogs who come here for more than the beer.

Le Pont de la Tour
Butlers Wharf, 360
Shad Thames SE1
071-403 8403

Open: lunch

The aptly named Pont de la Tour, at the moment of writing London's most fashionable restaurant, is the brainchild of Sir Terence Conran, the man behind the Conran Shop, Habitat, Bibendum (see Knightsbridge) and, along the river, the Blueprint Cafe (see separate entry). The concept at Butler's Wharf is that it should

midday–3 p.m., dinner
Mon–Sat
6 p.m.–midnight, Sun
6–11 p.m.
Credit: A, Amex, DC, V
Average: restaurant
£70, bar and grill £40

be able to offer people every service they should want: bar, restaurant, bakery and various other shops, and the various outlets all look very well together. Le Pont de la Tour itself looks like a beautiful ocean liner and if it's not the best restaurant in London it is certainly the best-looking.

The chef, David Burke, is Irish and has mixed French food with a touch of the Celtic. Main courses average around £15 for a fish dish. There is also a set menu at £25 a head. The wine list is perfect and, needless to say, *très* expensive.

Prospect of Whitby

57 Wapping Wall E1
071-481 1095

Open: Mon–Sat
11.30–3 p.m.,
5.30–11, Sun
midday–3 p.m.,
7–10.30 p.m.
Credit: A, Amex, DC, V
Average: £10

This Chef and Brewer pub, the oldest riverside pub in London, was first built in 1520, and rebuilt in 1549. It was once a popular meeting place for thieves and smugglers. During the summer they frequently have live music which varies from jazz to fifties and sixties pub standards. It's never too bad, but if it bothers you, you can always go into the beer garden and be comforted by the weeping willow. The beers include a decent selection of real ales and some average lagers. Traditional English pub food is available – steak and kidney pie, Lancashire hot pot and fish pie, all served with potatoes and vegetables, cost between £3.50 and £4.50.

The River Cafe

Thames Wharf, Rainville
Road W6
071-381 8824

Open: lunch, Tue–Fri
12.30–2.30 p.m., Sat,
Sun 1-3 p.m.; dinner
Mon–Fri
7.30 a.m.–9.15 p.m.
Credit: A, Amex, V
Average: £80

This is where London's cultural and culinary elite come to be seen – it's impossible to get a table here unless you know somebody who knows somebody. Bookings are taken months in advance for dinner and weeks in advance for lunch, but once they get into the understated dining room, once a canteen for local workers, people obviously seem to think it's worth it. Against my better judgement I have to agree with them. The food is based on North Italian cooking and connects simple meat dishes with even simpler salads. Everything here is uncomplicated – there are only a few good Chiantis to choose from and never more than half a dozen dishes – but it is an experience you will remember.

The restaurant is the child of Ruthie Rogers, who has brought everything she learned in Italy alive here. Her husband, architect Richard Rogers, has his offices next door and his influence is very apparent in the lack of any kind of formal decoration in the restaurant. It's an incredible place that has set new standards in London foodieland. It overlooks the Thames and in the summer there are half a dozen or so tables available outside.

The Rogue's Kitchen
St Marychurch Street
SE16
071-237 7453

Open: Mon–Sat
8–11 p.m.
No credit cards
Average: £12

Situated on the ground floor of a block of flats and selling Creole food, the Rogue's Kitchen comes as quite a surprise. The menu is simple and dishes such as rabbit stew and pecan pies are good – but it is the prices that make it even better. Up west, in the centre of the city, food like this would cost around £10 a dish, but here prices can be half that. Jambalaya, blacked red fish and blackened tenderloin of lamb are all £7, starters are about £2.50 and desserts £2. Though the restaurant is unlicensed you can bring your own wine and they don't charge corkage. The service is good and the atmosphere is totally unpretentious.

Studio 6
Gabriel's Wharf, 56
Upper Ground SE1
071-928 6243

Open: Mon–Sat
11 a.m.–11 p.m., Sun
midday–10.30 p.m.
Credit: A, Amex, V
Average: £17

Surprisingly for an area so rich in history and culture, Waterloo seems to lack just about every facility. It is very difficult to find a good restaurant or a cheap cafe here and there are very few pubs, good, bad or indifferent. Studio 6, inside the large wooden building on Gabriel's Wharf, however, is the perfect bar for a drink before or after a trip to the South Bank complex, firstly because hardly anybody knows about it and secondly, it's rather good. It has a very relaxed and cool atmosphere and jazz and blues are played here throughout the day. In the evenings there's a substantial list of cocktails available if you fancy something different.

The food here is a mixture of Mediterranean and American: burgers, salads and potato skins are all good and reasonably priced at around £5 a main dish.

The Tall House
134 Southwark Street
SE1
071-401 2929

Open: Mon–Fri
9 a.m.–4 p.m., lunch
from midday
Credit: A, Amex, V
Average: restaurant
£30, brasserie £18

The Tall House is about the only place in the Waterloo area where you can have a good cup of coffee in the morning. This huge building has a first-floor restaurant and a cellar bar. The brasserie menu changes regularly and the menu is kept quite simple, with dishes such as chilli con carne or good vegetable soup. Upstairs the food is a bit more serious, and so are the prices. John Dory, salmon fishcakes or steamed fruit parcels average out at around £10 for a main dish – about twice the price you will pay downstairs. The bar is not a bad place

at all for a stiff drink before a cultural evening at the South Bank Centre.

ENTERTAINMENT

Hammersmith Apollo
Queen Caroline Street
W6
081-741 4868

Credit: A, V

The Apollo was once the Hammersmith Odeon, London's premier rock venue. This ex-cinema was used by nearly every rock band and musician of any standing, from Van Morrison to Van Halen. Its attraction is that it is big enough to hold 2,000 people but small enough to have an intimate atmosphere and a good feeling between band and audience. The balcony is where the less committed fans go, and the main auditorium is left for those who want to interact. Both are great for seeing what is going on. On the way to the venue you will have to make your way past many illegal merchandising stalls trying to sell cheaper versions of the T-shirts, posters and so on available inside – I advise that you ignore them and buy inside. You'll still probably be ripped off but at least you'll know that what you've bought is official.

Tickets for concerts are available at the door and at main ticket outlets, and you've a good chance of catching what you want to see as the acts who come here tend to play several dates.

The London Dungeon
28–34 Tooley Street
SE1
071-403 0606

Open: April–Sept
10 a.m.–5.30 p.m.,
Oct–March
10 a.m.–4.30 p.m.
Credit: Amex
Admission: adults £6,
children £3.75

The darker side of London's history, which is usually hidden in exhibitions and guidebooks, is positively revelled in here: this is the London of blood-curdling sacrifices and plagues, not to mention torture and beheadings. This is the place to come to find out about Jack the Ripper or Charles I.

It's all very well done here; the models and reconstructions can actually be quite frightening. When the Dungeon first opened people thought it would never be a success, but in fact it has become one of London's most popular attractions. Children sometimes find it all a bit much, even though it's aimed at them – so tread carefully. There's a gift shop selling the usual souvenirs and so on, and also a cafe where you can get coffee and sandwiches and the occasional hot meal.

Mermaid Theatre
Puddle Dock EC4
071-410 0000

The Mermaid Theatre was founded by Sir Bernard Miles, then a minor actor who felt comfortable in anything from musical comedies to Shakespeare and who arrived here from managing a small theatre in a

Credit: A, Amex, V

back garden in Swiss Cottage. Built in 1959 with generous donations from City benefactors, the theatre's original aim was to entertain City workers, providing an early supper and performance for those needing to catch suburban trains home. This policy, matched with Miles's eclectic taste, made the theatre an instant success. In recent years the theatre has been used by the Royal Shakespeare Company to put on home-grown productions and, despite its out-of-the-way location, it remains as popular as ever. The view from the southern bar is spectacular, and the sight of the rapid Thames cutting and chopping the banks leaves one in no doubt about its strength. Tickets cost between £4 and £17.

National Film Theatre
South Bank Centre SE1
071-928 3232

Credit: A, Amex, V
Admission: £3.95,
concessions £2.75

Mainly on show here are foreign specialist films, with seasons of movies concerning specific directors, genres or themes, all intelligently put together. The bar and cafe, which sells basic food including a variety of vegetarian dishes, is all right, but you can't help feeling that the whole place could do with having a bit of money spent on it to bring it up to date. The NFT is always full of film aficionados who often look like leftovers from the sixties. But the most important thing is the terrific selection of films on offer, all of which are in great condition. You need to be a member, but daily membership can be had for 40p.

The Queen Elizabeth Hall and the Purcell Room
Belvedere Road SE1
071-728 8800

Credit: A, Amex, DC, V

The Queen Elizabeth Hall sits next to the bigger and uglier Royal Festival Hall. The difference between the two, apart from size (the Queen Elizabeth Hall holds 1,100; the Royal Festival Hall 3,000) is the atmosphere – it is less formal here and therefore perfect for recitals and small orchestral and chamber-music concerts as well as poetry readings. In recent years opera companies such as Opera North have attracted new audiences with their radical versions of classic operas such as *Carmen* and *Cosi Fan Tutte*, and there are two ballets a year performed here. The Purcell Room is a magical venue which is used mainly for soloists, and you can come in the afternoons and sit through rehearsals for free.

There is a rather ordinary cafe here which opens at 10 a.m., and also an exhibition space which shows prints and watercolours from travelling exhibitions – some of the work on display is for sale.

Riverside Studios

Crisp Road W6
081-748 3354

Open: Mon–Sat
10 a.m.–7 p.m., Sun
midday–7 p.m.; gallery,
Tues–Sun 1–8 p.m.
Credit: A, V

Hidden behind the river's north bank in Hammersmith, this arts complex is something of a secret. It is made up of a cafe, a bar, an exhibition space, a bookshop and a theatre space, and over the last few years has quietly put on some great performances of new dance and performance work – sometimes it seems as if the things the ICA (see Westminster and St James's) sets out to do happen here instead. Highlights of recent years have included shows by Anselm Kiefer, who needed a big and rather unconventional space to show his remarkable lead books, and by Scottish artist Ken Currie, whose work transformed the place into a realistic piece of Hell. The cafe is vegetarian and the menu changes each day, serving up decent if unimaginative food.

The Royal Festival Hall

Belvedere Road SE1
071-928 8800

Credit: A, Amex,
Connect, DC, V

This controversial classical-music concert hall was designed by Sir Robert Matthew and J. C. Martin in 1951. The brutalist architecture has never been much of an attraction for Londoners, but once inside the hall is surprisingly comfortable and functional. The stage has room for 200 players and can be used not only for choral and orchestral concerts but also for film and ballet performances. The Royal Festival Hall's organ was designed by Ralph Downes and installed in 1954. The hall itself can seat as many as 3,000, depending on the type of concert and staging, and despite the terrible appearance of the building the acoustics inside are perfect and engaging.

The Royal National Theatre

The Lyttelton, The Olivier, The Cottesloe, South Bank SE1
071-928 2252

Credit: A, Amex, DC, V

The idea of a national theatre was first put forward in 1848 but it was not until 1903, when Harley Granville Barker made a determined effort, that any progress was made. In 1951 the Queen Mother laid the first stone for Denys Lasdun's design and the first performance in the National Theatre did not take place until 1976. The National has set limits on how much they pay the actors, but manages to attract the best talent from home and abroad. There is a policy of promoting international as well as British theatre.

The Olivier is the biggest of the National Theatre's three auditoriums and it is very wide. It's here that the most lavish productions are staged, including a revival of the classic *An Inspector Calls*.

The Lyttelton is slightly smaller and has a conventional proscenium arch; recent productions here include the highly successful *The Madness of George III*, starring Nigel Hawthorne, and the dramatic revival of Rodgers and Hammerstein's *Carousel*.

Like the Royal Shakespeare Company's Pit theatre, the Cottesloe is an experimental space where new work is often performed for the first time. Several different plays can be seen here during the week, and the standard of work is usually very high.

GAZETTEER

Sights and Sites

ARCHITECTURE AND PLACES OF INTEREST

Albany House W1 118
All Saints Road W11 216
Arlington House NW1 243
Barbican Centre EC2 305
Battersea Bridge SW3, SW11 384
Battersea Power Station SW11 351
Bayswater Road W2 216
Belgravia SW1 143
Boltons, The SW10 159
Bond Street W1 47
Brick Lane E1 330
BT Tower W1 7
Buckingham Palace SW1 118
Camberwell College of Art SE5 366
Camberwell Grove SE5 366
Canary Wharf E14 384
Carnaby Street W1 85
Cavendish Square W1 67
Cenotaph SW1 118
Centre Point W1 7
Chelsea Physic Garden SW3 143
Cheyne Walk SW3, SW10 143
Chinatown W1 85
Cleveland Row SW1 119
Commonwealth Institute W8 173
Cromwell House N6 263
Earls Court Exhibition Centre SW5 159
Economist Building SW1 119
Edwardes Square W8 173
Exmouth Market N1 306

Finsbury Circus EC2 307
Finsbury Square EC2 307
Gray's Inn Square WC1 8
Hammersmith Bridge SW13, W6 386
Hammersmith Terrace W6 386
Harley Street W1 67
Highpoint Flats N6 265
Houses of Parliament SW1 119
Hungerford Bridge WC2, SE1 387
Jermyn Street SW1 120
Kensington Church Street W8 175
Kensington Palace Gardens W8 176
Kensington Palace W8 176
Kensington Town Hall W8 177
Kensington Village W8 177
Kenwood House NW3 265
Leicester Square WC2 86
Limehouse E14 388
Lincoln's Inn WC2 8
Lloyds Building EC3 308
London Bridge EC4, SE1 389
Lubetkin Flats EC1 281
Maudsley Hospital SE5 368
Melbury Road W8 178
Monument EC3 308
Mount Street Gardens W1 47
Notre Dame de France WC2 87
Piccadilly Circus W1 122
Piccadilly W1 122
Portland Place W1 67
Regent Street W1 68
Royal Agricultural Hall N1 282

CHURCHES AND CEMETERIES

GREEN SPACES

Mount Street Gardens W1 47
Parliment Hill NW3 266
Primrose Hill NW1 244
Regent's Canal Towpath NW1
    245

Regent's Park NW1 245
Ruskin Park SE5 369
Saint James's Park SW1 125
Soho Square W1 88

Eating, Drinking and Sleeping

CAFES AND BRASSERIES

This section covers those places which offer you the chance to sit over a cup of coffee and a cake rather than a full meal, though many offer excellent food as well.

Alfredo's Snack Bar N1 283
Angel, The N1 283
Arts Theatre Cafe W1 24
Bar Italia W1 90
Birley's EC3 314
Cafe Delancey NW1 247
Cafe Ezra Street E2 332
Cafe Figaro SW1 127
Cafe Grove W11 217
Cafe Gstaad W8 180
Cafe on the Hill SW2 370
Cafe Pelican WC2 25
Cafe Sante WC2 25
Cafe Soho W1 91
Copenhagen Patisserie NW3
    268
Cordon Brown WC2 26
Dome, The N1 284
Dome, The W1 69
East West EC1
Emporio Armani Express SW3
    199
Everyman Cafe NW3 268
Express, L' SW1 199
First Out WC2 12
Fungus Mungus SW11 354
Haagen Daz WC2 27

Hampstead Tea Rooms NW3
    269
Jacaranda Garden SW9 370
Joe's Cafe SW1 201
Joe's Cafe SW3 200
Julie's Wine Bar W11 182
Lauderdale House Cafe N6 270
Lisboa W10 221
Louis Patisserie NW3 270
Maison Bertaux W1 96
Maison Bouquillon W2 222
Maison Pechon W2 222
Maison Sagne W1 70
Marine Ices NW3 250
Market Cafe, The E1 334
Massarella's Ice-Cream Parlour
    and Creperie W1 71
Mike's Cafe W11 223
Minema Cafe Bar SW1 201
Muffin Man, The W8 183
Notarianni and Sons SW11 355
Oshobasho Cafe N10 270
Patisserie Bliss EC1 286
Patisserie Valerie W1 96
Picasso's SW3 147
Place Below, The EC2 316
Queen's Cafe W1 54

RESTAURANTS

Here you will find places to have a full meal. The section is divided into three parts: places where two people can eat for £15 or less; restaurants costing between £16 and £35; and those restaurants where a meal for two will cost more than £35. In all cases the price quoted reflects the average cost for two *without* wine or other drinks.

Under £15
Alfredo's Snack Bar N1
Ambrosiana Creperie SW10 160
Bengal Bertie's N6 267
Cafe Grove W11 217
Cafe on the Hill SW2 370
Cafe Pushkar SW9 370
Cooke, F N1 333
Cosmo Restaurant NW3 268
East West EC1 315
Ed's Easy Diner W1 93
Fungus Mungus SW11 353
Indian Veg N1 286
Indian YMCA W1 13
Jacaranda Garden SW9 370
Kosher Luncheon Club E1 334
Kramps SW5 162
Love Shack SW4 355
Luigi's SW10 162
Makan W10 222
Market Cafe E1 334
Navigator Restaurant SW5 162
Nazrul E1 335
Notorianni and Sons SW11 355
Rock and Sole Plaice WC2 29
Rogue's Kitchen SE17 397
Stick and Bowl W8 184
Stockpot SW3 203
Wagamama WC1 14
Windmill Wholefoods SW6 164
Woodlands W1 71
Wren in St James's, The W1
   131

Under £35
Al Hamra W1 49
Andrew Edmunds W1 89
Angel, The SE16 393
Ashley's Bar and Grill Room
   (grill room) EC2 313
Bar Gansa NW1 247
Battersea Village Rickshaw
   SW11 352
Bersagliera, La SW3 145
Bibendum Oyster Bar SW3 198
Bloom's E1 332
Blues Brothers SW4 353
Bonjour Vietnam SW6 160
Bouchée, La SW7 198
Brasserie du Marché W10 217
Break for the Border W1 90
Buchan's SW11 353
Cafe de Colombia W1 50
Cafe Italien W1 11
Cafe Rouge N6 267
Cafe Royal (brasserie) W1 90
Canal Brasserie W10 218
Caruso SW6 161
Casale Franco N1 284
Chez Solange WC2 26
Clifton, The E1 333
Costas W8 219
Criterion Restaurant W1 128
Cypriana W1 11
Daphne NW1 248
Daquise SW7 199
Deal's Restaurant SW10 145

Balls Brothers SW1 127
Belgo NW1 247
Belvedere, The W8 179
Bertorelli Room W1 10
Bill Bentley's SW3 197
Blue Elephant SW6 160
Blueprint Cafe, The SE1 393
Brixtonian SW9 369
Brown's Hotel W1 49
Cafe Royal W1 90
Camden Brasserie NW1 248
Caprice, The SW1 127
Carapace, La NW3 267
Casper's W1 50
Chez Gerard W1 11
Cibo W14 180
Clarke's W8 218
Connaught, The W1 50
Corney and Barrow EC2 314
Cozys EC2 314
dell'Ugo W1 92
Dog House, The W1 93
English House, The SW3 146
Famiglia, La SW10 146
First Floor W11 219
French House, The W1 94
Gavroche, Le W1 50
Gay Hussar, The W1 94
Grapes, The E14 395
Green House, The W1 52
Guinea, The W1 52
Harvey's SW17 354
Heal's Restaurant W1 12
Hiroko W11 181
Ivy, The WC2 27
Joe's Cafe SW3 200

WINE BARS
Angel, The N1
Balls Brothers SW1 127

Julie's Wine Bar W11 182
Kaspia W1 53
Kensington Place W8 221
Koto NW1 250
Launceston Place W8 182
Maggie Jones W8 182
Malabar W8 222
Museum Street Cafe WC1 13
Neal Street Restaurant WC2 29
Nico Central W1 69
Odette's NW1 50
Olivo SW1 147
190 Queensgate SW7 202
Orso WC2 29
Pomme d'Amour, La W11 184
Pont de la Tour SE1 395
Quaglino's SW1 129
Red Fort, The W1 98
Ritz, The W1 130
River Cafe, The W6 396
Rouxl Brittania EC2 317
San Frediano SW3 148
Scott's Restaurant W1 55
Signor Zilli W1 98
Simply Nico SW1 131
Soho-Soho W1 98
Star of India SW5 202
Stephen Bull's Bistro and Bar
    EC1 317
Suquet, Le SW3 203
Sweetings EC4 318
Tatsuso EC2 318
Teppanya Kisan SW6 163
Turner's SW3 203
Wakaba NW3 271
Wodka W8 184

Bar Gansa NW1 247
Blues Brothers SW4 353

Shopping

ACCESSORIES

ANTIQUES

BOOKSHOPS

Dover Bookshop WC2 31
Economist Bookshop SW1 132
Elgin Books W11 227
Forbidden Planet WC1 16
Foyle's WC2 103
Freedom Bookshop E1 338
French's Theatre Bookshop
  W1 16
Grey House Books SW3 150
Heywood Hill Booksellers W1
  58
Index Book Centre SW9 373
Keith Fawkes NW3 273
Mellor and Baxter W8 189

Offstage NW1 254
Shipley Specialist Art
  Booksellers WC2 107
Silver Moon Women's
  Bookshop WC2 107
Skoob Books WC1 17
Sports Pages WC2 108
Stanford's WC2 37
Thomas Heneage SW1 134
Tintin Shop WC2 38
Travel Bookshop, The W11 233
Vanburgh Rare Books WC1 18
Walford, G. W. N1 292
Waterstones W8 190

CLOTHES

Most of the shops listed sell both men and women's clothing; however, those who sell only male or female clothes are marked (m) or (f). The same convention is followed for shoes.

Agnés B. (f) SW3 204
Ally Cappellino W1 100
Amazon W8 185
American Retro W1 100
Azagury (f) SW1 204
Beller's N1 288
Ben de Lisi (f) W1 101
Boy SW3 148
Browns W1 55
Chipie NW3 272
Christian Lacroix (f) SW1 204
Comme des Garcons W1 56
Destroy WC2 31
Douglas George Davies (m)
  SW10 165
Duffer of St George (m) W1
  102
Emporio Armani SW3 206
Fisher, S. W1 56
Freedman and Tarling Ltd (m)

W1 57
Garage, The SW3 150
Giorgio Armani SW1 206
Hackett (m) SW6 166
Hennes (f) W1 74
Hermes W1 58
Hyper-Hyper W8 187
Jasper Conran Shop (f) SW3
  267
Jigsaw (f) SW3 208
John Pearse (m) W1 103
John Richmond W1 104
Jones WC2 32
Joseph SW1 208
Katherine Hamnett SW1 208
Kookai (f) WC2 32
Margaret Howell (f) SW3 208
Mark Powell (m) W1 105
Marks and Spencer W1 74
Monsoon (f) WC2 33

Morning (f) WC2 33
Moss Bros WC2 33
Mulberry W1 74
Nicole Farhi NW3 273
Pam Hogg (f) W1 105
Paul Smith (m) WC2 36
Phase Eight (f) SW10 167
Polo – Ralph Lauren W1 59

Rigby and Peller (f) SW3 210
Simpson W1 133
Swanky Modes (f) NW1 255
Timothy Everest (m) E1 342
Venus (f) WC2 38
Whistles (f) W1 77
William Hunt (m) WC2
World's End SW10 152

DEPARTMENT STORES AND SHOPPING CENTRES

Arding and Hobs SW11 356
Barkers of Kensington W8 186
Bon Marché SW9 372
Harrods SW1 206
Harvey Nichols SW1 207

Liberty W1 104
Peter Jones SW1 151
Selfridges W1 75
Whiteley's W2 234

FLOWERS, PLANTS AND GARDENS

Beryl Williams Florist NW3 272
Columbia Road Market E2 337
Evans and Sons Ltd E2 338
Flower Stand, The SW3 150

Garden Studio, The E2 339
Harper and Tom's Flowers
  W11 229
Rassels Nursery W8 189

FOOD AND DRINK

Algerian Coffee Shop W1 100
Ambala Sweet Centre E1 336
Beigel Bake E1 336
Bibendum NW1 252
Biggles W1 73
Boulevard, Le SW10 164
Camden Coffee Shop NW1 252
Cannelle SW10 164
Chelsea Catering Company
  SW10 165
Cullens W11 187
Freshlands Wholefoods EC1
  319
Frumpkin and Co. Ltd W1 74
Garcia and Sons W11 228
Gazzano and Son EC1 290
Harts the Grocer SW10 150

Jones Dairy E2 340
Lea and Sandeman SW10 166
Lidgate, C. W11 188
Lina Stores W1 105
Luigi's Deli SW10 166
Maison Blanc W11 188
Mr Christian's W11 230
Neal's Yard Dairy WC2 35
Olga Stores N1 291
Oshushi No Yoshino W1 133
Paris and Rio's E2 340
Pasta Place, The NW3 273
Paxton and Whitfield SW1 133
Peppercorns NW3 274
Randall and Aubin W1 107
Sainsbury's NW1 254
Steve Hatt N1 291

Chelsea Farmers Market SW3 149

Columbia Road Flower Market E2 337

Garage, The 150

Golborne Road Market W10 228

Gray's Antique Market W1 57

Hyper-Hyper W8 187

Inverness Street Market NW1 253

Kensington Market W8 188

Leadenhall Market EC3 319

New Covent Garden Market SW8 357

Nine Elms Sunday Market SW8 358

Northcote Road Antiques Market SW11 358

Petticoat Lane E1 340

Portobello Road Market W10, W11 231

Spitalfields E1 341

MUSIC

Black Market Records W1 102

Dub Vendor W10 227

Honest Jon's W10 229

Music and Video Exchange W11 230

Music Kiosk SW9 373

Rough Trade W11 232

Tower Records W1 134

Unity Records W1 109

Virgin Megastore W1 76

NEW AGE

Ganesha SW10 165

Mysteries WC2 34

Over the Moon SW6 166

SECOND-HAND CLOTHES

American Classics SW10 148

Cenci WC2 30

Flip WC2 31

Glorious Clothing Company N1 291

SHOES

Anello and Davide WC2 30

Church's Shoes (m) W1 56

Holt Shoes NW1 253

Manolo Blahnik SW3 150

Natural Shoe Store WC2 34

New & Lingwood (m) SW1 132

Oliver Sweeney SW1 209

Patrick Cox SW3 151

Shelly's WC2 36

SPORTS SHOPS

Bicycle Workshop, The W11 225

Cycle Logical W1 73

Gidden Ltd, W. & M. W1 (equestrian) 57

Lonsdale Sports Equipment Ltd W1 (boxing) 105

Low Pressure W11 (surfing) 229
Slam City Skates WC2
 (skateboarding) 37
Snow and Rock W8 (climbing
 and skiing) 189

Soccerscene W1 108
Sports Pages WC2 (books) 108
Yellow Jersey Cycles NW1 255
YHS Adventure Shop WC2
 (camping, climbing) 38

THEATRICAL SHOPS

Anello and Davide WC2 30
Charles H. Fox Ltd WC2
 30
Cinema Bookshop WC1

French's Theatre Bookshop
 W1 16
Offstage NW1 254
Theatre Zoo WC2 37

TOILETRIES

Crabtree and Evelyn W8 186
Floris Ltd SW1 132

George F. Trumper W1 57
Penhaligon's W1 59

TRAVEL SHOPS

Stanford's WC2 37
Trailfinders W8 190
Travel Bookshop, The W11 233

Virgin Megastore W1 76
YHS Adventure Shop WC2 38

MISCELLANEOUS

Anything Left-handed W1
 101
Altantis European Ltd E1 (art
 supplies) 336
Broadhurst & Clarkson & Co.
 EC1 (astronomy) 289
Cornflake Shop W1 (specialist
 hi-fi shop) 15
Cover Girl Shoes N1 (quality
 transvestite clothes and
 shoes) 290
Cutler and Gross SW1
 (spectacles) 205
Dogs' Home, The SW11
 (unwanted and abandoned

 pets in search of a good
 home) 357
Elvisly Yours E1 (everything
 for fans of the King) 337
Fiddles and Sticks W11
 (musical instruments repair
 service) 227
Get Stuffed N1 (taxidermy)
 290
Mann, N. WC2 (framing
 service) 33
Shhh E1 (women-only sex
 shop) 341
Smythson W1 (stationery) 60

Entertainment

ARTS CENTRES

BAC SW11 359
The Barbican Centre EC2 305

Institute of Contemporary Arts SW1 135
Riverside Studios W6 400

CINEMAS

Camden Parkway Cinema NW1 256
Camden Plaza NW1 257
Clapham Picture House SW4 359
Coronet Cinema W11 235
Electric Cinema W11 235
Everyman Cinema NW3 274
Gate Cinema W11 236
Kensington Odeon W8 190

MGM Cinema SW10 168
Minema SW1 210
National Film Theatre SE1 399
Plaza Cinema SW1 136
Renoir Cinema WC1 19
Scala Cinema N1 296
Screen on the Green, The N1 297
Whiteley's UCI W2 238

CLUBS

Annabel's Club W1 60
Bass Clef, The E1 343
Cafe de Paris W1 109
Chelsea Arts Club SW3 152
Circa W1 61
Cobden Working Men's Club W10 235
Double Bass, The SW5 167

Embargo SW3 153
Embassy Club W1 61
Fridge, The SW2 374
Madame Jojo's W1 111
Paradise Club N1 295
606 Club SW10 154
Turnmills EC1 324
Wag Club, The W1 113

COMEDY/VARIETY

Brick Lane Music Hall E1 343
Hackney Empire E8 344

Jongleurs NW1 258

COMMERCIAL GALLERIES

Anderson O'Day W11 235
Andrew Usiskin NW3 274
Anthony D'Offay W1 60
Cartoon Gallery WC1 18

Fine Art Society, The W1 61
Hamilton's Gallery W1 62
Jill George Gallery W1 110
K Gallery NW3 275
Karsten Schubert W1 18

Marlborough Fine Art Ltd W1
62
Photographers' Gallery, The
W1 40
Raab Gallery W1 63
Robin Symes Ltd W1 136

Slaughterhouse Gallery, The
EC1 323
Special Photographers' Co.
W11 237
Todd Gallery W11 237
William Jackson Gallery W1 63

MUSEUMS

Bank of England Museum EC2
304
Bethnal Green Museum of
Childhood E2 330
Black Cultural Archives SW9
366
British Library WC1 6
British Museum WC1 6
Buckingham Palace SW1 118
Burgh Museum NW3 263
Cuming Museum SE17 368
Design Museum SE1 385
Dickens House WC1 7
Fulham Palace SW6 385
Geffrye Museum E2 331
Globe Museum SE1 386
HMS *Belfast* SE1 387
Horniman Museum SE23 368
John Wesley's House and
Chapel EC1 307
Keats House NW3 265
Kelmscott House W6 388
Kensington Palace W8 176

Kenwood House NW3 265
Lambeth Palace SE1 388
Lauderdale House N6 266
Leighton House W14 177
Linley Sambourne House W8
178
London Dungeon, The SE1 398
Madame Tussaud's NW1 244
Marx Memorial Library EC1 281
Museum of London EC2 309
Museum of Mankind W1 47
Natural History Museum SW7
195
Percival David Foundation
WC1 9
Pollocks Toy Museum WC1 9
Science Museum SW7 196
Sir John Soane's Museum WC2
Tower Bridge SE1 391
Tower of London EC3 312
Victoria and Albert Museum
SW7 197

MUSIC VENUES

Bass Clef, The N1 343
Brixton Academy SW9 374
Camden Palace NW1 256
Duke of Wellington N1 293
English National Opera WC2 39
Falcon, The NW1 257
Forum, The NW5 257

Grand, The SW11 359
Hammersmith Apollo W6 398
Hare and Hounds, The N1
294
Jazz Cafe NW1 258
Marquee, The WC2 111
Pizza on the Park SW1 210

Queen Elizabeth Hall and the Purcell Room SE1 399
Ronnie Scott's W1 112
Royal Festival Hall SE1 400
Royal Opera House WC2 41

St John Smith Square SW1 136
606 Club SW10 154
Subterrania W10 237
Wigmore Hall W1 77

PUBLIC GALLERIES

Commonwealth Institute W8 173
Hayward Gallery SE1 387
National Gallery WC2 121
National Portrait Gallery WC2 122
Queen's Gallery SW1 123

Royal Academy of Arts W1 48
Serpentine Gallery W2 179
Tate Gallery SW1 125
Wallace Collection, The W1 68
Whitechapel Art Gallery E1 331

SPORTS AND HEALTH

Brixton Recreation Centre SW9 374
Central YMCA WC1 18
Chelsea Football Club SW6 167
Community Health Foundation EC1 321
Hampstead and Highgate Bathing Ponds NW3 274
Highbury Fields N4 294

Hurlingham Club SW6 168
Ironmonger Baths EC1 321
Jubilee Hall WC2 40
Mayfair Hotel Gymnasium W1 62
Porchester Centre W2 236
Queens Club W14 168
Queen's Ice-Skating Club W2 237

THEATRES

Almeida Theatre N1 292
Apollo Theatre W1 109
Comedy Theatre SW1 134
Gate Theatre W11 236
Globe Theatre W1 110
Grace Theatre at the Latchmere, The SW11 360
Hampstead Theatre NW3 258
Kings Head Theatre N1 294
Lilian Bayliss Theatre EC1 294
Little Angel Marionette Theatre N1 295

Lyric Theatre W1 111
Man in the Moon Theatre Club SW3 153
Mermaid Theatre EC4 398
New End Theatre NW3 275
Old Red Lion Theatre Pub EC1 295
Palladium Theatre W1 112
Pit, The EC2 321
Royal Court SW1 153
Royal National Theatre SE1 400
Royal Shakespeare Company EC3 322